Adlerian
Therapy

Adlerian Therapy

Theory and Practice

Jon Carlson, Richard E. Watts, and Michael Maniacci
Foreword by Albert Ellis

American Psychological Association • Washington, DC

First Printing August 2005
Second Printing November 2008
Third Printing August 2012

Published by
American Psychological Association
750 First Street, NE
Washington, DC 20002
www.apa.org

To order
APA Order Department
P.O. Box 92984
Washington, DC 20090-2984
Tel: (800) 374-2721; Direct: (202) 336-5510
Fax: (202) 336-5502; TDD/TTY: (202) 336-6123
Online: www.apa.org/books/
E-mail: order@apa.org

In the U.K., Europe, Africa, and the Middle East, copies may be ordered from
American Psychological Association
3 Henrietta Street
Covent Garden, London
WC2E 8LU England

Typeset in Goudy by Stephen McDougal, Mechanicsville, MD

Printer: Edwards Brothers, Inc., Lillington, NC
Cover Designer: Naylor Design, Washington, DC
Technical/Production Editor: Kristen S. Boye

The opinions and statements published are the responsibility of the authors, and such opinions and statements do not necessarily represent the policies of the American Psychological Association.

Library of Congress Cataloging-in-Publication Data
Carlson, Jon.
    Adlerian therapy : theory and practice / Jon Carlson, Richard E. Watts,
Michael Maniacci. — 1st ed.
        p. cm.
    Includes bibliographical references and index.
    ISBN 1-59147-285-7
    1. Psychotherapy. 2. Adlerian psychology. I. Watts, Richard E. II. Maniacci, Michael.
III. Title.

    RC480.5.C3565 2005
    616.89'14—dc22   2005010986

British Library Cataloguing-in-Publication Data
A CIP record is available from the British Library.

Printed in the United States of America
First Edition

CONTENTS

FOREWORD

Although I have hardly read all the scores of books and articles on Alfred Adler and his Individual Psychology that Carlson, Watts, and Maniacci have cited in this book, I think that I can safely say that *Adlerian Therapy: Theory and Practice* is a truly outstanding volume. It is more comprehensive and thoroughgoing, I think, than any other book on Adler. I am happy to salute it!

First, as to comprehensiveness: The book covers the whole range of Adler's theory of how people largely disturb themselves and what they and their therapists can do to help them refuse to do so. It deals at length with Adlerian personality theory, but it also goes into detail with Adler's strategies, techniques, and tactics, including his brief therapy, couples and family therapy, play therapy, and group therapy. In each case, a specific history of Adler's method is given, and full descriptive material is presented, including some verbatim conversation between therapists and clients.

Additionally, *Adlerian Therapy: Theory and Practice* compares Adler's techniques, some of which he originated almost a century ago, with several modern therapeutic methods, such as constructivism and solution-focused therapy. In these and other cases, it is convincingly shown by the authors that Adler's pioneering early 20th-century views surprisingly predated several of today's most popular "innovations." Throughout the book, Adler is frequently shown to have been well ahead of his time in proposing new kinds of treatment.

As the readers of this book might wish, Adler's progressive political and social views are nicely presented. His major contributions of profound social interest, emphasis on the importance of client–therapist relationship, and encouragement of human compassion are consistently dealt with in several parts of the book. Adler is shown to be unusually broad-minded and tolerant in these respects. Moreover, his social theorizing and his therapy practices are steadily presented in a highly integrated fashion. Adler is shown to be not only a rare therapist for his day but also a worldwide social educator of rare skill.

I particularly like the authors' exposition of Adler's self theories and his origination of the view, which was radically different from Freud's, that human problems are usually closely related not to sexual disturbances but to self-rating and power issues. Even sexually, people commonly rate themselves as "inferior" or worthless because they assess their *attractiveness* and their sexual *performances* as inadequate; they then overgeneralize that their *entire person* is "no good" or "worthless." In my practice of rational–emotive behavioral therapy, I have for many years stressed that people foolishly rate their whole self instead of merely evaluating their performances. They thereby create what Adler called *inferiority feelings*. They overgeneralize by condemning other individuals and groups for their actions and thereby create rage, hatred, feuds, and wars. People's self-loathing can be reduced by their acquiring unconditional self-acceptance in spite of their failings, and their hostility to others can be minimized by their acquiring unconditional other-acceptance in spite of other people's wrongdoings. Rational–emotive behavioral therapy does very well with clients and readers by encouraging them to adopt these two major philosophies. But without Alfred Adler's teaching similar attitudes from the 1920s onward, I doubt whether I and rational–emotive behavioral therapy would so thoroughly have them today.

Once again, Adler was a remarkable therapist and educational pioneer. *Adlerian Therapy: Theory and Practice* does a fine job of comprehensively reminding us of that. May it help to preserve and enhance Alfred Adler's reputation for centuries to come.

Albert Ellis, PhD
President, Albert Ellis Institute
New York, NY

PREFACE

People. You come into the world in the hands of others and you leave
the world in the hands of others.

—African proverb

The importance of interpersonal relationships in our lives was not lost
on Alfred Adler. Freud and others tried to understand behavior and personality as existing solely within each individual person. They acted as though
we lived and could be studied in isolation. Adler believed that we find our
place in a world of others and that we must be understood in that same context.

None of the authors of this book knew Adler. Only the senior author,
Jon Carlson, knew his son Kurt, daughter Alexandra, and granddaughter
Margot. It is interesting that a relative stranger could have such an impact
on us.

Most of Adler's ideas are almost 100 years old. His followers have made
numerous modifications to tailor his ideas to fit a different world. With each
new generation of Adlerians, the approach is modified. The notable exception is the San Francisco psychotherapist Henry Stein. Henry continues to
practice and endorse classical Adler. This book is not about classical Adlerian theory and therapy but rather is our attempt to go beyond Adler and
create an integrated Adlerian approach suitable for today's world. This approach is based in Adler but incorporates the effective tools of other contemporary theories.

We are indebted to the many who came before us and taught us so
much about the work of Adler. Those who stand out are Don Dinkmeyer,
Rudolf Dreikurs, Harold Mosak, Bernard Shulman, Ray Corsini, Merle Ohlsen,
Dorothy Peven, Ed Stormer, Leo Gold, Mansford Sonstegard, Oscar
Christensen, Rollo May, Virginia Satir, Ken Weig, Abraham Maslow, Albert
Ellis, Frank Walton, Heinz and Rowena Ansbacher, Bob Powers, Bronia
Grunwald, Edith Dewey, Loren Grey, Maurice Bullard, Ray Lowe, Cameron
Meredith, Eva Dreikurs Ferguson, Guy Manaster, Bill Pew, Ron Pancner,
Lydia Sicher, James Croake, Kurt Adler, and Alexandra Adler. We are also

indebted to our contemporary Adlerian colleagues, who help us grow with their friendship and professional contributions. These include Len Sperry, Don Dinkmeyer Jr., James Bitter, Claire Hawes, Art Freeman, John West, Frank Main, Roy Kern, Betty Lou Bettner, Bill Nicoll, Gary and Joyce McKay, Kevin Leman, Lou Losoncy, Amy Lew, Daniel Eckstein, Gerald Mozdzierz, Marion Balla, Robert Sherman, Bob McBrien, Mike Nystul, Charley Huber, Mim Pew, Jane Griffith, Harold McAbee, Buzz O'Connell, Kathy Walton, Leo Gold, Bob Armstrong, Bill Curlette, Erik Mansager, Mel Markowski, Steve Maybell, Art Clark, Jerry Corey, Tim Evans, Stephen Hirschorn, Don Kelly, Terry Kottman, Rich Kopp, Becky LaFountain, John Newbauer, Art Nikelly, Paul Peluso, Michael Popkin, Randall Thompson, Mark Stone, Judy Sutherland, Jim Sulliman, Evelyn Wachman, Julia Yang, Bryna Gamson, Mary Wheeler, Al Millirin, and Steve Slavik. Although this is only a partial list, it seems to highlight the amount of professional collaboration and social interest among those who practice the psychology of Alfred Adler.

We are grateful to Albert Ellis for taking the time in his 90th year of life to write the Foreword to this book. Ellis has been an inspiration to us throughout his long and productive career. We are deeply honored by his participation in this book.

Laurie Johnson deserves extra recognition for her preparation of the manuscript and attention to details during all stages of the manuscript's development.

Finally, we thank the staff at the American Psychological Association Books Department for making this project a labor of love. Special thanks go to Susan Reynolds, Susan Herman, Kristen Boye, Margaret Schlegel Sullivan, Julia Frank-McNeil, and Gary VandenBos. Additional thanks go to our outside reviewers: Richard R. Kopp, PhD, of Alliant International University/California School of Professional Psychology in Alhambra, California, and Jeff Tirengel, PsyD, of Cedars-Sinai Medical Center in Los Angeles.

Adlerian Therapy

INTRODUCTION

So many people are trying to find happiness, satisfaction, and meaning in today's world. Some are looking to science, others to religion, and many more to psychotherapy. This is not a new search but rather seems to be the quest of the ages. Where does this missing wisdom come from?

Many of us think of our parents and grandparents when we think of wisdom. They seem to possess time-tested ideas and solutions. Think about it: Whom would you choose to seek out for guidance? Would you choose a bright young doctor or a seasoned veteran?

As we ponder the future of psychotherapy, we have turned to a seasoned veteran in the form of Alfred Adler. At the time of his death, he was a very popular source of practical help. His books were on the bestseller lists, and his lectures were sold out in Europe and the United States. Adler was not interested in being a legacy or creating a school of thought. He was interested in making the world a better place. He was a blue collar person who was interested in the hands-on aspect of work with people and not conducting research for evidence-based practice. He believed in "giving psychology away" and frequently conducted family counseling sessions in front of an audience. He observed that we all have similar problems and therefore the audience members could solve their problems right along with the family onstage. He referred to this educational intervention as *spectator therapy*. His ideas were broad enough to cover the main ideas and strategies of many valuable and contemporary schools of psychotherapy.

Some people may be questioning whether schools of psychotherapy are outdated or even necessary. Rudolf Dreikurs (1960) noted that it is impossible to not have a theory of human nature and that even therapists who claim they are eclectic still have a theory, that of eclecticism. The question, then, is not whether to have a theory but how useful the theory is and how well one understands the theory.

Regardless of the theory that a person holds, he or she should know it well, and one of the best ways to learn a theory is in relation to another system. Adlerian, or Individual Psychology, is a good system to learn, especially if the goal is to be able to access and integrate the other major approaches. By clearly understanding Adler's system, it is possible to understand and access the other schools of thought. In this book, it will be easy to see how Adlerian ideas bridge cognitive, cognitive–behavioral, rational–emotive, constructivist, solution-focused, and other social constructionist approaches to psychotherapy.

To function in today's psychotherapy community, it is necessary to be able to integrate the many good approaches to helping so that one can reach the wide variety of clients who seek assistance. By understanding the wisdom of Adler, it is possible to use the best of today's contemporary approaches. Through an understanding of Adler, you will be a better cognitive, cognitive–behavioral, or constructivist therapist in that you will be able to work more effectively and with a greater variety of problems.

It is helpful to note that the Adlerian approach is one that is best called *contemporary Adlerian psychotherapy*. We have taken Adler's ideas and made them applicable to today's world, that is, one that is consumer driven and regulated by managed care. The approach, therefore, needs to be more clearly focused, briefer, and more accountable than a classical Adlerian approach. There is an accompanying video/DVD entitled *Adlerian Therapy* (Carlson, 2005) that complements this book. The video depicts two different therapy sessions that provide a firsthand look at Adlerian therapy in action.

Adlerian theory allows the practitioner to understand the dynamics of the presenting problem and to develop a treatment formulation and plan that incorporate a wide variety of interventions. It is also likely that no two people using an Adlerian model will come up with the same treatment plan, although they will arrive at a similar treatment formulation. Much of the actual treatment depends on tailoring the intervention to both the clinician and the client.

We are hopeful that through gaining an understanding of Adlerian psychotherapy, you will be able to develop a more comprehensive understanding of your clients and will be able to use your existing theoretical orientation in a more effective fashion.

I

ADLERIAN THEORY FOR CONTEMPORARY THERAPISTS

We do not always learn from experience. Of course we learn to avoid certain difficulties and we acquire a certain conduct towards them, but the line along which we move is not changed thereby. . . . we make our experiences, by which it indicates that everyone is master of the way in which he utilizes his experiences.

—A. Adler, 1956, pp. 211–212

Perhaps Adler's greatest gift is a comprehensive theory that has withstood the test of time. His pragmatic conceptualization of human behavior and change processes makes it possible to integrate the many valuable insights of the contemporary theories of psychotherapy.

This section begins with the contemporary relevance of Adler's ideas, the major constructs and how they can improve professional practice. We provide a brief discussion of Adler and his life before we discuss how these ideas fit with other current approaches. The final element of this section provides a deeper grounding in the theory that allows for the integration of so many important approaches.

1

WHY SHOULD PSYCHOTHERAPISTS
BE EXCITED ABOUT ADLER?

In 1994, Prochaska and Norcross presented results of a Delphi study in which they asked 75 psychotherapy experts to predict the near future of the field of psychotherapy. In terms of interventions and modalities, the consensus was that psychotherapy would become more directive, psychoeducational, present centered, problem focused, and brief in the next decade. Concomitantly, aversive, relatively unstructured, historically oriented, and long-term approaches were predicted to decrease. In terms of therapy formats, individual, couples, family, and group therapy were seen as continuing their upward swing, but the largest transformation was expected in the length of therapy: Short-term therapy was on its way in, and long-term therapy was on its way out. In terms of theoretical orientations, respondents predicted that integrative, eclectic, systems, and cognitive persuasions would thrive but that classic psychoanalysis, humanistic approaches, and existentialism would not (Prochaska & Norcross, 1994, p. 486).

A follow-up Delphi study by Prochaska and Norcross (2003) produced almost identical results. Given contemporary psychotherapy theory and practice, Prochaska and Norcross's reported results are impressively accurate. In this chapter, and throughout the book, we describe how Adlerian theory and therapy are specifically tailored to meet the needs of today's practitioner of brief, integrative, present-oriented, problem-focused therapy in all formats. In addition, Adlerian therapy is integrative and eclectic, and it solidly resonates with postmodern approaches, such as constructivist and narrative therapies (Watts, 2000). Moreover, Adler's Individual Psychology presents a theoretically consistent system, which is particularly important for beginning clinicians and for seasoned clinicians who feel uncomfortable with a patchwork approach to integrative practice.

In this chapter, we describe how Adlerian psychology meets the needs of contemporary counselors and psychotherapists. Then we provide an introduction to the theory and therapy that are discussed in detail in the remaining chapters of the book, introducing key terms that will be used throughout. Finally, for readers who want to know more about the man who developed this forward-looking theory and therapy, we provide a brief biography of Alfred Adler.

CHARACTERISTICS OF ADLERIAN THERAPY

Many practitioners and educators—as well as managed-care boards—may be unaware that Adlerian psychotherapy is brief and time limited, present and future oriented, directive, integrative, and eclectic.

Brief and Time Limited

Adlerian therapists have a long history of doing psychotherapy briefly. Adler was an early proponent of brief or time-limited therapy, typically limiting each client's number of sessions to 20 or fewer (a tradition commonly practiced by contemporary Adlerians). In addition, many of the techniques used by many contemporary brief therapy approaches are similar or identical to ones created by Adler. In a comparative analysis of nine brief therapy approaches, Dinkmeyer and Sperry (2000) demonstrated that the Adlerian approach is very similar to cognitive–behavioral, experiential, and systemic brief therapies, "yet it shares with the [brief] psychoanalytic approaches an appreciation of early experiences on current functioning and use of insight as a treatment strategy" (pp. 230–231). For further discussion of Adlerian perspectives on brief therapy, see chapters 8 and 9.

Present and Future Oriented

Adlerian therapy has often been misunderstood as having a past-oriented focus. Although affirming that the past is certainly—and often significantly—influential, Adlerians do not believe that the past determines one's present or future. Some theoretical perspectives state that the past determines the present and, consequently, individuals in the present are products of their past. Other perspectives focus solely on the immediate present (i.e., how it is perceived) and place little or no emphasis on the past or future. Adlerians' theoretical position is that present-centered anticipations of—and aspirations for—the future largely predicate the way in which people remember the past and function in the present (Manaster & Corsini, 1982). According to Singer and Salovey (1993),

> Adler, alone among all theorists in the clinical and experimental circles, argued for the centrality of memory to the understanding of personality. He proposed that one's earliest memories are merely reflections of the most valued current tendencies and life goals of the individual. Memories are revised and shaped in the service of one's enduring attitudes. Rather than veridical accounts of past experiences, they are tendentious fictions that encapsulate in their manifest content what is now most important to the person. (p. 19)

Manaster and Corsini affirmed that there is significant interaction among the past, present, and future and that all three perspectives are salient for understanding clients in psychotherapy: "No one can deny the effects of the past, no one can deny the importance of the [present] moment, and no one can deny the force of the future. But which of these three views of time is the most likely to lead to understanding ourselves and others?" (p. 5). The Adlerian position affirms that individuals are "continually creating (or recreating)" themselves and are always "in the process of becoming" (Mosak & Maniacci, 1999, p. 20). Thus, Adlerian therapy emphasizes a present and future orientation rather than one focused on the past.

Directive

Adlerian psychotherapy is directive and action oriented. Adlerians use active–directive teaching or psychoeducation in which the advice and information are presented in a direct fashion. Adler strongly supported social reform and community outreach programs, and he was an early proponent and developer of psychoeducational and prevention principles and procedures. He worked with troubled adolescents and their families and was the primary force in establishing child guidance and marriage clinics for the general public and teacher education programs in public schools. Consequently, by 1934, there were 28 child guidance clinics operating in Austria, where Adler had lived and practiced. Adler's ideas regarding psychoeducational means were developed and extended in America by Rudolf Dreikurs. Adlerians have developed psychoeducational materials for prevention of difficulties and as an adjunct to psychotherapy. These materials include couple enrichment programs, parent and family education programs, and teacher education programs. A further discussion of Adlerian psychoeducational methods is presented in chapter 12.

Integrative and Eclectic

The Adlerian approach is different for each client and situation. Adlerians are interested in questions such as "Who or what is best for this particular individual?" and "What works, for whom, and under which particular circumstances?" Adlerians are technical eclectics, just like Arnold Lazarus (2000):

> Thus, [multimodal therapists] care *not* to attempt to fit the client to a predetermined treatment. . . . In multimodal therapy, there is a deliberate attempt to determine precisely what type of relationship or what type of interactive posture each client will respond to. The multimodal orientation emphasizes therapeutic flexibility and versatility above all else. There is no unitary way to approach people's problems. (p. 345)

Adlerian therapists tailor therapy according to the unique needs and situations of clients. A vital aspect of Adlerian therapy is its integrative flexibility. Adlerians can be both theoretically integrative and technically eclectic while remaining consistent.

> Indeed, an Adlerian therapist might operate exactly as a psychoanalyst, a client-centered therapist, and a rational–emotive therapist on the same day with three different clients. Thus, with client A, the therapist may simply listen and let the client spew forth whatever is on her mind; with client B, the therapist may forcefully dispute the client's misconceptions. . . . We Adlerians are not limited in any way in our operations: everything depends on the therapist's judgment; while our theory is solid, our methods vary. In short, there is no [one correct] "Adlerian way" of doing psychotherapy or counseling which excludes techniques, as long as the technique "fits" the theory and the client or patient. Indeed, Adlerians are liberal with regard to therapeutic interventions. (Manaster & Corsini, 1982, p. 148)

Different clients may require different therapeutic metaphors. One client may prefer, or be best served by, cognitive–behavioral techniques; another may prefer solution-focused procedures; and yet another may prefer systemic or narrative oriented methods. Adlerian therapy allows the therapist to tailor therapy specifically to clients' unique needs, situations, and expectations rather than forcing clients into one therapeutic or technical framework. The Adlerian approach provides a solid base for integrating diverse treatment modalities and formats (A. Adler, 1929, 1956, 1979; Carlson & Slavik, 1997; Maniacci, 2003; Mosak & Maniacci, 1998; Sherman & Dinkmeyer, 1987; Sperry, Carlson, & Kjos, 2003; Sperry, Carlson, & Peluso, 2005; Watts, 2003a, 2003b; Watts & Carlson, 1999; Watts & Pietrzak, 2000; Watts & Shulman, 2003). More detail about how contemporary approaches to psychotherapy are consistent with the Adlerian approach is offered in chapter 2.

ADLERIAN THEORY AND CHANGE PROCESS

Human Behavior Is Socially Embedded

Human behavior was seen by Adler as goal oriented and socially embedded. Nobody exists outside society. We are born into social groups called *families*.

We are all social beings, and therefore all behavior is socially embedded and has social meaning. People are trying to belong and fit into the social milieu. The outside world shapes our consciousness, as does the world of the family. Through studying interactions with others we can understand how someone is fitting in or seeking to be known in the social world. When someone continues to have the last word in a conversation, for example, one could speculate that that person wants to be the boss, to be in charge.

Mental health is measured in terms of *social interest*: one's willingness to participate in the give-and-take of life and to cooperate with others. Healthy people are those who help others. They are people who look outward instead of inward. Social interest is the opposite of self-interest and concern for one's own good.

Each person is born into a human group and will need to find his or her place in a family constellation. The interactions among family members are the most important factor in creating one's personality. Each child is born into a unique position within the family. This position creates the subjective place from where the child will see and interpret world and life. Each child develops a unique way of viewing the world even though he or she grows up in the same surroundings as his or her siblings.

The Adlerian approach focuses on sibling relationships and psychological birth order. Adler identified five psychological positions: (a) oldest, (b) second of only two, (c) middle, (d) youngest, and (e) only. One's actual birth order is less important than the individual's interpretation of his or her place in the family.

Every family has a unique mood or tone; this is called the *family atmosphere*. The adults in the family also have values and opinions. The combination of atmosphere and values tells children what is important in the family. Children can usually tell whether sports, music, reading, work, religion, and so on, are important to the parent. If a child sees that the parents talk about problems together, he or she learns to value cooperation. When a child sees that parents argue and refuse to compromise, he or she learns that fighting and getting one's own way is the way to solve problems.

We Screen Ideas Through Our Own Life Style

According to Adler, every idea that is accepted by an individual is screened through his or her own *life style* (literally, his or her style of dealing with life) and the idealized picture of him- or herself. We are all self-creating beings. Adler stressed the importance of choice and believed that people are able to make their own choices. We always have the capacity to choose differently; most of us, however, do not use this ability and tend to make the same choices (good or bad).

People can best be understood by realizing that each person has an individual, subjective view of the world. No two people see the world in exactly the same fashion. It is important to understand that what a person sees becomes his or her reality and truth. What one person might view as a fair situation someone else believes is totally unfair. As we develop in life, we are put in many different situations. For example, for a person who grew up in a family that made a living from snow plowing and removal, snow is viewed as a good thing, whereas a person who fell and broke his or her arm while walking down snow-covered stairs might look at snow in a different way. These viewpoints become beliefs and are at the heart of how we live our lives. We interpret situations from our own unique point of view. We live our life and act as if our view of the world is correct. When our views are distorted, our thinking becomes faulty, and our behavior becomes inappropriate. As a Zen poem puts it, to her lover a beautiful woman is a delight; to an ascetic, a distraction; to a wolf, a good meal.

Each of us travels through life in a unique manner. Each person's life style is created in the first few weeks of life. This style is formed partly by seeing how other family members react to different behaviors and attitudes and partly from conclusions that the child draws. The life style is the characteristic way that we act, think, and perceive and the way we live. It is from the life style that we select the methods for coping with life tasks.

The Life Style Is Built on Private Logic

Private logic is composed of ideas conceived in childhood, which may or may not be appropriate to later life. Adlerians believe that "you are what you think." The life style is built on deeply established personal beliefs or constructs that are referred to as *private logic*. As we develop, we establish ideas about what is right and wrong on the basis of our subjective personal experience. If, for example, a person's early life experiences were painful, then he or she is likely to develop mistaken ideas or faulty logic. When a child does not have a useful way to feel significant to the family, he or she will find a way to fit in that is negative and useless. For example, the child might believe that the best way to get attention is to misbehave or have a temper tantrum. Social interest affects our life style. When we have social interest, we find our place in life in a fashion that is good for all; we develop a life style in which we think of others and not just the self. At the root of our problems is faulty thinking.

Human Behavior Is Goal Oriented

Our behavior has the goal of moving from a feeling of minus to a feeling of plus, from inferiority to superiority. Each individual determines what is a plus and what is a minus. Adler believed that there are three basic life tasks: (a) work, (b) friendship, and (c) love–intimacy. To be mentally healthy, it is necessary to master each of the tasks. The work task is addressed when what we do for work is meaningful and satisfying. The friendship task is addressed when we have satisfying relationships with others. The love or intimacy task is addressed when we learn to love ourselves as well as another. It has also been suggested that we need to master the recreation and spiritual tasks of life. The recreation task involves developing the ability to have fun and enjoy life. The spiritual task involves finding one's place in the cosmos. This might involve formal religious practice or a belief in some other higher power.

Humans constantly move toward goals, regardless of whether they are aware of it. All humans have goals, but everyone's goals will differ. To make progress, a person needs consciousness to plan his or her movements. Adler believed that people moved both physically and psychologically. Humans are constantly in motion, moving toward private, often unconscious goals. The pace, direction, and manner of psychological and bodily movements tend to form a personal pattern; observing that pattern can help one predict someone's future actions. There is logic, for example, behind a child's attention-seeking behavior. An attention-seeking child believes that he or she does not count or is not important and needs others to "be somebody." Therefore, the child acts out so that he or she will be noticed by others and thus will count or be somebody. The drive has the potential for good or evil. Movement and consciousness, mind and body, are inseparable.

Adler believed that all behavior is goal directed. People continue to strive for the future and what they believe is important or significant. If we can understand an individual's goals, then it becomes possible to predict his or her behavior and responses to situations. Therapists can work with clients to change their goals, thereby modifying clients' motivation.

Early recollections—the memories of specific incidents in childhood (under age 10)—are a key to finding out about life style. According to Adler, these memories "are, for the client, his 'story of my life,' a story he repeats to himself to warn him or comfort him, by means of past experiences, to meet the future with an already tested plan of action" (A. Adler, 1956, p. 351). These earliest recollections reveal beliefs and mistaken ideas that may form the basis for the way the client subsequently shaped his or her life. They also explain the person's present attitudes, outlooks, and motives. An individual's dreams are an expression of his or her life style and do not have universal outside meaning.

Children and, later, adults work toward specific goals. These include attention, power, revenge, and inadequacy. Once the goal of misbehavior is understood, the parent can understand how their responses often support the behavior they are hoping to eliminate.

Children who have a goal of attention usually do things to be noticed. The parent reminds, nags, scolds, and feels annoyed. The child usually stops the behavior temporarily but soon misbehaves again (see Table 1.1).

Children who have a goal of power usually do things to be the boss or have the last word. Parents tend to punish, fight back, or give in and feel angry. The child continues to misbehave, defies the parent, or does what is asked in a slow and sloppy fashion.

A child who has a goal of revenge usually does things to hurt others so that they will understand how the child feels hurt. The parent's response is to "get back" at the child and punish the child, and the parent then feels hurt and mad. The child misbehaves even more and keeps trying to get even.

A child with a goal of display of inadequacy usually does not do much. The parent tends to give up, agree that the child is helpless, and feels hopeless. The child does not respond or improve.

Some children may use different goals at different times or in different situations, whereas other children may favor one of the four goals. The four goals of misbehavior (attention, power, revenge, and display of inadequacy) are immediate goals of behavior and not life style goals.

Adler noticed that people try to compensate for their perceived inferiority. People who have (or believe they have) a deficiency will try harder to overcompensate for the problem. For example, Jim Abbott, who had only one arm, became a baseball player. Wilma Rudolph, who had polio and was not supposed to be able to walk, became the world's fastest runner. The "masculine protest" is a manifestation of the drive to power by which boys and girls struggle to overcome perceived inferiorities on the grounds of gender. Overcompensation provides the catalyst needed to push the boundaries of life.

Although we may appear to be moving toward particular goals, we may, in fact, be escaping past dramas. By (unconsciously) using the original mode that helped in an earlier situation, we are hoping to escape further pain, even though there is not necessarily a present threat. It is inevitable that the original mode will influence the present outcome and that the result may not always be healthy.

HOW DID ADLER SEE CHANGE TAKING PLACE?

Adler firmly believed that change was both possible and desirable. Men and woman who become blocked in their emotions need to change. They

TABLE 1.1
The Goals of Misbehavior

Child's faulty goal	Child's goal	Parent's feelings and reaction	Child's response to parent's attempts at correction	Alternative for parents
I belong *only* when I am being noticed or served.	Attention	Feeling: Annoyed. Reaction: Tendency to remind or coax.	Temporarily stops misbehavior or disturbs in another way.	Ignore misbehavior when possible. Give attention for positive behavior when child is not making a bid for it. Avoid undue service. Realize that reminding, punishing, rewarding, coaxing, and service are undue attention.
I belong *only* when I am in control or am boss, or when I am proving no one can boss me!	Power	Feeling: Angry, provoked, as if one's authority is threatened. Reaction: Tendency to fight or give in.	Active- or passive-aggressive misbehavior is intensified, or child submits with "defiant compliance."	Withdraw from conflict. Help child see how to use power constructively by appealing for child's help and enlisting cooperation. Realize that fighting or giving in only increases child's desire for power.
I belong *only* by hurting others as I feel hurt. I cannot be loved.	Revenge	Feeling: Deeply hurt. Reaction: Tendency to go retaliate and get even.	Seeks further revenge by intensifying misbehavior or choosing another weapon.	Avoid feeling hurt. Avoid punishment and retribution. Build trusting relationship; convince child that she is loved.
I belong *only* by convincing others not to expect anything from me; I am helpless.	Display of inadequacy	Feeling: Despair, hopelessness; "I give up." Reaction: Tendency to agree with child that nothing can be done.	Passively responds or fails to respond to whatever is done. Shows no improvement.	Stop all criticism. Encourage any positive attempt, no matter how small; focus on assets. Above all, don't give up.

Note. From *Systematic Training for Effective Parenting (STEP)* (p. 19), by D. Dinkmeyer, G. D. McKay, and D. Dinkmeyer Jr., 1998, Circle Pines, MN: American Guidance Service, Inc. Copyright 1998 by American Guidance Service, Inc., www.agsnet.com. Reprinted with permission.

must take responsibility for their behavior. When their mistaken goals are revealed, they can choose to pursue them with vigor. The process begins with the creation of a positive relationship between the therapist and the person seeking help. Adler believed that collaboration between client and therapist was necessary for change to take place. To emphasize the importance of equality, Adler literally came out from behind the Freudian couch and had the therapist and client face one another. Adlerian psychotherapy methods break the process down as follows:

- Through therapy you can learn about your mistaken goals. Once you are aware of these, you can make one of two choices: (a) change or (b) not change. The relationship between the therapist and client should be one of mutual respect.
- Through knowing your mistaken goals you begin to recognize patterns in your motivation and, as a result, develop insight. Encouragement helps you change your behavior.
- Because new behavior may work better than the old behavior in new situations, you may be able to replace your old private logic with a new common sense.
- As the new common sense grows, you will also show more social interest, and the end result of this is that you also gain a greater sense of belonging.
- Feeling a sense of belonging also means feeling equal to other people, which also means that you are encouraged. In other words, you grow more confident of your place in the world. You feel better about everything.
- Because you feel better about things, you become brave enough to take risks even if it means making mistakes. You have gained the courage to be imperfect. Your new insights, coupled with the new courage to act, add up to change.

WHO IS ALFRED ADLER?

Now that you have a sense of Adler's theory and therapy, you may want to know more about Alfred Adler, the man. He was a physician, educator, practical philosopher, and best-selling author. His life was packed with contrasts. He trained as a physician, became a psychologist and educator, and was a feminist and skilled public speaker. Adler was a friend of Trotsky's but received support and backing from millionaires. Adler believed in personal freedom, social responsibility, and the rights of children and women.

Adler was born on February 7, 1870, in Vienna, Austria. He was the second of six children. His father was a corn trader. Alfred was not a healthy child. He suffered from illnesses and physical problems. As if this were not enough, he was run over twice on the Vienna streets. He was a poor student, and his teacher urged his father to apprentice him to a shoemaker. Adler became motivated to compensate for his learning weakness. He rose to the top of his class. These experiences were catalysts that moved Adler toward a decision to study medicine so he could fight suffering and disease.

Adler became a physician. He began by studying ophthalmology and then moved on to neurology. It is not surprising that he was interested in perception and how one views the world before studying neurology. He also became interested in philosophy and politics, especially socialism and the ideas of Karl Marx. His first publication was a booklet titled "Health Book for the Tailoring Trade," and it criticized the labor conditions and the living conditions of the workers and their families (see Hoffman, 1994). Adler also suggested corrective measures that called for improved housing and a limit on the number of work hours allowed during the week.

Adler was actually more of a humanist than a socialist. He was more interested in the relationships that would be created in a community of equals. He certainly supported socialist ideas, such as the need to improve the living conditions of the poor, but he was also a proponent of the power of each individual to change his or her own life. He believed that education and skill training would make it possible for people to solve their problems and live life in a more satisfying fashion. He had a passionate concern for the common person and was against all forms of prejudice. Adler's ideas are compatible with current guidelines of the American Psychological Association and the American Counseling Association that relate to treatment with regard to diversity of race, gender, ethnicity, and sexual orientation.

Adler married Raissa Epstein, who had a major influence on his life. She was an active Russian socialist and feminist who was very liberal-minded. Among her acquaintances were Leon and Nathalia Trotsky, who became close family friends. It is likely that their collective influence led Adler to present a paper to the Vienna Psychoanalytic Society in 1909, "On the Psychology of Marxism" (Hoffman, 1994).

Adler and Raissa had four children. Kurt and Alexandra followed their father into psychotherapy and practiced in New York City for many years. Cornelia, the middle child, was an artist. The eldest daughter, Valentine, was politically and socially active, like Raissa. She and her husband perished in a Russian gulag just prior to Adler's death. Many speculated that his heart was broken when he heard of Valentine's death. He died shortly thereafter of a heart attack while lecturing in Scotland.

At the time of his death, Adler was very well known. He wrote in a simple, nontechnical style. His first book of popular psychology, *Understanding Human Nature*, was one of the best-selling books of the era, and Adler was in great demand as a public speaker (A. Adler, 1957). Adler was teaching people to recognize how negative behavior could limit their lives and providing outlines on how they could change and improve the quality of life. Adler believed that people needed training in how to live life as equals or in a democratic manner. He believed this training could occur through the written word and spoken word, and not just through therapy.

Adler was a product of his times. He endured many personal and professional hardships. The social movement from autocratic to democratic living was occurring in Europe, and Adler found himself at the forefront with his own liberal views as well as the revolutionary ideas of his wife and friends. He realized that people had been raised in an autocratic (pecking order) system and therefore needed skills to learn to live as equals. Although people believed in the concepts of democracy, they did not know how to treat one another in a democratic or equal fashion. Men talked down to women, adults to children, bosses to employees, rich to poor, and so on. He concentrated on helping parents and teachers educate children differently. He believed that by changing these basic relationships it would be possible to change the entire society.

CONCLUSION

Adler's approach to understanding human behavior integrates thinking, feeling, behaving, and systemic approaches. It is a complete approach that allows one to understand people in the way they want to be understood. People cannot be divided into component parts but are indivisible and need to be considered holistically.

The Adlerian approach is one that shows great respect for all people regardless of gender, ethnicity, behavior, and so on. It is a truly democratic approach that respects the notion that all people are equal and deserve to be treated in that fashion. Adlerians advocate for social justice and the rights of all people.

Adler highlighted the importance of understanding people within their social context. It is not possible to understand them in isolation; everything they do pertains to their social context. This understanding allows therapists to operate on a variety of levels to create change.

Adler realized that an individual's culture helps to create his or her rules, roles, and outlook. He stressed the importance of understanding the cultural context of each person. This understanding will dictate the nature of the intervention. Today's multicultural world makes these ideas especially relevant.

Finally, Adler's approach is simple and practical. The ideas are easy to understand and to use in one's therapy practice and one's daily life. This does not mean, however, that Adler's approach is not powerful.

Adler provided the world a clear understanding of how a socially healthy way of life could be established and maintained. He believed that the healthiest and only sensible goal in life, and its accompanying life style, was social cooperation. He stressed the basic importance of social interest and how serious problems occur when social interest fails to develop.

This book will provide readers with an in-depth understanding of how Adler's ideas can be applied to the practice of counseling and psychotherapy as well as consultation and psychoeducation.

In chapter 2, we describe how many current therapy approaches fit in with Adlerian theory and practice. In chapter 3, we describe the personality theory relevant to psychotherapy, which we introduced in this chapter, in much more depth.

In chapter 4, we discuss the therapeutic relationship from an Adlerian perspective and the essential role of encouragement in supporting the client in the formation and alliance and throughout therapy. In chapters 5 and 6, we turn to assessment. In chapter 5, we discuss psychopathology and how Adlerian thinking can be in tune with the *Diagnostic and Statistical Manual of Mental Disorders* (4th ed., text revision; *DSM–IV–TR*; American Psychiatric Association, 2000). In chapter 6, we broaden the topic of assessment to the ongoing working assessment of personality and presenting problems, and in chapter 7 we present goals and strategies that are used in the day-to-day practice of Adlerian therapy.

In chapters 8 through 12 we show how the theory and practice presented in previous chapters can be applied to a variety of therapy formats. In chapter 8, we describe brief individual therapy from an Adlerian perspective. We do the same thing, for brief couples therapy, in chapter 9. In chapter 10, we describe how group therapy for adults is conducted using Adlerian principles.

Chapter 11 focuses on young children and how to work with them in an Adlerian play therapy format. Chapter 12 also focuses on children in the context of school and family and how consultation and psychoeducation from an Adlerian perspective work. This last chapter represents in a concrete way Adler's abiding belief that individuals cannot be understood without reference to their social context. It also demonstrates his devotion to bringing psychology to the people in great numbers because many more people can be reached through consultation and psychoeducation than through psychotherapy.

We hope these chapters will encourage you to integrate Adlerian principles into your practice, whether you work with individuals, couples, families, or groups. We believe that an understanding of Adlerian theory and practice will help you to achieve more effective results with all of these clients in a brief period.

2

THE CONTEMPORARY RELEVANCE
OF ADLERIAN THERAPY

As we noted in chapter 1, there is a remarkable similarity between Prochaska and Norcross's (1994, 2003) Delphi results and the contemporary practice of Adlerian psychotherapy in that Adlerian therapy is a psychoeducational, present- and future-oriented, time-limited (i.e., brief), and integrative and eclectic approach. In regard to specific theoretical orientations, Prochaska and Norcross (1994, 2003) noted that their results suggest that cognitive and systemic theoretical approaches would continue to grow and thrive. Here again, we see significant similarity with Adlerian psychotherapy because the Adlerian model clearly integrates cognitive and systemic perspectives, and it solidly resonates with postmodern approaches (Watts, 2000).

In this chapter, we begin by discussing integrative areas of common ground between Adlerian psychotherapy and cognitive, systemic, and postmodern approaches. We then address the congruence between Adlerian therapy and both multicultural and positive psychology perspectives. In the section entitled "Validation of Adlerian Therapy," we discuss how the common—or nonspecific—factors of successful psychotherapy outcome research remarkably support the Adlerian approach to psychotherapy. Last, we touch on the topic of how Adler's theories were out of step with the prevailing metaphors of his time and note how contemporary theorists have integrated his theories into their practice.

ADLERIAN THERAPY AND COGNITIVE, SYSTEMIC, AND POSTMODERN PERSPECTIVES

Cognitive and Cognitive–Behavioral Approaches

The fact that Adlerian psychotherapy has substantial common ground with cognitive and cognitive–behavioral approaches is well documented in the Adlerian literature (e.g., Dowd & Kelly, 1980; Mosak & Maniacci, 1999; Shulman, 1985; Sperry, 2003; Watts, 2000, 2003a; Watts & Critelli, 1997). A number of non-Adlerians have noted, in a general sense, the influence of Adler on contemporary cognitive therapies. For example, Raimy (1975) iden-tified Adler as the first phenomenological, cognitive theorist and therapist in the modern era. Sundberg and Tyler (1976) acknowledged Adler as hav-ing pioneered a cognitive approach to psychotherapy and noted that many present-day theorists and practitioners are emphasizing cognitive and social aspects of personality similar to those discussed by Adler. Murray and Jacobsen (1978) explicated the cognitive focus of Adler's approach and credited him with being the forerunner of many modern cognitive therapies, including those developed by George Kelly, Albert Ellis, and Aaron Beck. According to Corey (1991), "contemporary cognitive–behavioral therapy looks much like Adlerian therapy" (p. 164).

Ellis (1970), founder of rational–emotive behavior therapy (REBT), noted that "Alfred Adler, more than even Freud, is probably the true father of modern psychotherapy" (p. 11). Ellis (1989, 2000) has identified Adler as the foundational modern-era precursor to REBT and stated that "it is highly probable that without [Adler's] pioneering work, the main elements of [REBT] might never have been developed" (Ellis, 1973, p. 112):

> The work of Adler was important to the development of [REBT] in sev-eral respects. Adler was the first great therapist to really emphasize infe-riority feelings—while [REBT] similarly stresses self-rating and the ego anxiety to which it leads. Like Adler and his Individual Psychology, [REBT] also emphasizes people's goals, purposes, values, and meanings. [REBT] also follows Adler in regard to the use of active–directive teach-ing, the stress placed on social interest, the use of a holistic and human-istic outlook, and the employment of highly cognitive-persuasive forms of psychological treatment. (Ellis, 1973, p. 130)

Beck (1976), the developer of cognitive therapy, cited Adler as the earliest of the attitudinal therapists who "focus[ed] on the person's ideas—

his introspections, his observations of himself, his plans for solving problems" (p. 22).

> Alfred Adler's Individual Psychology emphasized the importance of understanding the patient within the framework of his own conscious experiences. For Adler, therapy consisted of attempting to unravel how the person perceived and experienced the world. (Beck, Rush, Shaw, & Emery, 1979, pp. 8–9)

Freeman (1981) cited Adler as the "earliest of the cognitive therapists" (p. 228) and indicated that Beck and Ellis both credit their training in Adlerian psychology and psychotherapy as foundational to their development of their respective cognitive models of psychotherapy (Freeman, 1993). Freeman and Urschel (2003) addressed the similarity between Adlerian and cognitive psychotherapies:

> It is interesting to present Adlerian concepts to psychology students or to mental health professionals who have been trained in a cognitive behavior therapy [CBT] model. The responses can be categorized into three main types. The first type of response involves extensive note taking. To this group, the material is new, interesting, useful, and relevant. The second type of response is manifested by those who sit back and simply nod. After all, these ideas make sense and appear to be consistent with CBT. What's new? A third response involves a mild protest. After all, who is this Adler fellow to co-opt so many of the CBT ideas? (p. 71)

The similarities between cognitive–behavior therapy and Adlerian therapy are "rooted in [a] shared conceptual framework of examining the rules of life that each person acquires" (Freeman & Urschel, 2003, p. 73).

According to Sperry (2003), there are at least three basic components of Adlerian psychotherapy that are generally recognizable in cognitive therapy. These include (a) a therapeutic focus on life style convictions, or what cognitive therapists call *underlying schemas*; (b) a therapeutic relationship that emphasizes cooperation and collaboration; and (c) therapeutic change, or the process of reeducation and reorientation.

> Although the term "cognitive restructuring" did not come into vogue until much later, this was Adler's aim. Adler . . . at one point describes the goal of therapy as replacing large errors (in cognition) with smaller ones, "and to reduce these even further until they are no longer harmful." (Mosak & Maniacci, 1999, p. 153)

Sperry's (2003) observations are particularly salient regarding the relationship between Adlerian therapy and the cognitive therapy approach known as *schema-focused therapy* (Young, 1999) or simply *schema therapy* (Young, Klosko, & Weishaar, 2003). A developmentally oriented cognitive therapy, schema therapy focuses on the role of maladaptive schemas that are developed in early childhood in response to difficult family experiences and other abusive or traumatic events. Oberst and Stewart (2003) noted that the significance of these early maladaptive schemas for the development of subsequent psychopathology is remarkably similar to the Adlerian position regarding the role of the family atmosphere and other early childhood influences on the development of problematic aspects of what Adler called the *schema of apperception* and *private logic* within the life style (one's style of being, relating to others, and relating to world and the tasks of living). Thus, as Oberst and Stewart indicated, children who experience abuse, neglect, hatred, or pampering may, very early in life, develop core schemas of themselves as "damaged, unworthy, deserving of negative treatment, and so forth. The private logic of these individuals may evolve and operate in ways that perpetuate the dysfunctional and self-defeating [life styles] resulting from the experience of distress early in life" (Oberst & Stewart, 2003, p. 138).

The Adlerian term *life style convictions* is essentially similar to cognitive therapy's underlying schemas, and thus maladaptive life style convictions parallel schema therapy's notion of maladaptive schemas. According to Oberst and Stewart (2003), Adlerian therapy and developmentally oriented cognitive therapy practitioners (e.g., schema therapists) may "focus on the early, conscious decisions that people made about how to respond to their distressing experiences as a way to build insight about their private logic or their maladaptive schemata" (p. 138):

> That is, Adlerians . . . and some cognitive therapists . . . believe that clients, even as children, make conscious decisions about the meanings of challenging events they experience and about how they will respond emotionally and behaviorally . . . [and] these decisions may elude discovery as they are covered over by the passage of time and with the evolution of subsequent schemata. (pp. 138–139)

Young et al. (2003) indicated that schema therapy is an integrative approach that blends elements from cognitive–behavioral, Gestalt, constructivist, and psychodynamic and psychoanalytic perspectives. Adlerian therapy is an integration of cognitive, systemic, existential, and psychodynamic perspectives. Given their shared integrative underpinnings, it is not surprising that schema therapy and Adlerian therapy share many similarities.

Systemic Approaches

According to Sherman and Dinkmeyer (1987), Adler most likely developed the first professional couple and family counseling and family education models, and these were used in child guidance centers in Europe from immediately after World War I until 1934, when Nazi German officials forced them to close. Consequently, there is an ample literature discussing the similarity or integrative compatibility of Adlerian therapy and family systems approaches by both Adlerian and family systems authors (e.g., Broderick &

Schrader, 1991; Carich & Willingham, 1987; Carlson & Dinkmeyer, 1999; Christensen, 1993; Evans & Milliren, 1999; Kern, Hawes, & Christensen, 1989; LaFountain & Mustaine, 1998; Nichols & Schwartz, 1995; Sperry & Carlson, 1991; Sperry, Carlson, & Peluso, 2005; Watts, 2000).

According to Sherman and Dinkmeyer (1987), "Adler's concerns, ideas, and methods cut across what today are called structural, strategic, communications, experiential, behavioral, cognitive, multigenerational, and ego psychology approaches to the family" (p. xi). To support this statement, Sherman and Dinkmeyer asked six family therapy experts—each from a different theoretical framework—to rate the degree of emphasis or acceptability of 66 family therapy concepts, change methods, and techniques according to their specific theoretical perspective. The six approaches represented were (a) Adlerian, (b) human validation process (Satir Model), (c) Mental Research Institute (MRI), (d) rational–emotive, (e) structural, and (f) strategic family therapies. Sherman and Dinkmeyer indicated that their hypothesis, that "Adlerian theory in particular overlaps to a high degree with most other [family] theories," was supported. They reported that on 92.4% of the 66 items, the majority of the other five approaches and the Adlerian approach were in agreement regarding whether the items were accepted or rejected. The authors concluded that there is significant overlap and convergence between Adlerian therapy and systemic approaches.

Many family therapy authors agree that Adlerian therapy and various family therapies share considerable common ground. For example, Foley (1989) stated that Adler significantly influenced family therapy and that Adlerian therapy and family therapy share many similarities:

> [Adlerian therapy's] emphasis on the family constellation is a major concept borrowed by family therapists. Adler's approach was holistic, as is family therapy. The use of paradox, a major weapon in family therapy, has its roots in Alfred Adler.... The freedom to improvise is a feature of family therapy and . . . has roots in Adler. (p. 458) . . . Adler emphasized the conscious, the positive, and the ability to change. This typifies family therapy. . . . Oscar Christensen, an Adlerian family therapist, says "Adler would view behavior as movement, communication, movement toward others, and the desire to belong—the desire to be part of". . . . This is a description of family therapy. (p. 460)

Goldenberg and Goldenberg (2000) agreed that Adlerian therapy is conceptually similar and compatible to family therapy formulations:

> Adlerian theory emphasizes the social content of behavior, the embeddedness of the individual in his or her interpersonal relationships, and the importance of present circumstances and future goals rather than unresolved issues from childhood. Both Adlerian psychotherapy and family therapy take a holistic view of the person and emphasize intent and conscious choices. Adler's efforts to establish a child guidance move-

ment, as well as his concern with improving parenting practices, reflects his interest beyond the individual to family functioning. (p. 379)

Adlerian authors Carlson, Sperry, and Lewis (1997, 2005) and Sherman (1999; Sherman & Dinkmeyer, 1987) have noted that Adlerian psychotherapy's emphasis on holism, nonlinearity, cognition, purposeful or goal-directed behavior, and social embeddedness clearly parallels systemic perspectives:

> Both individuals and social systems are holistic, and individuals seek significance by the manner of their behavior in social systems. The basic social system is the family. It is from the family that individuals learn how to belong and interact. (Carlson et al., 1997, p. 42)

Postmodern Approaches

As noted earlier, Adlerian psychotherapy is an integration of cognitive, systemic, existential, and psychodynamic perspectives. Consequently, it resembles many contemporary cognitive and constructive approaches. The relationship between three popular postmodern approaches—constructivist therapy, solution-focused brief therapy (SFBT), and narrative therapy—and Adlerian therapy has been addressed to varying degrees in the literature, and substantial common ground between the postmodern therapies and Adlerian psychotherapy has been demonstrated.

Constructivist Therapy

Adlerian and constructivist theories both affirm that humans are creative agents in the construction of their own personalities and the subsequent perceptions and interpretations of themselves, others, and the world (Carlson & Sperry, 1998; Watkins, 1997; Watts, 2000; Watts & Critelli, 1997; Watts & Shulman, 2003).

> Human beings live in the realm of *meanings*. We do not experience things in the abstract; we always experience them in human terms. Even at its source our experience is qualified by our human perspective. . . . Anyone who tried to consider circumstances, to the exclusion of meanings, would be very unfortunate: he would isolate himself from others and his actions would be useless to himself or to anyone else; in a word, they would be meaningless. But no human being can escape meanings. We experience reality only through the meaning we ascribe to it: not as a thing in itself, but as something interpreted. (A. Adler, 1931/1992, p. 15)

According to Carlson and Sperry (1998), the realization that individuals coconstruct the reality in which they live and that they are also able to question, deconstruct, or reconstruct reality for themselves is a fundamental tenet not only of Adlerian psychotherapy but also of other constructivist psychotherapies (p. 68).

G. Kelly (1955), creator of personal construct psychology and psychotherapy, noted the similarity between his "superordinate constructs" and Adler's "style of life" (p. 88). Mahoney (1991, 2003) has noted that both Kelly and Adler were significantly influenced by Hans Vaihinger's (1925) book, *The Philosophy of "As If."* Mahoney (1991, 2003) stated that Vaihinger emphasized that human cognitive processes serve a purposeful, instrumental, and functional significance for survival and activity in the world. According to Vaihinger,

> Consciousness is not to be compared to a mere passive mirror, which reflects rays according to purely physical laws, but "consciousness receives no external stimulation without moulding it according to its own nature." The psyche then is an organic formative force, which independently changes what has been appropriated, and can adapt foreign elements to its own requirements as easily as it adapts itself to what is new. The mind is not merely appropriative, it is also assimilative and constructive. . . . [Thus, Vaihinger argued that] the object of the world of ideas is not to portray reality—an utterly impossible task—but rather to provide us with *an instrument for finding our way about more easily in this world.* (cited in Mahoney, 1991, pp. 98–99)

Both Adler and Kelly drew on Vaihinger's work for the notion of *fictions*, subjective thought constructs that, although not necessarily corresponding with reality, serve as useful tools for coping with the tasks and problems of living.

Higgins (2002) stated that "constructivist therapies have been practiced since the early 20th century" and cited Adler's approach to therapy as the first constructivist therapy. Furthermore, Michael Mahoney (2002, 2003) and Robert Neimeyer (2003), both well-known constructivists, have acknowledged Adlerian psychology and psychotherapy as a constructivist theory and approach to therapy. In addition, the literature addressing the similarity and potential for integration between Adlerian and constructivist therapies has grown significantly in recent years (e.g., Carlson & Sperry, 1998; Jones & Lyddon, 2003; Mahoney, 1991, Maniacci, 2003; Master, 1991; Oberst & Stewart, 2003; Scott, Kelly, & Tolbert, 1995; Watts, 2000, 2003b; Watts & Critelli, 1997; Watts & Shulman, 2003).

Solution-Focused Brief Therapy

Watts (1999; Watts & Pietrzak, 2000) reviewed the literature written by proponents of SFBT and found no substantive mention of Adlerian therapy. Nevertheless, a wealth of common ground between the two approaches has been identified (LaFountain, 1996; LaFountain & Garner, 1998; Watts, 1999; Watts & Pietrzak, 2000). For example, Watts (1999; Watts & Pietrzak, 2000) identified striking similarities between the assumptions and characteristics of the encouragement process as used in Adlerian therapy and the therapeutic process of SFBT. For further discussion of this topic, see chapter 8.

Narrative Therapy

A review of narrative therapy literature, as with SFBT, produced no mention of Adlerian therapy (Watts, 1999). However, in a special issue of the *Journal of Individual Psychology* (Schneider & Stone, 1998) entitled "Narrative Therapy and Adlerian Psychology," Adlerians do identify substantial common ground between the two approaches. Narrative and Adlerian approaches resonate on the issue of social constructionism, and they share common therapeutic methods, albeit with different nomenclature.

According to Singer and Salovey (1993), Adler was the earliest personality theorist and psychotherapist to discuss the central role and use of self-defining or narrative memory in psychotherapy. They noted that the essence of what many contemporary authors have to say about meaningful memory was said by Adler in the first three decades of the 20th century. Similarly, Disque and Bitter (1998) noted that we live "storied" lives:

> As humans, we not only experience life directly through our senses, but we also transform it in an effort to make meaning out of what we experience. We live constantly with other human beings, and as such, we frame all that we do in the context of social relationships. The ordering of the meaning we experience in our lives with others most often takes the form of a story or narrative about who we are; who others are; what we are worth to ourselves, others, and the world; and what conclusions, convictions, and ethical codes will guide us. . . . Adler was one of the first to recognize this process in human development. He called the ordering of our experiences into a teleological narrative our lifestyle, our unique way of being, of coping, and of moving through (and approaching) the tasks of life. (p. 431)

What we know is influenced by the frames through which we view events. Everything we know depends on how we interpret and assign meanings (Neimeyer, 1995). Knowledge is derived from looking at the world from a particular perspective and is in the service of some interests rather than others. "If I ask about the world, you can offer to tell me how it is under one or more frames of reference, but if I insist that you tell me how it is apart from all frames, what can you say?" (Goodman, quoted in Gergen, 2001, p. 11). Narrative therapists Parry and Doan (1994) noted that neurobiological research indicates that one of the brain's primary functions is to create a model of the world, an internal blueprint or road map. The brain's function of creating an internal blueprint or road map is variously labeled by cognitive constructivist approaches as *core ordering processes, personal construct systems, personal meaning organization, underlying schemas,* and the like. It is important to note, however, that social constructionist therapies (e.g., narrative therapy) disdain the structural language used by cognitive constructivist therapies and the individualist implications thereof. They instead use literary metaphors such as narratives or stories. Regardless of the language or root metaphors used by cognitive constructivist or social constructionist therapies, they, like Adlerian psychotherapy, are nevertheless addressing the individual's personal metanarrative for apprehending and responding to life; that is, how humans construct or make meaning of their experiences (Watts, 2003a, 2003b; Watts & Phillips, 2004).

Bridging Postmodern Perspectives:
A Contemporary Adlerian Perspective

As Dinkmeyer and Sperry (2000) indicated, "there is increasing interest in emphasizing the commonalities and converging themes among psychotherapy systems" (p. 9), and psychotherapy integration is the prevalent focus among many psychotherapy theorists, researchers, and practitioners. Adlerian therapy clearly resonates with cognitive, constructivist, and social constructionist perspectives. In recent years, several authors have broached the idea of bridging cognitive constructivist and social constructionist theories and psychotherapies (Botella & Herrero, 2000; Botella, Herrero, Pacheco, & Corbella, 2004; Martin & Sugarman, 1997, 1999; Neimeyer, 2000). Botella and Herrero (2000), Botella et al. (2004), and Neimeyer (2000) have suggested that this integrative bridge might be usefully labeled *relational constructivism*. It has been suggested that Adlerian psychology and psychotherapy, understood as a relational constructivist approach, is situated within the dialogic space between cognitive constructivist and social constructionist perspectives in a flexible, integrative manner (Watts, 2003b; Watts & Shulman, 2003).

It might be helpful at this juncture to provide brief, operational definitions for *cognitive constructivism* and *social constructionism*. Both perspectives may be considered constructive or constructivistic in the sense that both stress the ongoing processes of psychological organizing, disorganizing, and reorganizing (Mahoney, 2003). According to cognitive constructivist perspectives, the primary focus is on the role of the individual in learning and psychological development. As Martin and Sugarman (1999) noted,

> (Cognitive) constructivists conceive of hypothetical learning mechanisms or processes intrinsic to the nature of human individuals. These mechanisms or processes are believed to preside over the individual's development, serving to construct, manipulate, transform, and append the various mental representations and organizations that comprise the individual's cognitive architecture. (p. 9)

Social constructionist perspectives, on the other hand, state that the focus of learning and psychological development is fundamentally conversational and interrelational:

> Psychological activity . . . is seen to arise from, and to reflect our immersion in, discursive social, relational practices. It is through our involve-

ment in such practices that we acquire, develop, convey, and confer upon others the symbolic cognitive tools through which we manage our psychological engagement with the world. The means for organizing thought and forging and expressing experiential and imaginal constructions derive from our attunement to relational practices, the most conspicuous being conversations. (Martin & Sugarman, 1999, p. 8)

According to the Adlerian approach, "persons must be ultimately understood in social context; it is in relationships that humans have their meaning. . . . Psychological theories tend to be either individualistic or collectivistic—in the former community disappears; in the latter, the individual disappears" (Jones & Butman, 1991, p. 237). Adlerian theory, on the other hand, is "a healthy balance of the individual rooted in relationships" (Jones & Butman, 1991, p. 237).

The Adlerian perspective agrees with social constructionism regarding the sociocultural origins of human psychological development, and it affirms cognitive constructivism's emphasis on the importance of humans as active agents creatively involved in the coconstruction of their own psychology (Carlson & Sperry, 1998; Mosak & Maniacci, 1999; Watts, 2003b; Watts & Shulman, 2003). Adlerian theory and therapy agree with Martin and Sugarman's (1997) position that "although humans exist in a sociocultural world of persons, a distinguishing characteristic of personhood is the possession of an individual agentic consciousness" (p. 377). It is true that some constructivist and social constructionist theorists and theories disdain individualism and state that it is impossible for humans to escape being situated in some relational matrix. However, if there is no self-reflexive individual, and situatedness is indeed inescapable, then it is a spurious notion to think that we can engage in what Gergen (1999) called the "emancipatory potential of discourse analysis, that is, inquiry which causes us to reflect critically and creatively on our own forms of life" (p. 80). The conviction expressed by social constructionists that all that is meaningful stems from relationships has no particular utility for one's present situation, because "the constraints of that situation will not be relaxed by that knowledge" (Fish, quoted in Korobov, 2000, p. 368). Thus, the value of a relational constructivist position such as Adlerian psychology and psychotherapy is that it accounts for both the social-embedded nature of human knowledge and the personal agency of creative and self-reflective individuals within relationships (Watts, 2003b; Watts & Shulman, 2003).

The Adlerian perspective, in agreement with Martin and Sugarman (1997), states that the individual arises from the social but is not the same as, nor is it reducible to, the social. Adlerian theory is a holistic perspective, one that does not view humans in a reductionistic manner. The Adlerian approach affirms that knowledge is socially embedded and relationally distributed but does not empty the self. It embraces a "both/and" position, accounting for and affirming that knowledge and experience is a coconstruction of self and others in a socially embedded matrix (Carlson & Sperry, 1998; Watts, 2003b; Watts & Shulman, 2003).

Adlerian therapy also remarkably parallels constructive approaches to psychotherapy in regard to therapeutic practice. Whereas it is true that constructive approaches certainly have their differences, they share with Adlerian psychotherapy the following clinical–practical characteristics: They place strong emphasis on developing a respectful therapeutic relationship, they emphasize strengths and resources, and they are optimistic and future oriented. Given the aforementioned areas of common ground between Adlerian therapy and the constructive approaches, it is not surprising to discover many similarities in regard to the process of therapy. Although a detailed explication of the similarities is beyond the scope of this chapter, it is important to note that, among many points of common ground, Adlerian and constructive therapies share similar perspectives regarding maladjustment, client reluctance or resistance, the therapeutic alliance, and facilitating change. Adlerian therapy is not focused primarily on, or driven by, techniques and therefore has long been a technically eclectic approach. Consequently, Adlerian therapists place a strong emphasis on developing and maintaining an encouragement-focused therapeutic alliance and tailoring therapy according to each client's unique needs, circumstances, and expectations (Carlson & Slavik, 1997; Carlson & Sperry, 1998; Mosak & Maniacci, 1998; Watts, 2003b; Watts & Carlson, 1999; Watts & Phillips, 2004; Watts & Shulman, 2003).

Adlerian psychotherapy fits well within the contemporary integrative *zeitgeist* of psychotherapy. As a relational and constructivist psychology, Adlerian therapy affirms that humans cannot be understood apart from their social context and the relationships therein; "it is in relationship that humans have their meaning" (Jones & Butman, 1991, p. 237). Adlerian therapy inclusively affirms both the collectivistic and individualistic aspects of human functioning. The Adlerian view of humankind is "a healthy balance of the individual rooted in relationships" (Jones & Butman, 1991, p. 237). In both theory and practice, the Adlerian approach clearly resonates with both cognitive constructivist and social constructionist approaches and could be correctly identified as a relational constructivist approach, one that might usefully bridge cognitive constructivist and social constructionist therapeutic perspectives.

ADLERIAN PSYCHOTHERAPY: CONTEMPORARY MULTICULTURAL CONSIDERATIONS

The research results presented by Prochaska and Norcross (1994) at the beginning of chapter 1 appear to be, for the most part, both congruent with the demands of managed care and supported by contemporary outcome research (Friedman, 1997; Hoyt, 1995; Hubble, Duncan, & Miller, 1999b; Lambert & Barley, 2001; Sauber, 1997; Sexton, Whiston, Bleuer, & Walz, 1997). However, one important issue the research did not address is that of multicultural considerations in psychotherapy. One significant addition in Prochaska and Norcross's (2003) follow-up study was the emphasis on multicultural issues in psychotherapy. The demographics of North America—especially in the United States—are changing at an exponential rate. Thus, if any approach is to be considered a relevant psychotherapy for contemporary society, it must successfully address issues of multiculturalism and social equality (Watts, 2000).

With the increasing emphasis on multiculturalism, many therapists have been drawn to constructive approaches because of these approaches' focus on the social embeddedness of humans and, consequently, human knowledge. Adlerians and Adlerian theory addressed social equality issues and emphasized the social embeddedness of humans and human knowledge long before multiculturalism became a focal issue in the helping professions. Adler campaigned for the social equality of women, contributed much to the understanding of gender issues, spoke against the marginalization of minority groups, and specifically predicted the Black power and women's liberation movements (Ansbacher & Ansbacher, 1978; Dreikurs, 1971; Hoffman, 1994; LaFountain & Mustaine, 1998; Mozdzierz, 1998; Watts, 2000). In addition, Adlerian theory played an influential positive role in the outcome of the historic *Brown v. Board of Education* decision of 1954:

> Kenneth B. Clark headed a team of social scientists who called on Adlerian theory to explain the need for equality in American society. Their argument against separate-but-equal schools swayed the highest court in its decision that ruled in favor of the plaintiffs. (LaFountain & Mustaine, 1998, p. 196)

Adlerian psychotherapy is clearly relevant for working with culturally diverse populations in contemporary society. According to Gerald Corey, the Adlerian approach is "certainly compatible with many of the macrostrategies for future delivery of service to culturally diverse populations" (quoted in T. J. Sweeney, 1998, pp. 33–34). Arciniega and Newlon (1999) noted that the characteristics and assumptions of Adlerian psychology are congruent with the cultural values of many racial–ethnic minority groups and affirmed that the Adlerian therapeutic process is respectful of cultural diversity. Adlerian therapy goals are not aimed at deciding for clients what they should change about themselves:

> Rather, the practitioner works in collaboration with clients and their family networks. This theory offers a pragmatic approach that is flexible and uses a range of action-oriented techniques to explore personal problems within their sociocultural context. It has the flexibility to deal both

with the individual and the family, making it appropriate for racial and ethnic groups. (Arciniega & Newlon, 1999, p. 451)

The Adlerian psychology and psychotherapy literature addresses a wide range of multicultural issues, including culture, ethnicity, gender, racism, sexual orientation, and social equality (e.g., Ansbacher & Ansbacher, 1978; Brack, Hill, Edwards, Grootboom, & Lassiter, 2003; Carlson & Carlson, 2000; Chandler, 1991; Chernin & Holden, 1995; Dreikurs, 1971; Duffy, Carns, Carns, & Garcia, 1998; Frevert & Miranda, 1998; Hanna, 1998; Hedberg & Huber, 1995; Herring & Runion, 1994; Miranda & Umhoefer, 1998; Newlon & Arciniega, 1983; Reddy & Hanna, 1995; Roberts, Harper, Tuttle Eagle Bull, & Heideman-Provost, 1998; Salzman, 2002; Schramski & Giovando, 1993; Sperry, 1995).

A rapidly growing dimension of multiculturalism includes attention to and appreciation of the role of religion or spirituality in the lives of clients. The field of counseling and psychotherapy has made a 180-degree turn, from a position of disdain and avoidance to one that is beginning to appreciate the influence of spiritual issues on cognition; emotion; and, ultimately, behavior (Propst, 1996; Watts, 2001, 2003b; Watts & Shulman, 2003). According to Mahoney (1995), "issues of value—good–bad, right–wrong, and sacred–profane" will become increasingly central in the future of psychotherapy, "with the dimensions of religiosity and spirituality taking on new meanings in psychological assessment" (p. 55).

A key value for many clients is their personal spirituality. Without understanding their clients' spiritual perspective, therapists are "operating with a vital value system and possibly even a member of the family, God, left at home and ignored" (Grizzle, 1992, p. 139). Spirituality is a vital area for therapists to understand, because clients' spiritual beliefs typically provide the value system by which they view themselves, others, and the world (Watts, 2001, 2003b; Watts & Shulman, 2003).

Historically, most systems of psychology have had either a neutral or negative position toward religion and spirituality. Adlerian therapy, however, has been quite open to addressing religious and spiritual issues. The topic is addressed somewhat regularly by authors in the *Journal of Individual Psychology* (e.g., Mansager, 2000).

According to Manaster and Corsini (1982), "the most common Adlerian position toward religion is positive, viewing God as the concept of perfection. . . . For Adler, religion was a manifestation of social interest" (p. 63). Mosak (1995) noted that "Adler's psychology has a religious tone. His placement of social interest at the pinnacle of his value theory is in the tradition of those religions that stress people's responsibility for each other" (p. 59). Mosak (1995) mentioned that when Adler introduced the concepts of value and meaning into psychology via his 1931 book *What Life Should Mean to You*, the concepts were unpopular at the time. The cardinal tenet of Adlerian theory is social interest, something Adler equated with the mandate to "love one's neighbor as oneself" and the Golden Rule. Furthermore, Mosak (1995) identified spirituality as one of the five major tasks of life:

> Although Adler alluded to the *spiritual*, he never specifically named it. But each of us must deal with the problems of defining the nature of the universe, the existence and nature of God, and how to relate to these concepts. (p. 54)

ADLERIAN THERAPY AND THE POSITIVE PSYCHOLOGY MOVEMENT

According to Mosak and Maniacci (1999), the basic tenets of Adlerian psychology and psychotherapy have become mainstreamed into contemporary thought—particularly in psychology—yet Adler's pioneering influence is only rarely mentioned. This is evident in the recent positive psychology movement.

In the preface of the *Handbook of Positive Psychology*, the editors (Snyder & Lopez, 2002) describe the positive psychology movement as a "new approach" because "psychology and its sister disciplines . . . focus on the weaknesses in humankind" (p. ix). In affirming the positive qualities of humankind, the editors stated that "*no science, including psychology, looks seriously at this positive side of people*" (p. x).

Chapters in the *Handbook of Positive Psychology* (Snyder & Lopez, 2002) include discussions of topics that are in the Adlerian literature. Higgins (2002) and Mahoney (2002) both briefly noted that Adler's approach was, and is, a constructivist personality theory and psychotherapy; however, no substantive mention of Adlerian psychology or psychotherapy as a pioneering positive psychology is offered in the book. For example, in the opening chapter of the *Handbook*, "Positive Psychology, Positive Prevention, and Positive Therapy," Seligman (2002) stated that the goal of positive psychology is to move from a preoccupation with pathology to a more balanced perspective that includes the idea of "a fulfilled individual and a thriving community" by emphasizing "the possibility of building strength as the most potent weapon in the arsenal of therapy" (p. 3). In his conclusion, Seligman stated, "I well recognize that positive psychology is not a new idea. It has many distinguished ancestors" (p. 7). The two examples of ancestors he mentions are Gordon Allport and Abraham Maslow. Although Adler is not listed as a forefather of positive psychology, the goal of positive psychology has been a historical Adlerian position.

Many aspects of the positive psychology movement specifically align with Adlerian theory and therapy. Examples include the following shared emphases: normal human growth and development; prevention and education rather than merely remediation; a shift away from the medical model perspective; a focus on mental health and clients' strengths, resources, and abilities rather than psychopathology and clients' disabilities; and holism, wellness, multiculturalism, and social justice (A. Adler, 1956, 1979; Ansbacher, 1992; Mosak & Maniacci, 1999; T. J. Sweeney, 1998; Watts, 1999, 2003b; Watts & Shulman, 2003). This list of shared emphases is by no means exhaustive.

Cowen and Kilmer (2002) offered a critique of positive psychology's lack of attention to the precursory literature:

> [Positive psychology's] major current limitations include: (a) a relative insulation from closely related prior work in primary prevention and wellness enhancement; (b) its lack of a cohesive undergirding theoretical framework; and (c) its primarily adult, cross-sectional approach which does not sufficiently reflect key life history and developmental pathways and determinants of specific positive outcomes. (p. 449)

The authors criticize the positive psychology literature for its "insulation from closely related prior work" regarding prevention and wellness, and its lack of developmental perspective, yet they do not mention the Adlerian literature, which is closely related, prior, developmental, and includes prevention and wellness perspectives. Furthermore, Adlerian theory could serve as the useful "cohesive undergirding theoretical framework" that Cowen and Kilmer suggested is lacking in positive psychology.

Adlerian psychology is a growth model that emphasizes the holistic, phenomenological, teleological, and field-theoretically and socially embedded aspects of human functioning. It is an optimistic perspective that views people as unique, creative, capable, and responsible. In the post-Freudian phase of his career, Adler progressively moved from a primary focus on abnormal human behavior to one emphasizing normal human development. Adlerians eschew the medical model orientation to maladjustment and embrace a nonpathological perspective. Clients are not sick (in the sense of having a disease) and are not identified or labeled by their diagnoses. Because Adlerians believe the growth model of personality makes more sense than the medical model, they see clients as discouraged rather than ill. Thus, Adlerians are not about curing anything; therapy is a process of encouragement. In fact, Adlerians consider encouragement a crucial aspect of human growth and development (Manaster & Corsini, 1982; Mosak & Maniacci, 1999).

Whereas they have focused on prevention rather than simply remediation, Adlerians have functioned extensively in education. Throughout his career, Adler was actively involved in public health, medical and psychological prevention, and social welfare. He wrote, lectured on, and advocated for children at risk, women's rights and the equality of the sexes, women's rights to abortion, adult education, teacher training, community mental health, family counseling and education and the establishment of family counseling clinics, experimental schools for public students, and brief psychotherapy (Mosak & Maniacci, 1999). Adlerians have continued Adler's emphasis on prevention and education. For example, they have been perhaps the strongest proponents of child guidance and parent and family education and have written extensively on parent and family education, couple enrichment, and teacher education.

Adlerian therapy is a positive psychology and an approach to therapy that emphasizes prevention, optimism and hope, resilience and growth, competence, creativity and resourcefulness, social consciousness, and finding meaning and a sense of community in relationships. Indeed, Adlerian therapy has a long history of being a positive psychology and psychotherapy.

VALIDATION OF ADLERIAN THERAPY

Watkins and Guarnaccia (1999) correctly noted that although there is a solid body of research literature addressing (and supporting) central constructs of Adlerian psychological theory, research studies on Adlerian psychotherapy are "few, far between, and hard to find" (p. 226). They suggested that Adlerian psychotherapy research might benefit from the development of an Adlerian treatment manual that could be used in therapist training and as a guide to research. They further stated that "Such manuals are not a panacea, and problems attendant to them must be borne in mind. . . . Yet they could be one viable means of allowing [Adlerians] to . . . research the Adlerian therapy process, its effects, its outcome" (Watkins & Guarnaccia, 1999, p. 227).

Whereas Adlerians have historically preferred an idiographic or case study method (Mosak, 2000), Edwards, Dattilio, and Bromley's (2004) recent suggestion—that clinical practice and case-based research be included as a significant contributor to evidence-based practice—may be of particular interest to Adlerians. Similarly, the burgeoning qualitative research methodologies may also prove useful for studying Adlerian psychotherapy. Regardless of the methodologies researchers choose, Adlerian psychotherapy certainly will benefit from additional research.

This not to say, however, that there is no research supporting Adlerian psychotherapy. There is a wealth of current research that clearly—albeit indirectly—supports the process and practice of Adlerian therapy. For example, as we explained in chapter 1 and at the beginning of this chapter, the results of Prochaska and Norcross's (1994, 2003) research are remarkably similar to the contemporary theory and practice of Adlerian psychotherapy. Thus, Prochaska and Norcross's (1994, 2003) results are consistent with, and provide support for, the fundamental tenets of Adlerian psychotherapy.

Perhaps even more remarkable is the significant common ground between Adlerian therapy and the research addressing the transtheoretical factors commonly identified in the successful psychotherapy outcome literature (e.g., Hubble et al., 1999b; Lambert, 1992; Norcross, 2002; Prochaska & Norcross, 2003; Wampold, 2001). Mental health professionals have long observed that different approaches to psychotherapy share common elements or core features. According to contemporary research literature, 40% of the variance in successful outcomes is accounted for by extratherapeutic and client factors (i.e., what clients bring to therapy, e.g., attitudes, motivation, strengths and assets, social support, etc.). Thirty percent of the variance is accounted for by therapeutic relationship factors (i.e., the counseling relationship and therapeutic alliance developed between the client and therapist). Fifteen percent of the variance in successful outcomes is accounted for by placebo, hope, and expectancy factors (i.e., the hope and expectancy of success generated in therapy); and 15% of the variance is accounted for by model/technique factors (i.e., the therapist's theory and techniques; Hubble et al., 1999b; Lambert, 1992; Wampold, 2001).

Adlerian Therapy and the Transtheoretical Factors of Successful Outcomes

Prochaska and Norcross (2003) stated that,

> Despite theoretical differences, there is a central and recognizable core of psychotherapy . . . [that] distinguishes it from other activities . . . and glues together variations of psychotherapy. The core is composed of *common factors* or nonspecific variables common to all forms of psychotherapy and not specific to one. More often than not, these therapeutic commonalities are not specified by theories as being of central importance, but the research suggests exactly the opposite. (p. 6)

We would argue that Adlerian therapy resonates enormously with the common factors of successful outcomes and that these common factors are indeed specified by Adlerian therapy as being of central importance. Next we offer a brief description of the points of common ground between Adlerian therapy and the common factors of successful psychotherapy outcomes.

Extratherapeutic/Client Factors

According to the research literature, client factors exert the greatest impact on psychotherapy outcome. These factors consist of what clients bring to therapy and the influences and circumstances in clients' lives outside of it (Hubble, Duncan, & Miller, 1999c).

Adlerian therapy stresses the importance of attending to what clients bring to therapy; especially their strengths, assets, and resources. According to Adler (1913/1956), "The actual change in . . . the patient can only be his own doing" (p. 336). Consequently, therapists must believe that clients have the requisite capabilities to solve their problems (Mosak, 1979). Hubble, Duncan, and Miller expressed (1999a) this well:

It is perhaps best summarized by Alfred Adler when he said he approached all clients, "fully convinced that no matter what I might be able to say . . . the patient can learn nothing from me that he, as the sufferer, does not understand better" (Adler, 1913/1956, p. 336). Approaching clients in this manner not only helps to combat discouragement and instill hope but, as Adler also noted, "make[s] it clear that the responsibility for . . . cure is the patient's business" (Adler, 1913/1956, p. 336). (p. 411)

Therapeutic Relationship Factors

Extratherapeutic/client factors have the most significant influence on the results of psychotherapy. It is clear, however, that therapeutic relationship factors play a crucial role in successful outcomes. According to Asay and Lambert (1999), the research demonstrates that positive outcomes in psychotherapy are clearly related to therapist relationship skills and are essential for building and maintaining a strong therapeutic alliance.

Of all the common factors, Adlerian psychotherapy most strongly resonates with the emphasis on the therapeutic relationship. Adlerian psychotherapy, a relational approach, consists of four phases. The first and most important phase, called the *relationship* phase, clearly focuses on establishing a strong client–therapist alliance. Furthermore, and consistent with the positive outcome research literature, Adlerians believe that therapeutic efficacy in other phases of Adlerian therapy is predicated on the development and continuation of a meaningful therapeutic alliance.

Therapeutic relationship variables are so important in Adlerian therapy that we devote an entire chapter to the topic (see chap. 4). In that chapter, we more fully delineate the common ground between Adlerian therapy and the therapeutic relationship factors. We also address how the encouragement-focused therapeutic process of Adlerian therapy attends to both the extratherapeutic/client factors and the hope and expectancy factors.

Placebo, Hope, and Expectancy

Asay and Lambert (1999) noted that clients come to therapy because they have lost hope; not only are they "demoralized about having problems," but they also "have lost hope about being able to solve them" (p. 44). They noted that expectancy of success generated in therapy is powerful because it helps provide clients with hope that their problems can be solved.

Mosak (2000) described the Adlerian therapeutic process in terms of "faith, hope, and love" (p. 67), that is, expressing faith in the client, developing the client's faith in him- or herself, and both the client and therapist having faith in the therapeutic process; engendering hope in clients who present with varying levels of hope of improvement; and love, in the broadest sense, in that the client experiences a relationship with a caring, empathic, nonjudgmental, genuine human being. Adlerian therapy is an optimistic and encouragement-focused approach to psychotherapy.

Encouragement, in Adlerian therapy, is both an attitude and a way of being with clients. The encouragement-focused process helps build hope and the expectancy of success in clients by demonstrating concern, active listening, and empathy; communicating respect and confidence; focusing on strengths, assets, and resources; helping clients generate perceptual and behavioral alternatives; focusing on efforts and progress; and helping clients see the humor in life experiences (Watts & Pietrzak, 2000). According to Dreikurs (1967), presenting problems are "based on discouragement" and, without "encouragement, without having faith in himself restored, [the client] cannot see the possibility of doing or functioning better" (p. 62). Adler (1913/1956) once asked a client what he thought made the difference in his successful experience in therapy. The client replied: "That's quite simple. I had lost all courage to live. In our consultations I found it again" (p. 342).

Model/Technique Factors

According to Hubble et al. (1999c), model/technique factors may be viewed from two perspectives:

> In a narrow sense, model/technique factors may be regarded as a belief and procedures unique to a specific treatment. . . . In concert with Frank and Frank (1991), [we] interpret model/techniques factors [sic] more broadly as therapeutic or healing rituals. . . . They include a rationale, offer an explanation for clients' difficulties, and establish strategies or procedures for following them. Depending on the counselor's theoretical orientation, different content is emphasized. Nevertheless, most therapeutic methods or tactics share the common quality of preparing clients to take some action to help themselves. In particular, counselors expect their clients to do something different—to develop new understandings, feel different emotions, face fears, or alter old patterns of behavior. (p. 10)

Prochaska and Norcross (2003) stated that there is a pervasive misconception suggesting that psychotherapists who align themselves with a specific theoretical orientation are "dogmatic and antiquated" and "are unwilling to adapt their practices toward the demands of the situation or the patient" (2003, p. 6). According to Hubble et al. (1999a), affirming that common factors do account for the majority of change in psychotherapy does not mean that one must practice a "'model *less*' or 'technique*less*' therapy" (p. 408); instead, they suggested that therapeutic models informed by the common factors attend to and implement what works to facilitate change. Furthermore, as Lambert and Barley (2001) suggested, improvement of psychotherapy may more readily occur when therapists increase their ability to relate to clients and tailor treatment to individual clients.

The Adlerian model of psychotherapy clearly includes a rationale, offers an explanation for clients' difficulties, and possesses strategies or procedures to prepare clients to take some action to help themselves. In agreement with Hubble et al. (1999c), Adlerian therapists "expect their clients to do something different—to develop new understandings, feel different emotions, face fears, or alter old patterns of behavior" (p. 10).

Furthermore, Adlerians are technical eclectics (Manaster & Corsini, 1982), and a vital aspect of Adlerian therapy is its integrative flexibility (see Watts, 2003a, 2003b). Different clients may require different therapeutic relational emphases and different therapeutic metaphors. Adlerian therapy allows the therapist to tailor therapy to the client's unique needs and expectations, rather than forcing the client into one therapeutic or technical framework (A. Adler, 1929, 1913/1956, 1979; K. Adler, 1972/1989; Carlson & Slavik, 1997; Maniacci, 2003; Mosak & Maniacci, 1998; Watts, 2003a, 2003b; Watts & Carlson, 1999; Watts & Pietrzak, 2000; Watts & Shulman, 2003).

The common ground between Adlerian psychotherapy and the common factors outcome research is indeed remarkable. The Adlerian model of psychotherapy, in agreement with that research, emphasizes the foundational importance of the counseling relationship and model and technique flexibility for attending to extratherapeutic and client factors (e.g., clients' strengths and abilities) and for building hope and expectancy of successful experiences in psychotherapy.

CONCLUSION

As we will discuss at some length in the concluding chapter of this book, Adler's theories, which exhibited tremendous creativity and foresight, were out of step with his contemporaries, particularly Freud, and also out of step with the dominant metaphors of that time. When a theory is out of step with the dominant metaphors of its time, its constructs and methods may, inevitably, be undervalued, even as its useful features are assimilated into emerging perspectives of a later day. As will be demonstrated throughout this book, looking at how Adler's theory is used and therapy is practiced by contemporary Adlerian therapists has much to offer beyond what has been borrowed and integrated into other contemporary approaches.

Is Adlerian therapy relevant for contemporary psychotherapy practice? Given the contemporary status and direction of the field of psychotherapy suggested by Prochaska and Norcross (1994, 2003), the increasing emphasis on multicultural understanding and applications, the positive psychology movement, and the research on the common factors of successful therapy outcomes, the answer is strongly affirmative. Contemporary therapeutic perspectives are steadily progressing toward a position that is congruent with the Adlerian perspective.

Adler died in 1937 having created a personality theory and approach to therapy so far ahead of its time that contemporary cutting-edge theories and therapies are only now discovering many of Adler's fundamental conclusions, typically without reference to or acknowledgment of Adler. (Watts, 1999, p. 8)

3

ADLERIAN PERSONALITY THEORY AND PSYCHOTHERAPY

In chapter 1, we began with a brief discussion of development and change and introduced some basic terms used by Adlerians to describe the dynamics of these processes. In this chapter, we go into more depth to ground readers in the theory that will unify any integrative practice of psychotherapy. We begin with a discussion of the life style, a cornerstone of Adlerian theory and the focus of much of Adlerian psychotherapy. We discuss the influence of biology and of psychosocial dynamics (including psychological birth order and parenting styles) on the development of the life style.

Next, we discuss self-concept and worldview, highlighting how convictions derived from these can result in the kinds of problems people bring into therapy. In the same vein, we discuss how feelings of inferiority can lead to problems when individuals are discouraged rather than encouraged in their formative years. Safeguarding mechanisms, such as symptoms, interpersonal distance-seeking, and even emotions, come into play as people seek to defend their mistaken convictions, even at the expense of their own and others' happiness.

LIFE STYLE AND MEANING-MAKING

For as long as people have been alive, humans have been meaning-makers (A. Adler, 1931). What meaning they make of what they perceive—and conceive—has been a matter of conjecture and, at times, outright debate (if not conflict). The basis of all meaning humans make has been located in one of two areas (which are not mutually exclusive): (a) in themselves or (b) in some spiritual being. Psychology professionals have spent the better part of the last century focusing on the former. For those who see meaning as having its genesis in human creation, the quest has been to understand the way people create meaning, and therefore its corollary, value, in life.

Adlerians have their way of understanding the meaning- and value-making that operate in people (A. Adler, 1931, 1933/1964). Whereas other theorists have used terms such as *psyche*, *personality*, *ego*, or *self*, Adlerians have used the phrase *style of life* (A. Adler, 1956; Powers & Griffith, 1987; Shulman & Mosak, 1988; Stein & Edwards, 1998). The style of life, often shortened to *life style*, is that which creates meaning and value. It serves many purposes, three of which we highlight here.

First, style of life is a *guide*. Life can be difficult, joyful, pleasant, confusing, dangerous, and just about anything else. Without some kind of guide, or direction setter or compass, humans would be at the mercy of forces they could not manage. Imagine what life would be like if humans had no way of organizing their movements through it. At best, survival would be compromised.

Second, the style of life is a *limiter*. Humans do not do certain things that fall outside the species-specific guidelines. Just as biology limits what certain species can and cannot do, the life style limits what any one individual will do or not do. For instance, Bob is a calm, peaceful man. His personality—his character, if you will—limits the range of responses he will master and demonstrate in certain situations. Just as one would not expect a dolphin to walk on land, one would not expect a human to live in the ocean; thus, psychologically, we would not expect Bob to be an agitator or highly aggressive man (unless there were extenuating circumstances). He would not think of it and, if he did, he would probably be at a loss for how to be aggressive, never having trained himself to act in this manner. If every person had to learn everything to survive, then there would be no survival. Biology limits what a species is capable of doing; psychology, and its subset, personality (or life style), limits what in the individual's unique developmental environment needs to be mastered to survive. It simply is inefficient to have to learn everything. People's life styles limit learning to what is deemed necessary.

Third, the life style is a *predictor*: It gives us security and a sort of rhythm to life. In our meaning-making and value-creating, we need not only structure and guidance but also predictability and regularity. As a predictor, the life style allows us to develop habits—in other words, habitual responses that no longer need cortical control. Jane knows how to respond, and she knows when to respond, because she is able to predict what will happen next. If she had to learn this anew every time, her decisions and responses would become far too time consuming. Prediction leads to comfort and efficiency. Humans predict what will happen not only in the next moment but also in the longer term future. The life style is the rule of all rules for how humans prepare themselves for life's contingencies (Mosak & Maniacci, 1999). Given what they have experienced, they come to conclusions about how to belong in their environment. They learn. As becomes evident in the following sections, assuming that *environment* applies only to external operations and events is too narrow; there is an internal environment to which we must respond as well.

How does the life style do what it does? Adlerians believe that there are three main operations that take place: (a) biased apperceptions, (b) self-reinforcement, and (c) arrangement.

Perhaps the most pervasive mechanism of the life style is *biased apperception*. Humans are biased in what they perceive. Perceptions themselves have meaning attached to them. For example, if I do not believe I made any mistakes in typing this manuscript, then I will not even perceive one. If I believe my wife is a difficult, controlling woman, I will not even notice behaviors that disprove that assumption and, if I did notice them, or if they were forcefully pointed out to me, I would probably be able to explain them away in a manner that would allow my biases to remain intact (see chap. 5). Biased apperceptions operate nonconsciously; people are not aware of them. As an example, a frequent exercise used with clients or students entails asking them to list all the things that are physically touching them. The list starts out including clothing, and furniture, and then after some time moves to hair, maybe jewelry and, after awhile, people typically say that is all. Very few, if any, list the air as something that is touching them. The air is so ubiquitous people forget to notice it—until there is an unexpected change in air temperature or pressure; then it is noticed. Much the same happens with biased apperceptions. People do not notice them until something unexpected occurs, and then they may notice that their biases are not facts. It is at such times that learning occurs and, as we discuss in the next chapter, it is at these times that certain people go out of their way not to learn.

Another way the life style functions is by being *self-reinforcing*. If people see only what their life styles allow them to see, then they also seek out that which will confirm their expectations. Although this might seem like hair-splitting, there is a difference between biased apperceptions and self-reinforcement. The former describes what is perceived, whereas the latter describes what is sought after. If Carl believes authority is bad, not only is that what he will see, but it also is what he will look for and, possibly, even create. This last point leads to the next operation of the life style.

The life style is an *arranger*. It prompts others into behaving in ways that will confirm its assumptions. It creates experiences to verify expectations. If Carl cannot find enough evidence that authority is bad, then he may nonconsciously provoke (i.e., arrange for) authority figures to be bad. He is then justified in his beliefs.

To summarize, imagine the following scenario. Peter develops his life style within his family of origin and in his neighborhood and community. He grows, and it is time for him to "leave the nest." Depending on what Adlerians refer to as his *courage*—or, more accurately phrased, how *encouraged* he is—Peter has five options:

1. He can stay at home with what is familiar. The opportunity for growth will most likely be very limited.
2. He can move a short distance from home but still maintain most of his primary relationships and sphere of activity in and around his old neighborhood. Again, growth is limited, but it is somewhat better than in Scenario 1.
3. He can leave the comfort of home but move to areas where situations and people are very similar, if not almost identical, to what he knew at home. He left home geographically, but not psychologically.
4. Peter can leave the comfort of home, and even move to areas where situations and people are very different, but then spend the next several months (if not years) trying to seduce them into being like the people and situations he left at home.
5. Finally, he can leave home and try new things. Peter can attempt to learn new things, and have new experiences. His life style expands and adapts. He grows.

HOW THE LIFE STYLE DEVELOPS

Whereas other texts detail with far greater specificity the various factors that lead to the development of the life style (Powers & Griffith, 1987; Shulman & Mosak, 1988), in this chapter we highlight four factors: (a) biology, (b) degree of activity, (c) psychosocial dynamics, and (d) goodness of fit (Mosak & Maniacci, 1999).

Biology

Four principal biological factors influence the development of the life style: (a) organ inferiority, (b) needs, (c) processing neurodynamics, and (d) goals. All have been previously discussed in the literature to some extent or another (A. Adler, 1956).

Organ Inferiority

Organs or organ systems can be vulnerable. If they are functionally or structurally deficient, trouble with adaptation can occur. Of note, however, is the relativity of such a statement. Although an organ or organ system may be deficient, in the right environment such a deficit need not lead to trouble. We consider this in greater detail in the section on goodness of fit.

Adlerians believe that when an organ is genetically inferior, *compensation* takes place. The compensations are of three types (Dreikurs, 1967; Maniacci, 1996b). The first type is *somatic compensation*: If one kidney is deficient, then the other kidney hypertrophies to compensate. Second, *sympathetic compensation* occurs: The body may readjust its posture to protect the unimpaired kidney. Third, *psychic compensation* may develop: The person may foster traits of timidity or hesitation so that he or she can limit his or her range of activity, thus further protecting the unimpaired organ.

The third realm of compensation, psychic compensation, is most relevant to this chapter. Psychic compensation can, and frequently does, affect the formation of the life style. Children who inherit diabetes frequently develop a style of life around the issue of getting; sometimes they develop a life style type Adlerians refer to as "the getter" (A. Adler, 1956; Mosak, 1977). They arrange the assumptions and convictions about the world and their place in it to focus on what and how much to get. This is understandable, given their medical condition. How they use such a life style is another matter, which we address later in this chapter.

Needs

We are biological beings. Biology is served, or the organism dies. Adlerians have documented four needs all infants must satisfy to survive (Forgus & Shulman, 1979). These are not psychological in origin, although over time they do yield significant psychological effects. If these needs are not met, the infant experiences what is called "failure to thrive." The needs are met in one of three ways. First, they can be appropriately met. Second, they can be neglected, leading to danger. Third, they can be met too well, leading to difficulty. An example would be hunger. The child can be appropriately fed, which leads to healthy growth. Second, the child can be neglected and not fed enough, leading to potentially severe consequences, such as malnutrition. Third, the child can be overfed, leading to obesity or any number of medical complications.

The four basic needs have been summarized into the following categories: (a) nourishment and contact, (b) protection and safety, (c) mastery, and (d) sensory variation. Through over- or understimulation, these needs become hierarchically arranged. Once the hierarchy is established, it becomes fixed for life.

Processing Neurodynamics

Adlerians have documented six styles of processing information (Forgus & Shulman, 1979). Briefly summarized, they are the following:

1. Internal versus external locus of control.
2. Narrow versus extensive scanning.
3. High versus low tolerance for ambiguity.
4. Field independence versus field dependence.
5. Sharpeners versus levelers.
6. Reflective–analytic versus impulsive–global.

Internal–external locus of control describes how people process data relevant to their sense of control. People with an internal locus of control see the locus of action as stemming from within themselves; people with an external locus of control see it as coming from outside. Upon losing a toy, some children will feel they lost it because of their carelessness, whereas others will feel they lost it because others did something wrong. The former are internally controlled, the latter externally.

Narrow versus extensive scanning describes how people search the environment for relevant data. Narrow scanners limit the search parameters, whereas extensive scanners search far and wide. Using again the example of losing a toy, some children look only in one small area, whereas others tear apart the whole house.

High or low tolerance for ambiguity describes how people tolerate frustration. For some people, there are not many things that stress them out. For others, even slight discrepancies lead to a state of overload. Children with a high tolerance for ambiguity who lose a toy will not exhibit much physiological distress, whereas those with a low tolerance will perspire, increase respiration, and exhibit general hyperarousal.

Field independence and dependence describes how people orient themselves to external stimulation. Field-independent people carry themselves into situations (generally) maintaining their attitudinal sets, whereas field-dependent individuals adapt easily to situational demands. Children who are field independent and lose their toys will react according to their goals and intentions, regardless of who is around or what is happening, whereas field-dependent children will moderate their responses according to the situation around them.

Sharpener versus leveler refers to how people process incoming data. Sharpeners accentuate the differences and highlight the fine details in what they perceive, whereas levelers downplay such perceptions and minimize the differences. Using again the example of a child who has lost a toy, sharpeners will describe in exquisite detail what the toy looked like, where they looked for it, how they felt, and so forth, whereas levelers will respond minimally, saying things like "I don't know—it's somewhere."

Finally, *reflective–analytic versus impulsive–global* describes how individuals think through challenges. Reflective–analytic people think logically and sequentially and are methodical in their approach, whereas impulsive–global people are quick to act, follow their intuition, and can be somewhat haphazard. A reflective–analytic child who has lost a toy will retrace his or her steps, think things through, and have a systematic search pattern, whereas an impulsive–global child will run around, look here and there, and tear through the area rapidly.

Goals

Through interaction with the environment and inherited predispositions, the aforementioned needs (nourishment and contact, protection and safety, mastery and sensory variation) become socialized. Although children are, during the earliest perinatal developmental periods, initially passive responders to their internal and external environments, they soon become active interactors with their worlds. They learn and begin to anticipate. Their styles of life begin to operate. No longer do they passively receive data; at some early point they begin to shape the input, either directly, by "training" their caretakers to respond in certain ways, or indirectly, biasing their perceptions to process only certain types of data. At this (admittedly still unclear) point of development, the four basic needs become goals (Forgus & Shulman, 1979):

1. Nourishment and contact becomes the goal of attachment.
2. Protection and safety becomes the goal of security.
3. Mastery becomes the goal of competence.
4. Sensory variation becomes the goal of cognition.

As noted, these needs become hierarchically arranged, and therefore so do the goals. How they are arranged becomes the structure of the individual's personality, the person's style of life.

Some people's hierarchy looks like this: competence, cognition, security, attachment. For these people, being the best, especially in areas involving thinking and information, leads their lives. When they are the best and know a lot, they feel safe. Only then will they consider interpersonal bonding.

Another person's hierarchy might look this way: attachment, security, cognition, competence. These people will want to be bonded to others, and that leads them to feel safe. Once this happens, then they can think clearly and believe they can handle things.

These are only two ways the goals can be arranged; there are many other possibilities. Through the processes of articulation and differentiation, the goals manifest themselves differently through different developmental periods. Let us examine one goal and its possible manifestations. Attachment, in most cultures, starts out in young children as dependency. This is appropriate. With time and learning, dependency differentiates and changes. It lessens and becomes affection. Affection is initially directed to caregivers and close relatives, but it expands as the child's social network widens. Affection spreads to peers, teachers, even pets. Affection develops and, in many cultures, evolves into friendships. As adolescence approaches, friendships develop into love relationships. Those love relationships articulate and differentiate on trajectories as well, such as genital excitement with many possible peers; to possessive attachment to a single peer; to a mature, stable love relationship with a significant other in what Adlerians label *interdependence*. How the attachment motive articulates and differentiates is a matter of cultural variation, temporal history, early training and response, and environmental opportunity. Just as the attachment motive goes through these changes, so too do the other motives. In general, in Western cultures, security progresses from insecurity to safety and self-assuredness, competence progresses from incompetence to self-reliance, and cognition develops from ignorance to knowledge.

These goals become matched with processing neurodynamic styles. For example, imagine but one hierarchical variation of the four goals with one each of the six processing styles: attachment, cognition, competence, and security with the following processing styles: internally controlled, extensive scanning, low tolerance for ambiguity, field independent, sharpener, and reflective–analytic.

The narrative description of this person might be as follows: This is a man who loves people (attachment motive), but he is a man who needs to be right (an idiosyncratic version of the cognition motive he learned at home from his family of origin). He believes that with information (cognition motive), he can win people over (attachment motive) and that will lead him to feel powerful (an idiosyncratic version of the competence motive) and safe (security motive). He does this by taking too much responsibility for everything (internal control), and by managing everything he and others do (extensive scanning), and he gets very angry if others do not give him the information or control he wants (low tolerance for ambiguity). He prides himself on being his "own man," who expects life to operate on his terms (field independence), and he is a nitpicker who demands perfection from himself and others (sharpener). He thinks way too much; has far too many activities he organizes and thinks about; and he reports that, without the help of alcohol, he cannot "shut down" his mind at night (reflective–analytic).

Such a description, although detailed, can be elaborated on in even greater specificity by discussing how this particular man articulates and differentiates each motive in his own manner. By looking at him this way, the astute clinician can project backward to the possible developmental influences on him and whether he is over- or understimulated with any particular need. In chapter 6, we detail how Adlerians use assorted data (e.g., developmental history, early childhood recollections, initial interview data, psychological test material, etc.) to locate people on each of these dimensions.

Degree of Activity

After biology, another factor that influences the development of the life style is degree of activity (A. Adler, 1956; Ansbacher, 1977; Mosak &

Maniacci, 1999). Whereas organ inferiority, needs, processing neurodynamics, and goals are principally biological factors, degree of activity is a transitional concept. It is situated in between the more clearly biologically loaded factors and the more clearly psychosocial factors, which we discuss next.

By *degree of activity*, Adlerians mean the amount of energy people use in adapting to life's challenges. Adlerians have traditionally described people as having either a low or high degree of activity, with some shades of difference between these two poles. Children who prefer to sit and read all day clearly have a different degree of activity than those who would rather run around and play outside. The degree of activity can sometimes even be noticed in the amount of sleep some individuals require, and how they actually sleep during the night, with some people characterized as deep sleepers, who do not move much, and others characterized as light sleepers who toss and turn and have restless nights. How much of this factor is related to nutrition, endocrine functions (especially thyroid function), and hormonal/sexual processes in general is not clear, because some of it does seem to be learned in response to early socialization influences. For instance, many boys are socialized to be more active than girls, despite whatever biological predispositions they may have. Regardless of the origin, degree of activity is an influence, and although it is not typically addressed in great detail in the Adlerian literature, its effect is important, especially in regard to the last factor we address: goodness of fit with one's important early caretakers and environment.

Psychosocial Dynamics

The interactions children have with their environments, particularly their siblings, parents, and other caretakers, and the neighborhood and community (including peers, school personnel, and others) are crucial in the development of the style of life. In the following sections we provide an overview of each.

Role of Psychological Birth Order

Adler (1956) was one of the first theorists to incorporate the concept of birth order into his work. Since then, Adlerians have made considerable use of the concept in their clinical and psychoeducational work (e.g., Leman, 1985). There are two definitions of *birth order* (Shulman & Mosak, 1988). One is called *ordinal position*; it refers to the actual order of birth of the siblings. The other is called *psychological position*, and it refers to the role the child adopts in his or her interactions with others. Adlerians use the latter definition. An example will clarify the differences and demonstrate how the two definitions can lead to different conclusions about the same family. Imagine the Smith family, with the following sibling constellation: Bill, 14 years old; Mike, 12 years old; Gail, 6 years old; and Joey, 3 years old. In ordinal psychology, Gail is a third-born and Joey a fourth-born. There are no consistent findings about what kinds of traits third- or fourth-borns develop. In the psychological position, the picture is different. Bill is an oldest born, Mike is a second-born, Joey is a youngest born, and Gail is a blend of an only child (the only girl) and oldest born. Why an oldest? Adlerians believe that age differences of 5 years or more produce subgroups. Gail would most likely be the eldest of the second group. What are the rules that determine psychological birth order role? Although other texts address this dynamic in considerably greater detail, here we present the guidelines in brief.

First, as stated previously, siblings typically are born within 5 years of each other. Age differences greater than that tend to put children into distinct subgroups, for two primary reasons: First, at age 5, school begins, and a new child coming into the family will not have as much direct contact with the school-age sibling; in a cognitive sense, a newborn and a 5-year-old are in different worlds. Second, handicaps or disabilities in one child may alter the psychological roles. If the first-born boy (ordinal position) has Down syndrome, then psychologically he may take on the role of youngest born (psychological position), while the second-born boy (ordinally) may take on the role of oldest born (psychologically). Third, gender may play a part. If the parents model strong sex role differences, then in the preceding example Gail will probably be able to find her place as the only girl. If they downplay sex role differences, then she may not see much difference in masculine and feminine roles, and she may take on the role of a middle child (along with her brother Mike). Finally, ordinal positions have no blends. One cannot simultaneously be a second- and fourth-born. Numbers are categorical concepts, not dimensional ones. Psychological positions often do occur in blends.

Adlerians discuss five psychological birth order positions (Pepper, 1971). Succinctly stated, they are only children, oldest borns, second-borns, middle children, and youngest borns.

Only children never have to share their worlds with other siblings. They grow up using parents (or significantly older siblings) as models. Hence, they tend to be perfectionists who are used to having their way. They set their goals exceedingly high and tend to prefer polite distance from people. *Oldest borns* are used to being number one. They were typically voted in their class yearbooks "most likely to carry their own caskets to their graves," in that they are used to doing things themselves. They are in charge and like being that way. Oldest borns tend to be analytical, detailed, and methodical, and they usually overvalue control. *Second-borns* play a teeter–totter game with oldest borns, in that where one goes up, the other goes down. If the oldest born is good in math, the second-born will typically choose to ignore math and focus on something the oldest born ignores, such as sports. Just as this occurs with academics, it also occurs with personality traits. Second-borns tend to be rebellious and independent, to dislike order, and to be responders (rather than initiators, like their elder sibling). *Middle children* are diplomats; they are people pleasers who dislike conflict but desire fairness and justice for all. They often feel squeezed by their siblings and complain that they have neither the rights and privileges of oldest borns nor the pampering and attention of youngest borns. *Youngest borns* are frequently excitement seekers who crave stimulation and are masters at putting others into their service. They are used to having things done for them, and they know how to play people's emotions quite well. Additionally, youngest borns can often become the most ambitious in the family; because they feel so far behind, they desire to catch up with the older ones to prove they are no longer the babies.

Parenting Styles

Parents and caretakers play an obviously crucial role as well (Powers & Griffith, 1987). Parents generally (although not universally) set the tone for discipline, establish the family atmosphere, model problem solving, and demonstrate the key family values. We write "generally," because siblings and other adults can alter significantly any of these. For example, having a sibling with autism can radically alter the family atmosphere, values, and discipline. So, although parents usually set the family dynamics in motion, siblings can have a profound influence on them as well.

With regard to discipline, parents can have numerous styles, some of which we highlight here. Parents can be authoritarian and too controlling. This will elicit different responses from different children, if they perceive their parents to have those characteristics. Some children will respond to an authoritarian disciplinary style with compliance and lack of initiative, whereas others will respond with rebelliousness. Parents also can be too laid back and permissive. Should the children perceive them that way, they may choose to become too self-centered and learn to put their own needs ahead of everyone else. Other children in that same situation will become parentified children and attempt to discipline the other children themselves in an attempt to bring order.

The *family atmosphere* is the emotional tone of the home (Dewey, 1971). Some homes are calm and pleasant, whereas others are stormy and conflictual. Once again, the children's perception of the atmosphere is crucial: Children learn to develop coping styles for the various atmospheres in the home. In general, in chaotic atmospheres children tend to become anxious, as if they have to be ready for anything. In stormy and conflictual ones, they tend to become very assertive (if not aggressive) themselves, or be numb and develop a high threshold for stimulation. We address this dynamic in greater detail in chapter 6, when we examine the role of the childhood family atmosphere on the adult's prevailing mood.

Parents are models for problem-solving styles. Many parents are good problem solvers, and others are poor ones. Some children never see their parents solve problems because the parents overprotect them from such things. Other children observe only limited solutions to problems, such as yelling or screaming. Many parents tell children what *not* to do, without demonstrating or teaching what *to* do. The effects of this on children are fairly obvious.

Last, parents establish values. Values can be one of two types: (a) stated and (b) unstated. Stated values are exactly that—stated. Children are told not to lie, to be honest, to share, to eat their food, and so forth. Unstated values are more difficult to detect but have an important role as well. These are the values that are enacted without being stated, such as lying on certain occasions, yelling in order to get one's way, and disrespecting others in tone or attitude without actually speaking badly about them. As children develop, they will be able to linguistically access the stated values fairly easily; the unstated ones may haunt them and affect their decision making without conscious, linguistic awareness.

Neighborhood and Community

Children are influenced by factors outside of the home as well (Powers & Griffith, 1987). Considering the parents as the sole influence on their children is an antiquated notion. The role of peers, school personnel, neighbors, coaches, friends and their families, and clergy has only recently begun to be taken seriously. For many children, the first significant contact with adults other than their parents happens when they go to school and meet teachers. Children are still young and learning, and although much of their life style is established by age 5, there still can be changes made by strong, dominant figures at school. These factors need to be assessed; they often provide clues to understanding the nuances of an individual's life style.

Goodness of Fit

The last major influence on the life style is the notion of goodness of fit. This basic proposition is very much overlooked in the developmental literature. The key to all of the factors we have just described is not necessarily their presence or absence but rather the degree to which the dynamics of the child match the dynamics of the caregivers and community. For example, a very athletic, coordinated child will blossom in a community that has the resources and structure to provide her with the needed outlet for her talents. A child with a high tolerance for ambiguity will do better in a chaotic atmosphere than will a child with a low tolerance for ambiguity. A child with a dominant goal of cognition will do well in an environment that is stimulating, but a child with a dominant goal of attachment will do better in a stimulating environment that includes plenty of time for bonding and sharing. Children from an orthodox Jewish family will not have as easy a time as their Catholic peers in a strict Roman Catholic neighborhood. It is the interface between the children's goals and needs and the resources in their environments that is the key. Too much emphasis on either factor to the exclusion of the other will skew the data and present a distorted picture.

Adlerians believe that the life style is relatively fixed by about age 5 (A. Adler, 1956; Ansbacher, 1977). Does that mean that it does not change after that? The answer to that is both yes and no. The answer is yes in that the basic convictions, the rules governing how to belong, can change if a therapeutic event occurs. A therapeutic event does not have to take place in psychotherapy, and frequently it does not. A person who believes he is unlovable can have a therapeutic-like conversion if he finds someone who loves him. That loving person may genuinely change the life of the person who heretofore believed himself to be unlovable. The answer is no, however, in that whether people actually change their fundamental convictions about life, or simply change the way they use those convictions, is still open to debate. We discuss this issue in more detail in chapter 7.

In concluding this section on the development of the life style, we must make one more point: Whereas the core convictions of the life style are set by around age 5, the methods of operation generally are not. Sally may believe that her main goal in life is to be competent, and she may articulate that by believing she has to be the best at everything she does, particularly if she is an oldest born from a highly competitive family that values success and achievement and lives in an affluent neighborhood. Although that goal may be set by around age 5, how Sally implements that goal is still a matter for experimentation and opportunity through adolescence and into early adulthood. She may be able to be the best academically if she has good teachers, a supportive atmosphere, a good intellectual level, and so forth, or, if relevant opportunities are open to her, she might decide to be the best athlete. She may also take that goal and use it quite differently, such as by being the best shoplifter in the gang. Teenagers may seem to have extreme identity shifts throughout adolescence, but from the Adlerian perspective their goals typically do not change. What changes are the ways they attempt to achieve those goals. They will experiment until they find a way suitable to them. One way we typically teach this point to parents and professionals is by asking someone to pick a destination, such as New York. Now we ask that person to list as many different ways to get there as possible, such as plane, train, automobile, bus, walking, bike, and so on. In each scenario, the goal remains the same, but the method of getting there changes. So too is it with teenagers.

LIFE STYLE, SELF-CONCEPT, AND CONVICTIONS

Until now, we have examined the life style from a macroanalytical perspective. It is time to tighten our focus and examine it more closely. The life style can be divided into two main parts: (a) convictions about what is and (b) convictions about what should be (Mosak & Maniacci, 1999; Shulman & Mosak, 1988).

Convictions about what is entail two categories: (a) the self-concept and (b) the worldview. Convictions about what should be entail two categories as well: (a) the self-ideal and (b) ethics.

The self-concept is the sum total of all the beliefs about who "I am." They typically can be phrased as completing the following sentences: "I am ____" and "I am not ____." The following are some examples:

- I am short.
- I am a winner.
- I am not smart.
- I am Irish.

The worldview contains all the beliefs about the "not me." It can be stated with phrases such as "Life is ____" or "People are ____." The worldview can be subdivided into two main categories: (a) people (men, women, authority, etc.) and (b) life (the world, institutions, etc.). The following are some examples:

- Life is hard.
- People are cold.
- Women are fun.
- Men are tough.
- School is good.

These convictions are learned through mirroring by caregivers and actual experience with life. For example, if a child feels weak, and the parent confirms that feeling, then the child may develop the conviction "I am weak." If the child tries to lift something and can actually lift it, then the child receives confirmation from the world and may believe "I am strong." Both of these convictions are articulations of the competence motive. A person's convictions are, in general, reality based.

One's convictions about what should be are not necessarily reality based. They are not learned from direct experience or through mirroring by a caretaker; instead, they are learned through a repeated pattern of frustration with the environment and idealizing comments from caretakers. Some examples of self-ideal statements are

- I should be strong.
- I should not be a loser.
- I should be happy.

Some ethical convictions might be

- People should be good.
- Life should be fair.
- It is wrong to hurt people.
- It is right to be kind.

Like self-ideal statements, ethical convictions emphasize what should be; they are ideals, not about the self but about the world and people. If a child experiences frustration when reaching for something, then she may develop the self-concept "I am short" and, from there, the ideal quickly develops that "I should be tall." Similarly, she may believe that because she cannot reach something, "Life is unfair" and, therefore, "Life should be fair." When caretakers provide feedback about what the child is, self-concepts are fostered; similarly, when they provide feedback about what the world is, the worldview is fostered. However, when they emphasize what should be, such as by saying, "Yes, I know you will do it—keep trying," they are feeding into the self-ideal. The child has not yet done the thing she is being encouraged to do but is being told she will be able to do it if she keeps trying; hence, the ideal, as yet to be attained nature of the convictions.

An example of the core dynamics of the life style of one type of adult can be summarized as follows:

- I am weak.
- I should be strong and free from being trapped.
- Life is a jungle, and it is a dog-eat-dog world.
- People should look out for themselves.
- Therefore, I will bite first before I am bitten and keep all my options open.

These statements summarize the core convictions of people who usually are diagnosed as having antisocial personalities. They have disturbances in the attachment motive, seeing bonding as something potentially dangerous and limiting. They have overemphasized the competence and security motives, so much so that those motives color the attachment motive to an extreme degree. They tend to be sharpeners, global–impulsive, field independent to an abnormal extreme, externally controlled, and extensive scanners, and they exhibit a high tolerance for ambiguity. In other words, they are excitement seekers, quick to react without thinking, behave without consideration for the situation, blame others and life for their problems, and are careful to observe and take note of everything around them almost in a paranoid fashion; they can live quite well for the moment, not concerned about what their lives will be like 5 years hence. Given these dynamics, clinicians can begin to hypothesize the formative influences on these individuals. If the competence and security motives are distorted and overemphasized, then it is safe to assume that they had disturbances in their needs for protection and safety and mastery. They probably frequently were neglected in these areas, and they perceived (or actually experienced) a severe lack of safety (i.e., they were threatened) and similar lacks in a sense of personal mastery (i.e., they were out of control). Neurodynamically, they probably either inherited or were trained (or both) to have high tolerances for pain; hence, they did not learn quickly from physical experiences. They either inherited or were trained (or both) to seek out too much stimulation. We could continue, but the point is clear: By assessing the motives and processing styles, clinicians can accurately describe personalities using Adlerian principles.

The Basic Positions

People can be encouraged or discouraged (A. Adler, 1956; Dreikurs, 1967). If they are encouraged, they will risk doing things about which they are unsure, if it leads them to growth. If they are discouraged, they will not take risks; they will hold onto their convictions and not seek to change or grow. They will play it safe. Any threat to their convictions is seen as a hostile challenge to be strenuously avoided. People who are encouraged do not perceive the world as a hostile place. They are willing to risk being wrong, because this is not a threat to their self-concept and self-ideal.

Social interest, otherwise known as *community feeling* (A. Adler, 1933/1964; Ansbacher, 1992; Mosak & Maniacci, 1999), is the topic we address in more detail in the next chapter. For the purposes of this chapter, we address it in the context of the life style. Convictions can be enacted in one of two ways, either prosocially or not. By *prosocial* Adlerians mean that individuals move through life in such a way so as to foster the growth and development of others, not hinder them in self-centered, hostile ways. I may have a self-concept that states I am weak, but I do not have to hurt others to prove I should be strong. I can help others, and that may prove I am strong. When social interest and community feeling are displayed, people are encouraged and encouraging to others.

What hinders the development of social interest and community feeling? A closer look is required to lay the groundwork for chapter 5, which focuses on maladaptive behavior. A distinction must be made between *inferiority feelings* and *inferiority complexes*, and a brief discussion of the concept of inferiority in general is necessary before it can be explored (Mosak & Maniacci, 1999).

Inferiority is objective, can be measured, and is contextual. This means that people can quantify it, observe it, and realize that it can change depending on what is being used as the standard of measurement. Shortness can be measured, and it is observable. However, it is relative. A 5-foot, 10-inch man is short compared with someone 6 feet tall; hence, with height as a barometer, he is inferior. Yet, next to someone who is 5 feet, 3 inches tall, that same man is now taller; he is superior.

Inferiority feelings are global, subjective, and evaluative. In direct language, they are generalizations that tend to be held onto despite evidence to the contrary. For example, the 5-foot, 10-inch man mentioned in the preceding paragraph may feel short no matter who is in the room with him. Inferiority feelings are not related to actual inferiorities. Very often, objectively measured intelligent people feel dumb, attractive people feel ugly, competent people feel helpless, and so on.

Inferiority complexes are behavioral manifestations of inferiority feelings. Someone may feel inferior but not act that way. When he or she acts on those feelings in such a way as to avoid exposing those feelings, Adlerians say that person has an inferiority complex. For example, because the 5-foot, 10-inch man just discussed feels short (i.e., inferior), he refuses to leave his house. He has an inferiority complex. Inferiority complexes come in two types: (a) normal and (b) psychopathological. Normal inferiority complexes restrict behavior in minor ways that do not interfere with functioning in the tasks of life (work, social, and love and sex). Psychopathological inferiority complexes restrict functioning in major ways, thus interfering with the tasks of life. For example, Mary might be terrified of snakes. Because of her intense fear of them, she refuses to handle them or even be near them. This would be an inferiority complex. However, if she can still work, love, and socialize without any disruption to her life, the complex is considered normal. She will not run into many snakes in her job as a banker. If she works at the reptile house at the local zoo, then she is going to have trouble. That would lead to an abnormal (psychopathological) inferiority complex.

Anybody, at any time, can encounter a situation in which he or she feels inferior. How that person deals with feeling inferior becomes the key issue, but first a clarification is in order.

When the self-concept falls short of the self-ideal, the resulting cognitions are called *feelings of inferiority, low self-esteem,* or a *poor self-concept.* When the self-concept falls short of the worldview, the resulting cognitions are called *feelings of inadequacy.* When the self-concept falls short of the ethical convictions, the resulting cognitions are called *guilt feelings.* All of these terms are synonyms for *inferiority feelings.* If "I am dumb" when "I should be smart," I feel low self-esteem. If "I am someone who cries" when life demands that "Real men don't cry," I feel inadequate. If "I am a liar" when "People should be honest," I feel guilty. As is evident, these are not feelings per se; instead, they are discrepancies in convictions.

If I am encouraged and display social interest and community feeling, then I will engage in problem solving when faced with discrepancies in convictions. I will take a "Yes, I can" attitude and either engage indirect problem solving or compensate in one of three ways. First, I may compensate in the area in which I feel inferior. If I am afraid of snakes, I will overcome that fear. Second, I can choose to compensate in another area, such as by forgetting about snakes but becoming a really excellent dog trainer. Finally, I can overcompensate: Not only do I overcome my feelings of inferiority by handling snakes, but I also go take that job at the reptile house (the one Mary quit).

When I am discouraged, I will engage in what Adlerians call *safeguarding mechanisms* (A. Adler, 1956; K. Adler, 1967). Other systems of psychotherapy and personality call them *defense mechanisms.* I will be more interested in protecting my convictions and not changing them than in learning from them and growing. I become static in my development. Adlerians have described numerous safeguarding mechanisms. Some of the original ones Adler (1956) first articulated are described in the following sections.

Symptoms

Symptoms are arranged nonconsciously. If people do not want to face intensified feelings of inferiority (regardless of their particular manifestation), they can develop symptoms, such as phobias, somatic complaints, obsessions, or the like. They are not aware they are creating these symptoms. In the next chapter, we discuss in greater detail how and why symptoms happen.

Excuses

Unlike symptoms, excuses are consciously created. When asked to do something they do not want to do, people may use all sorts of denials, rationalizations, and the like.

Aggression

Adlerians talk about aggression as a safeguarding mechanism and delineate three types: (a) depreciation, (b) accusation, and (c) self-accusation. With depreciation, insecure people put others down as a way of avoiding a challenge. If they cannot elevate themselves, they can put others down. In that way, they have some sense of elevating their self-esteem. Another, more subtle form of depreciation is through idealization. Some people develop ideals to depreciate others, such as by saying "I would marry if I could only meet the right person." If this is done as a safeguarding mechanism, these people are putting down people they actually meet in favor of some ideal that does not exist. Accusation is much more blatant. It is a direct blaming of others for a person's own shortcomings. Self-accusation is a way of hurting oneself in order to hurt others. For example, these people can beat themselves up, sometimes literally, to make others feel bad.

Distance-Seeking

Adlerians discuss distance-seeking as a form of safeguarding. Four of the more common ones are (a) backward movement, (b) standing still, (c) hesitation, and (d) creating obstacles. In backward movement, individuals distance themselves from tasks that they believe would expose their feelings of inferiority. One example would be someone who enrolls in school only to drop out before the first examination. Another would be someone who, out of fear, breaks off an engagement days before a wedding. In standing still, people go only so far—and then stop. Some people write half a novel and then stop out of fear of it being rejected by publishers. Some couples date for years without ever moving to a more committed stance. Hesitation entails a back-and-forth movement, such as getting engaged, breaking it off, and then getting engaged (to the same person even) again, or writing the first 20 pages of a paper, tearing it up, and then doing it all again, and tearing it up again. Creating obstacles involves making movement, but only after some major task is accomplished. Some examples would be not going back to school until after all the bills are completely paid off, or getting married after people become completely financially independent.

Anxiety

Another safeguarding mechanism is when people frighten themselves out of doing things. They could simply decide not to do these things, but then they might have to face their complexes and admit them. With anxiety as a mechanism, they claim they are too afraid to try.

Exclusion Tendency

The exclusion tendency operates by having people restrict their movements in life. People who have exclusion tendencies operate only where they are guaranteed of success. Everything else is excluded, and therefore they protect their self-esteem to the exclusion of personal growth.

Psychological Processes

Given this information, some familiar psychological processes can be reinterpreted in light of Adlerian dynamics. The ones on which we focus for the purposes of this chapter are conscious and unconscious, memory, and emotions.

Adlerians feel there is no opposition between what is conscious and unconscious (Adlerians prefer the term *nonconscious*). Both are in service of the dominant motive and the movement toward that goal. What I am not aware of will not impede my movement toward my goal (Nikelly, 1971a). In fact, by making myself not aware of certain things, I may even enhance my movement toward my goals. The particular motive hierarchy will determine what is conscious and what is unconscious. For instance, if Juan's motive hierarchy is cognition, security, competence, attachment, then he will probably be relatively unaware of many dynamics relating to bonding and affiliation. As we detailed in the beginning of this chapter, his life style will limit, direct, and select information in a prescreening type of way to maintain systemic integrity. He will be exquisitely aware of certain topics, such as facts, information, and details, and blithely unaware of others.

Just as such processes happen with external data—in other words, stimulation from the outside world—so too do they happen with internal data, such as memory. If people scan the environment and, through biased apperception, select only that which reinforces their convictions, then they also do that with regard to their personal history. They will select or distort their memories to justify their current convictions (Mosak, 1977). Memories are not simply remembered or recalled; they also are perceived and interpreted, much like physical sensations that arise from the body. Some people interpret chest pains as gas, whereas others interpret them as a heart attack. Both interpretations may have nothing to do with the actual origin and meaning of the pain and in fact may represent psychological interpretations of actual physical events. Much the same happens with memory. People probably will never have accurate representations of their historical past. They will have only their impressions, their interpretations, of their own past, as seen through their life styles. We discuss this in greater detail in chapter 6.

Finally, Adlerians see emotions as being in service of the life style, not something that interferes with it (Dreikurs, 1967). People do not experience emotions that disrupt their life styles; they create emotions to facilitate their styles. All emotions serve a purpose and, by knowing a client's life style, clinicians can see how the emotions are being used. Adlerians are not as interested in what causes the emotion as in searching for how the emotions fit in the person's overall life style. Anger is one example. It is used to either push people away or convince them to give in. Another example is apathy. It is used to create power. If people do not care about anything, it is difficult to control them. Love is an emotion generated when people want to move toward something forcefully. Someone whose dominant motive is attachment will love people. Another person who has a dominant motive of security will love safety. An extensive scanner will be angered by boredom, whereas a person with a high tolerance for ambiguity will be just fine with it.

CONCLUSION

In this chapter, we have examined what the life style is, how it operates, how it develops, and the types of conclusions to which it leads. The life style is a dynamic system that structurally has two parts: (a) a motive hierarchy and (b) information-processing neurodynamics. How the motive system is arranged, differentiated, and articulated, and which processing styles dominate, comprise the key structures of who and what we are. This system is acquired through biological predisposition, organ inferiority, degree of activity, psychosocial dynamics, and goodness of fit. Through this matrix of influences, convictions about what is and what should be are formed; maintained; and, at times, rigidly defended in the face of challenging situations. At their best, such processes create a sense of cohesion, consistency, and success; at their worst, they can, and often do, lead to hurt, suffering, disorder, and difficulties in living. It is to these last circumstances that we turn next in our exploration of the issue of maladaptive functioning.

II

ADLERIAN THERAPY IN CONTEMPORARY PRACTICE

All methods of Individual Psychology for understanding the personality take into account the individual's opinion of his goal of superiority, the strength of his inferiority feelings, the degree of social interest, and the fact that the whole individual cannot be torn from his context with life— or better said, from his context with society.

—A. Adler, 1956, p. 327

The concepts presented in these chapters apply to all of the Adlerian therapy formats. Adler's development of social interest is one such idea. Social interest can help practitioners develop deep compassion and concern when working with others. Adlerians learn how to go beyond the concept of engagement and relationship into a deeper level of appreciation of others.

Adlerian ideas about diagnosis and assessment will allow practitioners to work in a more efficient and effective fashion. Today's psychotherapeutic climate requires that one have familiarity with the *Diagnostic and Statistical Manual of Mental Disorders* (4th ed., text revision; American Psychiatric Association, 2000) and how it not only can be helpful to our understanding of people but also can help them change. Adlerians have developed treatment protocols for the various *Diagnostic and Statistical Manual of Mental Disorders* diagnoses that are made possible through effective assessment.

Adlerian theory and assessment strategies provide the foundation for the final section, which describes goals and techniques. Because Adler's ideas are so practical, this section is a treasure trove of strategies and tactics. Each one is clearly presented and organized by the stage of therapeutic treatment.

4

ESTABLISHING THE
THERAPEUTIC RELATIONSHIP

Research over the past 40 years has consistently supported the idea that, apart from client and extratherapeutic factors, the best predictors of successful therapeutic outcomes are client–therapist relationship factors. According to Sexton and Whiston (1994),

> Of all the techniques, client–counselor characteristics, and procedures that have been studied, it is only the [therapeutic] relationship that has consistently been found to contribute to success of the therapeutic process. . . . Thus, research has confirmed what was widely recognized: The success of any therapeutic endeavor depends on the participants establishing an open, trusting, collaborative relationship or alliance. (pp. 6–7)

Factors such as therapist relationship attitudes and skills (e.g., genuineness, unconditional positive regard, and empathy) are fundamental to establishing a good client–therapist relationship and are positively related to successful outcomes; approximately 30% of improvement is attributed to the client–therapist relationship (Asay & Lambert, 1999; Bachelor & Horvath, 1999; Frank & Frank, 1991; Hubble, Duncan, & Miller, 1999c; Lambert & Barley, 2001; Norcross, 2002). In fact, as Lambert and Barley (2001) noted, client–relationship factors consistently correlate more highly with successful client outcomes than do specific therapy techniques. Thus, "it seems without a doubt that a positive therapeutic relationship is a necessary (but probably not sufficient) component of all effective psychotherapy" (Bachelor & Horvath, 1999, p. 161).

In discussing the importance of the therapeutic relationship, the psychotherapy research and practice literature often acknowledges Carl Rogers as the first theorist and therapist to emphasize the crucial importance of developing a warm, accepting, and empathic relationship with clients (e.g., Bachelor & Horvath, 1999; Day, 2004; E. W. Kelly, 1994; Lambert & Barley, 2001). For example, E. W. Kelly (1994) stated that the research of Rogers and those who expanded Rogers's work in research and practice not only emphasized the client–therapist relationship as "the major therapeutic component of the [psychotherapy] process but also made reasonably concrete how this relationship is achieved" (p. 150). Although it is true that Rogers's important work significantly increased the field of psychotherapy's attention to and value of a warm and empathic client–therapist relationship, he was not the first theorist or psychotherapist to emphasize its importance (Ansbacher, 1990; Watts, 1995, 1998).

An obscure fact in the history of psychotherapy is that Rogers studied with Alfred Adler in 1927–1928, when Adler was a visiting instructor and Rogers was a doctoral intern at the now-defunct Institute for Child Guidance in New York City. Shortly before his death, Rogers stated,

> I had the privilege of meeting, listening to, and observing Dr. Alfred Adler. . . . Accustomed as I was to the rather rigid Freudian approach of the Institute—seventy-five-page case histories, and exhaustive batteries of tests before even thinking of "treating" a child—I was shocked by Dr. Adler's very direct and deceptively simple manner of immediately relating to the child and the parent. It took me some time to realize how much I had learned from him. (quoted in Ansbacher, 1990, p. 47)

Except for two brief, nondescript statements (Rogers, 1967, 1980), however, Rogers apparently did not mention Adler in his writings, and the previous quotation appears to be the only acknowledgment Rogers ever made regarding Adler's influence. However, drawing from primary source materials, Watts (1995, 1998) has demonstrated that there are remarkable similarities between Adler's multifaceted descriptions of social interest—especially in terms of the role of the therapist—and Rogers's descriptions of the therapist-offered core conditions of therapeutic change.

ROGERS'S CORE CONDITIONS AND ADLER'S SOCIAL INTEREST

Of the therapist-offered core conditions of empathy, unconditional positive regard, and congruence, empathy was the first that Rogers (1951) identified and explicated. In his seminal article "The Necessary and Sufficient Conditions of Therapeutic Change" (first published in 1957), Rogers (1989) added to empathy the core conditions of congruence and unconditional positive regard.

Empathy and Social Interest

In describing empathy, Rogers (1951) stated,

> It is the counselor's function to assume, in so far as he is able, the internal frame of reference of the client, to perceive the world as the client sees it, to perceive the client himself as he is seen by himself, to lay aside all perceptions from the external frame of reference while doing so, and to communicate something of this empathic understanding to the client. (p. 29)

According to Rogers (1989), the condition of empathy occurs when

> the therapist is experiencing an accurate, empathic understanding of the client's awareness, of his own experience. To sense the client's private world as if it were your own, but without ever losing the "as if" quality— this is empathy, and this seems essential to therapy. (p. 226)

Raskin and Rogers (1989) also noted that unconditional positive regard is communicated to clients through empathy: "Being empathic reflects an attitude of profound interest in the client's world of meanings and feelings as the client is willing to share this world" (p. 157).

In a 1927 publication, Adler (1956) described social interest in terms of empathic understanding:

> By social interest or social feeling, we understand something different from that which other authors understand. When we say it is a feeling, we are certainly justified in doing so. But it is more than feeling; it is an evaluative attitude toward life. . . . We are not in a position to define unequivocally, but we have found in an English author a phrase which clearly expresses what we could contribute to an explanation: "To see with the eyes of another, to hear with the ears of another, and to feel with the heart of another." (p. 135)

Adlerians have subsequently affirmed Adler's perspective regarding the role of empathy in social interest. O'Connell (1965) noted that social interest "covers the intellectual, affective, and behavioral aspects of the optimal relationship to others, namely, understanding, empathizing with, and acting on behalf of others" (p. 47). Ansbacher (1991) added that individuals with developed social interest are able to "understand and appreciate [clients'] subjective experiences, their private worlds, and their opinions. Such an individual is tolerant, that is, he is reasonable, understanding, able to empathize, to identify" (p. 36).

Unconditional Positive Regard and Social Interest

In his 1957 publication on the core conditions, Rogers described unconditional positive regard:

> To the extent that the therapist finds himself experiencing a warm acceptance of each aspect of the client's experience as being a part of that client, he is experiencing unconditional positive regard. . . . It means a prizing of the person . . . as much acceptance of ways in which he is inconsistent as ways in which he is consistent. It means caring for the client . . . as a separate person, with permission to have his own feelings, his own experiences. (1989, p. 225)

In a 1929 publication, Adler stated that individuals acting in accordance with developed social interest not only have feelings of self-worth and value, courage, and optimism but also treat others in an egalitarian manner, viewing others as equals and as people of value and dignity who are worthy of respect (A. Adler, 1956). Adler (1956) emphasized the "unconditional expression of social interest on the part of the psychotherapist" (p. 341)—in other words, offering clients an encouraging therapeutic atmosphere where clients feel permission to be truly themselves with the therapist. Adler (1956) further noted that the therapist's task is to

> give the patient the experience of contact with a fellow man, and then enable him to transfer this awakened social interest to others. . . . The consultee must under all circumstances get the conviction that in relation to the treatment he is absolutely free. He can do, or not do, as he pleases. (p. 341)

Adlerians have echoed Adler's position regarding developed social interest as evinced by caring, respect for, and acceptance of others. Manaster and Corsini (1982) stated that "true social interest relates to all people at all times in all ways (p. 58). . . . The essence of social interest is the Golden Rule: Do unto others as you would have them do unto you" (p. 64). Mosak (1989) presented the biblical mandate to love one's neighbor as oneself as a parsimonious illustration of social interest. Following Mosak's lead, Watts (1992) addressed the parallels between social interest and the Koine Greek word *agape*, meaning "unconditional love." The behavioral characteristics of agape—perseverance, benevolence, trustworthiness, humility, altruism, unselfishness, and optimism—parallel both Adlerian descriptions of social interest and Rogerian descriptions of the core conditions, especially unconditional positive regard.

Congruence and Social Interest

Rogers (1989) stated that *congruence* means that within the therapeutic relationship the therapist is "freely and deeply himself, with his actual experience accurately represented by his awareness of himself. It is the opposite of presenting a facade, either knowingly or unknowingly" (pp. 222–223).

> When I can accept the fact that I have deficiencies, many faults, make lots of mistakes, and am often ignorant when I should be knowledgeable, often prejudiced when I should be open-minded, often have feelings which are not justified by the circumstances, then I can be much more real. (Rogers, 1969, p. 228)

Raskin and Rogers (1989) provided further clarification:

> The therapist does not deny to himself or herself the feelings being experienced and the therapist is willing to express and to be open about any persistent feelings that exist in the relationship. It means avoiding the temptation to hide behind a mask of professionalism. . . . Congruence refers to the correspondence between the thoughts and the behavior of the therapist; thus, genuineness describes this characteristic. The therapist does not put up a professional front or personal facade. (pp. 171–172)

Of the three core conditions, Adler's descriptions of social interest are the least explicit regarding what Rogers called *congruence*. Adler (1956, 1979) suggested that therapists with developed social interest possess self-awareness and relate to clients with compassionate honesty (i.e., genuineness). These ideas, which are implicit in Adler's writings, however, have been explicitly discussed by subsequent Adlerians. Manaster and Corsini (1982) stated that people with developed social interest have the courage to be imperfect; that is, they have "learned how to accept themselves with their frailties and weaknesses" and believe they are acceptable, albeit imperfect (p. 49). Mosak (1989) noted that people with developed social interest are genuine; they are "willing to commit to life and the life tasks without evasion, excuse, or side shows" (p. 80). Therefore, just as Rogerian therapists strive to be models of empathy, warmth, and genuineness for clients, so also Adlerian therapists strive to be models of social interest.

> Adlerian therapists represent themselves as "being for real," fallible, able to laugh at themselves, caring. . . . If the therapist can possess these characteristics, perhaps the [client] can, too, and many [clients] emulate their therapists, whom they use as referents for normality. (Mosak, 1989, pp. 90–91)

The therapist-oriented core conditions do indeed parallel the attitudes and behaviors of social interest. Mosak (1989) stated that people with social interest are "socially contributive people interested in the common welfare and, by Adler's pragmatic definition of normality, mentally healthy" (p. 67). Thus, by providing clients with a therapeutic environment permeated with what Rogers called the core conditions, therapists model social interest and lay the foundation whereby clients feel safe to grow toward greater mental health and well-being.

KEY ASPECTS IN ESTABLISHING
THE THERAPEUTIC RELATIONSHIP

Decades of research indicate that the provision of therapy is an interpersonal process in which a main influential component is the nature of the therapeutic relationship (Lambert & Barley, 2001). According to Bachelor and Horvath (1999), the therapeutic relationship

> appears to be formed early in therapy, probably within the first few sessions. Close attention should be paid to the client's early perceptions and reactions and to the establishment of a positive relationship with the client at the beginning of therapy. (p. 161)

Furthermore, the client–therapist relationship itself can represent a therapeutic intervention. Bachelor and Horvath indicated that "The experience of a trusting and safe environment facilitated by the therapist's availability, responsiveness, and constancy, in which clients can explore past and present feelings and interactions, may initiate change" (p. 161).

These comments significantly resonate with the Adlerian perspective regarding the therapeutic relationship. Adlerian psychotherapy, a relational approach, consists of four phases. The first and most important phase, entitled *relationship*, clearly focuses on establishing a strong client–therapist alliance. Furthermore, and consistent with the aforementioned outcome research literature, Adlerians believe that therapeutic efficacy in the other phases of Adlerian therapy is predicated on the development and continuation of a meaningful therapeutic alliance. Establishing a strong therapeutic relationship is crucial because it is the most influential component of change in psychotherapy. The therapeutic relationship in Adlerian therapy begins with the initial contact with clients and may continue intermittently for years. In the remainder of this chapter, we focus on three key aspects of establishing the therapeutic relationship or alliance in Adlerian therapy: (a) initial logistical issues, (b) developing and maintaining the therapeutic relationship, and (c) collaborative formulation of therapy goals.

Initial Logistical Issues

Adlerians, like other clinicians, must address important logistical issues at the outset of therapy, not only ethical and legal issues but also issues that significantly affect the initial effort to establish a strong, positive therapeutic alliance. In his writings, Adler addressed—albeit briefly—many of these crucial logistical issues. For example, he stated, "all the necessary questions—the visiting time, the question of fees, free treatment, the physician's pledge to secrecy [confidentiality], etc.—should be regulated immediately and be strictly adhered to" (A. Adler, 1956, p. 345). Following Oberst and Stewart (2003), we now address three key logistical issues that are significantly influential for the initial development of the therapeutic alliance: (a) duration and frequency of therapy, (b) fee structure, and (c) nonsession communication.

Duration of Therapy

Adlerian psychotherapy is not primarily a brief therapy or a long-term psychotherapy. It is a flexible, integrative, eclectic approach, and Adlerian therapists tailor treatment to the unique needs and situations of clients. Therefore, if brief therapy appears to be appropriate and is negotiated between the therapist and client, then brief treatment ensues. However, if the client desires longer term therapy, and the therapist deems it appropriate, then longer term therapy begins (Dinkmeyer & Sperry, 2000). Adler typically limited the number of sessions he saw clients to approximately 20 or fewer. In discussing the duration of therapy, Adler stated the following:

> An Individual Psychology treatment, if properly carried out, should show at least a perceptible partial success in three months, often even sooner. . . . Still one can add: "If you are not convinced in one or two weeks [two sessions per week] that we are on the right path, I will stop the treatment" (1956, p. 344). . . . You might say right at the beginning, "It will take eight to ten weeks" [two sessions per week]. In doubtful cases: "I don't know. Let us begin. In a month I shall ask you whether you are convinced that we are on the right track. If not, we shall break off." I have often proposed this in difficult cases. (1979, p. 201)

The approximately 20 or fewer sessions-per-episode limit recommended by Adler is consistent with the practice followed by most contemporary Adlerians (Dinkmeyer & Sperry, 2000; Maniacci, 1996a; Sperry, 1989). Nevertheless, specific details regarding the duration and frequency of treatment—as well as the length of individual therapy sessions—is negotiated between the therapist and client and is ultimately contingent on the treatment goals collaboratively developed by the client and therapist.

Fee Structure

Adlerian therapists, like other clinicians, should discuss their fee schedule with clients at the outset of therapy as well as address issues such as cancellations or the client's failure to attend sessions (A. Adler, 1979; Oberst & Stewart, 2003). In agreement with Adler (1956, 1979), Oberst and Stewart (2003) stated that therapists should refrain from demanding exorbitant fees and that care should be exercised "in determining the appropriate charge if a sliding scale fee is used" (p. 55). Adler (1956) stated that pro bono treatment "should be given in a manner which does not allow the patient to feel that there is any lack of interest in his case" (p. 345). Adler's thoughts are salient to sliding fee scale clients as well. In addition, Adler (1956) warned against receiving gifts or accepting favors from clients and expressed caution regarding "making payments contingent upon success for the treatment" (p. 345). Finally, Adler (1979) noted that, should a client find it difficult to pay for therapy, the therapist should not allow him or her to continue therapy and accumulate a large unpaid bill. Adler suggested that a client in this particular situation should be provided an appropriate referral based on his or her specific financial situation. Oberst and Stewart (2003) correctly noted that "Although managing issues of fees may seem commonsensical, clients can and do create therapeutic issues in this domain that can be challenging to resolve" (p. 55).

Communicating With the Therapist Outside of Therapy

When and how the therapist may be contacted apart from scheduled appointments is an important relational boundary issue and should be addressed very early in the therapeutic relationship. Oberst and Stewart (2003) suggested that, as part of establishing appropriate relational boundaries, therapists should explain to clients what type and means of nonsession contact is permitted. Except in the rare cases of genuine emergency, therapists do not perform between-session treatment by telephone or electronic means. If the therapist's policy regarding nonsession communication is not stated clearly at the outset of therapy, there could be a significant—but unnecessary—subsequent rupture in the therapeutic alliance should a client attempt a nonsession communication.

Developing and Maintaining the Therapeutic Relationship

At the beginning of the therapeutic process, it is useful to inform clients about the qualities and characteristics of the therapeutic relationship. As Dinkmeyer and Sperry (2000) indicated, clients may have little knowledge of this kind of relationship or may have misperceptions and faulty expectations. In Adlerian therapy, the roles of the client and therapist as equal, collaborative partners in the psychotherapy endeavor must be made clear. It is crucial that the clients understand that they have an active coworker role in therapy. The Adlerian literature describes the client–therapist relationship using words such as *cooperative, collaborative, egalitarian, optimistic,* and *respectful.* Adler (1956) stated that therapists should not "insist upon any superior rank or right" with clients and should not allow clients to place them in some expert role such as "teacher, father, or saviour" (p. 338). Adler (1979) stressed that, from the outset of therapy, the therapist must help the client understand that the responsibility for change is the client's: "The most important therapeutic aid of the [therapist] is always the patient himself," and the job of the therapist is to help the client "pull himself out of the swamp by his own bootstraps" (pp. 192–193). The recent research indicating that extratherapeutic or client factors account for the greatest amount of the variance in successful therapy outcomes strongly supports Adler's point (see, e.g., Hubble, Duncan, & Miller, 1999b).

Adler's emphasis on social interest, as it pertains to psychotherapy, is clearly evinced in the qualities and characteristics that help develop a strong therapeutic relationship. According to Adler (1956)

> Psychotherapy is an exercise in cooperation and a test of cooperation. We can succeed only if we are genuinely interested in the other. We must be able to see with his eyes and listen with his ears. He must contribute his part to our common understanding. We must work out his attributes and difficulties together. . . . Thus, cooperation between patient and consultant . . . is of paramount importance, and from the start all measures should be taken to promote the cooperation of the patient with the consultant. Obviously this is only possible if the patient feels secure with the physician. The task of the physician or psychologist is to give the patient the experience of contact with a fellow man, and then to enable him to transfer this awakened social interest to others. . . . For the psychologist the first rule is to win the patient; the second is to never worry about his own success. . . . The patient's social interest, which is always present in some degree, finds its best possible expression in the relation with the psychologist. (pp. 340–341)

In reflecting on these comments from Adler, E. W. Kelly (1994) stated

> What stands out in this description of the therapeutic relationship is its nontechnical humanness. . . . [The therapeutic relationship] . . . is seen as peculiarly human, having the character of a genuinely person-to-person meeting. It is "winning," based on "genuine interest," aiming at "cooperation" (both within and outside of therapy), requiring the [therapist] to "see with [the client's] eyes and listen with his ears," moving toward a "common understanding" and representing an experience of distinctively human contact. (p. 140)

According to Asay and Lambert (1999), the therapeutic relationship must facilitate clients' abilities to "call on their own resources in solving problems" (p. 46):

> Helping clients to marshal their abilities and resources in the therapeutic enterprise begins with the therapist's attitude about the client's role in the change process. Communicating a belief and hope in the client's ability to change and an optimistic expectation that change will indeed occur is essential, especially in the beginning of treatment. Likewise, communicating the expectation that clients will be active participants in the therapeutic process who share responsibility for the type and amount of change implies that they are taken seriously by the therapist and are viewed as competent and capable of change. . . . The client's sense of efficacy is also enhanced [when the therapist inquires] about changes the client may have noticed within sessions or between sessions and how these changes may be related to the client's efforts in therapy.

> Therapists should also feel free to point out the positive changes and
> differences that they see in their clients and continue to communicate
> the expectation that more change is likely to occur. . . . [This affirma-
> tion] helps to reinforce the clients' faith in their ability to improve. (pp.
> 46–47)

Adlerians clearly agree. In developing the therapeutic relationship, Adlerian therapists focus on developing a respectful, egalitarian, optimistic, and
growth-oriented therapeutic alliance that emphasizes clients' assets, abilities, resources, and strengths. These qualities and characteristics are embedded in what Adlerians have historically called *encouragement*, or the therapeutic modeling of social interest.

For Adlerians, encouragement is both an attitude and a way of being
with clients in therapy. Dreikurs (1967) noted the essential necessity of encouragement in psychotherapy. He stated that presenting problems are "based
on discouragement" and without "encouragement, without having faith in
himself restored, [the client] cannot see the possibility of doing or functioning better" (p. 62). Adler once asked a client what he thought made the
difference in his successful experience in therapy. The client replied: "That's
quite simple. I had lost all courage to live. In our consultations I found it
again" (A. Adler, 1956, p. 342).

Adlerians consider encouragement a crucial aspect of human growth
and development. This is especially true in regard to psychotherapy. Stressing the importance of encouragement in therapy, Adler (1956) stated: "Al-
together, in every step of the treatment, we must not deviate from the path
of encouragement" (p. 342). Dreikurs (1967) agreed: "What is most important in every treatment is encouragement" (p. 35). In addition, Dreikurs stated
that therapeutic success was largely dependent on "[the therapist's] ability to
provide encouragement" and that failure generally occurred "due to the inability of the therapist to encourage" (pp. 12–13).

> Encouragement focuses on helping counselees become aware of their
> worth. By encouraging them, you help your counselees recognize their
> own strengths and assets, so they become aware of the power they have
> to make decisions and choices. . . . Encouragement focuses on beliefs and
> self-perceptions. It searches intensely for assets and processes feedback
> so the client will become aware of her strengths. In a mistake-centered
> culture like ours, this approach violates norms by ignoring deficits and
> stressing assets. The counselor is concerned with changing the client's
> negative self concept and anticipations. (Dinkmeyer, Dinkmeyer, &
> Sperry, 1987, p. 124)

*Therapist Behaviors for Developing and Maintaining
the Therapeutic Relationship*

Adapted from Allred and Poduska (1985) and Dinkmeyer and Sperry
(2000), the following description of therapist behaviors—when expressed

with warmth, empathy, and respect—are useful in establishing and maintaining a strong therapeutic relationship.

Encouraging. Encouraging behaviors include reassuring clients; active listening; reflecting feelings; paraphrasing; collaborative goal setting; acknowledging clients' efforts; recognizing clients' strengths and competencies; and other statements that emphasize the egalitarian, optimistic, and growth-oriented nature of the relationship.

Informing. Informing behaviors include providing information about the structure of therapy in general and, specifically, individual sessions; providing information or using self-disclosure to help normalize a client's situation; and providing information where clients may have an information deficit or erroneous information.

Discovering. Discovering behaviors include asking reflective questions for information about clients' thoughts or behaviors and reflecting or summarizing clients' thoughts or behaviors and asking for clients' feedback.

Interpreting. Interpreting behaviors include seeking clarifications of clients' meanings, offering tentative hypotheses or educated guesses about the meanings or purposes of clients' behavior, and summarizing tentative interpretations.

Confronting. Confronting behaviors include reflecting discrepancies between verbal or nonverbal communication (metacommunication), using immediacy to communicate about something that is occurring in the here-and-now relationship, engaging in dialogue about potentially discouraging thoughts and perceptions, and respectfully challenging destructive emotions and behaviors.

Considering. Considering behaviors include collaboratively and reflectively helping clients create, explore, and assess the viability of perceptual, emotional, and behavioral alternatives.

Proposing. Proposing behaviors include asking clients to practice or rehearse behaviors indicative of perceptual, emotional, or behavioral alternatives they have considered; asking clients to engage in behaviors indicative of perceptual, emotional, or behavioral alternatives they have considered; and negotiating with clients regarding specific changes.

Evaluating. Evaluating behaviors include asking questions regarding clients' follow-through on tasks to which they have committed; asking clients to evaluate the progress they have made; and providing clients with feedback statements regarding their progress, or lack thereof.

Importance of the Continuing Therapeutic Alliance

Asay and Lambert (1999) stated that the basic qualities and skills that help develop the therapeutic relationship "are the foundation on which all other skills are built" (p. 43) and help facilitate "the element of collaboration between therapist and client, including the consensual endorsement of therapeutic procedures, [that have] shown to be an essential part of the development of a strong therapeutic alliance" (p. 44). In addition, Lambert and Barley (2001) affirmed that additional success in psychotherapy may result as therapists learn to improve their abilities to relate to clients and to tailor that relationship to individual clients (see also Norcross, 2002; Safran & Muran, 2000).

Adlerian therapists agree that the therapeutic alliance is foundational for all aspects of therapy, including selection and implementation of techniques. Because of its emphasis on the critical role of the therapeutic alliance, Adlerian therapy is not a technique-driven approach. Adlerians are technical eclectics and, consequently, tailor their treatment to their clients' unique needs and circumstances. Dreikurs (1967), however, warned therapists to avoid being overly enamored with techniques. He suggested that a primary focus on techniques, instead of the therapeutic relationship, can do irreparable harm to the therapeutic process. Thus, Adlerians emphasize that techniques are most usefully employed, and have the greatest opportunity for influence, within a safe and trusting relational context. Regardless of the therapist's technical acumen, clients typically need the safe base of a positive therapeutic alliance in order to do significant work.

Lambert and Barley (2001) stated that the therapeutic alliance is often understood as having three components: (a) bonds, (b) goals, and (c) tasks. *Bonds* include the relational attachment developed between the client and therapist based on acceptance, confidence, and trust. *Goals* are the goals of therapy collaboratively developed and endorsed by both the client and the therapist. *Tasks* are the in-session (or assigned homework) behaviors and procedures that constitute the actual therapeutic work. Consequently, a continuing focus on the qualities and skills that initially develop the client–therapist relationship is essential throughout therapy because "[it is] the foundation on which all other skills and techniques are built" (Asay & Lambert, 1999, p. 43). Asay and Lambert (1999) noted that the progress of therapy is largely determined by the therapist's ability to develop and maintain strong therapeutic relationships, particularly with more difficulty or challenging clients:

> Therapists who are able to communicate warmth, understanding, and positive feelings toward the client and can facilitate a reasonable dialogue leading to understanding and agreement about therapeutic goals, techniques, and roles will be more likely to effect a positive treatment alliance. (pp. 47–48)

Adlerians agree with Lambert and Barley's (2001) and Asay and Lambert's (1999) conclusions regarding the importance of the ongoing therapeutic relationship. As noted elsewhere, Adlerian therapists believe that therapeutic efficacy in later phases of Adlerian therapy is predicated on the development and continuation of a strong therapeutic relationship. A relationship based on mutual trust and respect may help clients feel safe enough to engage in the ongoing therapeutic process. A strong therapeutic relationship is important in the second phase of Adlerian therapy, when the therapist seeks to assess and understand the client's life style. In a trusting, respectful relationship, clients may be more forthcoming in sharing their story, and, consequently, therapists will have a more thorough text to assess. Furthermore, continuing attention to and development of the client–therapist relationship is particularly necessary in the insight and reorientation phases, in which a client's maladaptive core convictions and relational patterns emerge and are addressed and the client is encouraged to reflect on and enact different ways of thinking, feeling, and behaving. The therapist's ability to continually attend to and deepen the therapeutic relationship may significantly affect the client's willingness to examine potentially maladaptive aspects of underlying schemas and his or her willingness to consider and engage in perceptual, emotional, and behavioral alternatives (in and out of therapy).

Dreikurs (1967) indicated that the therapeutic relationship, properly established, may be the first relationship in which "the give-and-take of life can be accepted in good grace. Here the patient learns that he can stand the friction and clash of interests without disrupting the relationship" (p. 8):

> This type of relationship with its give and take, its resilience in conflict and its endurance under the impact of hostility can well form a pattern for future and more satisfactory relationships. . . . The training of a better form of relationship is one of the goals and objectives of psychotherapy. (p. 67)

The therapeutic relationship is one permeated by mutual trust and respect, where the therapist offers empathy, warmth, and acceptance and creates an atmosphere of hope and encouragement and where clients feel understood and develop an optimistic sense that their life can be different. Dreikurs (1967) noted that this kind of relational atmosphere is crucial, particularly "in moments of relapse, or at times when a plateau is reached" (p. 8).

Collaborative Formulation of Therapy Goals

A crucial early aspect of the therapeutic relationship in Adlerian psychotherapy is the collaborative formulation of specific, cocreated therapy goals. Clients and therapists partner together to develop a plan or contract addressing what clients want from psychotherapy, how they plan to get what they want, what is impeding them from attaining their goals, and how they can use their strengths and capabilities to bring their goals to fruition. The plan or contract also delineates the responsibilities that these equal partners—clients and therapists—in the therapy process are to assume. Progress in therapy is not possible without an alignment of clearly defined goals, and the therapy process is effective only to the degree to which it addresses issues that "the client recognizes as important and wants to discuss and change" (Dinkmeyer & Sperry, 2000, p. 77).

Oberst and Stewart (2003) suggested that, although some initial agreement about the purposes of therapy may be achieved in the initial session, it often takes several sessions before the client and therapist are able to clearly define the therapeutic goals. There are at least three reasons for this. First, sometimes a client's stated problem is not the actual problem (Dinkmeyer & Sperry, 2000; Oberst & Stewart, 2003). Clients will often present an initial issue to determine whether the therapeutic situation is safe. When sufficient trust has been established, clients are more forthcoming with their problems. Developing an atmosphere of trust and respect not only helps clients at the beginning of therapy but also lays the foundation for work in the subsequent phases. Second, although therapists may rather quickly discover maladaptive aspects of life style convictions, many clients desire a chance to tell their stories before they are ready to develop therapeutic goals (Oberst & Stewart, 2003). By attending well to clients' stories, therapists can help clients feel understood and accepted, and they may gain greater insight regarding strengths and capabilities that may be missing in the clients' present narrative. Third, clients may come with extremely low expectations about their chances for change or excessively high expectations of psychotherapy (Dinkmeyer & Sperry, 2000). When clients come to therapy with strong negative perceptions about themselves or others, they often believe that their situations are not amenable to change. Before establishing specific goals, therapists must strive to engender hope and anticipation of change with these clients. On the other hand, some clients come to psychotherapy with unrealistically high expectations. Establishing specific goals with these clients must wait until after the therapist helps them gain more reasonable expectations of therapy. As we discuss shortly, this may require therapists to more clearly delineate roles and responsibilities in psychotherapy. In addition, therapists should never make any guarantees—explicitly or implicitly—about successful therapy outcomes. Adler (1956) stated that therapists "should never, not even in the most certain cases, promise [success], but rather only the possibility of [success]" and they should "ascribe the work and the success of the therapy to the patient at whose disposal [therapists] should place [themselves] in a friendly way, as a coworker" (p. 338). Therapists should stress the importance of ongoing evaluation of progress in psychotherapy and the potentiality of collaboratively renegotiating goals as needed.

Adlerian psychotherapists can facilitate the goal-setting process by inquiring about the circumstances that precipitated the scheduling of the appointment for psychotherapy. Questions might include "What brings you in to see me today?" or, later, after the client has shared some about the occasion for the session, "How will your life be if you did not have this problem?" Follow-up questions include "What kind of person would you like to be 6 months from now? How about a year from now?" (Oberst & Stewart, 2003, p. 58) and may be revealing in regard to the client's hopes or expectations for a successful outcome. Additional questions that help focus goal setting even further include "Of the several important problems you have shared, which one is most troubling for you?" or "Which one are you most ready to begin working on?"

Paradoxically, an additional way to facilitate the initial goal-setting process is for the client and therapist to consider the criteria for termination of psychotherapy. Typically a part of the goal-setting agreement process, the criteria for termination address the question "What has to happen to signal that the work is nearing completion?" (Oberst & Stewart, 2003, p. 59).

> Although the exact moment and criteria for terminating work may change as the treatment proceeds and clients' goals evolve, the current era of managed care requires that therapists attune themselves to opportunities to punctuate their work. . . . The criteria for termination may be achieved of tangible, external goals or, alternatively, may emerge through a felt sense that the time is near for completing the treatment. (Oberst & Stewart, 2003, p. 59)

An important aspect of the goal-setting process in Adlerian psychotherapy is to clearly communicate to clients, especially ones new to therapy, what is expected of them. According to Oberst and Stewart (2003), therapists should tell clients what they may experience in psychotherapy and delineate clients' responsibilities:

> Some clients may view going to the therapist the same way they do their dentist—a little bit of pain, but the doctor does most of the work. Unlike other forms of health care, therapy requires clients to work in the traditional sense of the word (i.e. being willing to explore and sit with painful emotions, realizing one's limitations, etc.). This orientation, too, will help to prevent clients from heaping the bulk of the responsibility for change on the therapist. (p. 59)

This communication of expectations is important not only at the beginning of therapy but also, and equally so, throughout the therapeutic process. For example, sometimes the therapist may note that a client is not focused on the problem, is evading a topic, or is not attending to a comment offered by the therapist. The therapist might help the client refocus by using immediacy to indicate what is happening in the present moment of the relationship—in this case, how the client avoids particular issues. When the therapist helps a client refocus on the task, he or she is also reemphasizing the client's responsibility in psychotherapy (Dinkmeyer & Sperry, 2000).

Sometimes, however, a client may demonstrate behaviors similar to ones just described because of goal misalignment; that is, the client and therapist are not in agreement regarding the goals or direction of therapy. According to Dreikurs (1967),

> The proper therapeutic relationship, as we understand it, does not require transference, but a relationship of mutual trust and respect. This is more than mere establishment of contact and rapport. Therapeutic co-

operation requires an alignment of goals. When the goals and interests of the patient and therapist clash, no satisfactory relationship can be established. Winning the patient's cooperation for the common task is prerequisite for any therapy; maintaining it requires constant vigilance. What appears as "resistance" constitutes a discrepancy between the goals of the therapist and those of the patient. In each case, the proper relationship has to be re-established, difference resolved, and agreement reached. (p. 7)

As Dreikurs (1967) noted, so-called *resistance* in psychotherapy is often goal misalignment. When there is disagreement regarding therapeutic goals, at the beginning of therapy or later, clients are reluctant to genuinely continue in the therapy process. In this case, continued focus on the therapeutic relationship is crucial to facilitating a collaborative and cooperative therapeutic environment in which the client feels sufficiently safe and trusting to work toward goal realignment or modification and, thus, continue work on the concerns that impede him or her from successfully engaging the tasks of living.

CONCLUSION

An extensive body of research—from Rogers's work in the late 1940s and early 1950s to more recent studies (Asay & Lambert, 1999; Bachelor & Horvath, 1999; Burns & Auerbach, 1996; Frank & Frank, 1991; Lambert & Barley, 2001)—offers significant support for the fundamental importance of the client–therapist relationship in successful psychotherapy outcomes. This research indicates that developing and maintaining a positive therapeutic relationship is a necessary factor in psychotherapy efficacy. Consequently, most approaches to psychotherapy emphasize, to varying degrees, the importance of the therapeutic relationship or alliance.

Adler, in the early decades of the 20th century, emphasized the immense importance of developing egalitarian, respectful, optimistic, and growth-focused therapeutic relationships that focus more on clients' assets and capabilities than their deficits and disabilities. The first and most important phase of Adlerian psychotherapy is entitled *relationship*, and it addresses the establishment and maintenance of a strong therapeutic alliance. Adlerians understand that success in subsequent phases of Adlerian therapy—analysis, insight, and reorientation/reeducation—is clearly predicated on developing and continuing this therapeutic relationship. Adlerians pay more attention to the client–therapist relationship than they do to techniques or interventions; therefore, they tailor their treatment to the unique needs and situations of their clients.

Adlerian psychotherapy's emphasis on the therapeutic relationship is consistent with Adler's emphasis on human relationships. Individual (or

Adlerian) Psychology is a relational psychology, and the cardinal tenet of Adler's theory is *Gemeinschaftsgefuhl*, which is translated as "social interest" or "community feeling." Thus, Dreikurs (1967) stated that between the therapist and the client "there exists, after all, a human community" whose purpose is to help the client (pp. 30–31). Establishing and maintaining the therapeutic alliance, this "human community," is the foundational task for successful outcomes in Adlerian psychotherapy.

5

AN ADLERIAN PERSPECTIVE ON PSYCHOPATHOLOGY: USING THE *DSM*

In chapter 3, we discussed how personality is conceptualized from an Adlerian perspective. Adlerians view personality from a goal-directed, interpersonal, phenomenological, and holistic perspective. All people are striving for goals in a social context that, from their point of view, give their life meaning and purpose. From their vantage point, life makes sense when they do what they do the way they were raised to do it. That such a manner of living should bring grief not only to themselves but also to others, is difficult for them to realize.

Why do people make life so difficult for themselves and others? Since antiquity, people have been trying to answer that question. Adlerians believe they have an answer: They have given the wrong meaning to life (A. Adler, 1931). Some individuals are born with inadequate equipment. Adlerians refer to that as *organ inferiority*. Some grow up in discouraging childhood situations. Adlerians refer to those situations as being *pampered* or *neglected*. Some people, it seems, never had a chance to learn how to attach the correct meaning to life. Still, there is another factor most theories leave out of their assumptions: creativity. The use people make of their circumstances is as important as, and often more important than, the circumstances themselves.

THE CONCEPT OF SOCIALLY USEFUL
AND SOCIALLY USELESS MOVEMENTS

Adler (1956) theorized that adaptation was crucial to survival. He believed that because humans were so poorly physically equipped, compared with most animals, they had to rely on something else. That "something else" was each other. Humans are social animals. When they bond, they flourish; when they are isolated, they do not. Communication and the ability to *abstract*—to project into the future occurrences that had not yet happened—led humans to learn not only from experience but also from each other. People could learn without having to experience for themselves. The adaptive value was enormous. Humans could learn through the experiences of others, and this may have been one of the key elements in humanity's success. There was, however, one catch: Each person had to have a group from whom to learn, and the other group members had to accept that person.

To maintain group cohesion, each member had to have responsibilities and pull his or her load. Even infants had work to do: They had to suck at the nipple—milk simply would not flow on its own—and they had to communicate (albeit vaguely) when something was needed. To gain the benefits of group wisdom (the cognitive motive), protection (the security motive), and survival training (the competence motive), individuals needed to belong to the group (the attachment motive) and had to contribute to whatever extent they could. Individualistic, self-centered striving not only put each member at risk but also failed to contribute to the well-being of the group. If the group did not survive, no individual did, either.

When Adler (1956, 1933/1964) wrote about socially useful and socially useless behavior, this is the context he meant. Thousands of years of evolution have left their mark. People still need to contribute. As their contribution to the general welfare of the group increases, so does their personal success. There is no dichotomy; questions such as "Should I be for myself or others?" miss the point. Humans are interconnected. Although some contemporary Adlerians tend to prefer the terms *constructive, nonconstructive,* and *destructive* to the classical *useful* and *useless* (Mosak & Maniacci, 1999), the point is the same. The inseparable bond humans have with each other is the key ingredient to survival.

The Larger Context of Overall Adaptation: Community Feeling and Social Interest

Individuals who grasp the notion of adaptation, who see no such me-or-them dichotomy, are exhibiting community feeling and social interest. They understand the interconnectedness of humanity; they know it is not "me or them"; it truly is "us." The overall empathic bond is the *community feeling*, and the action that derives from that feeling is the *social interest*

(Ansbacher, 1992; Mosak & Maniacci, 1999; Stein & Edwards, 1998). Betty cares for her neighbors (community feeling) and shows it by being kind and considerate (social interest).

Both concepts are global and species specific. They aim for species survival and long-term, overall adaptation. They are unchanging and universal—in other words, they are not subject to cultural interpretation and historical context. What is good for all people, at all times, regardless of their particular circumstances? What is good for all people, everywhere? These are the types of questions Adlerians ask when assessing whether people's actions are displaying social interest.

Situational Dynamics: The Concept of Common Sense

Such a global, universal notion is admittedly tough to grasp and certainly not always so clear in application. The concept of common sense explains why. Adlerians speak of common sense in the situationally specific, cultural, and historical context (A. Adler, 1956). It is hard for any individual to transcend his or her cultural and historical context. It is important to adapt to that situational context and to share in the common sense of the group, as it is currently defined. As Adler grew to know all too well, living in Vienna in the 1920s and 1930s and witnessing the rise of Fascism and the Nazi party, the common sense is certainly important in defining what is healthy, adaptive, and socially useful, but it can also be tragically and monumentally wrong, causing great pain and horror. There had to be another concept over and above common sense in determining mental health and adaptation; hence his formulation of the concepts of community feeling and social interest (A. Adler, 1933/1964).

The Tasks of Life

Adler (1956) noted that there were three main areas of life that required cooperative movement: (a) work, (b) social, and (c) love tasks. Later Adlerians have added three others: (a) getting along with oneself, (b) finding a place in the cosmos, and (c) parenting and family tasks (Mosak & Maniacci, 1999). For space considerations, here we address only Adler's original three, and even these we discuss briefly and only with regard to their clinical applications.

People have to work. *Work* can be defined in a variety of ways, not simply as a paying job. Helping around the home can be work, as can doing well in school. No individual can survive on his or her own. No one human possesses all the requisite knowledge to be totally self-sufficient. People need each other to produce goods and services. Physicians cannot make their own clothes and simultaneously practice medicine very well. Farmers cannot design and build the equipment they need and still find time to work their land.

Humans need to get along with each other. As we noted in the beginning of this chapter, there is a fundamental social contract that requires we cooperate. Civility, kindness, and mutual respect make everything function easier and better. This is the social task.

Humans cannot reproduce by themselves; this requires two sexes. To get along with others and to reproduce requires effort and teamwork. Bonding in general, be it heterosexually or homosexually, with or without children, requires cooperation, empathy, and compassion. Of all the life tasks, that of love and sex is often the most difficult to fulfill. In the other two tasks, some distance can be maintained as they are accomplished. This is not the case with love and sex. Also, although this task is far easier today to fulfill than it was, say, in the 1920s, when Adler first wrote about it, love and sex are still exceptionally challenging for many individuals and provide one of the greatest tests of common sense and community feeling.

What gets in the way of meeting the life tasks? Why do some people have a hard time displaying common sense and social interest? The answer to these questions is because in their apperceptive schema, something is different. That something is the nature of the way they construe life, themselves, and their place in the world.

Private Logic

All individuals have ways of construing themselves, their world, and their place in it that are unique to them (Dreikurs, 1967; Nikelly, 1971a). Not everybody has the same amount of common sense, primarily because not every family is perfect. Not all children are equally well prepared to use what they have learned at home and with their families in the real (i.e., outside) world.

Adlerians classify thinking into two categories: (a) common sense and (b) private sense (Nikelly, 1971a). Private sense has become more commonly known in the Adlerian literature as *private logic* (and, in some texts, as *private intelligence*). Simply put, it does not make common sense; it is idiosyncratic, personal, and at times bizarre. Not all private logic runs counter to community feeling and social interest. Some private logic, such as personal preferences or tastes that do not match those of the times, is unique but not harmful. Individuals are cognizant enough to understand their idiosyncrasies and recognize when they need to keep them to themselves and not disrupt the group or sidetrack group dynamics too much. In short, they allow others to have their own way, too, and they do not feel too inferior for being different; even if they do, they problem-solve and compensate cooperatively and usefully.

Other people are not so socially interested. Their private logic not only runs counter to common sense but also does not allow for problem solving or cooperative compensations. Their private logic is more than idiosyncratic; it is self-centered, and they do not usefully compensate for it. They construe life and themselves in ways that do not facilitate group cohesion, adaptation, and survival. They see life not only differently but also in ways that Adlerians consider socially disturbing.

Styles of Striving and Movements Through Life

Individuals who strive to find their place in the group cooperatively, displaying social interest and community feeling, rely on prudent judgment. When this may not be the best barometer, they have that larger, more universal perspective—a sort of wisdom that defies categorization but is inevitably useful. They are displaying community feeling. They move through life *with* others.

Other people do not do this. Their private logic, at crucial times and in crucial ways, lacks that larger perspective and even runs counter to it. Consider these two self-ideal statements:

A. I should be number one.
B. I should always be number one, no matter what.

Both are articulations of the competence motive, and both have some degree of private logic to them. How so? Think about it. Does survival really depend on being "number one"? Of course not. Both statements are not common sense, yet Statement B is special. Not only is it clearly private in logic, but it also is hostile and rather extreme.

Private logic of the type displayed in Statement B can be categorized along the following guidelines (Ansbacher, 1977). It is *dichotomous*, or what Adler referred to as displaying an "antithetical mode of apperception." This type of thinking is categorized by dichotomies such as either–or, black–white, yes–no, and so on. With rare exception, however, life and the world exist along a continuum, not in dichotomous categories. This type of private logic is inflexible, not adaptive. It is categorized by an insistence that "It is either this way, or not at all." It views life vertically, not horizontally. By *vertical*, Adlerians mean the construal of people as above or below, superior or inferior, master or slave. Who is on top of whom? Who is better or worse? This type of thinking increases feelings of inferiority and inferiority complexes, not minimizes them. It decreases group cohesion, not enhances it. Horizontal thinking sees people as fundamentally different but equal, with each contributing something unique and useful to the group. Everybody is on the same level; hence, there is little need for safeguarding or defensiveness when confronted with inferiorities. Finally, this type of private logic operates at the expense of others, not with others. For a person who uses the logic depicted in Statement B, his or her striving comes only if others do not do well. This style of thinking is far too self-centered. It almost inevitably leads to what has become known as *psychopathology*.

THE *DSM* AND ADLERIAN PSYCHOLOGY

The relationship of the *Diagnostic and Statistical Manual of Mental Disorders* (4th ed., text revision; *DSM–IV–TR*; American Psychiatric Association, 2000) to Adlerian psychology has been documented before, most recently in a special issue of the *Journal of Individual Psychology* (Sperry, 2002). In this chapter we cannot and will not cover all that material in similar depth, but we do offer a fairly detailed overview (Maniacci, 1999, 2002; Maniacci & Sackett-Maniacci, 2002; Sperry & Maniacci, 1992).

The *DSM* is descriptive and atheoretical (as much as any point of view can be), and it attempts to be empirical. Diagnoses are included in the manual only after extensive peer review, field testing, cross-referencing with other professionals (including those from other disciplines and countries), and replication by at least a second team of researchers. Despite all such attempts, it is flawed, as any work published by a committee will eventually become. There are too many diagnoses (more than 500); far too many cases of diagnostic overlap between categories; and, in a surprisingly large number of cases, poor interrater reliability. Even something that attempts to be atheoretical and remain at the level of description will have, as any philosopher worth his or her degree will tell you, a theoretical stance. The unacknowledged perspective is an uneasy melding of radical behaviorism and the classical medical model of diagnosis by matching and exclusion.

In spite of these flaws, the *DSM* is the best available classification system on the market. Without it, teaching, communicating with other professionals, and conducting research would be almost impossible. At some time, in some way, people must be categorized, or learning becomes impractical. To learn every possible manifestation of psychopathology in its idiosyncratic presentation—that is, on a case-by-case basis—would be foolhardy. Students in training would never learn about clinical depression, they would learn about Mr. Smith or Ms. Williams. They will never see Mr. Smith or Ms. Williams; they will see Ms. Greene or Mr. O'Malley. What do they do then?

The scientific method is one of humanity's greatest achievements. Something truly "unbiased" can be achieved only with the scientific method; at the least, bias can be radically minimized through the process of consensual validation, peer review, and replication. For the scientific method to be used, terms must be defined in a clear, objective manner. Without such agreed-on terms, no one can be sure what is being observed. That is where the problem begins. The diagnoses of the *DSM* both eliminate and create problems. The diagnoses are the bases of comparison and measurement, yet it is difficult for many clinicians and researchers to consistently agree on many of the diagnoses.

Adlerian psychology is occasionally descriptive, but it is mostly explanatory. Like any personality theory, it attempts to explain why things are occurring, not simply describe what is occurring. There is a place for both.

Recent clinicians have attempted to maintain the descriptive methodology of the *DSM* while incorporating the explanatory principles of Adlerian psychology. Such an (admittedly) uneasy process has yielded some pretty workable results. It is not perfect, but it is functional, and even a bit helpful if used properly.

The *DSM* is arranged systematically, from the most biologically loaded disorder to the least, with Mental Retardation being listed first, and Conditions Not Attributable to a Mental Disorder listed last. Adlerians would conceptualize such an order as an example of organizing disorders with the most organ inferiority to least. Those at the front of the book clearly have the strongest evidence for organic impairment, whereas those at the back have the least. With crucial exceptions (which we detail at the end of this chapter), the *DSM* is a catalogue of inferiority complexes. What the *DSM* labels as Dysthymic Disorder Adlerians might call the Dysthymic (Inferiority) Complex. What the text describes as the Obsessive–Compulsive Disorder could be called the Obsessive–Compulsive (Inferiority) Complex.

Complexes are behavioral manifestations of inferiority feelings that interfere with meeting the life tasks. Interestingly enough, one of the central tenets of the *DSM* is that, to be considered a "mental disorder," the problems must interfere with functioning. This is exactly the Adlerian position on psychopathology; that is, that these complexes interfere with the tasks of life (Sperry & Carlson, 1996).

For psychopathology to be diagnosed (to use *DSM* language), or to understand how these safeguarding mechanisms are being used in a socially useless manner (to use Adlerian language), two dynamics must be detailed: (a) the role the individual plays in producing complexes and (b) the role life or the world plays in producing complexes.

The Individual's Part

The individual brings two factors into the psychopathology equation: (a) biological vulnerabilities, in the form or organ inferiorities, and (b) life style vulnerabilities, in the form of basic mistakes (Dreikurs, 1967). We now examine each in depth.

As we explored in the previous chapter, nobody has a perfect biological makeup. Something, somewhere, goes wrong along the developmental process. Should the deficiency be inherited (something now most often called *genetic*), the law of compensation (Dreikurs, 1967; Maniacci, 1996b) will occur along three dimensions: (a) somatic, (b) sympathetic, and (c) psychic. If the deficiency is not inherited, then there may be no compensations. How and why this is the case is explained best by using an analogy.

Imagine resting your elbows on a table at which you are sitting. Interlock your fingers so as to form a crude arch. At sea level, there will be approximately 14 pounds of pressure per square inch upon your arch. It handles the pressure well; there are no signs of stress or cracks in the structure. Next, have someone increase the pressure by placing objects upon the arch, right where the fingers interconnect. The heavier the objects become, the more pressure the structure is under. At some point, the arch will begin to show fatigue, as the structure cannot distribute the energy efficiently throughout the supporting columns (the arms). The arch will begin to collapse. Where will it collapse? Why will it collapse at that particular point in time?

No structure is perfect. Every structure has inherent weak points and, when put under enough stress, they yield to pressure, and cracks appear. When these cracks appear is a matter of time and pressure. How the structure was built and designed, along with the type and quality of material, will be critical to understanding how the pressure was handled. The human body can be conceptualized in much the same way. The organ inferiorities are the body's structural weak points and, when put under enough pressure—or, in modern language, stress—cracks will appear. Breakdowns of form and function will occur. No body is totally immune.

Psychologically, almost exactly the same analogy can be used. What was discussed structurally with reference to the body can be applied to the mind. Under enough stress, the mind will crack, so to speak, at its weakest points. The core convictions of the life style that are most rigid, inflexible, and subject to disconfirmation because of their extreme character are vulnerable to stress.

What is *stress*? As theorists and researchers have pointed out, stress is anything that requires an organism to adapt (Mosak & Maniacci, 1999). Distress is that which is noxious to the organism. In its efforts to adapt, the organism expends energy and exhausts itself if the distressing event is not resolved either by fight or flight. The organism must then adapt, that is, alter its programming, to better deal with such stress the next time it occurs, or survival is compromised.

As we discussed in the last chapter, it is often the case that people do not constructively compensate for mistaken convictions in the life style. Learning does not readily occur because of an overreliance on safeguarding mechanisms. People cling to their beliefs rather than risk changing them or being exposed to the group as being even more inferior than they already perceive themselves to be. The paradox is that by doing so they bring more stress into their lives. What Adlerians describe as "errors"; "basic mistakes"; "interfering ideas"; or "interfering attitudes, beliefs, behaviors" are those convictions that cause the most trouble (A. Adler, 1956; Dreikurs, 1967; Powers & Griffith, 1987; Shulman & Mosak, 1988).

The relationship of organ inferiority to basic mistakes needs to be noted. In effect, what organ inferiorities are to the body, basic mistakes are to the mind. Almost universally, one leads to the other. Either the actual inferiority itself or the perception of it can affect the formation of the style of life (Maniacci, 1996b). For example, genetic deficiency in hearing, especially if undetected by caregivers, can lead children into trouble. The children's over-reliance on visual input (a sympathetic compensation) can lead them to not sufficiently realize the extent of their auditory defect. When they consistently miss things in conversations, they may resort to safeguarding mechanisms, such as depreciating peers, and thus create conflict with peers. Their failure to admit the extent of the problem (i.e., deal openly with their actual inferiority because of feelings of inferiority) will create a vicious circle, leading to more and more discouragement. With enough adverse experience, they may develop an almost paranoid style, becoming suspicious and thereby doubting others' veracity when they say "But we did tell you!" They may even be accused of lying by caregivers who sincerely believe the children are "just not listening." In this case, it is that they are not hearing. That is how organ inferiority can affect the formation of the style of life if there are not adequate compensations in all three domains (somatic, sympathetic, and psychic).

What role does the world, or life, play in producing psychopathology? In the following section we examine the concepts of challenges, stressors, shock, and trauma.

The World's Part

Radical constructivists believe there is no reality, only perception (Watts, 2003b). Philosophers and theorists who are more existentially oriented disagree (Maniacci, 2003). Reality exists, even if it is known only through perception. Adlerians tend to be more existentially oriented. They do not deny the existence of the world; instead, they study the interrelationship of people and the world. The existentialists even have a central concept called *being-in-the-world* that emphasizes the inseparability of the two. A woman walking across a dark room in the middle of the night does not have to perceive the end table in order to stub her toe on it. There was no perception of the table, but oh, how it hurt anyway. The perception of the table did not create the experience; the experience created the perception. Given this orientation, the role the world plays in producing psychopathology can be explored.

Life presents challenges. Plans go awry, schedules get disrupted, and people disappoint each other. Adlerians believe that life presents challenges that must be met. Some of the biggest challenges are the tasks of life. These are interpreted as challenges because people are encouraged. They are task focused, not prestige focused. They are focused on what they are doing, not on how they are doing. They therefore engage in problem solving and compensation.

Challenges become stressful when core convictions are confronted (Dreikurs, 1967). If my self-ideal depends on my being intelligent, then losing an athletic contest probably will not be stressful. Getting a bad grade most likely will be very stressful, because my movement toward my goal of being smart has been called into question.

Some stressors are traumatic. Adler (1956) preferred the word *shock*. Something that is shocking so challenges the life style that individuals understandably pause. Their world has been rocked. They become disoriented and need to ground themselves again and reaffirm their place in the world. Such traumatic events are both idiosyncratic to the individual life style and general to people as a whole.

The more rigid the conviction, the greater the chance that someone can be shocked or traumatized. Anyone can be traumatized, for horrible things do happen. However, some people's rigidity and inflexibility cause them to be more easily traumatized than others. When these people are shocked, Adlerians have noted a curious phenomenon: They cling to the shock effect. Why would they do that?

People cling to the shock effect to safeguard themselves (A. Adler, 1956; Mosak & Maniacci, 1999). It is a form of distance-seeking. It is as if they believe that if they never move past that particular point in time, they can prevent the traumatic event from happening again. Stan believes he has to be taken care of in order to belong (an articulation of the attachment motive). He is shocked when he loses his caretaker, and he does not replace that person. He may freeze at that point. His developing symptoms will serve the purpose of safeguarding him. How? The point at which he freezes is the point at which he was last taken care of; he refuses to move on in life. Stan clings to his caretaker's memories and photographs, refuses to leave the home, and thinks obsessively about the caretaker and how they were together. He courts symptoms of agoraphobia. Bad things happen to people when they venture too far from home, so he believes he had better stay put. Others start to come to him rather than he having to go out to them.

A technical point is in order. Many people, including some novice Adlerians, believe that when people seek distance, they stop moving toward their goals. That never happens! People are always moving toward their long-term, life style goals—their self-ideal statements remain intact. They hesitate, move backward from, or stand still before life tasks. People avoid confronting tasks in order to maintain their overall movement toward their life style goals. If Tamara believes that in order to have a place in this world, she has to avoid being hurt (an articulation of the security motive), a discouraged way of maintaining that movement is to avoid doing anything she might perceive as risky. "Nothing ventured, nothing lost," she feels. Her hesitation before tasks actually allows her to move toward her goal of security.

Psychopathology as Breakdown and Central Themes

Do people have breakdowns? That is an intriguing question. From an objective point of view, yes, they do. From the Adlerian point of view, no, not quite. They are still moving toward their goals. Here is an example from one of Adler's early coworkers, Wolfe (1934):

> Everyone knows what a knock-out is. A prize-fighter takes a terrific punch on the chin. He lies unconscious in the ring while the referee slowly counts him out. The prize-fighter has been so badly hurt that his body cannot function normally. Nature in her infinite wisdom has suspended his vital activities to keep him from killing himself. . . . However ignominious the knock-out may be from the prize-fighter's personal point of view, it is a life-saving device so far as nature is concerned. . . . If he were only as wise as nature, he would understand that his knock-out is an emergency measure, designed to save him from the untoward results of his own physical folly.
>
> A nervous breakdown may be described as a personality knock-out. In the arena of life we are sometimes exposed to sudden or intolerably severe shocks. . . . In a nervous breakdown the whole personality declares a moratorium of normal activities. . . . The nervous breakdown is a . . . warning that you have broken the basic laws of human conduct. (pp. 1–2)

Wolfe's (1934) example is still accurate. The breakdown people experience is not what they or others typically believe it is. People are not prepared to move ahead and face greater challenges if they do not adapt (i.e., change) to suit the new situation. They should stop themselves. While the boxer discussed previously is unconscious, his body is recovering. We can only hope he learns his lesson and either improves his boxing skills or faces less superior opponents. For him to prevent another knockout, he must change. If he does not, he is in for trouble.

In a psychological sense, much the same can be said about psychopathology. It is a safeguarding mechanism that prevents further harm, but only if people learn their lessons. If they continue with the same erroneous life style, they will get "knocked out" again.

People tightly grip their life styles. As we mentioned in the previous chapter, life styles bring consistency and predictability to people. Their life styles can be seen to cluster around certain themes (Mosak, 1977). The theme of "getting," mentioned in the preceding chapter as one possible outcome of children with diabetes, will dominate the problem-solving system of individuals. If they desire to get as much as they can, then they will develop the requisite traits that will allow that to happen. Traits are not the building blocks of personality; they are in the service of the goals and motives of the style of life and are developed after the fundamental conclusions about what is and what should be are formulated. Just as personality traits are secondary to life style convictions, so too are symptoms. The particular patterning of symptoms will be selected on the basis of a number of factors, such as organ inferiority; compatibility with life style convictions; and situational dynamics, such as the impact such symptoms will have upon their target audience.

After all, if the symptoms do not effect the types of readjustments in the social networks they are designed to produce, they may be abandoned and new ones selected. Through trial and error, some will be kept and others discarded. Once they are kept, certain predictable patterns in symptoms will emerge, and diagnostic labeling can be attempted.

The Classical Categories and Their Adlerian Interpretations

Earlier versions of the *DSM* divided psychopathology into three main categories: (a) neuroses, (b) psychoses, and (c) personality disorders. These categories were helpful, but the task force assigned to nomenclature avoided such language because of the psychoanalytic overtones. The neurotic disorders included what are now categorized as the anxiety disorders, dissociative disorders, somatoform disorders, and dysthymia. The psychotic disorders included what are now labeled the schizophrenic disorders, bipolar disorders, delusional disorders, and major depression with psychotic features. The personality disorders, although arranged somewhat differently (into personality trait disorders and personality style disorders), comprised many of the same disorders found in the text today, including (but not limited to) antisocial, narcissistic, obsessive–compulsive, and paranoid personality disorders. Diagnosis was based on both the symptom presentation and the psychodynamic formulation of the clinician. Because of the considerable disagreement among professionals about which theory should provide the basis for the psychodynamic formulation, that element was dropped from consideration.

Adlerians, however, still use psychodynamic theory in their formulations (Maniacci, 1996a, 2002). When restored to the process, it enriches the diagnostic formulation (Dreikurs, 1967; Sperry & Carlson, 1996).

Neurotic Psychodyamics

From an Adlerian point of view (Maniacci, 1996a), when people use neurotic psychodynamics they display a consistent patterning to their life styles. The main issue for them is what Adlerians call "training in prestige politics." When confronted with a challenge, encouraged people—that is, people who use common sense and display community feeling and social interest—respond with a "Yes, I can" attitude. They take their self-esteem off the line and focus on what needs to be done, not how well they are doing it. If they have feelings of inferiority in any of the aforementioned manifestations, they use those feelings to move ahead and develop useful coping strategies. That is not the case with people who use neurotic psychodynamics. These people respond with a "Yes, but I'm sick" attitude. Structurally, their common sense is strong, but so is their private logic. Encouraged people have far more common sense than private logic, and the private logic they do have is benign. As the proportion of private logic increases relative to common sense, so too does the likelihood of rigidity, inflexibility, and the like.

The "Yes, but I'm sick" attitude is designed to excuse people from tasks on which they believe they will be exposed as inferior. How they look in other people's eyes is crucial to them. They are hypersensitive to criticism, and therefore they are very self-conscious. To the extent that they are so self-conscious, it is evident that the main processes are not unconscious in neurotic dynamics, as early psychoanalysts hypothesized. Their main safeguarding mechanisms will be symptoms and excuses.

Neurotic mechanisms arise in relatively uniform ways. During childhood, there are common-sense, healthy models available. These children, however, are strong willed. They want what they want the way they want it. That, however, is not the key problem. As Adlerians phrase it, these children are chasing two rabbits at once. On the one hand, they want things their way; yet on the other hand, they want approval and support, hence the "training in prestige politics." To have both can be difficult. These children's solution is elegant but troubling: They act as if they are complying with authority figures' wishes while pursuing their own agenda. They do what they should, but they feel oppressed and held down. When they rebel and assert themselves, they declare disability or illness as a way of mitigating the conflict. The stress eventually leads to symptom formation. "I know I should have studied more for the test, but I felt so tired," is one way they justify not living up to their standards. They eventually incorporate others' injunctions to do well, all the while maintaining their desire to do things differently. They may not want to do well in school but, to maintain approval, they "try" but are sidetracked by symptoms. "It's not me that messed up—it's not my fault!" they can then declare. They got to do what they wanted to do—not study—and still appear as if they did want to study. The compromise is costly.

People who use neurotic psychodynamics are filled with lots of "should"s and "must"s that are held over from childhood. They want to have their cake and eat it too. Symptoms become sideshows, rationalizations, for why they have not done the things they did not really want to do in the first place. They wanted approval (a variation of the attachment motive), but they did not want to do what it took to get it because of their strong will to pursue their own agenda (a variation of the competence motive).

Psychotic Psychodynamics

There is a consistent patterning to psychotic psychodynamics as well. The role of organ inferiority is very pronounced with these disorders. It both encourages the movement away from common sense and maintains the current level of common sense. The main issue for these individuals is an early and pervasive training in escapism (Maniacci, 1996a). Fantasy becomes more satisfying than reality and, given their potential organic inferiorities, once they begin to consistently withdraw from external stimulation and follow their internal cues, it becomes harder and harder for them to come back; at some point, many of these individuals stop wanting to come back. They can be among the most discouraged individuals with whom clinicians work. The response they give to life's demands is clear: "No!" If they meet the tasks at all, it is in their own idiosyncratic, private logic kind of way. People with paranoid schizophrenia do not regularly fulfill the social task in consensual ways. They maintain that others are out to get them. They withdraw and look down on those whom they perceive as hostile.

People using psychotic psychodynamics do have common sense, but their proportion of private logic to common sense is tipped too far in favor of private logic. They have been trained, and have trained themselves, to rely on private logic as a sort of security blanket when they are challenged. They did have common-sense role models as children; they simply preferred their own private worlds to reality. Their ideals were more satisfying, and in the end, more isolating, than actual transactions with people and attempts at accomplishing tasks. When reality too harshly clashes with their idealizations, these individuals are genuinely afraid and lost. Many an adolescent has rehearsed and practiced how to approach someone of the other sex and ask for a date. When adolescents who are vulnerable to psychosis because of genetic vulnerabilities, neurochemical dysfunction, and life style rigidity do approach these idealized potential dates, they are crushed, if not outright humiliated, if rejected. All the self-statements about being inadequate, inferior, and not having a place come rushing into awareness. Instead of learning to do better, they learn a different lesson: to not do that again. In their fantasies, they never get rejected, crushed, or humiliated. It is easier, and more satisfying, to stay there. The small steps they take lead them down a dangerous road that their neurochemistry facilitates. They withdraw. As stress returns, and it always returns to these adolescents, it becomes easier and easier to manage by constructing elaborate fantasies rather than dealing with reality. They become more rigid and inflexible in their thinking and more and more unsuccessful in life. If they are fortunate enough, they have close caretakers who can look after them. However, if they are not challenged to strengthen their common sense and develop the requisite skills and useful compensations (of which medication may be one choice), these well-intentioned caretakers actually increase these people's distance-seeking from life. They make it easier for them not to adapt. We examine this in greater detail in chapter 6.

Psychotic psychodynamics are based on goals that are out of proportion to reality, because these goals have been formed without enough feedback from the consensual world. These individuals do not use realistic feedback to attenuate their ambitions and desires. Left unchecked, these people believe not only that such constructions are attainable but also that they would be attainable if only these individuals were somehow better. The inferiority feelings are profound when they realize that they cannot attain their goals. Their ideas about themselves and the world (a variation of the cognition motive) are more important to them than the world itself. They are genuinely scared when reality intrudes on them, and they retreat for safety (a variation of the security motive) into their private worlds.

Personality Disorder Psychodynamics

Individuals using personality disorder psychodynamics have consistent patterns as well. They have been trained in determination (Maniacci, 1996a). Whereas the neurotic psychodynamics are based on the "two rabbits" of wanting their own way and wanting to look good in others' eyes—and psychotic psychodynamics are centered on inappropriate goal setting, frustration, and fearful escape into fantasy—personality disorder psychodynamics are grounded in no such conflict. These individuals believe that their way is the right way. Their conflict, more so than any other disorder, is based on trying to convince the world that it and other people are wrong. They are as strong willed as those with any of the disorders discussed thus far, even more so. When confronted with challenges for which they are unprepared, their characteristic response is "Yes, but I'll do it my way." Their primary safeguarding mechanisms are aggression and depreciation.

These people usually did not have too many common-sense models in childhood. If such models were there, these people ignored them. The social press from the neighborhood and community only reinforced the messages they believed they received at home. They grew up believing their private logic was common sense, and therefore, everybody who did not agree with them was wrong. For example, a person with obsessive–compulsive personality disorder might have grown up believing that life should be orderly and that he should be in control. There were many instances when he was not only reinforced for believing this but also was rewarded with success. The rewards happened not only at home but also at school, with peers, and in the neighborhood. When circumstances changed, and he was no longer required to be so much in control, he would not shift. He would not adapt to the changes life gave him. His inflexibility in the face of disconfirming evidence, however, did not lead to the panic of a psychotic individual, or the tension of a neurotic individual; this man with a personality disorder grew angry and demanding. He believed that other people should adapt to his style, not the other way around.

It is sometimes said that these people do not suffer like the individuals in the other two categories. That is erroneous. They do suffer, but as a secondary phenomenon. They suffer because of the conflicts that arise with the world, not primarily because of their internal conflicts. They tend not to feel the stings of inferiority feelings in the way people in the other two categories do. They feel angered, get into conflicts, and then feel inferior. This is the reverse of what typically happens in the other categories. With neurotic and psychotic psychodynamics, the strong feelings of inferiority come first, and the conflicts with others are anticipated, and their safeguarding mechanisms are designed to reduce those conflicts and still allow them to have their way.

This is not the case with people who have personality disorders. They believe they are right, and they have difficulty empathizing with others. Their lack of common sense both protects them from some of the pain the other categories feel and exposes them to even more pain, later in the cycle. Neurotic and psychotic disorders tend to be cyclical because these individuals do have common sense to return to after they have attained some degree of stability from their symptoms. People with personality disorders never quite return to a stable state; they just move ahead until the next situation confronts them with how wrong other people can be. In between, they are simply confused by others' naiveté.

An Adlerian Interpretation of the Five-Axis System

In this chapter, we have presented an Adlerian view of psychopathology incorporating the language of the *DSM*. There is another component to the *DSM* that can be interpreted and used from an Adlerian perspective (Maniacci, 1999, 2002): the five-axis system.

To be more comprehensive, the *DSM* allows clinicians to diagnose mental disorders using either a five-axis system or not. Should clinicians choose, they can simply list the most prevalent disorder, or they can be more holistic and examine the client from a multiaxial perspective. The five axes are as follows:

- Axis I: Clinical Syndromes and V Codes
- Axis II: Personality Disorders and Mental Retardation
- Axis III: Medical Conditions Relevant to the Axis I and II Disorders
- Axis IV: Psychosocial Stressors
- Axis V: Global Assessment of Function Scale

What were once termed the *neurotic* and *psychotic* disorders would be listed on Axis I; personality disorders would be on Axis II. Axis III would describe whatever medical concerns need attention in the management of the Axis I or II disorder. Axis IV would list what stressors seemed to precipitate, or co-occur with, the first appearance of the disorder. Axis V asks clinicians to rate the client's overall level of functioning on examination (according to a scale of 0–100 provided in the manual). A typical diagnostic formulation would look like this:

- Axis I: 300.02 Generalized Anxiety Disorder
- Axis II: 301.6 Dependent Personality Disorder
- Axis III: Leg fracture (per physician diagnosis)
- Axis IV: Psychosocial Stressors: recent divorce and leg injury from accident
- Axis V: Global Assessment of Function: 55

Ms. Cahill is 40 years old, not sleeping, and worrying excessively (Axis I). The anxiety, ruminating, and tension are affecting her ability to function (Axis V). She is a rather dependent, unassertive woman (Axis II) who had recently experienced a divorce from her husband of 18 years and shortly thereafter fell off a ladder while attempting a home repair and broke her leg (Axes IV and III). What would the Adlerian formulation be?

An Adlerian would conceptualize the five axes this way:

- Axis I: The Arrangement
- Axis II: The Life Style
- Axis III: Organ Inferiority or Organ Jargon
- Axis IV: The Shock
- Axis V: A Barometer of the Life Tasks

Axis II addresses issues of the life style. It represents the pervasive, patterned responses to life that characterize the individual. Even when no diagnosis is listed on Axis II, clinicians are encouraged to list personality traits or styles, which is also in keeping with the Adlerian perspective. It is adaptable until life presents it with a challenge for which it is unprepared. That would be the shock, listed on Axis IV. That is the challenge for which the clients are unprepared. Any organ inferiority, or organ jargon, would be listed on Axis III. *Organ jargon* is what the life style will express with the body when words are not used. Axis I would be the symptoms, or safeguarding mechanisms, clients use to deal with the Axis IV challenge. These mechanisms are designed to keep the life style intact in the face of the shock. Axis V catalogues the effect such symptoms are having on the life tasks.

Ms. Cahill's case formulation would be as follows: Ms. Cahill is someone who values closeness and believes that to find her place in the world, she should be loved (Axis II). She relied on her husband to provide for her, and in return she was very devoted (Axis II). Her belief system was too rigid, however, and when he left her for another woman, she was stressed beyond her capacity (Axis IV). Nonetheless, she attempted to take care of herself and her home, but she injured herself doing a task he would have normally done (Axis III). The symbolic meaning: She can no longer stand up for herself and stand on her own two feet. She is acting as if she is in severe danger and is behaving as if she has to prevent another hostile attack from a cruel world (Axis I). This is both punishing her husband for his actions (she is angry and feeling out of control but cannot express herself for fear of pushing even more people away) and communicating to her children and family of origin how much she needs them not to leave her as her husband did. She is not functioning on her own, and therefore her children and her mother and a brother have stepped in to help her (Axis V). Her dominant motives are attachment and security. She is most deficient in the competence motive. She feels she is at the mercy of life and other people (external locus of control) and waits for them to initiate and set the tone (field dependent). She plays down her own needs and desires and overlooks signs of conflict or displeasure (narrow scanning and leveling). She frightens easily when she is unsure of how to operate (low tolerance for ambiguity), and she will panic and haphazardly try to make things better without any clear plan of how to do it (impulsive–global). Developmentally, she was the youngest born and the only daughter of older parents who babied her; she was "Daddy's girl" and "Mother's little helper." She was encouraged to be cute, affectionate, and not self-sufficient. She was charming and engaging, and that made her feel safe and warm.

The Diagnostic Categories and the Concept of Inferiority Complexes

When all things are considered, inferiority complexes are chosen to safeguard the life style and prevent further attacks on the person's already-taxed self-esteem. Such a decision is made in minute steps, over a long period of time, without fully realizing the consequences along the way. The tasks of life are avoided to maintain the fiction of attachment, competence, security, or knowledge (i.e., cognition).

Not every disorder listed in the *DSM* is an inferiority complex (Maniacci, 1996b, 2002). Some disorders are not chosen. One example is mental retardation; another is dementia. These conditions do adversely affect functioning in the life tasks, but they are not arrangements in the classical Adlerian sense. There may even be life style factors involved in some manifestations of some of the disorders, such as senile dementia, but their causative significance is minimal compared with the biological processes underlying these mainly physical disorders.

For inferiority complexes to arise—or, in *DSM* terminology, for (psychologically based) mental disorders to appear—they must be solutions or attempted solutions to psychosocial stressors. The Axis I conditions must be attempts at resolving, even in a private logic kind of way, the stressors, so that the line of movement prior to the onset of the disorder is maintained after the disorder appears. If there is no such consistency in the line of movement, there is a very good chance the underlying processes are more biological than psychosocial.

Central Themes and the Interrelatedness of Psychopathology

Psychopathological disorders shift presentations. Adlerians have a theory why: Symptoms, and symptom clusters, will shift even though the underlying life style convictions remain unchanged (Mosak, 1977). As we detailed in the previous chapter, there can be many ways to attain the same goal. Simply because behavior changes does not mean underlying convictions change.

Self-ideal statements can be clustered and categorized into central themes. For example, the self-ideal statement "In order to have a place in this world, I should be in control," would be indicative of the central theme of what Adlerians refer to as *controllers* (A. Adler, 1956; Mosak, 1977). Another example would be "In order to have a place in this world, I should be liked." That would be indicative of someone who needs to be liked, also known as a *pleaser*. A person who needs to be superior would believe that "In order to have a place in this world, I should be the best." These themes can produce what are known as *types*. Psychological types have existed since antiquity, and Adlerians have discussed them at length (Mosak, 1977; Mosak & Maniacci, 1999). As people perceive difficulty in moving toward their goals, they may shift behaviors to continue with their lines of movements, in much the same way drivers change directions when they are faced with physical impediments in the roadway. They are still heading toward the same general destination, but they have selected another route to get there.

To cite one example, people with obsessive–compulsive disorders have elements of paranoia. They also experience bouts of depression. Although obsessive–compulsive disorder, paranoia, and depression are, diagnostically, three separate disorders, psychodynamically they have one central theme in common: All of them value control. One of their self-ideal statements (and people can and do have more than one self-ideal statement) is that "In order to find my place in this world, I should be in control." What is evident is that obsessions and compulsions, paranoia, and depression are all perceived to be ways to maintain control. That is why clients with depression often obsess and ruminate, and even get a bit paranoid; that is also why paranoid clients are so obsessive and get so pessimistic about life and people. All have the dynamic of control in their life styles (Mosak, 1977).

With two self-ideal statements, the range of possible behaviors increases. Consider these two self-ideal convictions: "In order to have a place in this world, I should have excitement"; and "In order to have a place in this world, I should get what I want." In typology terminology, we refer to these types as *excitement seekers* and *getters* (Mosak, 1977). Some possible diagnostic presentations that may appear when these two convictions are rigid and lacking in common sense and community feeling include pathological gambling, binge eating disorder, and substance abuse and addictive disorders. All three disorders can produce excitement, commotion, and a whirlwind of activity as individuals set out to get their kicks. With more community feeling and common sense, they could be successful salespeople, restaurant owners and head chefs, or entertainers.

CONCLUSION

In this chapter we have examined psychopathology from the Adlerian perspective. It is compatible with the *DSM* and can enhance the diagnostic process through adding an explanatory dimension to the procedure.

Adaptation is not only a matter for psychology. It is rooted in biology and evolution. An individual's ability to bond with the group increases the chances of survival not only of the individual but also of the species (group). Such an increase in survival is predicated on affiliation, mutual protection, the communication of skills and strategies for survival, and information about how to use those skills. When these processes are functioning well, everybody benefits. When bonding is done in a self-centered, uncooperative, rigid manner, everybody can suffer. People must focus on using the common sense of the community while maintaining one eye on the greater good for all, not just in this time and place. When this is done, there is little chance of maladaptive behavior.

6

THE WORKING ASSESSMENT
IN ADLERIAN THERAPY

Adlerians give considerable attention to assessment. They focus on two areas in exquisite detail: (a) how people are functioning in the here and now, in their current worlds, and (b) how people came to see and operate in their worlds. Adler (1956) referred to the first assessment as the *general diagnosis* and labeled the second type the *special diagnosis* (Powers & Griffith, 1987). In the language of contemporary Adlerians, these are known as the *initial interview* and the *life style interview* (Maniacci, 1999). In this chapter, we explore both.

GENERAL DIAGNOSIS: THE INITIAL INTERVIEW

In an initial interview, several things must be accomplished. First, Adlerians conduct both an assessment and diagnostic interview. In an assessment interview, Adlerians try to determine what makes a person "tick." They want to know what is right about a person, what works well. What may be the key values and priorities of this person? The diagnostic portion of the interview is focused on the opposite: What makes this person "sick"? What is wrong, or misunderstood, by this individual and therefore leading him or her into difficulty? It is in this portion of the process that diagnostic labels and categories are generated.

Second, Adlerians are interested in determining how much of the individual's distress is related to his or her dynamics, versus how much is related to situational dynamics. This can be difficult to tease out. Often, both dynamics are causing a problem. Eddie has been given a rough time by life lately. He lost his job, and his wife is leaving him. Certainly, these are situationally related dynamics that would affect most people. What is Eddie's part in both these issues? Has he led his life in such a way so as to precipitate both these problems? Even if the answer is "no," that he has not done anything to precipitate either of these situations, an Adlerian would want to know how Eddie is handling these crises. What use is he making of these situations? Does he need support in handling these difficult situations?

Third, if the situation is weighted far more in favor of individual dynamics than situational ones, the next topic to assess is how much of the individual dynamics are related to life style factors versus non-life-style factors. This requires some elaboration.

Some people get themselves into trouble because of faulty motivation. Others get into trouble because of faulty education. Both are related to distorted, or erroneous thinking, but they are different, and far too often they are lumped together. An example may clarify the distinction. Sheri is a mother with three young children. She is having trouble with her parenting. She is being far too strict and controlling. The kids are rebelling, and Sheri is becoming even sterner. The situation is hard for everyone. If Sheri's lack of parenting skills is the primary dynamic, then psychoeducation, guidance, and bibliotherapy will prove helpful. Like most people in this scenario, she can learn new tactics, and gain in understanding, and the situation will be resolved. However, it is possible that it is not an educational deficit. Sheri knows the right things to do, but she does not want to do them. The right tactics do not fit her life style convictions. In this case, Sheri's problem is related to her life style. Without some change in her psychological dynamics, she will not implement the needed tactics in her family dynamics; therefore, the situational dynamics will remain bothersome.

Fourth, Adlerians want to determine the individual, life style dynamics to yet another degree. Are they related to neurotic dynamics or to personality disorder dynamics? This is a crucial difference. If neurotic dynamics are dominant, there will be a clear avoidance of some task in the picture. For instance, in the case of Sheri, Adlerians would want to know if she is using her troubles with the children as a sideshow, as a way of creating obstacles, or distance, from something she fears will expose her as inferior. For example, Sheri is afraid to focus on her marriage. She believes, in her private logic, that if she does, she will be a miserable failure, like her mother and sister. She creates the obstacle of trouble with the kids to keep the attention off her marriage. She can engage in what Adlerians have referred to as "buying double insurance" (Mosak & Maniacci, 1999, p. 92), a safeguarding mechanism that works the following way. People buy insurance in case something goes wrong. They would therefore buy double insurance in case anything goes wrong *or right*. Students will buy insurance, so to speak, for examinations, by studying. They will buy double insurance by *not* studying. Then, if they pass the examination, they can say how smart they were, that they were able to pass without studying. If they fail, they can claim disability: They did not have time to study. In either case, their self-esteem is preserved. If Sheri is buying double insurance, she is using a neurotic dynamic. She will arrange to have trouble with the children so she can preserve her self-esteem in her marriage. If she maintains the marriage, she can say how good she and her husband are as a couple, despite all the difficulties with the kids. If the marriage fails, she can say it is not her fault, that who could keep it going with all the hassles with the kids? "Yes, I'd love to have a better marriage, but my kids are in the way of us being happy," she might declare.

If Sheri's difficulties are related more to personality-disorder dynamics than to neurotic ones, the picture is different. There will be no neurotic-like avoidance of a task. She will genuinely believe in her stern, controlling style and will be flabbergasted by anyone who does not do parenting her way. She may have obsessive–compulsive personality disorder. She will believe that "Parenting should be done my way!" Again, without a change in life style, she will not use the new parenting skills. The psychotherapy in personality-disorder cases is different than in neurotic ones.

Fifth, Adlerians will assess yet another variety of individually oriented dynamics. As we have seen, person versus situation dynamics can be weighted to the person side with or without life style factors involved. If life style factors are involved, Adlerians will attempt to determine whether there are more personality disorder or neurotic dynamics. Last, Adlerians will assess whether, if individual dynamics are involved, any part of it is more biologically loaded than psychosocially loaded. What is the role of potential organ inferiorities or handicapping conditions? Are medical or somatic factors in any way responsible for the individual's dynamics? For example, are Sheri's aggressive outbursts with her children based on psychological factors or biomedical ones? Could she have a neurological problem? Could they be related to medication or substance abuse problems? What consultations would be needed to rule out these factors?

There are many sources available that discuss how to actually conduct an initial interview (K. Adler, 1967) and, within the Adlerian tradition, actual questionnaires have been published that detail the types of questions Adlerians use to determine the previously mentioned dynamics (A. Adler, 1956; Dreikurs, 1967; Maniacci, 1999; Powers & Griffith, 1987). Because of space limitations, such questionnaires are not reproduced in this book. Instead, a more general overview is provided.

THE INITIAL INTERVIEW: THE SIX KEY DOMAINS

For a thorough clinical assessment to be accomplished, six key domains need to be addressed (Maniacci, 1999): (a) identifying information, (b) presenting problem, (c) background data, (d) current functioning, (e) treatment expectations, and (f) clinical summary. We examine each in turn, but first we offer an important caveat: Obviously, no questionnaire can cover every situation adequately. There may be many instances when no questionnaire at all is needed. These areas, we believe, should be assessed, but how they are assessed is as much a matter of clinical judgment as of clinical necessity. Thus, the following sections should serve as guidelines, not hard-and-fast rules.

Identifying Information

"Who are you?" is the central question of this section. Clients are encouraged to describe who they are without any focus on their problems. Name, address, date of birth, marital status, children, occupation, education level, military service, religion, and a brief medical/health history are some of the topics to be covered. The therapist should also note the names and ages of the client's parents, siblings, and spouse. Finally, an emergency contact person's name and telephone number should be recorded. Why are these questions necessary, and why is this section listed first?

The bias is clear. People are more than their problems. Adlerians want to know who the person is before they focus on what is wrong. Some interesting dynamics can be revealed with these seemingly innocuous questions. For example, does the person initially present for therapy on or near his or her birthday? Is there something about this calendar date that is significant? Does the first name "match" the last name? For example, is the client's name Michael Gonzales? Why not "Miguel"? Is he trying to anglicize his name? If so, why? Is he estranged from his family of origin? Are they encouraging him to be more "American"? Did the person marry within his or her ethnic group? Is his or her spouse the same age, or significantly older or younger? Has the person had previous marriages?

Where does the person live relative to where he or she works? Does he or she have a long commute? Does the occupation level match the neighborhood where the person works? If not, how is this explained? Is the neighborhood diverse or ethnic? Does the person's ethnic background match the neighborhood? How could this be a factor? Does the person's education level match his or her occupation? If not, why is there a difference?

Who is the client's emergency contact person? Why did the client choose that person—why not someone else? Why would the client allow this person to see his or her "inferiorities"?

Does the person take care of his or her health? Does the person know what medications he or she is taking? Is the person aware of any side effects of medication he or she is currently taking? Is the person aware of his or her own health history? Is the person an educated, proactive consumer or a passive health recipient?

What is the birth order of the person? Is the individual named after either parent? Are any family members deceased? When and how did they die?

These questions already begin the assessment process. The answers can start the detective work in motion, especially if the clinician records the answers in session rather than having the client fill out the answers ahead of time. Body language can be crucial during the assessment.

Presenting Problem

In this section, the focus turns to the problem for which the client is seeking assistance. What brings you here, and why now? For how long has this been an issue, and what have you done about it in the past? When is it better or worse? Who is most affected by it? What else was going on in your life when this problem first emerged? Who does not know you have this problem? Why not? Additionally, any questions related to the *Diagnostic and Statistical Manual of Mental Disorders* (4th ed., text revision; American Psychiatric Association, 2000) could be used to determine the presence or absence of various diagnoses.

In this section the therapist asks the client to do three things: (a) specify what is wrong, (b) notice what makes it better or worse, and (c) establish a social context for the disorder.

Clients need to be able to discuss what is wrong; otherwise, psychotherapy is not going to be very helpful. Do they take responsibility for their disorder? Does it come and go without their having any hand in it? Can they see their role in creating or maintaining it, or in making it better or worse?

Does the client see a pattern to the onset of symptoms and their dissipation? Have they noticed what this pattern is? How much insight or psychological-mindedness do they have? Have they noticed who is most affected by their symptoms? This is a classic Adlerian question. Because symptoms are believed to serve a social purpose, knowing who is most affected by the symptoms can yield some interesting data. Many clients will respond by saying, "I'm most affected by it," but Adlerians will keep pressing, by saying, "I know. But after you, then who is most affected?" and the targeted person will eventually be revealed. Inquiring about who does not know about the symptoms is interesting as well, especially when the client is asked, "Why don't they know?"

Background Data

This domain covers a brief psychosocial history and is not intended to replace the more detailed, long history that will be obtained in the life style interview. It answers the following questions:

- For how long has this problem bothered you?
- What kind of person were you when you were young?
- Has the presenting problem or anything like it happened during childhood or adolescence?
- What was your early social life like?
- Who was your best friend, and why?
- What teachers did you like, and why? What teachers didn't you like, and why?
- What were your grades like?

Also in this section are questions about previous therapy:

- Were you in psychotherapy before? For how long and with whom were you in treatment?
- What worked in that treatment, and what did not?
- Why did you stop?
- What did you like about your previous therapist, and what didn't you like?
- What did you learn?

These questions examine not only whether the presenting problem might be long standing (and thereby personality based) but also how clients learn and relate to others.

Through childhood and adolescence, clients choose certain peers to relate to and others to avoid. Similarly, clients will report learning well with some types of teachers, and disliking (or even hating) other types of teachers. Why? It may be related to life style factors and can provide a clue about how the psychotherapist should attempt to relate and teach the client. If Gina reports that her best friend was Margaret, because she was funny and kind, Gina may be telling the interviewer that, in order for her to feel connected, the interviewer should be kind and funny. Similarly, if Gina says she learned best in Ms. Doll's class, because she was strict but fair, and she hated Ms. Danny's class, because she seemed to be uninterested in her students, Gina may be describing the interpersonal conditions under which she will be willing to learn. This is also rich material that can be used in psychotherapy.

The reasons clients stopped previous therapy may reveal why they could potentially stop their current therapy. Also, knowing what worked in previous therapies and what did not, and what the client liked about previous therapies and therapists and what he or she did not like, can help clinicians tailor treatment. At this point, the interviewer shifts the focus, and the type of data that are sought changes somewhat. Whereas the previous data may have been elicited in a more free-flowing manner, the next section usually turns out to be more structured.

Current Functioning

Thus far, the questions have tended to focus on what Adlerians call the *subjective condition*, that is, the client's feelings, pain, and previous circumstances. This section focuses on what Adlerians call the *objective situation*. The main focus is to examine how the client functions in the tasks of life, or "How has the presenting problem affected or not affected you in these areas?" Again, for space and topic limitations, we focus on only the three main life tasks.

Work

What do you do for a living? If you do not work, what do you do with the free time? Why did you choose that occupation? How do you feel about it? How do you get along with bosses, coworkers, and subordinates? If you could change anything about your work, what would it be?

Social

What do you do for fun? What is your social life like? Who is your closest friend? Why is that person your closest friend? What makes someone a friend? How do you relate to your community? If you could change anything about your social life, what would you change?

Love

Describe your current romantic relationships. If you do not have any, how do you explain that? What is your attitude about sex? What do you think about love? What makes someone masculine or feminine? Describe any difficulties you have in this area. What would you change in this area if you could change anything you wanted?

These questions examine how the client is interpreting and responding to the life tasks. Is there one task the client seems to be having trouble with more than others? Is he or she having trouble with all of them? Is the client functioning well in all of them, and does he or she think he or she is functioning well? Many clients will be functioning well but not seem to know it. What might that mean for their life styles?

Treatment Expectations

Whereas the domain covering the client's presenting problems examines what is wrong, this domain looks at what the client wants to do about it. They are not the same issue. A woman may go into a shop because she needs a pair of pants. That is what is wrong—or, in other words, the presenting problem. She may want someone to show her where the sale items are, or what the new fashions are, or she might simply want to be left alone until she looks around and decides she is ready for help. This last dynamic would be the treatment expectations. The general thrust of this section is to ascertain "Given the presenting problem, what would you like to do about it?"

Some of the questions asked in this domain include the following: What would be different in your life if you didn't have this problem? Why do you think it is happening? How do you explain it to yourself? What would you like us to do about it? How long do you think it will take to solve it? How will we know when we're done? Should anyone else be involved? One final question some Adlerians include in the initial interview is this: In your opinion, who is the most famous person of all time, and why?

This domain is designed to help clinicians align goals. It is important for clients to be headed in the same direction, and at roughly the same speed, as psychotherapists. That is what these questions are designed to determine. If a client believes that she is depressed because of biochemical abnormalities, or genetics, or hormones, then clinicians need to inquire why she is seeking a psychotherapist. The answers to these problems lie with physicians, not psychotherapists. If clients feel their mood swings are caused by marital and family dysfunction, when asked "Who else should be involved?" they should say "spouse and family." If they do not, the psychotherapy will run into difficulty. Along the same line, if they believe their worry and tension are caused by the stress at work, then clinicians should formulate a treatment plan that takes such an explanation into account. Clinicians who hear that, yet still come back with something like, "Your anxiety is caused totally by your biochemistry," or "totally by your erroneous thinking," will be leaving clients feeling misunderstood. If nothing else, such clinicians are just being inattentive. The clients will feel heard if at least some of their formulation is being considered and given credence.

Two questions deserve special attention. One is called "The Question" by Adlerians (A. Adler, 1956; Mosak & Maniacci, 1998). It asks "What would be different in your life if you didn't have this problem?" In chapter 7, we explore in greater detail the various uses of this question. At this point, only one dimension will be explored. The answer to this question typically reveals what is being avoided by using the presenting problem. For example, one client may say, "If I didn't have this anxiety, I'd be able to work better." He may be using anxiety as a safeguarding mechanism (see chap. 5) as well as using it to buy double insurance. Another client may respond with "If I weren't so depressed, I'd be able to be nicer." She may be using depression to cover up some aggression and depreciation tendencies.

The other question, "Who is the most famous person of all time, and why?" leads to a glimpse of the style of life in many instances (Lombardi, 1973; Maniacci, 1999). A core value is frequently identified. One of the most common responses to such an inquiry is "Jesus Christ." The particularly intriguing part is why the person names Jesus Christ. Some people will say "Because everyone knows him," whereas others will say "Because he gave his life for us." Notice the different reasons. In the first case, the answer has to do with attention and being noticed, both articulations of the attachment motive. In the second case, the answer has to do with sacrifice and service for others, both articulations of the security motive.

Clinical Summary

This is the section that puts it all together. Clinicians are asked to answer the following types of questions. Is the presenting problem more biologically or psychosocially based? Should consultations or supervision be sought? What is the client's line of movement, both before and after the presenting problem began? Against whom is the presenting problem directed? What style or styles should the psychotherapist consider using in relating to this client? What seems to be a central, organizing value for this client? What is being avoided by this presenting problem? Are any life tasks being evaded? What are the client's explanations for why this is happening? What treatment formats should be considered, and for how long? What five-axis diagnoses should be considered?

CLINICAL EXAMPLE

The following is a summary of a hypothetical client. It is designed to demonstrate what a completed summary might look like. Readers should be able to follow along with the narrative and understand from where the data were derived.

Carl is a 28-year-old Caucasian who has been married to his first and only wife for 5 years. They are expecting their first child in 3 months. He works as a salesman and has a degree in business. His mother is his emergency contact. He is the youngest of four children and is the only male in his family of origin; he has no significant medical history and is on no medication.

Carl presents with anxiety, tension, and worry. He is not sleeping, and he traces the onset of his symptoms to the beginning of his wife's pregnancy. She has a high-risk pregnancy and requires bed rest. He reports that he and his wife are most affected by his symptoms, because they worry her, and she and his mother at times have to calm him down. She believes that he is too worried about this pregnancy. He reports that his anxiety gets better when he has a drink and people calm him down.

Carl describes himself as having been an anxious child. He related well to other children only if they would play at his house. His best friend was his mother. No one understood him like she did. He had outside friends, but no one very close. He liked teachers who were orderly, directive, and kind. He has never had psychotherapy.

His work is unaffected. Carl is very successful. He makes the deals while his two assistants, both female, close the deals for him. He gets along well with his boss, also a woman. Socially, he has many friends and goes out two times per week on average. They spend time watching games while his mother stays with his wife. Carl reports that his marriage is wonderful, but his wife can be demanding and is too impatient with him. She doesn't understand his stress and his need to "be one of the boys."

Carl maintains that, without his anxiety, he would be able to function better with his wife and be more rested and, therefore, better at work. He is unsure why he is anxious but feels it is related somehow to his wife's unsympathetic stance toward his pressures. He feels she should be involved. He reports that the most famous person of all time is Michael Jordan, because everyone admires him and treats him like royalty.

The clinical summary is as follows: Carl is a youngest born who believes the world should revolve around him. He relies on others, especially women, to take care of him. When they do, life is great, and when they do not, he does not know how to function. With his wife on bed rest, he has lost a main support, and his mother has stepped in to help. By creating anxiety, he is sidestepping the role of caretaker of his wife and allowing others to do it, while maintaining his line of movement as being the center of the world who does what he wants when he wants it. His diagnostic workup is this:

- Axis I: 309.24 Adjustment Disorder with anxiety
- Axis II: Narcissistic and histrionic traits
- Axis III: None reported
- Axis IV: Psychosocial stressors: wife's pregnancy
- Axis V: Global Assessment of Functioning: 70 (mild impairment)

TREATMENT PLAN

The treatment plan is a natural outgrowth of the general diagnosis. It has five components (Maniacci, 1999):

1. Crisis management
2. Medical/somatic interventions
3. Short-term goals
4. Long-term goals
5. Ancillary services

After an initial interview, which typically takes anywhere from 45 to 90 minutes, clinicians should be in a position to gather all of the previously mentioned data and form a treatment plan.

The first step is to manage any crises that are at hand. These can range from suicidal and homicidal threats, to acute psychotic reactions, to child or elderly abuse or neglect, with anything in between. Most crises will be a part of the Axis I diagnosis, and their management will help bring relief of those issues. In many cases, there are no crises to be managed, and therefore clinicians can move to Step 2.

Medical/somatic interventions are just that. A physician referral is often required to assess, verify, or rule out the presence of a strong biological loading not only in the presenting problem but also in the client. A client may not complain about somatic factors; nonetheless, they may be present and in need of attention. Medication evaluations, if they were not already covered in the crisis management step, also should be considered. This step is typically aimed at Axis I, II, or III diagnoses.

The short-term goals are considered next. These interventions will typically be targeted to the Axis IV dynamics, the psychosocial stressors. As clinicians help clients manage the stressors more appropriately, the Axis I issue often is resolved.

The long-term goals are directed to the Axis II factors. These are almost always long-standing issues that are not quickly or easily addressed. Even when a full-blown personality disorder is not diagnosed, clients may be hesitant to address their life style. Most simply want relief from their Axis I complaint.

Finally, ancillary services, which clinicians may provide, or refer out, are believed to be helpful in improving the Axis V functioning. Consultations with clergy, lawyers, or recommendations to support groups or 12-step groups, along with psychological or neuropsychological testing and the like, are usually recorded here.

To use the example of Carl, the youngest born with a pregnant wife, his treatment plan might entail the following:

- Crisis management: None. This situation is unsatisfactory but stable.
- Medical/somatic interventions: Referral to a psychiatrist for anxiolytic consultation.
- Short-term goals: There are three. First, Carl and his wife could use some brief marital counseling to reduce their tension. Second, Carl needs to practice active listening and empathy skills to be more compassionate with his wife and their situation. Third, progressive relaxation and deep breathing should be taught so Carl can learn to manage his anxiety more effectively. This has the added benefit of teaching him some skills the couple can use during labor and delivery.
- Long-term goals: None are required, but two are strongly recommended. First, Carl should undergo a life style assessment to

clarify his personality dynamics. Second, he is encouraged to engage in individual psychotherapy of moderate length (about 25–30 sessions) to help modify his self-centered stance. His motivation for such a recommendation probably will not be very great, but it should be made, even if he decides to cooperate at a later date.

- Ancillary services: Two are recommended. One is to bring in Carl's mother for a family session, and although she is to be thanked and appreciated for her support, she is to be encouraged to back off and allow Carl to handle more of the load. The other is for Carl to attend some new-parent support groups in his area so he can be better prepared for the upcoming challenges of fatherhood.

MOVEMENTS WITHIN TREATMENT: ONGOING ASSESSMENT (PART I)

Once the initial interview, clinical summary, five-axis diagnosis, and treatment plan are completed, the next phase begins. The plan is presented to the client or clients, and modifications are negotiated. This phase of the assessment entails evaluating whether the plan is being followed. Collaboration with the plan occurs in two ways: (a) over the course of treatment and (b) in each particular session. There are three possible ways for the clients to react (Maniacci 1996a, 1999).

First, clients can stick to the plan. If they do, no particular intervention over and above the agreed-on plan is needed. Clinicians should provide guidance and support and reinforcement for the collaboration. In Adlerian terms, clients are moving toward the treatment goals.

Second, clients can move near, but not quite toward, the treatment goals. Some process work is required. Clinicians can offer feedback and gently nudge clients back on track. Active interventions on the part of the clinician are required; otherwise they themselves are not sticking to the agreed-on plan.

Third, clients can move away from the goals. This can happen for (usually) three reasons. One is that they no longer agree with the plan, often because new information or new situations have arisen. In such a case, the plan should be modified. Second, clients or clinicians may have been mistaken, and a part or parts of the plan are inappropriate or just plain wrong. Again, the plan should be corrected. Third, clients may be displaying in-session dynamics that are mirroring their life style issues. Psychoanalytically oriented theorists refer to these as *transferential reactions*. The focus of the sessions, at this point, needs to change. Clinicians need to gently but firmly confront the clients with their incongruent behavior. They agreed to one thing, but they are doing another. Almost universally, the way they handle such confrontations in session will mirror how they handle such confrontations out of session. Safeguarding mechanisms will be prevalent, and clinicians will be pressed into reacting in ways significant others in the clients' lives react. This needs to be closely monitored, and here, especially, good supervision by a senior colleague or partner is invaluable. Multiple psychotherapy (Mosak & Maniacci, 1998), a technique practiced by Adlerians, is often very helpful at this point. Having another clinician sit in—with the client's approval, of course—can very often get the therapy back on track. Real growth is gained when clients learn how what they have done in session is the same as what they do outside of session. Instead of being ridiculed, attacked, or abandoned, clients can experience acceptance and encouragement, but nonetheless persistence, from the psychotherapists as both attempt to examine and resolve the client's rejection of the agreed-on plan. This can be exceedingly challenging work, but wonderfully rewarding as well.

THE SPECIAL DIAGNOSIS: THE LIFE STYLE INTERVIEW

Not all clients will benefit from a life style interview. In many situations, it is not needed. Sometimes it is bypassed because the life style is not deemed to be a factor in the management of the case. At other times it is bypassed because the life style issues are so clear that a formal assessment is redundant, and at other times, it is not bypassed as much as it is delayed. There may be too many other pressing issues, such as crisis management or good old-fashioned comfort and guidance, that need to be addressed first. The life style interview will be done at a later date. At other times, the life style interview will be done, but somewhat informally, in a more conversational, relaxed manner without the formal assessment being announced as such (K. Adler, 1967; Stein & Edwards, 1998).

When the life style interview is formally undertaken, the data typically can be collected in two to three 45-minute interviews. Some clinicians use standardized forms for the data collection (e.g., Powers & Griffith, 1987; Shulman & Mosak, 1988), whereas others use plain paper. Some Adlerians provide feedback about the data during the collection, and others wait to prevent formal summaries, in written format, at the end of the process. Many times, an Adlerian psychotherapist who collects the data creates the summary; in other cases, a second Adlerian psychotherapist is brought in to help summarize the data, sometimes live, in the presence of the client, or privately, in supervision.

The life style interview is a semistructured process for understanding the developmental influences on the style of life. There are usually 10 sections to the data collection. The first nine pertain to information the client provides from birth up to puberty and is called the *family constellation inter-*

view. The last section, the collection of early recollections, covers the client's life up to the age of 10. Not all of the questions that make up the life style interview are presented herein, but enough will be given to provide the overall flavor of the data being sought.

The *sibling array* is explored first. The client and the client's siblings are described, rated on a series of traits, and discussed with regard to questions like "Who was most like you?" and "When you were a child, what were your fears?"

The client's *physical development* is explored next. "What was your body like as a child?" and "How was your health?" are two of the topics explored.

Next, the client's *school experience* is examined. Questions about grades, relations with teachers, and favorite and least favorite subjects are asked.

In the next subsection, the client is asked about what *meanings were given to life*. "What were your religious beliefs?" and "What were your favorite daydreams or stories?" are asked, along with "If you could have changed anything from childhood, what would you have changed?"

The client's *sexual development* is explored next. Some of the questions have to do with preparation for puberty, sexual abuse or sex play, and attitudes about masturbation and sexuality in general.

The next subsection entails asking about the client's *social development*. How did the client get along with peers, who were his or her friends, how were friends made, and so forth, are some of the topics covered.

Parental influences are covered in detail. Each parent is described in depth, as is each parent's approach to affection, praise, discipline, and favoritism. The parents' marriage is explored, as is their affection with each other, how they handled conflict, and other such topics.

The role of the *neighborhood and community* during the early developmental years is discussed. What was the ethnic makeup of the client's neighborhood? How did the family fit in? What were the socioeconomic factors?

Other role models and alliances is the last subsection explored in this part. Were there other adults or people in the client's life who have not been discussed yet? Who were they, and how were they important?

The last section is the *collection of early recollections*: the discrete, earliest memories the client can recall under the age of 10. There are three guidelines: First, the memory must be a single, one-time event. Second, it must be visualized. Third, it must have two parts specifically articulated: (a) what was the most vivid part of the recollection and (b) how did the client feel during the recollection? Usually, approximately eight memories are collected.

At the end of the process, two summaries and two lists are generated (Dreikurs, 1967; Powers & Griffith, 1987; Shulman & Mosak, 1988). The first summary is called the "Summary of the Family Constellation." It summarizes the data from the first nine sections. The second summary is called the "Summary of the Early Recollections." It is a summary of the themes and dynamics derived from interpreting the early memories as a projective technique. The first list generated has many labels, such as "Interfering Attitudes, Beliefs, Behaviors," or "Interfering Ideas." It is a list of convictions clients hold that Adlerians believe interfere with the client's functioning. The final list is "Assets and Strengths." It presents those beliefs that serve the client well and foster prosocial functioning. The Summary of the Early Recollections, Interfering Attitudes, Beliefs, Behaviors, and Assets and Strengths are all derived from the same material: the early recollections.

The Summary of the Family Constellation provides an overview of the early life influences on the client. It describes, in an almost historical manner, how the client experienced his or her development. More crucially, however, it describes what the client decided to do with such a developmental history. It is not enough to know that Patty's parents were abusive. Adlerians are very interested in how Patty explained their abuse to herself and what she decided to do about the abuse. Did she believe they were abusive because they were bad, or because she was bad? Did she think the abuse happened because they could not control themselves, or because they were doing what they thought was best? How did she decide to handle the abuse? Did she fight back? Did she turn to God or religion? Did she "go underground" and become covertly rebellious, or did she become overly cautious and attempt to please them at every turn? How did she handle her siblings? Were they abused, or abusive, and what were her explanations for those issues? These are some of the dynamics the Summary of the Family Constellation explores.

The early recollections present data of a completely different kind. Adlerians have long held that what people remember from under the age of 10 years is related not as much to the historical past as it is to the present (A. Adler, 1956; Clark, 2002). Early recollections are those memories individuals have held onto for years, even decades, as if to say, "These are the crucial events in my life and the lessons they have to teach me. I had better remember these!" Here is an early recollection of a client:

> Age 5. I was walking down the street. Someone came up to me, a man I didn't know, and gave me a quarter. He said, "Here, buy something for yourself," and left. *Most vivid part:* He gave me the quarter for nothing! *Feeling:* Excited and happy.

Of all the events that happen to people during childhood, why would this woman remember this so well? Adlerians believe because it reminds her of a very important value in her life today: She should "get." She is most likely what Adlerians refer to as a "getter." Notice the details of the memory. She does not do much. She gets for simply being there. Her reaction is to be happy. She probably also believes that men should give to her, because the person in the memory is a man. What was her presenting problem? She was depressed and suicidal. Her boyfriend of several years had left her, and she claimed she could not survive without him.

Let us look at another early recollection of a different client:

Age 7. I am riding my bike and not paying attention. I swipe a car with my arm. As I kept riding, I felt my arm become warm. When I looked down I realized I was bleeding. I jumped off my bike and frantically began wiping the arm in the grass, trying to stop the bleeding. It didn't work. *Most vivid part:* The bleeding and my trying to wipe it off on the grass. *Feeling:* Calm, at first, then terrified and frantic.

What is he saying to himself about life and his place in it? He is active, certainly, but he is careless. He does not notice he is hurt until there is considerable damage, and even then his attempts to deal with the hurt are futile, and even make matters worse. Why did he seek treatment? He had failed to quit smoking after seven attempts, including medications, hypnosis, and behavioral counseling. He wanted to try it again.

After examining several early recollections from the same client, themes emerge, and general patterns can be detected (Clark, 2002). These are summarized so as to emphasize what the client has held onto from the background described in the family constellation interview. Let us return to the case of Carl, from the section on the initial interview. His life style assessment provided the following summaries and lists.

Summary of Family Constellation

Carl is the youngest of four and the only boy; psychologically, he is a youngest born and crowned prince. He grew up in a family that valued masculinity, togetherness, and hard work. This was a calm family atmosphere, except for when Father was upset, and then all hell could break loose. Father ruled with an iron fist, but because he was regularly deferred to, he seldom had to get too mad. Mother acquiesced and believed that a conflict avoided was a conflict that never existed, and therefore she avoided protesting and acted as if everything was all right. Carl's sisters generally agreed, except for Jenny, the second-born, who was a rebel and challenged Father's rule. This got her in considerable trouble, and not even Mother could help her. Carl watched all this and learned too well. He was Father's favorite, and he knew it. In Father's eyes, Carl could do no wrong. Like Father, Carl worked hard and made his mark. This also entitled him, he believed, to special treatment, and special treatment he got. Mother defended him from his sisters and neighborhood bullies, and at times even helped Carl succeed in school by doing his homework. Carl was honest and often responsible, but in the end he was also self-focused and demanding, and he saw no problem with that. He felt himself to be strong and smart but, more important, he felt like a real man, and that carried a lot of weight in his neighborhood and family.

Summary of Early Recollections

Carl's early life recollections can be summed up as follows: Life is good when you get what you want and work hard for it. It is a man's world, and what a world it can be. Women should take care of men. I am hard working, and entitled to do what I want, and no one should stop me. When challenged, I do two things: I either get upset or I run away. In either case, it is important to follow my feelings and live for the excitement of the moment.

Interfering Attitudes, Beliefs, and Behaviors

- Carl believes he is the center of the world.
- He wants what he wants when he wants it.
- He sees emotional upset as a way to solve problems.
- He expects women to take care of him, whether they want to or not.
- Carl equates masculinity with superiority.

Assets and Strengths

- Carl can work hard.
- He loves women.
- He is not afraid of feelings.
- He knows what he wants.
- With time, Carl does learn.

The finished life style assessment would be presented to Carl for his feedback, corrections, comments, and reflections. The final copy would be typed and given to him to keep. In conjunction with the treatment plan, Carl would have a lot to think about, explore, and discuss. He would most likely feel very involved in his own treatment, a key aspect to Adlerian psychotherapy. Unlike most psychological tests, for which test security renders it impossible to discuss where the clinician got the material in the final report, the life style interview and initial interview data are easily explained and fairly easy to comprehend. Collaboration in the treatment process is enhanced.

The Motive System and Processing Styles Revisited

Not only can central themes and life style convictions be ascertained from the life style interview, but so too can the motive system hierarchy and processing styles (Forgus & Shulman, 1979). During the interviews, clinicians can listen not only for content but also for process. Is the client more reflective–analytic or global–impulsive during the data collection? Do the early recollections display elements of an internal or external locus of control? Does the telling of the family constellation material show the style of a sharpener or leveler? Does the client wait for too much direction (field dependence) in responding, or does he or she grasp the idea and run with it (narrow scanning)? What seems to be the client's central motive, especially in the early recollections?

In an oversimplification, let us look at four early recollections and see if we can find any motives and processing styles. These are actual memories from an adult male client in psychotherapy:

Age 4. Playing soldiers in my room. I set them up and had them kill each other. *Most vivid part:* They were green, and they stood up on their own. *Feeling:* Excited.

Age 5. My brother wanted my toy car. I said "no" and he smacked me until I gave it to him. *Most vivid part:* He kept hitting me. *Feeling:* Furious but helpless.

Age 5. It was snowing. My friends and I built a snow fort and hid in it. When cars drove by, we chucked snowballs at them and hid in the fort. *Most vivid part:* Chucking the snowballs. *Feeling:* Excited and sneaky.

Age 8. It was Thanksgiving and it had snowed something awful. We were waiting for dinner when our neighbor went out to use his snow blower. We heard a scream and ran to the window. There was blood coming out of the snow blower. He had gotten his hand caught in it. *Most vivid part:* The red blood on the white snow. *Feeling:* Cool; now this was exciting.

Self-concept: I am weak and can be hurt.

Self-ideal: I should be strong, aggressive, insensitive to pain, and sneaky.

Worldview: It is a cold world. Men can be cruel and hard.

Ethical convictions: Life should be exciting and fun. Look out for yourself.

Motive hierarchy: competence, security, cognition, and attachment.

Processing styles: impulsive–global, externally controlled, extensive scanner, sharpener, field independent, and high tolerance for ambiguity.

This man acts too quickly, without thinking. He sees himself at the mercy of life and other people. He is almost paranoid in his style, scanning the environment for two factors: (a) excitement and (b) danger. He craves excitement and courts it. He does not care about situational cues that much; if he wants to do something, he will. He can live with ambiguity quite well.

A final scan of the recollections will show the reason the motive hierarchy was arranged the way it was. He does not care about people. The attachment motive is clearly disturbed. He is overly concerned with being strong enough and safe, both variations on the competence and security motives. He craves excitement and stimulation, both variations of the cognition motive.

The Life Style Summaries and Treatment

What is the relevance of the material collected in the life style interview, and how can it help in psychotherapy, beyond what has already been presented? To tie it all together, we offer an explanation of how this is done. There are 10 factors in the Summary of the Family Constellation that have relevance to treatment planning (Powers & Griffith, 1987; Shulman & Mosak, 1988). We now briefly examine these factors.

Birth order explains how clients see life now. What is their psychological vantage point? Oldest borns see life from the vantage point of leaders and initiators. Middle children see life from the vantage point of peacekeepers. Birth order will help explain how clients approach challenges in life, including how they may approach treatment.

Family values explain what clients will probably experience as psychosocial stressors. If both parents valued something, that made it a family value. To disregard it was tantamount to deciding to not fit in the family. By understanding what the client's family values were, clinicians could understand what may be causing their clients stress as adults. For example, if education was a family value, it is understandable why clients will be stressed by examinations as an adult. To fail the tests could be perceived as violating the family values.

Family atmosphere is the prevailing emotional tone of the home. For adult clients in treatment, an awareness of the childhood family atmosphere can help explain their dominant moods. For example, if Justin grew up in a chaotic family atmosphere, he might develop an anxious mood. The anxiety in this situation would serve the purpose of keeping him on his toes, because he still believes as an adult that he must be prepared for anything that might happen.

The *gender guidelines* established by the parents will help establish clients' expectations about gender-related behaviors and timetables. For example, if the father is never home, the children may develop the idea that "real men aren't around." If the mother stays with such a man, the children may believe that "real women stay with such men." If the mother divorces the father when she is 40, the children may expect that, when they hit 40, their relationships should end. Such timetables should be noted and compared to dates found in the initial interview data, and they may explain why some clients seem stressed by certain birthdays, anniversaries, or dates.

The *place made by the client* explains how he or she solved problems or when and what safeguarding mechanisms were practiced. When challenged now, clients will usually resort to the same mechanisms they used in their family constellation.

The *place made by siblings* helps explain clients' expectations regarding significant others in their lives now. The roles siblings adopted in childhood will most often comprise the cast of characters clients seek out as adults. If Jane took on the role of leader in her family of origin, with her siblings following along, then she will look for her friends and coworkers to do much the same now. She may even try and train them to be like her siblings.

Other role models and alliances reflect the possible alternatives clients may have had in childhood to their family of origin. If everybody in the family was "crazy," but a couple of teachers were not, clients may not give up hope, knowing that somewhere, somebody could be there who is sane. Often, in psychotherapy, the healthy alternatives presented to clients in childhood can be the open doors clinicians can use to reach hesitant clients.

The *neighborhood and community*, as described in the family constellation interview, can help explain the client's capacity for empathy. If the client never saw or experienced certain situations or people, it may explain why he or she has difficulty stepping outside his or her own frames of reference now.

Adolescence and sexuality will help explain how clients received their initiation into the world of intimacy. What are their expectations for closeness, and how prepared are they for shame, distrust, intimacy, or pleasure? Frequently, clients' first experience with attempts at self-gratification and pleasure come in this area. Do they become ashamed of such things?

Constitutional and biological factors are the last issues addressed. How clients viewed their internal environments are revealed in the life style interview and family constellation summary. Did they see themselves as big and awkward or as small and swift? Did they feel their intelligence was a handicap or asset? This area may help explain why the clients do not see themselves as others see them now.

MOVEMENTS WITHIN TREATMENT: ONGOING ASSESSMENT (PART II)

Another assessment Adlerians conduct has to do with the types of safeguarding mechanisms that are used during treatment (Maniacci, 1996a). There are three general categories, each of which was discussed in chapter 5: (a) neurotic dynamics, (b) psychotic dynamics, and (c) personality disorder dynamics.

Psychotherapists know they are facing neurotic dynamics when the safeguarding mechanisms are primarily of an externalizing type. Clients claim sickness or disability as the reasons why they cannot cooperate. Their difficulty cooperating entails not only out-of-therapy situations but also in-session processes. When such clients are moving away from the treatment plan, they will declare that they are too upset, or depressed, or scared, to stick to what they already agreed with, and that, because of their illnesses, they should be excused from sticking to the treatment goals. This is the exact mechanism they use out of session with loved ones and coworkers. There are five responses psychotherapists should use at such times:

1. They should interpret what is happening: "We are getting sidetracked here. How did this happen?"
2. They should confront the "should"s clients are using. For example, clients will say, "I know I should do what we agreed to,

but I'm too scared." The response from the psychotherapist can be, "Who says you 'should'"?

3. Therapists are then in a position to explore "wants": "Why don't you tell me what you 'want,' instead of what you 'should'?"

4. Therapists can then give permission for clients to pursue what they want rather than what they should: "Look, I think you agreed to this plan because you believed you should. For too long you've agreed to what you should when all the while you still did what you want. Would you finally give yourself permission to stop that?"

5. Psychotherapists should remove all status considerations from the discussion: "I know it seems wrong to want what you want, but if you don't admit it to yourself—and me—that you want it, how can we proceed?" At this point, the block is resolved, the impasse is cleared, and the psychotherapy can usually proceed in a very fruitful direction.

When faced with psychotic dynamics, the safeguarding mechanisms are illogical. Clients move away from the treatment plan, and when confronted they become confused, bizarre, and disorganized. The way past such a point is fourfold:

1. Psychotherapists must be exceptionally supportive of the clients, even if they are not supporting the psychotic processes: "I know something is going on, because you're doing that again. You are working yourself up. Let's calm down and take a moment."

2. Clients need to be educated, again and again and again. Psychotic clients can be very slow learners when it comes to using common sense. Clinicians can say something like "This is happening again. Remember, we talked about this. That is a hallucination. Let's practice how to calm down and not let it run away with you right now."

3. Psychotherapists need to translate what is happening into common-sense terms and concepts: "You believe you're hearing voices telling you to kill yourself right now, is that correct? Could it be you feel threatened and want to move away from what is happening right now? Could that be what your auditory hallucination is saying to you?"

4. Clients, at that moment, need help building bridges back to the consensual world: "OK, I'm here. I can back off if that is what you want, but first you must tell me to do so in a way I understand. Just say we should stop, right now, and we will.

You don't need your voices to protect you. I will listen to you."

If the client uses common-sense modes of communicating at this point, the psychotic episode has been aborted and, with time, the entire process can be revisited and role played, this time using common-sense communication before the psychotic processes begin.

Finally, when faced with personality-disorder dynamics, psychotherapists often find themselves severely challenged, if not outright attacked. Depreciation and aggression are the primary mechanisms used (Maniacci, 1996a). Clients are too threatened to stick to the treatment plan, so they devalue the therapist and therapy. There are five steps to handling this:

1. Confrontation without aggression is central: "Listen, I know you're upset with me, but yelling at me won't solve anything. Can we hold on, please?"
2. Whenever feasible, clinicians should take a one-down position: "Look, I'm human. I make mistakes. If I've offended you, I'm sorry. Let's see where we got off track."
3. Be patient and be willing to be led: "I'm in no hurry. We've got time. If not in this session, there'll be others. What do you think I meant when I said we were off track? Here is how I saw it. . . . What do you think is happening?"
4. It is important, even when taking a one-down position, to maintain boundaries and limits: "Look, I asked you to calm down, and I admitted I'm human and make mistakes. If you continue being so hostile, I will end the session or wait outside until you calm down."
5. Explore the process and look for ways to get back on the plan: "Thank you. When you're ready, I'd like to explore how we got into that situation. If it comes up again, what should each of us do differently?"

This last statement is key. With people who have personality disorders, such situations regularly come up. As they learn to handle them differently in session, they will learn to handle them differently out of session. This is a long process, with many ups and downs. Clinicians need support, a strong gastrointestinal tract, and supervision to handle such times and situations. When they do, the change in clients can be rewarding.

ADLERIAN PSYCHOLOGY AND PSYCHOLOGICAL TESTING

Adlerians who are trained as psychologists can and do use psychological tests (Mosak & Maniacci, 1993). There are two guidelines in their use:

(a) the tests are used in a manner suited to the design and intention of the test and (b) the assumptions of Adlerian psychology are not violated. When both conditions are met, it can be a fruitful pairing.

Although the tests themselves are used in a traditional manner, the interpretations of the tests are done along holistic, interpersonal, teleological, and phenomenological lines. There is not enough space, and this is not the book, for a detailed look at such topics, but we do offer two examples of how traditional, standardized tests can be used from an Adlerian viewpoint. One such test is the Wechsler intelligence scales (with different versions for adults or children), and another is the Rorschach Inkblot Test. It is to these that we turn next.

The Wechsler intelligence tests (Sattler, 1982) are designed to provide three standardized scores: (a) Full Scale IQ, (b) Verbal IQ, and (c) Performance IQ. Depending on which version is used, the childhood or adult, there can be anywhere from 10 to 14 subtests. The Wechsler scales are well constructed, standardized, and normed. Each subtest has a series of questions or tasks that become gradually more difficult. The reward for knowing an answer is to have another question, an even harder question, asked next. When used by well-trained professionals in a sensitive and sophisticated manner, they can be a vital part of a psychological test battery. Only a couple of facets of the Wechsler scales are addressed in this book (Sattler, 1982).

Point totals are assigned for correct performance. Depending on the subtest, scores of 1, 2, or 3 can be assigned, with additional bonus points available for quick, accurate performance within specified time limits on some subtests. A score of 0 is also given if the answer is wrong. Clients are not given feedback about the accuracy of their responses and are not supposed to see the recording or scoring sheets. General encouragement is always appropriate, as is a kind, supportive attitude on the part of the examiner. Clients can usually tell when they are getting questions that are too hard. From an Adlerian perspective, a key point is how they handle those times, especially when their answers are wrong and receive 0 points. Clients are challenged. When faced with challenges for which they do not know the answers, do they feel inferior? How do they handle those feelings? Do they become anxious? Do they withdraw? Both are safeguarding mechanisms. Perhaps most fascinating is whether they will admit they do not know an answer. Many clients will never say "Gee, got me. I don't know that one." Those clients may act as if they know everything. They never say "I don't know," because that would interfere with their self-ideal. Others will too readily admit their inferiorities, and some even apologize for knowing so much and keeping the examiner too long. How the clients respond can be quite revealing.

Another factor is to examine the subtests themselves. Clients are given a wide range of tasks to perform, from building puzzles to answering general information questions. One subtest is the Comprehension subtest. It is a series of questions that ask clients to provide answers to given situations and specific problems, such as what to do if one finds a stamped, addressed envelope in the street or (for children) if someone smaller than the client tries to start a fight with the client. Responses reflect people's knowledge of conventional standards and wisdom (Sattler, 1982). From an Adlerian perspective, the Comprehension subtest is a measure of common sense. It shows the clients' ability (and, to some degree, willingness) to use common sense to solve problems. Clients who do well on this subtest clearly have common sense (their willingness to use it, however, is another matter). Clients who do not do well are lacking in common sense. They are using their private logic too often. The incorrect answers may be rather revealing and sometimes projectively significant.

Another psychological test is the Rorschach Inkblot Test (Exner, 2003). It is a standard series of 10 inkblots that are achromatic, shaded, or chromatic and presented to the clients in a standardized manner. Clients are asked to respond to the cards and elaborate on the question "What might this be?" By coding the responses and tabulating, one can compute the codes into scores, various ratios, percentages, and frequencies, which can generate hypotheses about clients. The final scores are compared to standardized and stratified data tables to determine deviations. In the hands of experts, the Rorschach can be a powerful tool.

We discuss two Rorschach codes in this book; one is used for location, and the other is used for a determinant. Although an Adlerian interpretation of the Rorschach Inkblot Test has been detailed in its entirety in another publication (Maniacci, 1990), in this book we explore only these codes.

There are three main parts to the Rorschach response (Exner, 2003): (a) location, (b) determinant, and (c) content. When someone looks at a card and says "That looks like a bat," the examiner must clarify what the client saw (content), where in the card the client saw it (location), and what made it look like that (determinant). For example, the previous response would begin to be coded this way: content—it looks like a bat; location—the whole thing; determinant—the shape and color of the inkblot. For this manual, the two codes on which we focus from an Adlerian perspective are (a) W, for location, and (b) V, for a determinant (*vista*, a type of diffuse shading; Hartings, 1976; Maniacci, 1990).

The examiner codes a W when clients report that the content they saw was located in the entire blot. "The whole thing," is the typical response to the inquiry "Where did you see that?" "The whole thing just looks like a Halloween mask." The amount of W seen in the 10 blots is documented in the various frequency tables. It is not only quite common, but also expected, that not every answer will be a W. Some responses will focus on the common details of the blot, others on uncommon details. From the Adlerian vantage point, the clinician considers what W might signify.

The W score is an indicator of ambition. Clients with too many W responses are trying to "do it all." How often clients use W can be an index of how they set goals. If they have a standard amount of W, they are most likely appropriate in their goal setting (Maniacci, 1990; Mosak & Maniacci, 1993). If they have far too many, they are most likely overly ambitious and set their goals too high, too often. Additionally, in what cards W is seen is important. Clients may attempt to find W responses in every card, often as a first response to each card, as if to say they always expect to be superior, no matter what the challenge. Yet another possibility is far too few W responses. These clients may be saying they are not ambitious at all. It can be one of the indicators of an inferiority complex. They may give up trying to have ambition, as if they were saying, "It is too difficult for me. I should take the easy way."

The V (vista) code is a determinant based on diffuse shading. The examiner codes a V when the response indicates the use of shading to create a sense of perspective, such as when clients say "That looks like a valley, off in the distance, because it's dark in the middle and lighter on the sides." The V response is rarely given; in fact, it is normal for V to not be in a protocol at all (Exner, 2003). It is present in the responses of both clinically depressed individuals and those who have successfully completed suicide and had taken the Rorschach earlier and, as Exner (2003) reported, is one of the key variables in both the Depression Index and the Suicide Constellation (an index of the risk for suicide). What does V mean to Adlerians?

The V code is an indicator of a potential inferiority complex (Hartings, 1976; Maniacci, 1990). It is the use of distance-seeking as safeguarding mechanism. One form of distance-seeking is moving backward (as discussed in chap. 3). When approaching a task for which they do not feel prepared, some individuals will move away from it, as if they are saying that they must back away. The V code is an indicator of just such movement. The client is literally seeing something in the blots from which he or she must back away because of its darkness. When V is used, something is probably wrong. The client is relying on distance-seeking to deal with it—or not deal with it, as the case may be. Why would a client seek distance, and what does that have to do with an inferiority complex? Remember, V implies not only distance but also a sense of perspective. The blots are two-dimensional; there is no perspective, so that is a projection by the clients. In trying to take perspective, the clients are measuring themselves and finding that they come up short. Because of their smallness in the face of life, they are creating distance. That is the key dynamic.

Although no single variable in the Wechsler scales or the Rorschach should be used to diagnose or assess someone, these are some ways individual aspects of each test can be interpreted from the Adlerian perspective. When placed within the context of complete protocols, these codes, responses, and subtests can help fill out a complete picture of an individual.

CONCLUSION

Assessment is crucial in Adlerian psychology. Be it the initial interview, the life style interview, psychological testing, or ongoing assessment of process, Adlerians apply their holistic, goal-directed, interpersonal, and phenomenological assumptions to the material. In this chapter, we have explored how Adlerians assess their clients and share those conclusions with those clients. The collaborative, interactive nature of Adlerian psychology is clearly present in this area. Clients are encouraged to work with Adlerians and see how the clinicians determined what they determined and to offer feedback to more accurately grasp what is happening with them and their lives. Once they become engaged in such a process, they have already begun the process of change, of taking their idiosyncratic, private perspective and examining it with others, in a social context, in an attempt to find more adaptable, common-sense ways of solving problems, working, socializing, and loving. That is the beginning of a journey toward community feeling and social interest, and it is this for which psychotherapists hope.

7

GOALS AND TECHNIQUES IN ADLERIAN THERAPY

Adlerians have developed numerous ways of helping clients in psychotherapy (Mosak & Maniacci, 1998). Before we examine some of them, a more detailed analysis of the goals of psychotherapeutic treatment is in order.

Adlerians see psychotherapy as a cooperative, egalitarian enterprise (A. Adler, 1956; Mosak, 2000; Peven & Shulman, 2002). Whenever possible, Adlerians attempt to engage clients in a dialogue about the goals of psychotherapy. For many clients, a good psychotherapeutic relationship is the first collaborative relationship they have genuinely, consistently experienced (K. Adler, 1967). It is therefore alien to them. They are not accustomed to seeing people along a horizontal plane, as equals. If they have had a vertical perspective, they see people along dimensions such as above–below, superior–inferior, or dominant–submissive. The endlessly fascinating aspect of this is how they are not even clearly aware they do this most of the time. They argue that they are justified in believing what they believe, and many times (if not most), they are. They have come by their convictions honestly, in that the world they perceive at present is the world they were trained to see and the one they trained themselves to see. If any of us were in their shoes, we would have come to the same conclusions.

129

When counselors or therapists begin the collaborative process, clients may balk. After all, they declare, the counselors or therapists are the professionals, and they should be in charge. "Fix me!" they demand. At the other extreme, they come to sessions expecting that they will be in charge, that the counselor or therapist will follow them. "It's my session and my money!" they declare. In either case, they are missing the point: This is a collaborative experience. The clinician and therapist have to do therapy together. Although there are times when it is not only appropriate, but also crucial, for clinicians to be in charge or let clients be in charge, those decisions are arrived at collaboratively.

One additional point must be made: Whereas clients are always in charge of themselves, psychotherapists are always in charge of the process (Mosak & Maniacci, 1998). There are no exceptions to this. Such a strong declaration needs clarification. Psychotherapy is a professional practice for which training and supervision are mandatory. Therapy is more than friendship, and it is not a casual encounter. Psychotherapists cannot control clients, but they have to be sufficiently professionally competent to manage the process. If they cannot manage the process of psychotherapy, then two issues need to be addressed. First, the therapist may be lacking in competence in a certain area or with a certain clientele. If so, additional training and supervision are required. Second, the client may be too domineering. There are many ways a client can dominate the process. Sometimes the domination can be overt, through threats, confrontations, and demands such as "You must do this my way!" At other times, the domination is more subtle, such as through tears, passivity, or inactivity, with indirect statements such as "I'm so helpless, and you must do it this way." In either case, if they are not careful, professionals may find themselves walking on eggshells and beginning down the slippery slope of losing control of the process. If that happens, most psychotherapy will run into trouble. Clients should not do the psychotherapists' jobs. That is not their role. They need to relax and let clinicians handle issues of process. Clients' attention should be on themselves.

THERAPISTS' GOALS

Adlerian therapists have one strategic goal in mind: to increase clients' social interest and community feeling. What that means is not easy to translate into daily practice, but the following are four criteria:

1. Decrease symptoms.
2. Increase functioning.
3. Increase the clients' sense of humor.
4. Produce a change in clients' perspectives.

In regard to Criterion 1, therapists are accountable to clients. Most clients, most of the time, want symptom relief. That is understandable and an appropriate goal. How that happens is a far more complex matter, but it should be a goal nonetheless. In regard to Criterion 2, there should be an increase in clients' functioning. They should be able to meet the tasks of life more efficiently and in a more satisfying way. In regard to Criterion 3 (a frequently overlooked goal), clients need to have a more humorous perspective. Humor (which we discuss in greater detail later) can be a sign of being confident and realizing that one's self-esteem is not on the line all the time (Mosak, 1987). Last, in regard to Criterion 4, the clients' views of something have to change. With some clients, the "something" is simply information. They thought something was "A" and now realize it is "B": "Oh, I thought if I yelled at my kids, they'd be better off. Now I realize how silly that sounds." For others, the something is more profound; they must change their life styles. It is not simply their perspective on the presenting problem, but their view of themselves and the world, that changes. If this is the case, clinicians will notice a change in clients' dreams and early recollections. Many of the themes they displayed in their dreams and early recollections will undergo a transformation. Sometimes, the transformation is subtle; sometimes, it is great. As clients change the way they view life and their place in it, their view of their internal world changes as well. They may add or delete minor details to their childhood recollections that yield new meanings to them, or they may completely forget the memories they told therapists at the beginning of the treatment (during the life style interview) and produce completely new memories, often declaring that these new memories are the ones they told therapists the first time (hence the need for accurate note-taking during the life style interview).

Here are two earliest recollections of the same adult female client at two different points in time. The first memory is from the life style interview, and the second is from a termination interview, 18 months later.

Age 3: I'm in my mom's arms. She bent over to pick something up and dropped me. *Feeling:* It hurt, and I screamed. *Most vivid part:* the pain.

Age 3: My mom was carrying me. She bent over to pick something up and started to drop me. I clung to her as best I could. I hit the floor. *Feeling:* It hurt but could've been worse. *Most vivid part:* It hurt, and she comforted me.

There are subtle but crucial differences between these two recollections. Life can still be painful, and the client is still relying on others for too much support, but if she falls, she is not hurt as badly, and she is more proactive now in trying to prevent her own fall. At least she does something. The "big error" with which she came into therapy is now smaller. Is there more work that could be done? Yes, but she is satisfied. She feels ready to be on call with her therapist. She also swears that the second version of the recollection is exactly what she told the first time. She can no longer remember the first recollection the previous way.

These are the Adlerian goals. Clients have their own goals, and it is to those we turn next.

CLIENTS' GOALS

Clients have as many different types of goals as trees have leaves. Many of them are perfectly acceptable and fit within the Adlerian therapist's treatment goals. Some do not. Some clients want to be average, some want to be above average, and some want to be the best (and we wish you good luck in trying to define that). Some really do not want to change themselves, yet they still want their symptoms to go away. They want the benefits the symptoms provide them, without having to change themselves. For example, Buster wants to put out minimum effort and receive maximum gain. He is what Adlerians refer to as a "getter." He really does not want to work much harder at school, but he wants his parents off his back and his grades to be higher. Needless to say, with Buster, a good deal of the therapeutic work is going to be accomplished before the therapy technically begins. The negotiating of the treatment plan and goals will be crucial, perhaps even the hardest part. If there is no alignment of goals, then the psychotherapy will go nowhere.

Psychoeducation about the nature of psychotherapy in general and Adlerian psychotherapy in particular is often quite helpful (Maniacci, 1999; Mosak & Maniacci, 1998, 1999). For example, the therapist might say: "Here is what I can offer and how I can offer it. How does this suit what you're looking for?" Once this is clarified, the therapy formally begins.

From an Adlerian perspective, three points in particular are worth noting. First, when it comes to clients' actual inferiorities, clients can be taught to either accept them or compensate for them. For instance, if Rachel has a cleft palate, she can either learn to accept it as is, or compensate through medical interventions, such as surgery. Second, when it comes to clients' inferiority feelings, clients can be encouraged to eliminate them through a change in their perceptions and ideas (discussed shortly), or live with them, acknowledging that feelings of inferiority are part and parcel of being human. Should they decide to live with them, it is pointed out that they need to differentiate between having the feelings of inferiority and what they do about those feelings. If everyone has such feelings sometimes, it is what one does about those feelings that count. Do clients make others responsible for them? Do they use safeguarding mechanisms, such as depreciation and aggression, to cope with them? It may be not the feelings, but how they handle those feelings, that changes. Finally, when it comes to inferiority complexes, Adlerians encourage clients to give them up. They are encouraged to take a more horizontal view of life and realize that the antithetical modes of apperception they have used as guiding points in life are unproductive at best and detrimental at worst. It is not that clients have to decide, for example, to be either dependent or independent. Such a dichotomous way of thinking misses the point. Clients need to accept interdependence. We are all tied to each other and, to some degree, accountable to each other.

Adlerians, with the proper training, use many formats in their work. It is not uncommon to switch, with the same client, from individual to group or family therapy, and vice versa. Psychotherapy tends to be brief, with the average number of sessions consistently being reported as around 20 (Kern, Yeakle, & Sperry, 1989). Multiple contacts, over long periods of time, are also fairly common. Adlerians do practice long-term psychotherapy. It depends on the case and the negotiation process, detailed earlier. The concept of collaboration is the key: Without it, the alignment of goals becomes impossible, and the treatment never starts off in an effective manner.

VERBAL MARKERS AND TARGETED INTERVENTIONS

Despite the all-too-common phraseology used in Adlerian psychology, there are some specific guidelines that are used.

Adlerian therapists listen for *self-concept statements*. As we discussed in chapter 3, when the self-concept falls short of the self-ideal, feelings of inferiority ensue. When the self-concept falls short of the worldview, feelings of inadequacy arise. When the self-concept falls short of the ethical convictions, guilt feelings are prominent. The different dynamics sound like this (Mosak & Maniacci, 1999):

> Inferiority feelings: I am weak. I am stupid. I am slow, or short, and so forth.
> Inadequacy feelings: I can't handle it. I'm incompetent. I'm not capable.
> Guilt feelings: I'm bad. I'm wrong. I'm evil, and so forth.

Why note these differences? When clinicians hear these different versions, they have a better idea where they can direct their focus. With inferiority feelings, they need to address self-concept/self-ideal dynamics. With inadequacy feelings, the focus is on self-concept/worldview dynamics. With guilt feelings, it is on self-concept/ethical conviction dynamics. For example, Keri keeps reporting thoughts such as "I'm bad. I keep messing up." Clinicians will want to explore her self-concept and ethical convictions. Does either need to change, or does her behavior need to change? Similarly, she may report "I just fall apart. I can't handle life." Her self-concept needs to be examined, but so does her worldview. Why does she see life as so overwhelming? Is she overestimating life's difficulty, or is she underestimating herself? Could she be doing both? When the clinician targets the interventions to the appropriate dynamics, therapy becomes far more efficient.

With these considerations in mind, it is time to explore some specific tactics Adlerians use in practice. We discuss these according to the concept of the *psychotherapeutic situation*.

AN ARRAY OF ADLERIAN TACTICS

Adlerians have written about the difference among *strategies*, *techniques*, and *tactics* (Mosak & Maniacci, 1998). Tactics are targeted to situations; strategies and techniques are not.

A therapeutic *strategy* is the overall, long-term goal of the psychotherapy. The strategic goal of Adlerian psychotherapy is to foster in the client a sense of community feeling. The strategic goal of psychoanalysis is insight, the strategic goal of cognitive therapy is to correct irrational or distorted thinking, and the strategic goal of behaviorism is to change behavior.

A *technique* is that which is used to get to the strategic goal. Some techniques in Adlerian psychotherapy are life style assessment, encouragement, and antisuggestion. In psychoanalysis, some techniques are dream interpretation, free association, and analysis of the transference. In cognitive therapy, some techniques are keeping thought records, cognitive disputation, and logical analysis. In behavior therapy, some techniques are the use of rewards, differential reinforcement of other behaviors, and systematic desensitization.

The term *tactics*, however, refers to when and how techniques are used. For example, Adlerians tend to use the life style assessment early in therapy, when clients and therapists need to better understand the core convictions that may be leading the clients to trouble. In psychoanalysis, analysts use free association to start off sessions or when dreams are produced, so as to better understand the potential nature of the repressed material. In cognitive therapy, thought records are kept so that the clinician can monitor the distorted thinking clients have that generates the dysphoric feelings. In behavior therapy, rewards are used when clients engage in behaviors that are agreed to be beneficial.

Tactics are situation specific. People interact with the world and with each other. In any interaction, there are three variables: Variable A, Variable B, and Variable C. In psychotherapy, Variable A is the therapist, Variable B is the client, and Variable C is the situation. We provide the following example to clarify.

Dr. Smith is the psychotherapist, and Mr. Jones is the client. Dr. Smith brings in his goals for the session, and Mr. Jones brings in his. There still remains Variable C, which very few, if any, textbooks address. Under what conditions do Dr. Smith and Mr. Jones meet this day? Is it late in the day for both of them, and therefore they are both equally tired? Is Mr. Jones mildly sick with a cold and not up to his usual self? In the immediately preceding session, was Dr. Smith given an especially hard time and is still a little rattled?

Situational variables are as important as therapist and client characteristics. As the existentialists are fond of saying, we are beings in the world. To deny the realities of existence is naive. Tactics are used by clinicians according to their strategic and technical goals and are directed to clients' issues at the time they are raised and in the manner in which they are raised. Specifically, how would an Adlerian handle a client's crying, early in treatment, if the crying were being used as a safeguarding mechanism? Depending on even more specific data, Adlerians might use encouragement, confrontation, or paradox. If the client were particularly discouraged (remember, this is early in treatment), the Adlerian might use encouragement. If the client were using the crying to avoid an important issue, then a different tactic, such as confrontation, might be needed. If the client claimed to be unable to control his or her crying, then a paradoxical suggestion to "Go on, really let it out—do more!" might be used. It would depend not just on the therapist's bias and client's presentation but also on relevant situational variables. Crying can be used in many different ways, in the pursuit of many different goals. The tactic is directed toward the situationally specific use of the crying, not the crying itself.

For tactics to be useful, they must be grounded in theory. Clinicians must have a sense of timing, and they must know their clients. Clinicians also must be considerate of situational variables, such as time, location, and stress. Tactics that may be appropriate for one situation may not be appropriate for another, even given the same client, the same symptom, and same therapist. Anxiety-reducing tactics that were very effective early in treatment with motivated clients may not be as useful later in treatment, with clients who are experiencing the consequences of not following through with the treatment plans. For example, Billy is reporting moderate anxiety before an examination. Teaching him relaxation and deep breathing might prove helpful and move the therapy along. He agrees to use it before the examination, but he does not, and his grade suffers. He comes to the next session anxious about his grade and his father's reaction. In this situation, it might be more therapeutic to use confrontation, not relaxation, with him. He might benefit from the anxiety *not* being lessened this time. It might increase his motivation to follow through with his agreements next time. It all depends on the situation.

What follows is an overview of some 24 tactics culled from the Adlerian literature (A. Adler, 1956; K. Adler, 1967; Carlson & Slavik, 1997; Dreikurs, 1967; Maniacci, 1999; Mosak, 2000; Mosak & Maniacci, 1998; Nikelly, 1971b; Peven & Shulman, 2002; Powers & Griffith, 1987; Stein & Edwards, 1998; Watts & Carlson, 1999). As we described earlier, they are grouped according to situations therapists encounter. Not every tactic described will work with every situation. In fact, in many psychotherapeutic situations there may never be a use for any formal sort of tactic. Listening, supporting, and reflecting feelings may be all that are required—unless, of course, listening, supporting, and reflecting feelings are considered tactics themselves.

Orienting the Client to Therapy

As we discussed in chapter 6, Adlerians strongly believe in collaborative treatment. To whatever extent feasible, clients are encouraged to help formulate goals and treatment plans, or at least to provide feedback early and often about the goals and treatment plans. When they ask, "So what do you think is happening with me? Why is this going on?", Adlerians are eager to provide an answer.

Presenting a Summary

Many Adlerians present clients with two summaries in the beginning of psychotherapy. The first is usually a summary of the initial interview data. As demonstrated in chapter 6, clients are given a brief overview of the six key domains: (a) identifying information, (b) presenting problem, (c) background data, (d) current functioning, (e) treatment expectations, and (f) clinical summary (including diagnosis and treatment plan). On the basis of this initial summary, clients and therapists are in a better position to decide whether they like each other, whether they can work together, and whether they agree with the formulation of the initial interview data.

The second summary clients are given is of the life style interview (should one be formally completed). In reality, this second summary is really two summaries and two lists: summary of family constellation, summary of early recollections, basic mistakes, and assets and strengths. This life style assessment helps detail how the clients came to be the way they are and what they have carried from childhood into adulthood that is both detrimental to them and beneficial.

Making Connections

Another way clients are oriented to treatment is to help them make connections. One such connection is between their expectations for how life should be and what they have experienced. The former is the life style summary, and the latter comprises the initial interview data. Given both sets of summaries, clients are told something like this: "Given how you were brought up and the conclusions you came to (life style material), this is what you were ill prepared for (initial interview data)." An admittedly oversimplified version might look like this:

> Edna, you were a strong, self-assured, oldest born who was used to being number one. This worked well for you until you lost your job because you made a serious mistake, and that dealt you a double blow— first, you were fired, and then you had to deal with the fact that you

made such a silly error. Neither one of those things you were prepared for in childhood.

The other type of connection Adlerians make with clients is their use of symptoms and safeguarding mechanisms and how they relate to life style material and initial interview data. "Given these life style convictions, you trained yourself to develop these mechanisms whenever you met these challenges." Again, an oversimplified version might look like this:

> Edna, as an oldest born in that chaotic, alcoholic family, you felt overly responsible for everything. Your parents took responsibility for nothing, so you took on too much as an overcompensation and no one could give you as hard a time as you gave yourself. You did that to regularly prove you weren't like them. Now, see, with what happened at work, you beat yourself up again and again, and given your family history of depression, you developed one yourself. That depression is really your way of saying you should never make a mistake—you should be perfect. You're furious at yourself.

Differential Diagnostics

There are two primary ways Adlerians conduct differential diagnosis (Mosak & Maniacci, 1998). The first is to use what Adlerians have come to call "The Question." The other is to seek congruency between life style convictions and symptoms. Both tactics address the situation when clients and clinicians want to know "Why is the client experiencing these symptoms?" As Adlerians have documented elsewhere (including in this book), medical consultation is always advised and should be considered in every treatment plan. Adlerians simply have an additional way of examining the question of differential diagnosis.

The Question

In the initial interview, clients are asked "What would be different in your life if you didn't have these symptoms?" There are three types of responses (Mosak & Maniacci, 1998).

One response reflects a clearly psychogenic symptom. When asked The Question, they provide a certain type of response. Let us use as an example symptoms of anxiety and panic. When asked, "What would be different if you didn't have these panic attacks?" the client responds "Gee, I'd be able to go to work." The response indicates a social purpose for the panic: One of the three life tasks is being evaded. The Adlerian clinician would help the client be better prepared for the work task, and the symptoms would probably subside.

Another response to The Question might indicate a more somatogenic symptom. If the client responds with something like "Gee, I don't know. I guess I wouldn't feel such tightness in my chest and shortness of breath," then the symptom seems to be serving no social purpose. No task is being deliberately avoided. Referral to a medical specialist would be in order.

Yet another response to The Question indicates a hybrid response, that is, a response that is probably somatogenic in origin but is being used for a social purpose. The client might respond this way: "Gee, I wouldn't feel such pressure in my chest and shortness of breath, and I'd really be able to focus on my work." Again, a medical specialist should be consulted, but even if there is clear-cut organic pathology it is probably being used to evade the work task.

Is There Congruency Between Life Style Convictions and Symptoms?

The client's symptoms should be congruent with the convictions of his or her life style. If they are, they are probably psychogenic in origin; if not, they are probably somatogenic (Maniacci, 1996b). The life style convictions of a pleaser are usually the following:

- I am in need of other people.
- I should make others happy and keep them close.
- People are all report card givers, and I have to work hard to get good grades.
- It is right to be kind and sensitive and care more for others than yourself.

Given these convictions, symptoms that have a psychological origin should not contradict any of these convictions. If any symptoms do, either there is tremendous external stress (and such extreme stress is rare), and therefore the symptoms are truly a product of situational variables, or there is a somatic basis for the symptoms. The pleaser would not do things to push people away or look bad in their eyes. If Constance were a pleaser, Adlerians would expect her to pull people toward her. If she is pushing them away, something is wrong—that is not like her. Either she is under extreme situational pressure (e.g., someone has a gun to her head) or she is physically ill, and her symptoms are biologically based (e.g., her aggression is secondary to a brain tumor).

Conflict Resolution

Adlerians do not see conflict as stemming from intrapsychic forces. Conflict occurs between people, or between people and situations. Dreikurs (1961) used to have a wonderful demonstration of the Adlerian view of conflict. He would ask people to grab their hands at chest level and pull as hard as they could. He would ask them to notice what happened. Their hands stayed dead center, moving neither right nor left. He would then ask why the hands did not move to either side, and people would say "because of equal and opposite forces." Dreikurs would smile and tell them to repeat the exercise, only this time, on his command, as they were struggling, he would tell them, "Pull them to the left, now to the right," and the hands would move. The hands stayed dead center not because of equal and opposite forces but because people choose to keep them there. They simply were not aware they were making that choice. Why are people choosing to create their own internal conflicts? Because they perceive that to move forward would threaten one of their convictions (Mosak & Maniacci, 1998). For example, Pierre has a wife and a girlfriend. He reports that he cannot choose because he is in conflict. Adlerians would say that to resolve this conflict would put him at risk. He is a getter who believes no one should ever say no to him. As long as he is in conflict, he gets to keep both his wife and girlfriend.

Empty Chair

In the empty chair technique, two chairs are set aside. The client is asked to sit in one chair and give one reason why something is favored, then immediately move to the other chair and give a reason why the other thing is favored. The client is instructed to keep moving between the chairs, giving reasons in each chair, until he or she feels "done." For example, Diane cannot decide between going on to graduate school or staying home and raising her children. She reports feeling in conflict. The two chairs were set up; one was designated her "graduate school chair," and the other was designated her "homemaker chair." Diane took turns sitting in each chair and giving a reason why she should choose one situation over the other. In the graduate school chair, she claimed she wanted to earn her master's degree. She then jumped to the other chair, stating that her kids needed her. She went back to the first chair, saying she loved school, and then back to the other chair, saying a mother's role is with her children. This went on for about 3 minutes until, tired, she dropped into one chair and said "I'm done, I can't think of any other reasons. I'm still stuck, I still can't decide!" It was pointed out to her she was in the graduate school chair. She burst out with a smile. As Adlerians repeatedly say, trust only movement. The chair in which the client finally rests reflects the real choice. Everything else is a sideshow. In Diane's case, she fully intended to go to graduate school, but felt she guilty (an ethical conviction/self-concept discrepancy). She felt she should be better educated (a self-ideal/self-concept discrepancy), and therefore she chose both: to go to graduate school but to create feelings of guilt to show what a good mother she was. In this way, she could satisfy both her self-ideal and ethical convictions. The empty chair is a wonderfully simple tactic that never fails to point out clients' underlying intentions.

Double Unbind

With the double-unbind tactic, clients are confronted with the illogic of their arguments. Hal reports that if he goes with his wife to the party, he will make her happy but himself miserable because he misses a ball game on television he wants to watch. If he stays home and watches the game, he will be happy, but he will make his wife unhappy, and again, he will end up miserable. He is in conflict. What should he do? He is in a self-constructed double bind: No matter what he decides, he will lose. It is pointed out to him that his conflict serves a purpose. If he struggles long enough and suffers long enough, his wife may take pity on him and let him stay, and his own pain over his decision will lessen her anger. Besides, if he takes too long to decide, she will go without him, and again, he can say "You can't blame me—I was trying to decide when you stormed out." He denies this—until he is placed into a double unbind. His therapist says to him "Look, according to you, no matter what you decide, you'll get grief, either from yourself or your wife. So the answer isn't to find the alternative without grief, it's to ask yourself: Which kind of grief do I want, mine or hers?" When he realized this, he grinned and declared, "Oh, to hell with it! If I'm setting myself up for grief either way, I might as well enjoy the game!" His show of good intentions being resolved, Hal watched the game, and did not even give himself grief.

Assuming Another's Perspective

As is discussed repeatedly throughout the Adlerian literature, one of the cardinal features of psychopathology is self-centeredness. By failing to demonstrate community feeling and social interest, clients repeatedly show the me-or-them dichotomy that leads them to trouble. At crucial points in treatment, clients need to be shown another's perspective (Mosak & Maniacci, 1998).

Higher Standards Than God

This tactic works especially well with pleasers, who are overly concerned with rejection. They often declare that to be rejected is horrible, akin to death. If they are religious, they are asked the following: Do you believe in God? If yes, do you believe God is the most perfect being? Yes? Then, do all people love God, and even the ones who do, do they love God always? Are there atheists? Well, here is God, the most perfect of all beings, and not even God can be accepted by all people, every time. If God tolerates atheists, can you? Or do you have standards higher than God? Can no one reject you? This usually puts the overambition into perspective quite nicely.

Social Consequences

When clients stubbornly hold onto troublesome convictions, Adlerians ask them to examine what would happen if all people held that same troublesome belief. As an example, consider Cheryl. She believes that, in order to have her place in this world, she should be superior in everything. Her therapist might ask her "What would happen if all people held that belief?" Cheryl would most likely respond that it would lead them to trouble, that the conflict and fighting between people would be disastrous. She is then asked to consider this. Imagine her children having this conviction. What would life be like for them? After all, if the conviction that she must be superior in all things is good enough for her to believe, why should this not be passed on to her children? Children are excellent observers but horrible interpreters, and if they see Cheryl with this conviction, at least one of the children will probably model her. Can she live with it? This puts her private logic into a social context, and therefore it becomes more amenable to change.

Confrontation Tactics

Adlerians believe that people are strong, and as long as a good relationship is maintained, clients can and should be confronted (Shulman, 1973). There are many situations when confrontation is necessary. The central thrust of all confrontations is the same: to provoke an immediate response from a client. That is the main difference between an interpretation and a confrontation. Interpretations require no immediate responses from clients, whereas confrontations do. Not all confrontations have to be done "with a hammer." Some confrontations can be done "with a feather."

Immediate Behavior and Movement

One way of confronting clients is to point out their immediate behavior and overall line of movement. "You look as if you feel attacked. Is that how you feel?" "You're turning away. Is that your way of telling me you don't want to face something?" Not only can clients be confronted with their immediate behavior, but also the consistency in their line of movement can be pointed out. "Your anxiety is certainly painful, but have you noticed how people react to you when you're anxious? It sort of reminds me of when you were a kid and got scared." "I know you feel threatened and suspicious, but have you ever noticed how that allows you to avoid certain things? Do you remember how you got out of doing certain things as a child when you were really upset?" These confrontations are designed to make connections but, as we mentioned, the key ingredient is the requirement of an immediate response from the client. They are pressured to respond to, and therefore address, an issue.

"When?"

Clients can be confronted with how much time they believe they need to change. "I know," says a client, "that I should change." The therapist can respond with "When?" That one word can powerfully point out the fact that nobody is immortal. Psychotherapy does not go on forever. When is the client going to change, or make that phone call, or give that apology, or write that book?

Paradoxical Tactics

To maintain symptoms, clients must actively fight against them. If people want to remain nauseated, then they must fight very hard to not be. Their fighting against it only makes it worse. Paradoxical tactics are designed to demonstrate how clients create their symptoms, nonconsciously, and use them for a purpose (A. Adler, 1956; Dreikurs, 1967; Mosak & Maniacci, 1998).

Antisuggestion

Adler (1956) used the term *antisuggestion* to describe paradox. He would instruct clients to try and make their symptoms worse. In the early 1900s, syphilis was a major problem in Vienna. Many male clients developed what was known as "syphilophobia." Because of their fear of syphilis, they refused to date and have relationships with women. Some even believed they had syphilis and, despite numerous examinations proving otherwise, they would not date, so as to not infect anyone. They used their fear of syphilis to avoid the love task. Physician after physician would assure and reassure them they did not have the disease, but they persisted in believing they had it. When they came to Adler, they would say "All these doctors have told me I'm safe, but what do they know? What if they are wrong? How could I live with myself if I gave such a disease to some girl?" Adler (1911/1924) would reply, "Yes, I see. You know, these tests aren't very precise; you probably do have it. You are wise to be so worried." With that, the clients began to argue back. "But Dr. Adler, all these tests can't be wrong, can they? Maybe I don't have it." As soon as Adler stopped fighting them, and encouraged their fears, they began to doubt their illness.

Spitting in the Soup

This rather distasteful phrase is a marvelous tactic that is efficient and effective (A. Adler, 1956). Put simply, clients are shown what their symptoms are providing them and then encouraged to keep using the symptoms. They may continue to have the symptoms, but they will not "taste" as good any longer. A female client who is very good at denigrating herself when she makes a mistake is told how superior she thinks she is: Only someone with such high standards would be so hard on herself; therefore, she must think quite highly of herself. A male client who is too worried what other people must think of him whenever he goes in public is confronted with his vanity: Obviously, everybody must be noticing him. This tactic also helps to put symptoms into perspective.

Encouragement Tactics

Encouragement is the converse of discouragement. According to Adlerians, to have courage means the willingness to take a risk even when the outcome is uncertain (Mosak, 2000). Self-esteem is not on the line; therefore, people can move ahead with confidence. To be discouraged is the opposite. People are unwilling to take a risk. They are too concerned with avoiding feelings of inferiority, so much so that they too sharply curtail their worlds. They need to be encouraged; that is, they need to be shown that they have a place in the world; they belong, even if they "fail." Even if they are actually inferior, they still have a place and still can contribute.

There are two directions on which to focus. Clinicians can encourage clients' self-concepts, or they can encourage clients' self-ideals. Therapists can say "Nice effort" and therefore encourage the self-concept by focusing on what was done. They can also say "I know you failed this time, but you'll get it next time. I believe in you." They are encouraging clients to do something they have not yet done, and that helps reinforce the client's self-ideal.

Lessons From the Past

One way that clients can be encouraged is by examining how they handled challenges in their past. Common examples are learning to walk, ride a bike, cross a street, and so forth:

> Remember learning to cross a street, how scary and potentially dangerous it was when you were a child? Yet you did it. You were not stopped by your fears then, and you don't have to be stopped now. Show the same faith in yourself now you showed then.

Minus to Plus

What clients perceive to be a minus can be reframed as a plus. They are therefore shown that it is not necessarily the trait, or belief, or attitude, but rather how they use it, that causes them grief. For example, Gail can be shown that her critical attitude could be a sign of good judgment, if she uses it to make wise decisions instead of using it to avoid decisions. She can keep that trait; she just has to use it prosocially.

Change Tactics

In the end, Adlerian psychotherapy is about change (Mosak, 2000). *Insight* is defined as a meaningful experience that leads to perceptual change and change in the line of movement (Mosak & Maniacci, 1998). Note the combination of perceptual change and behavior change. It is not enough that clients see things differently. They must also act differently. The old phrase "My head knows it but my heart still feels the same" is interpreted to mean that the client is in conflict. In other words, the client does not want to change but wants to create the impression with the therapist that the therapist is being heard but that the client is still going to do things his or her way.

Acting "As If"

Adler (1956) believed that all people create cognitive maps of their worlds and that these maps serve as guides for how to lead life. All of these maps are fictions, that is, constructs, that may or may not closely resemble the actual terrain. People act "as if" these maps were then real, and live accordingly. In what he called *the law of ideational shifts*, Adler (1911/2002) described the differences among (normal) caution, anxiety, and depression. With caution, people act as if what they feared *might* happen. With anxiety, they act as if what they feared *will* happen. With depression, they act as if what they feared *has* happened. The cognitive shift from might, to will, to has, is critical. Note the increasing degree of rigidity. All three constructs are fictions, and each serves a purpose. Therapists can use this dynamic. They can encourage clients to act as if their fears were not going to happen. Consider the following example.

Walter is shy. In Adlerian language, he uses shyness as a way of finding his place in the world. It is no longer serving him well, as it did when he was a child and others, seeing he was shy, found him cute and sought him out. Now he is alone, and no one seeks him out. He can be asked to think of someone he believes is assertive, and he picks his boss, Jack. He is then asked to imagine, and then role play, how Jack would handle difficult situations. Walter is then given this prescription. The next time he is feeling shy and does not know what to do, he can act as if he were Jack.

Task Setting/Homework

Adlerians ask clients to do things that will make improvements (Mosak & Maniacci, 1998). When done in session, this is called *task setting*; when it is done between sessions, it is called *homework*. With rare exceptions, clients are always given something to do in session and then something to do between sessions. Often, it is the same task, and having practiced the task in session makes it easier to do between sessions. Clients can be asked to meet friends, relax, work harder, and try new foods, or anything under the sun, as long as it fits into the treatment plan. Adlerians believe in holism, and therefore cognitive change does not always have to precede behavior change. Sometimes, the reverse can happen: By doing something different, clients may then produce the change in their beliefs.

Humor

As noted earlier, humor is important for many reasons. It is a sign, when used with community feeling, that clients are confident and at peace with themselves. It allows a certain perspective on oneself to be taken. Adlerian therapists frequently use humor in psychotherapy (Mosak, 1987).

Jokes

Jokes can often be very revealing. Finding out which jokes they think are funny, including asking them to tell the jokes they think are the funniest they've ever heard, can reveal much about that client's life style. Along the same lines, often therapists will be able to make points using humor and jokes that could not be made as effectively otherwise. Here is an admittedly bad joke that is quite useful in making a point to clients who believe they must know all the answers:

> A young man walks into a bar with a little dog under his arm. It is open mike night, and new talent is being asked to go up on stage and try out. The bartender asks the man what he is going to do, and the man replies he has a talking dog, a *real* talking dog, and if he can go up on stage, he will not only become famous, but he'll make the bar famous as well. The bartender warns him that it is a hostile crowd, and he had better be as good as he thinks he is. The young man goes up and asks the dog, "What does sandpaper feel like?" and the dog replies, "Rough!" The audience boos. Undaunted, the man asks his next question: "Tell me dog, what's on top of a house?" The dog replies, "Roof!" The audience gets ready to throw the kid out and, sensing trouble, the bartender leaps from behind the bar and rushes the stage, trying to protect the two hapless victims on stage, but it's too late. "Tell me, dog, who was the greatest New York Yankee of all time?" to which the dog replies, "Ruth!" Bottles are thrown, chairs are broken, and the man and his dog are beaten bloody and thrown into the street. Dazed and confused, the young man and the dog look at each other as the dog mumbles, "DiMaggio?"

Sometimes, success depends not on knowing all the answers, but what questions to ask.

Twisted Adages

Dreikurs had dozens of twisted adages he used with clients. These were aphorisms that were often quite funny but made an important point. Adlerians have continued with his tradition (Mosak & Maniacci, 1998). Some of the more memorable ones are the following:

- Those who can't be big, belittle.
- You know you've defeated someone when he calls you a name.
- Have you ever noticed you never get angry when you're winning an argument?
- You remind me of someone trying to sit on two chairs with one ass.
- Not doing the wrong thing is not enough, but it helps.
- There is no problem caused by democracy that cannot be cured by more democracy.

- When we feel inferior, the only way we feel equal is to make ourselves superior.

There are more, but the point is clear. Short, pithy statements are sometimes better remembered and more effective than long, convoluted interpretations. They can also be more enjoyable.

Imagery Tactics

Imagery is an effective way of creating motivation. Clients frequently motivate themselves by creating images that move them in certain directions. They imagine themselves failing, being rejected, being humiliated, and hurting. Working with such images can be constructive and a form of psychotherapy in and of itself. Two tactics that rely on client-generated images are the pushbutton tactic (Mosak & Maniacci, 1998) and early recollections.

Pushbutton Tactic

Clients, especially depressed ones, can be taken through the following exercise. First, they are asked to remember a time in the past when they felt successful, or loved, or happy. With their eyes closed, they are asked to re-create the image in their minds in detail, including focusing on the positive feeling. When they have the image in their minds, they are told to raise a finger in the air. Second, they are asked to remove the image and start anew. Now, they are asked to remember a time when they felt hurt, sad, or unhappy. They are to picture it in all its clarity and detail and to focus on the feeling. When they have it, again, they are to raise a finger. After a moment, the third and final part begins. They are told to wipe that image away and recall another time when they were happy, successful, or loved. It can be the same image as before, should they choose. When the memory is recalled in all its clarity, including the accompanying feelings, they are told again to raise a finger. They are asked whether they noticed anything. Images create feelings. By creating certain images, certain corresponding feelings occur. The Adlerian therapist then gives them pushbuttons to take home. the pushbuttons control the images they create. When clients push one button, they create negative images that negatively affect their feelings. With the other button, they can create positive emotions. The choice is theirs. When they come back for the next therapy session, the discussion can then focus on which button they have been pushing, and why. Although such a tactic will not cure a depression, it can certainly interrupt it and teach clients the role they play in maintaining, if not creating, their depression or negative feelings (Mosak, 2000).

Restructured Early Recollections

As we discussed in a previous chapter, early recollections reveal the core convictions of the life style. Like the pushbutton tactic, early recollections can be shown to clients to be images that create motivation. They can be changed as well. "If you could change this recollection to have it work out any way you would want, how would you change it?" The restructured recollections are often as revealing as the original ones (Maniacci, 1996a).

The recollections are typically restructured in either of two ways: via an (a) internal or (b) external locus of control. The difference is very important. When clients re-create the recollection without anything changing about them—that is, by having other people or situations change—it is a sign of an external locus of control. When they change, it is an indicator of an internal locus of control. The following are some examples.

> Age 4. I am riding my bike, and I hit a bump and fall off. I break my arm. *Feeling:* hurt and angry. *Most vivid part:* falling off.
>
> Restructured: I am riding my bike, and it's smooth sailing. I'm flying free as a bird. *Feeling:* cool, fun. *Most vivid part:* the ride.

Notice the change. The client, a young man, feels free when life presents no bumps. He does not know how to handle life's challenges. He wants to be free, but he doubts his ability to move through life smoothly. He does not change anything about himself in the restructured recollection. Life has to change for him to be happy. Although that is certainly understandable, it is a risky proposition, because what if life does not change? Consider the following example, from a different client:

> Age 6. First day of first grade, and I am walking to school and lose my pencil. It falls in the street and down the sewer. *Feeling:* scared; what if the teacher gets mad? *Most vivid part:* the pencil dropping from my hand.
>
> Restructured: I am walking to school. I put my pencil in my backpack just to be careful and everything is just great. *Feeling:* excited. *Most vivid part:* the walk.

Notice the change this man made. He changed. This man wants to be prepared, and he knows he can make mistakes that will embarrass him. If he could change anything, it would be to be more careful and take more responsibility. Compared with that of the other client, this is a very different perspective.

Adlerian therapists can explore with clients how the recollections are restructured. Clients' ability or inability to step outside their private logic can be highlighted. Some clients will restructure their recollection three, four, or even five times, each time re-creating the same basic problem. They are waiting for life to change. They hesitate to realize they must change. Restructuring early recollections can demonstrate this point very effectively (Maniacci, 1996a).

Motivational Tactics

Sometimes, therapy is not an issue of re-education. Clients know what to do; they need help in getting motivated to do it (Mosak & Maniacci, 1998).

Selling

Imagine someone coming into a department store and being approached by a clerk. When asked what she wants, the customer states that she wants a black dress. The clerk starts showing her different types of shoes. What will happen? Sooner or later the customer will leave, feeling misunderstood and not listened to. The clerk might have been able to sell her some shoes, if she had first followed the customer's lead and showed her some black dresses. Much the same process can be seen in psychotherapy. By starting where the client is, therapists can increase the chances of going where they want to go. A common situation occurs in couples counseling. Frequently, the husband wants more sex, and the wife wants more communication. The husband is initially reluctant to do the communication exercises, until a link is made. If he communicates more, perhaps he will have more sex. If he can be encouraged to see that he will get what he wants if he goes in the direction the therapist wants him to go, everybody will be better off.

The "Stick and Carrot"

Some clients are motivated by what is positive, whereas others are motivated by what is negative. Like a stubborn mule that will move only when a carrot is dangled in front of it, some clients need to see something very positive in front of them. Some mules will move only if they are whacked with a stick. These clients will move only when threatened. Psychotherapists have to be willing to use either, depending on the clients' preference. Some clients can be encouraged to try new behaviors because of the pleasure it might bring them. For others, focusing on the pain they will avoid if they stop the troublesome behavior can motivate them. In pragmatic terms, the notion of social interest is enough to stimulate movement in some clients. With other clients, the thought of increasing symptoms and even more dysphoria is enough.

Anxiety-Reducing Tactics

There are times when it is important to help clients calm down. If they are too anxious, they will not be able to learn (Mosak & Maniacci, 1998).

Naming the Demon

Sometimes, simply giving a name to what the client is experiencing is enough to calm him or her down: "I know you're scared, but what you're experiencing is called panic. It will stop shortly. Trust me." Not having words for what one is experiencing can be horrific. By giving words to their condition, or even situation, clients can experience relief. "I think you're going through mourning. This is a grief reaction." It has been said that by naming the Devil, the Devil loses his power. Much the same can be seen with this tactic.

Taking Over

There are times when clients genuinely need someone to take over, if for no other reason than that they are truly lost and need a new map. Especially in cases of psychosis, clients will need guides back to the consensual world. "OK, here is what we are going to do. First, we will . . . " With the notion of community feeling, Adlerians are generally fairly confident that they know what kinds of directions to give under the right conditions. Taking over means being active in providing the new map. In the therapist's professional opinion, waiting for the client to discover the right track may be too stressful at this time and in this situation. The right track needs to be directly and forcefully pointed out.

Countering Tactics

As clients progress in therapy, they will begin to incorporate the messages from therapists. Clients will begin to question their own assumptions. At such times, clients may need help countering their typical ways of thinking. This can be a wonderfully exciting time for them and their therapists, and this stage of the work can be fulfilling for both. Clients may need help formulating their new convictions (Mosak & Maniacci, 1998).

Alternative Explanations

As clients grasp the notion of "psychology of use," they become aware that they are motivated not only by what happens to them but also their perceptions of what happens to them. Once they grasp this, they are ready for the next phase. What use do they make of what they perceive?

One way of teaching this point is to ask clients to imagine someone driving by on the side of the road. The driver is speeding, while they are stuck in traffic. Why is the driver speeding along the shoulder of the road? How many alternative explanations can they supply? As they begin to play with the concept, they begin to grasp its significance. Although the events of their lives are certainly important, the meaning and explanations they attach to those events are just as important.

As clients catch on with the driving scenario, they can progress to more challenging situations. Why did their parents do what they did? How many alternative explanations can they come up with? Why did their teachers do what they did? Why did their siblings do what they did? The process can become rather disorienting and thereby allow some useful distancing from their habitual ways of construing the world. Clients' life styles begin to develop flexibility.

Substituting Useful Beliefs

Once they are accustomed to generating alternative explanations, clients can be urged to examine the usefulness of selecting certain alternatives over others. They can begin to detect biases in the ways they construe events. It is no coincidence that they happen to have consistent biases. They now begin to grasp the concept of the style of life in a very personal, very profound way. Be it through early recollections, family constellation data, or even their current functioning in the life tasks, clients begin to make the connections themselves that earlier were made with the help of psychotherapists.

Given the fictional nature of their convictions, clients can be asked to create new, more socially interested fictions:

> If you think that guy is driving like a maniac down the shoulder because he is an idiot, you'll feel lousy. That will serve to justify your bias that it's a dog-eat-dog world, and justify your behaving badly. What if you believed he was driving that way because his house was on fire, or his kid was ill? How would you feel then?

Clients can start to apply the notion of community feeling in a direct, experiential manner.

We have presented only some of the tactics Adlerians use in their professional work. There are many more documented in the literature, and interested readers are encouraged to refer to those texts (e.g., Carlson & Slavik, 1997; Mosak & Maniacci, 1998). Creativity is the key. Tactics are learned not only through teaching and supervision but also by having the courage to take risks and try new things. Adlerian therapists are generally open to responding to clients and situations in novel but professional ways that allow for both clients and therapists to explore new options.

CONCLUSION

Adlerians are interested in encouraging in their clients a sense of community feeling and in fostering their social interest. In psychotherapy, that is accomplished in many ways, some of them directly, many of them indirectly. By attempting to align goals, elicit feedback from clients, and target interventions to specific dynamics, Adlerians attempt to be brief and efficient. Adlerians also tend to be focused and active in the treatment, believing that they need to have a high degree of activity not only in life but also in psychotherapy. Tactics are directed to the situations in which clients and therapists find themselves, and they are designed to help both parties move past those situations.

III

APPLICATIONS TO SPECIFIC THERAPY FORMATS

The demands made on man by communal life are really just as self-evident as the demands of climate, the demands of protection against cold, and of building houses. . . . If the conditions of life are determined in the first instance by cosmic influences, they are in the second instance determined socially. They are determined by the fact that men live together and by the rules and regularities which spontaneously arise in consequence of this. The demands of society have regulated human relations which had already existed from the beginning as self-understood, as an absolute truth. For before the individual life of man there was the community. In the history of the human culture, there is not a single form of life which was not conducted as social. Never has man appeared otherwise than in a society.

—A. Adler, 1956, p. 128

This final section provides an in-depth application of Adlerian therapy to specific areas of treatment. This approach can be applied to all targets of psychological treatment, and we highlight just a few of them. We begin with a description of the brief nature of this approach and apply it to individuals and couples. This is followed by descriptions of group therapy, play therapy with children, consultation with teachers and parents, and psychoeducation.

8

BRIEF INDIVIDUAL THERAPY

Historically, brief treatment was not considered "real" therapy. It was considered inadequate or substandard, because so-called "real" therapy required long-term, ongoing treatment in order for clients to make significant change. Within the past 30 years, however, brief therapy—in its various forms—has become the treatment of choice. No longer considered an ancillary or inferior form of treatment, brief therapy is now the primary modality of therapeutic intervention.

The concept of brief treatment has a long history. In the early development of psychoanalysis, Freud reported treating clients in terms of weeks and months. However, as he developed his theory, the length of treatment expanded as well. Psychoanalysis became increasingly long as Freud and his followers "became fascinated with the psychological phenomena that would emerge . . . if the therapist remained an inactive, and neutral 'blank' screen, while the patient freely associated" (Hoyt, 1995, p. 291). Anchin (2003) noted that, between the 1920s and 1940s, several analysts developed frameworks to shorten psychoanalytic treatment through the use of more active methods. However, as Hoyt (1995) suggested, the political climate within psychoanalysis was not ready for such a significant change.

World War II brought major changes regarding the practice of psychotherapy. Hoyt (1995) indicated that before the war, psychotherapy was a long-term, ongoing experience that only the privileged could afford, and it was largely restricted to psychoanalytic and psychiatric practitioners. However, there were so many soldiers requiring services during World War II that there was an urgent need for short-term interventions and methods that would help ameliorate symptoms and improve functioning so that the soldiers might either return to their posts or to civilian life. The remarkable effectiveness of these interventions "contributed mightily to the legitimization of short-term treatment" (Anchin, 2003, p. 222).

In the decades following the Second World War, the development of brief approaches to psychotherapy continued to grow. In the early 1950s, psychoanalytically oriented brief therapy approaches were developed by Baliant and Malan in England; Mann, Sinfneos, and Wolberg in the United States; and Davanloo in Canada (Anchin, 2003; Hoyt, 1995). Also in the 1950s, a number of psychoanalytically trained therapists became disenchanted with the psychoanalytic method and began creating their own approaches emphasizing active procedures to facilitate more rapid psychological change. For example, Perls and his associates began developing gestalt therapy theory and techniques, Wolpe and Lazarus developed behavior therapy (Lazarus ultimately developed the behaviorally oriented, technically eclectic approach known as *multimodal therapy*), Kelly developed personal construct psychology and therapy, Ellis and Beck began work on their cognitive–behavioral approaches (rational–emotive therapy and cognitive therapy, respectively), and Berne began developing transactional analysis (Anchin, 2003; Hoyt, 1995).

Brief therapy gained its greatest impetus in 1963 with the federal Community Mental Health Centers Act, which viewed mental health as a public health problem and had a goal of making psychotherapy more accessible to all people, not merely the affluent. To follow the directive of this legislation—to make services accessible for all people—required that psychotherapy become more short term. Ten years later, the federal Health Maintenance Organization Act added further urgency to the mandate for brief psychotherapy. Consequently, proponents of the aforementioned therapies that began developing in the 1950s continued to develop and refine their approaches. In particular, the behavioral and cognitive–behavioral therapies are regularly included in discussions of contemporary brief therapy approaches. Furthermore, new brief therapy approaches developed after the historical mental health developments of the 1960s and 1970s. Brief, strategic-oriented therapies—influenced by the work of Milton Erickson and the communications-systems orientation—began to gain prominence. For example, Haley and Madenes developed strategic family therapy; Watzlawick, Weakland, Jackson, Fisch, and Segal developed the Mental Research Institute (MRI) brief family therapy approach; and de Shazer developed solution-focused brief family therapy. Psychodynamically oriented brief therapies, drawing on the work of Sifneos, Mann, Malan, and Davanloo, developed significantly as well (Anchin, 2003; Hoyt, 1995).

The third historically significant catalyst toward mandated brief therapy treatment occurred in the 1980s, with the "revolutionary restructuring of the mental health care system" (Anchin, 2003, p. 225):

> Increasingly, insurance companies responded to growing pressure to expand availability of mental health services and to the latter's rising costs through development of managed care systems, placing specific limits on the number of mental health visits—characteristically 6–20—allotted to subscribers. (p. 225)

The result of this revolution is that brief or short-term therapy has become the standard model of contemporary psychotherapy.

WHAT IS BRIEF THERAPY?

Brief therapy is defined in various ways, and its complexity makes it difficult to truncate into a simple definition. For example, Cooper (1995) stated that brief therapy is routinely defined in contrast to long-term therapy. Both concepts are, in the main, poorly defined primarily in terms of calendar time or total number of sessions. In clinical practice, however, "long-term treatment is often intermittent, while technically brief treatments may occur episodically over years with challenging problems such as severe abuse or trauma" (Cooper, 1995, p. 14). Nevertheless, two useful definitions of brief therapy include the following:

1. When a therapist and patient endeavor to get from Point A (the problem that led to therapy) to Point B (the resolution that ends therapy) via a direct, effective, and efficient route, we say that they are deliberately engaging in *brief therapy*. . . . Another closely related term is *time-limited therapy*, which emphasizes the temporal boundedness of the treatment. Synonymous with *brief therapy* is the phrase *planned short-term therapy*, meaning literally a deliberately concise remedy/restoration/improvement. (Hoyt, 1995, p. 281)
2. Brief therapy takes many forms but is characterized by the planned use of specific concepts and principles in a focused, purposeful way. It emphasizes efficiency as well as efficacy. Underlying its variety, [brief therapy] shares a set of clinical features and a value orientation. (Cooper, 1995, p. 13)

Taking selected key words from the previous definitions, one may create a third: *Brief therapy* is any approach to psychotherapy that is concise, deliberate, direct, effective, efficient, focused, planned, purposeful, and time limited. It is interesting that these words resemble the shared or dominant values and essential characteristics of the various approaches to brief therapy described by Cooper (1995) and Hoyt (1995).

Seven Shared or Dominant Values of Brief Therapies

Brief therapies prefer or emphasize pragmatism, parsimony, and the least intrusive method of treatment. Whereas the notion of a "cure" is not emphasized, the brief therapies focus on small steps because they often lead to bigger changes. These therapies focus on normal human development and view significant psychological change as inevitable. Thus, all behavior has utility and potentially positive dimensions. Clients' strengths and resources are emphasized, and their presenting complaints are taken seriously, but not always at face value. Brief therapies affirm that much, if not most, significant change occurs outside of (and even after) therapy. Practitioners of brief therapy espouse the belief that therapy is not timeless. They acknowledge that psychotherapy is sometimes helpful and sometimes hurtful, and they understand that psychotherapy is not the most important thing in the client's life, that it is more important for the client to be in the world than to be in therapy (Cooper, 1995, pp. 14, 23–24; Hoyt, 1995, pp. 284–285).

Seven Essential Common Characteristics of Brief Therapies

The shared values mentioned have direct implications for the clinical practice of brief therapy. In this section, we identify practice characteristics common to the various brief therapies. Brief therapies emphasize the rapid development of a positive therapeutic alliance through the establishment of a therapeutic atmosphere that is permeated by compassion and understanding. A clear therapeutic focus, with clearly defined and achievable treatment outcomes, is developed. Practitioners of brief therapy stress clearly delineated roles and responsibilities in the therapeutic relationship and a high level of therapist activity and client participation. There is a clear focus on a rapid initial assessment and the integration of assessment into treatment. Brief therapy clinicians both actively attend to clients' presenting complaints and emphasize clients' abilities, adaptive capacities, competencies, and strengths. Consequently, brief therapy clinicians work from an expectation of change and improvement and strive to develop that expectation in clients. They espouse a present (and future) orientation and focus on current client functioning and thinking–feeling–behaving patterns, as well as potential alternatives. Brief therapy clinicians are time sensitive; they structure the duration and frequency of sessions—and tailor treatment in a practical and eclectic manner—on the basis of the unique needs of the clients (Budman, Friedman, & Hoyt, 1992; Cooper, 1995; Hoyt, 1995, 2000).

Seven Assumptive Hindrances to Brief Therapy

The following are common assumptions—possibly operating outside of awareness—that often interfere with therapists practicing in the most efficient way possible.

More Is Better

Many therapists may believe that long-term treatment is superior to short-term therapy; however, research does not support this assumption.

Deeper Is Better

This assumption states that anything other than deep therapy is superficial and considers other therapeutic interventions—such as guidance, suggestion, skill training, reassurance, practical problem solving, and so on—as inferior or substandard care.

Less Active Is Better

This belief emphasizes the superiority of the psychoanalytic method whereby the therapist remains relatively aloof so as to investigate the client's early childhood issues and unconscious meanings. The activity, focus, and selectivity of brief therapists and clients are, again, considered superficial.

The Therapist Knows Best

The difficulty here lies in the potential confusion between therapists' desires to explore broadly and deeply clients' underlying issues and clients' desires to attend directly to the problems and situations that brought them to therapy.

Financially, It Is Better

The fee-for-service model may present a temptation to continue clients longer than is necessary because it is profitable and dependable.

Delaying Goodbye Is Better

The pleasures of intimate conversation, the lure of living vicariously by means of an extended relationship, the need to be needed, and difficulties with termination may encourage therapists to continue therapy longer than is necessary.

My Way Is Better

Therapists may resist the apparent intrusiveness of managed care on their clinical practice; in other words, managed care emphasizes brief therapy, and therapists may resist this because they believe they are having practice dictated to them (Hoyt, 1995, pp. 2–3, 286).

Reasons Supporting the Practice of Brief Therapy

As noted earlier, brief or time-limited therapy has become the primary therapeutic modality expected of therapists and the treatment of choice for clients. There are several reasons that may justify the practice of brief therapy.

First, clients expect therapy to be brief. According to research, clients expect therapy to be directive, structured, focused on problem resolution, and last a relatively small number of sessions; typically 6 to 10 (Garfield, 1986; Hoyt, 1995).

Second, not only do clients expect therapy to be brief, but also they do not stay in therapy very long. Clients' expectations of treatment length (6–10 sessions) parallel their actual time in therapy (6–8 sessions) far more closely than therapists' expectations of treatment duration. Furthermore, research suggests that the largest amount of treatment gain occurs early in the course of therapy (Cooper, 1995; Garfield, 1994; Hoyt, 1995; Stuart, 2000). The modal number of sessions is 1. Whereas most clients do not stay in therapy long, and many come only once, each session is extremely important, and "treatment must make a rapid difference to [clients]" (Cooper, 1995, p. 25).

Third, research consistently suggests that the effectiveness of brief therapy is at least as effective as longer term therapy:

> Those studies that have directly compared brief and long-term methods have found equal effectiveness. Since brief therapy requires less time (both therapist and patient) and therefore less social cost, it has been suggested that brief methods are equally effective and more cost efficient than long-term psychotherapy. (Koss & Butcher, 1986, p. 658)

With both acute and chronic concerns, brief therapy has demonstrated success equal to longer term therapy, provided that the therapy has a specific focus issue and that reasonable treatment goals have been established (Asay & Lambert, 1999; Cooper, 1995; Dinkmeyer & Sperry, 2000; Hoyt, 1995; Koss & Butcher, 1986).

Fourth, the influence and policies of third-party payors and managed-care providers (insurance companies, health maintenance organizations, employee assistance programs, etc.) have significantly affected the movement toward briefer therapies. By limiting payment to brief, time-limited, outpatient and inpatient treatments, such providers have, in effect, mandated brief therapy procedures (Cooper, 1995; Dinkmeyer & Sperry, 2000; Hoyt, 1995).

Finally, the exponential increase in the number of people presenting for psychotherapy has demanded movement toward briefer, more time-efficient approaches. In many community and educational settings, there has been a significant increase in therapy caseloads without concomitant funding increases. Because of insufficient staffing, therapists' caseloads increase and, consequently, brief, time-efficient psychotherapies are required (Bitter & Nicoll, 2000; Nicoll, 1999).

ADLERIAN ROOTS OF BRIEF THERAPY

Traditional psychoanalysts—except for rare exceptions, such as Ferenczi, Rank, Alexander, and French—were reluctant to embrace short-term approaches to psychotherapy because traditional psychoanalytic theory requires treatment durations of sufficient length that the development and working through of the transference neurosis can occur. The traditional psychoanalytic treatment method often requires years of therapy (Shulman, 1989). "Having left the psychoanalytic movement in 1911," Shulman (1989) stated, "Adler was not concerned with the length of psychoanalytic treatment; he was developing his own psychotherapeutic approach" (p. 34).

Adlerian therapy has always emphasized brief treatment. Ansbacher (1972/1989) stated that many of the "various formal or structural attributes of brief therapy found in the current literature have from the beginning been part of the Adlerian approach" (p. 27).

According to Manaster (1989),

> Adler . . . stressed the issue of time in relation to change and effectiveness, the implications of crisis [specific problems] for motivating the client to and through therapy and focusing, from the first session, on the client and therapist working together on the specifics—the uniquenesses—of the client's personality in relation to the initial problem. Logically, then, Adlerians utilize a theory conducive to brief therapy with which they have generations of experience. (p. 244) . . . More and more of our therapy is effective and brief because we act in the belief that change can occur for anyone of any diagnostic category at any time and we treat to effect the change sooner, because we attempt to make each session a therapeutic whole; and because we *intend* to do brief therapy. (p. 247)

Shulman (1989) defined *brief therapy* from an Adlerian perspective as "the attempt to help the patient in a short period of time" (p. 36). The key aspect of this definition of brief therapy, according Manaster (1989), is "not as much the specification of an upper limit to the number of sessions as it is the emphasis on brevity, the emphasis on keeping therapy short, if possible attempting to limit the time of therapy" (p. 244). Adler typically limited the number of sessions he saw clients to 20 or fewer. In discussing the duration of therapy, Adler (1979) stated the following:

> You might say right at the beginning, "It will take eight to ten weeks" [two sessions per week]. In doubtful cases: "I don't know. Let us begin. In a month I shall ask you whether you are convinced that we are on the

right track. If not, we shall break off." I have often proposed this in diffi-cult cases. (p. 201)

The 20 or fewer sessions per episode limit embraced by Adler is consistent with current research and is a tradition followed by most contemporary Adlerians (Ansbacher, 1972/1989; Dinkmeyer & Sperry, 2000; Maniacci, 1996a). Thus, Ansbacher (1972/1989) argued that Adlerian therapy is the first brief therapy approach.

Adlerian Psychotherapy and Contemporary Brief Therapies

Sperry (1989; Dinkmeyer & Sperry, 2000) compared Adlerian psycho-therapy with eight contemporary brief therapy approaches derived from psy-chodynamic, cognitive, behavioral, systemic, and experiential orientations. These eight brief therapy approaches include the following:

- *Psychodynamic*: Sifneo's short-term anxiety provoking psycho-therapy, Mann's time-limited psychotherapy, and Klerman's interpersonal psychotherapy.
- *Cognitive*: Beck's cognitive therapy.
- *Behavioral*: Weiss and Jacobson's brief behavioral marital therapy.
- *Systemic*: the MRI's brief therapy approach and de Shazer's solution-focused brief therapy (SFBT).
- *Experiential*: Budman's brief interpersonal–developmental–experiential (IDE) therapy.

In terms of indications and contraindications, Dinkmeyer and Sperry (2000) reported that Adlerian therapy, the MRI brief therapy approach, SFBT, and Budman's IDE therapy share a "much wider range of applicability" com-pared with the other approaches, particularly the psychodynamic brief thera-pies (p. 227). Regarding treatment selection, they stated that the Adlerian, interpersonal psychotherapy, cognitive, MRI, SFBT, and IDE approaches are considered appropriate for a majority of clients. They noted that all nine approaches share the general treatment goal of symptom reduction or relief and that "each approach has a specific outcome goal which is consistent with its basic premise" (Dinkmeyer & Sperry, 2000, p. 230). In terms of the thera-peutic relationship, Dinkmeyer and Sperry indicated that all nine approaches stress the importance of rapidly developing the client–therapist relationship; however, the definitions of this relationship vary depending on the therapy orientation. Adlerian and cognitive approaches suggest a collaborative and equalitarian stance, whereas the psychoanalytic and MRI approaches em-phasize a more authoritative therapist-oriented stance. The other approaches fall somewhere between these two positions. Regarding treatment strategies, Dinkmeyer and Sperry reported that the Adlerian and IDE approaches "are the most eclectic and pragmatic in terms of choice of techniques" (p. 230). In summary, there are many areas of common ground among the brief therapies and Adlerian therapy. Perhaps most noteworthy is that Adlerian therapy is very similar to the nonpsychoanalytic brief therapy approaches but concomitantly shares with the psychodynamic brief therapies "an appreciation of the influence of early experiences on current functioning and use of insight as a treatment strategy" (Dinkmeyer & Sperry, 2000, p. 231).

An Extended Comparison

Given the epistemological shift in psychotherapy toward a constructive perspective, it is not surprising to find that many ideas originally presented in the constructively oriented theory of Adler appear in contemporary psychotherapies, although typically couched in different nomenclature (Watts, 1999, 2003a). Constructive therapies include both more individually focused, cognitive constructivist approaches and more communally focused, social constructionist perspectives. Adlerian therapy is situated between and resonates with both cognitive constructivist and social constructionist therapies. Espousing a *both/and* perspective, Adlerian therapy affirms the cognitive constructivist notion of individual human agency and the social constructionist perspective regarding the sociocultural origin of human psychological development. In other words, it is a healthy balance of individuals situated in relationships (Watts, 2003b; Watts & Phillips, 2004; Watts & Shulman, 2003). This *both/and* perspective is especially relevant because "there is increasing interest in emphasizing the commonalities and converging themes among psychotherapy systems" (Dinkmeyer & Sperry, 2000, p. 9), and psychotherapy integration is the prevalent focus among many psychotherapy theorists, researchers, and practitioners.

Two of the most popular brief therapy approaches are the cognitive–behavioral therapies and SFBT, and both are situated within the constructive therapy continuum: Cognitive–behavioral therapies may be understood as cognitive constructivist perspectives (e.g., Ellis, 1998), and SFBT authors acknowledge that theirs is a social constructionist approach. The similarity between Adlerian and the cognitive–behavioral therapies is noteworthy. As we noted in chapter 2, Adler's influence has been acknowledged, more so in some cases than in others, by the creators and practitioners of the cognitive–behavioral approaches to psychotherapy.

Theorists and practitioners of SFBT, on the other hand, do not offer substantive acknowledgment regarding Adler's pioneering approach to therapy. This is particularly surprising given the significant common ground between Adlerian therapy and SFBT (LaFountain & Garner, 1998; Watts & Pietrzak, 2000).

Solution-focused brief therapy authors note that the field of psychotherapy has historically focused solely on pathology, on deficits and limitations of clients, and has ignored their strengths, abilities, and resources. According to these authors, a unique contribution of SFBT is an optimistic therapeutic process that affirms clients' strengths (DeJong & Berg, 2002; Littrell, 1998; O'Hanlon & Weiner-Davis, 1989). Whereas this may be true for some traditional approaches to psychotherapy, it is clearly not true for Adlerian therapy. From the beginning, Adlerian therapy has stressed an optimistic, encouragement-focused approach. Adler and subsequent Adlerians consider encouragement a crucial aspect of human growth and development and an especially important element in psychotherapy. Because of this shared optimistic, strength-based focus, SFBT remarkably parallels the Adlerian understanding of psychotherapy in many ways (Watts & Pietrzak, 2000). Three of these parallels are described next; they include (a) the therapeutic alliance, (b) perspective on client problems, and (c) facilitating client change. It is important to note that these three parallels resonate with the cognitive–behavioral therapies as well.

The Therapeutic Alliance

The relationship between client and therapist in SFBT, as with most of the constructive therapies, is variously described as "cooperative," "collaborative," "egalitarian," "mutual," "optimistic," "respectful," and "shared." In developing the relationship, the counselor focuses on developing a strong therapeutic alliance, trusting the client, and exploring client competencies. Most of the basic relationship skills used in building the alliance are not unique to SFBT, and procedures and interventions used in therapy are often futile without a strong client–therapist relationship (DeJong & Berg, 2002; de Shazer, 1985, 1991; Littrell, 1998; O'Hanlon & Weiner-Davis, 1989; Walter & Peller, 1992).

Adlerian therapy strongly parallels SFBT's position regarding the therapeutic alliance. All the words used in the SFBT literature to describe developing the therapeutic relationship are also used in the Adlerian literature (e.g., A. Adler, 1956; Dinkmeyer & Sperry, 2000; Dreikurs, 1967; Mosak, 1979; T. J. Sweeney, 1998). For Adlerians, a strong counselor–client relationship is usually developed when therapists model social interest. As noted in chapter 4, Watts (1998) demonstrated that Adler's descriptions of therapist-modeled social interest look very similar to Rogers's descriptions of the core facilitative conditions of client change: congruence, empathic understanding, and unconditional positive regard. The basic skills necessary to build the therapeutic alliance discussed in the Adlerian literature are essentially the same as those mentioned in the SFBT and other constructive therapy literature (see chap. 4 for further discussion of the therapeutic alliance).

Perspective on Client Problems

In agreement with other constructive therapies, SFBT espouses a nonpathological view of maladjustment. Clients present for counseling because they are demoralized or discouraged, not because they are sick and in need of a cure. One of the main tasks of the SFBT clinicians is to help in the process of restoring patterns of hope with clients who have essentially lost hope (DeJong & Berg, 2002; de Shazer, 1991; Littrell, 1998; Metcalf, 1995; O'Hanlon & Weiner-Davis, 1989; Walter & Peller, 1992).

The similarity of SFBT to that of Adlerian therapy regarding maladjustment is remarkable. Adlerian therapy does not espouse the medical model of maladjustment; consequently, Adlerians do not see people as psychologically sick but rather as discouraged. Psychotherapy is not about curing clients; instead, it is a process of encouragement (Manaster & Corsini, 1982; Mosak, 1979). According to Dreikurs (1967), encouragement is crucial in psychotherapy. He noted that clients' problems are based on discouragement and that, without encouragement, without restoration of faith in themselves, clients will not see any possibility of more adaptive functioning.

Facilitating Client Change

Practitioners of SFBT seek to help clients change their behaviors and attitudes from a problem/failure focus to a focus on solutions/success and to discover and develop latent assets, resources, and strengths that clients may have overlooked as they focused primarily on their problems and limitations (Davis & Osborn, 2000; DeJong & Berg, 2002; de Shazer, 1985, 1991; Littrell, 1998; Walter & Peller, 1992). According to O'Hanlon and Weiner-Davis (1989), solution-focused brief therapists try to do three things:

1. "Change the *doing* of the situation that is perceived as problematic" (p. 126). By helping clients change their present actions and interactions, they become enabled to attempt other, less typical actions that may enhance the likelihood of resolving difficulties rather than repeating unsuccessful patterns of behavior.
2. "Change the *viewing* of the situation that is perceived as problematic" (p. 126). Facilitating perceptual alternatives—both in and out of counseling—may produce changes in behavior and elicit untapped strengths and abilities.
3. "Evoke resources, solutions, and strengths to bring to the situation that is perceived as problematic" (pp. 126–127). Reminding clients of their abilities, resources, and strengths may create changes in behaviors or perceptions.

Littrell (1998) noted that solution-focused brief therapists help clients remember or develop patterns of thoughts, feelings, and behaviors:

> We code these patterns with names like "resources" or "abilities" or "inner strengths." Some patterns we rediscover from clients' pasts; some are currently being used but clients have not yet recognized them as such. We can also co-create new patterns that do not yet exist in clients' repertoire or we can modify current ones. (pp. 63–64)

Once again, we see that the commonality between SFBT and Adlerian therapy is substantial. Hoyt (1994) identified three clinical–practical characteristics that SFBT and other constructive approaches share: (a) they place strong emphasis on developing a respectful therapeutic relationship, (b) they emphasize strengths and resources, and (c) they are optimistic and future oriented. These characteristics mirror what Adlerians have historically called *encouragement*, or the therapeutic modeling of social interest (Watts, 1999, 2003b; Watts & Pietrzak, 2000; Watts & Shulman, 2003).

In agreement with SFBT and other constructive approaches, Adlerians are technical eclectics (Manaster & Corsini, 1982). The interventions specific to constructive therapies are either similar to or congruent with ones commonly used in Adlerian therapy. Thus, as part of the encouragement process, Adlerians use a variety of procedures based on the client's unique needs and situation (Carlson & Slavik, 1997; Dinkmeyer, 1972; Mosak & Maniacci, 1998; Neuer, 1936; T. J. Sweeney, 1998; Watts & Pietrzak, 2000; Watts & Shulman, 2003).

ADLERIAN MODELS OF BRIEF THERAPY

Although the Adlerian therapeutic model as originally conceived by Adler may be correctly understood as the first brief therapy, it is not primarily a brief or a long-term psychotherapy. Adlerian psychotherapy is a flexible, integrative, and eclectic approach, and Adlerian clinicians tailor therapy according to the unique needs and situations of clients. As Manaster (1989) indicated: "Adlerians attempt full and complete therapy in whatever time is available and in the shortest time possible" (p. 245). Nevertheless, Adlerians have been clearly thoughtful regarding the need for brief, time-limited therapy. According to a survey conducted by Kern, Yeakle, and Sperry (1989), Adlerian therapy tends to be brief, typically lasting between 16 and 24 sessions. Furthermore, there is an extensive body of literature addressing Adlerian psychotherapy as a brief therapy (e.g., K. Adler, 1972/1989; Ansbacher, 1972/1989; Carlson, 1989; Dinkmeyer & Sherman, 1989; Kopp, 1989; O'Connell & Stubblefield, 1989; Pew, 1989; Powers & Griffith, 1989; Shulman, 1989; Sperry, 1987, 1989; Vann, 1995; Watts & Pietrzak, 2000). Although Adlerians can and do engage in long-term therapy, when doing so is both clinically appropriate and desired by the client, by and large they conduct brief therapy (Maniacci, 1996a).

In recent years, Adlerians have developed several specific brief therapy approaches. Three of these are addressed next; they include Adlerian brief therapy (ABT; Bitter & Nicoll, 2000; Nicoll, 1999; Nicoll, Bitter, Christensen, & Hawes, 2000), problem-solving counseling (PSC; Nystul, 1999), and efficient Adlerian therapy (EFT; Slavik, Sperry, & Carlson, 2000). As with Adlerian therapy, in general, these three Adlerian-based brief therapy approaches clearly resonate with the common characteristics of brief therapies presented earlier in this chapter.

Adlerian Brief Therapy

Developed primarily by William Nicoll and James Robert Bitter, ABT is an integration of Adlerian psychology and systems theory. It resonates with the common characteristics of brief therapies in general and the two Adlerian approaches to brief therapy that follow in this chapter (PSC and EFT). The assumptions of human nature and behavior that guide therapeutic assessment and intervention in ABT are presented in a four-phase strategy schema based on a three-level conceptual framework for understanding clients (Bitter & Nicoll, 2000; Nicoll, 1999; Nicoll et al., 2000).

Conceptual Framework for Understanding Clients' Behavior

Arguably the most comprehensive of the Adlerian brief therapy approaches, ABT affirms that therapy begins by assessing and striving to understand the client's presenting problems and current behavior according to a three-tiered framework that Nicoll (1999) called "the three levels of system behavior" (p. 20). This framework is explanatory for behaviors at both the micro- and macrosystemic levels (e.g., individual, couple, family, cultural, etc.).

The first level of behavior identifies the client's specific behaviors and emotions in the social context in which they occur. At this level, the ABT practitioner focuses on actual client behavior and the concomitant feelings, that is, discovering when the complaint does—and does not—occur and how the client thinks, feels, and behaves regarding the presenting problem. In addition, the therapist assesses how the client's behavior may affect other individuals at various systemic levels (Bitter & Nicoll, 2000; Nicoll, 1999; Nicoll et al., 2000).

The second level of behavior addresses the purpose or function served by the client's feelings, actions, and interactions. Consistent with Adler's theory as a psychology of use, symptoms are believed to be maintained because they are attempted solutions that, in some manner, serve a purpose in the client's systemic context. The purpose of problems or complaints can often be discovered by situating the client's patterns of behavior in his or her social context and examining the interactional patterns between (a) the client and significant peoples in that context or (b) the client and his or her life expectations (career, marriage, social, spiritual, etc.). As the therapist follows the sequence of interaction, the purpose or function of the client's behavior gradually emerges (Bitter & Nicoll, 2000; Nicoll, 1999; Nicoll et al., 2000).

The third level of behavior involves investigating the client's idiosyncratic rules of interaction. At this level, the therapist seeks to discover the client's basic assumptions, core constructs, or personal metanarrative regarding self, others, and the world; that is, the Adlerian notion of life style. In sum, the life style consists of all those elements that, in aggregate, constitute how the client makes meaning of his or her existence. By discovering the life style convictions, the therapist may better understand—and help the client better understand—the underlying rationale or private logic that maintains dysfunctional interactional patterns, problems, and symptoms (Bitter & Nicoll, 2000; Nicoll, 1999; Nicoll et al., 2000). Bitter and Nicoll (2000) noted that at this level of behavior, second-order change becomes possible. Merely changing behavior or emotions can amount to nothing more than symptom substitution, or first-order change. However, when the therapist actively listens for, understands, and discloses the client's rules of interaction, the client may more readily understand the purpose of dysfunctional behavior, thus making the behavior more difficult for the client to maintain. Behavior patterns become more clearly focused, even predictable to some extent. Thus, a change in the rules of interaction typically produces second-order change and facilitates lasting changes at the other two levels of behavior (Bitter & Nicoll, 2000; Nicoll, 1999; Nicoll et al., 2000).

The Four-Phase Strategy Schema of Adlerian Brief Therapy

Adlerian brief therapy offers a four-phase strategy schema that provides the therapist with an overall framework for both individual sessions and the brief therapy process as a whole. These four phases and strategies are identified with the acronym BURP: behavioral assessment/description of the presenting complaint, underlying rules of interaction assessment, reorientation of the client's rules of interaction, and prescribing new behavioral rituals (Nicoll, 1999; Nicoll et al., 2000). These phases of therapy are fluid rather than discrete. Nicoll et al. (2000) stated that Adlerian brief therapists follow the four-phase process more in terms of a structured flow—rather than a mechanistic, lock-step manner—because modifications may be necessary according to each client's unique situation and needs.

Phase 1: Behavioral Assessment/Description of the Presenting Complaint

Consistent with Adler's (1956) recommendations, ABT clinicians begin by obtaining a detailed behavioral description of how the presenting problem or complaint manifests in the client's daily life. From the initial meeting with the client, and consistent with Adlerian theory, the therapist strives to have the client describe the presenting complaint in behavioral (actions and emotions) terms rather than pathology language that suggests that the client has a disease or disorder that he or she has little or no power to overcome. For example, Nicoll (1999; Nicoll et al., 2000) suggested that when a client says "I am depressed," the therapist might respond by asking the client to describe in behavioral terms specific times and situations when he or she felt depressed or sad. Phase 1 process questions can include "What did you do the last time this occurred?", "Who else was affected?", What did they do?", and "How did you respond?" (Nicoll, 1999, p. 23). These questions help the therapist better understand the client's presenting complaint and may facilitate commencement of the reorientation process (Phase 3) by changing the language the client used to give meaning to his or her situation.

Action-oriented questions and terminology empower clients by helping them move from a problem-focused perspective to a problem-solving one. By focusing on how a client responds, the therapist can begin to understand the client's feelings and behaviors, when and in what situations the feelings and behaviors manifest, and who (or what) is involved or affected by the client's affective and behavioral responses (Nicoll, 1999; Nicoll et al., 2000).

Phase 2: Assessment of the Underlying Rules of Interaction

As the therapist carefully attends to the client's description of the presenting complaint, the context in which it occurs, and the sequencing and recurring nature of problematic interactional patterns, he or she usually begins to understand the possible (or intended) purpose or function of the client's behavioral symptoms. In addition, the therapist may begin forming hypotheses about "the possible rules of interaction whereby the client perceives, attaches meaning to, and chooses behaviors in his or her life" (Nicoll, 1999, p. 24). Clients are not consciously aware of their underlying rules of interaction; thus, they are unaware of perceptual and behavioral alternatives. The goal of Phase 2, therefore, is to understand the client's rules of interaction that maintain the problematic behavior.

When the therapist understands the client's rules of interaction, the client's behavior makes sense; that is, symptoms follow logically from the rules of interaction. Thus, the therapist is able to align with the client as an ally. When the client feels supported and understood, he or she is likely to engage in working with the therapist toward change. However, the therapist recognizes that there are perceptual alternatives to the one currently held by the client. Nicoll (1999; Nicoll et al., 2000) noted that there are numerous interventions that help therapists rapidly gain an understanding of the client's underlying rules of interaction. Nicoll et al. identified a few examples: "early childhood recollections," "family stories and family genograms," and the "magical question" originally developed and described by Adler and Dreikurs and later used in SFBT (pp. 231–233). According to Nicoll, these techniques, and similar tactics and interventions, often provide useful metaphors for the presenting complaint. These metaphors can be used to create perceptual and behavioral alternatives in the third phase of ABT.

Phase 3: Reorientation of the Client's Rules of Interaction

Nicoll (1999; Nicoll et al., 2000) emphasized, however, that success in Phases 3 and 4 is predicated on thorough attention to the assessment strategies in Phases 1 and 2 and the accurate identification of the client's presenting complaint across all three levels of the conceptual framework for understanding client behavior. The goal of Phase 3 is to facilitate a cognitive or perceptual shift in the client's understanding of the presenting complaint. Without this perceptual shift, the client may engage only in first-order change, if any. It is true that lasting change involves second-order change processes: "a fundamental morphogenic shift in how the existing situation is understood and addressed" (Nicoll, 1999, p. 26). Once this perceptual shift has occurred, behavioral options consistent with the new perspective may be considered and implemented.

There are many techniques that may be used during the reorientation process and, according to Nicoll et al. (2000), these procedures "serve to reorient the client's current perceptions (rules of interaction) relative to the presenting issue(s)" (p. 234). Suggested techniques include reframing; relabeling; humor; confrontation; using metaphors; language changes; and questions and procedures from solution-focused and narrative therapies, such as externalizing the problem, looking for exceptions, and assuming a one-down or not-knowing position with clients (Bitter & Nicoll, 2000; Nicoll, 1999; Nicoll et al., 2000). Although there are myriad procedures and interventions that may be used in the reorientation process, the choice of techniques is predicated on the unique client and his or her presenting complaint and situation.

Phase 4: Prescribing New Behavioral Rituals

This final strategy phase of ABT consists of new behavioral tasks (or *rituals*) that the client performs outside of therapy. Because brief therapy is based on the premise that change typically occurs between sessions rather than within them, the client is expected to actively engage in the change process outside of therapy (Nicoll, 1999; Nicoll et al., 2000). Rituals may be defined as "regular, repeated actions that serve to reaffirm or maintain underlying rules of interaction" (Nicoll, 1999, p. 26). A client's symptoms may be viewed as ritualistic behaviors that functionally reaffirm his or her underlying rules of interaction and, as such, often develop into self-fulfilling prophecies. Therefore, when a client changes his or her perception regarding the presenting complaint (Phase 3), he or she will need to learn alternative behavioral options (rituals) to both reinforce the encouraging perceptual alternative and effectively address the presenting complaint (Nicoll, 1999; Nicoll et al., 2000).

Rituals are action oriented. In this last phase of ABT, new behavioral patterns or rituals are prescribed for clients to use when addressing the presenting complaint using the perceptual alternative (Nicoll, 1999; Nicoll et al., 2000). There are numerous types of rituals that may be used, depending on the needs of the client. For example, Nicoll et al. (2000) suggested "changing-the-choreography rituals," in which new interaction steps might be introduced into a repetitive sequence between marital partners for handling conflict, or "changing-the-actors rituals," in which a person is removed from—or included in—an ongoing, problematic interactional pattern to change the sequence (p. 238). These rituals and others (e.g., restoring positive rituals, connecting rituals, desensitization rituals, boundary-making rituals, etc.) involve "prescribing specific new behavioral interventions that are to be performed on a regular, repeated basis and that reaffirm the new meaning or understanding associated with the presenting issue through the reorientation process" (p. 238). Regardless of the strategies used, this phase of therapy emphasizes that clients are actively making changes in their lives outside of the therapeutic situation.

Nicoll et al. (2000) emphasized that the behavioral prescriptions are based largely on "a shift, change, or reorientation in the client's original rules of interaction" (p. 240):

> The reorientation strategy [or phase] is the key to change. . . . Only when the client can view his or her symptoms from a new perspective will he or she be prepared to seek and then employ alternative behavioral strategies. The new behavioral rituals that the therapist gives the client are directives for handling the presenting situation differently that simultaneously reaffirm this new perspective. (p. 240)

Problem-Solving Counseling

The Adlerian therapy model is remarkably flexible. It is both theoretically integrative and technically eclectic. Nystul's (1999) PSC model is one example of this integrative flexibility. Problem-solving counseling is an integration of Adler's approach to psychotherapy and reality therapy, developed by William Glasser (1998, 2000; see also Wubbolding, 2000). Nystul (1999) noted that his four-step problem-solving model is "both a time-limited, solution-focused method and an approach that generates an in-depth analysis of unconscious processes" (p. 40).

Problem-Solving Counseling: The Four-Step Model

Nystul (1999) stated that problem-solving approaches tend to be highly structured and "use [discrete] steps that can be taught to clients and used to prevent future problems. In addition, problem-solving methods are well-suited for short-term, time limited counseling because they are problem centered and solution-focused" (p. 33). Nystul (1999) indicated that his PSC model can be used at any point in the therapy process but that it is most useful as a type of intervention following the development of the goals of therapy.

Step 1: Identifying the Inefficient Approach. Nystul (1999) indicated that this step parallels that of reality therapy in that its focus is on the client's current behavior. Thus, the therapist asks "What are you doing? Is it working for you?" (Nystul, 1999, p. 34). The client and therapist collaboratively identify the issues that have the greatest influence on whether the client is able to reach his or her therapy goals. The final aspect of this first step is to help the client realize the control that the client has over his or her behavior.

Step 2: Exploring the Psychology of Use. According to Nystul (1999), the therapist at this juncture in the PSC model uses Adlerian principles and procedures to explore the client's purposes and goals to understand the psychology of use behind the client's inefficient approach to his or her problems. Nystul (1999) noted that people learn approaches to problem solving in childhood to meet their basic needs that often will not work in adolescence or adulthood. Because of their thoughts that justify these inefficient approaches (i.e., their private logic), they often continue to believe that childhood problem-solving approaches are required to meet their needs as adolescents and adults. Therapists can investigate the client's psychology of use and private logic by exploring the client's early memories of his or her use of the inefficient approach and identifying the needs that were met. According to Nystul (1999), the process of exploring the client's psychology of use promotes at least two positive outcomes in therapy. First, exploring the psychology of use "is encouraging and communicates respect to clients in terms of identifying the payoffs associated with inefficient approaches" (Nystul, 1999, p. 35). Second, it helps in the process of normalizing clients' behaviors:

> From the perspective of the psychology of use and private logic, it is predictable and normal to expect clients to behave in ways they believe meet their needs. Normalizing has a positive effect . . . in that it promotes a strengths perspective and avoids tendencies toward self-criticism, catastrophizing, and other negative tendencies. (Nystul, 1999, p. 35)

Step 3: Enhancing the Client's Motivation. Step 3 in the PSC model involves engaging the client in a cost–gain analysis to help him or her understand the cost incurred by using the inefficient approach and what he or she can gain by giving it up. In conducting the cost–gain analysis the therapist often helps the client focus on one primary significant cost, known as the *paradoxical point*:

> The paradoxical point is the point in a person's life when an efficient approach becomes an inefficient one (or, as Glasser would say, a behavior that is no longer working for them). . . . Once clients become aware of the paradoxical effect of their inefficient approach, they will tend to be very motivated to give up that approach. (Nystul, 1999, p. 36)

Step 4: Developing a More Efficient Approach. This final step in the PSC process seeks to help clients select "a new approach that meets the needs identified in Step 2 without the cost associated with their inefficient approach" (Nystul, 1999, p. 36). The process involves the client selecting a new approach to modify or replace the inefficient one. This new approach has to be something that the client views as plausible and one with which he or she feels comfortable. The therapist can then help the client develop the thoughts, feelings, and behaviors required to successfully implement the new approach. Nystul (1999) stated that it is important, when possible, to "develop an approach that is consistent with the client's self-concept in order to minimize resistance. For example, if a client wants to be perceived as outgoing, then the new approach should incorporate outgoing characteristics" (p. 37). He also noted that the Adlerian techniques of acting "as if" and "catching oneself" are particularly useful at this juncture in the PSC model.

Efficient Adlerian Therapy

According to Slavik et al. (2000), EFT is not a truncated version of a longer term therapy. Adlerian therapy generally tends to be reasonably efficient, and the notion of efficiency seems to be "built into the purposes of Adlerian therapy and the typical training of Adlerian therapists" (Slavik et al., 2000, p. 250). However, they note that they developed the EFT model because of the demand for briefer, outcome-based psychotherapy. Although clearly derived from Adler's approach to psychotherapy, "this approach . . . has been tailored and adapted to the unique needs of North America" (Slavik et al., 2000, p. 250). Efficient Adlerian therapy is based on the assumption that all people are equal. Consequently, the therapist is more of a consultant than an expert on the client's life. Because of this premise of equality, which structures all of therapy, in EFT the client is trusted in the collaborative process of "matching solutions to situations" (Slavik et al., 2000, p. 250). Slavik et al.'s approach contains a six-element ("tactics") conceptual overview and a 10-step therapy process.

Tactics of Efficient Adlerian Therapy: The Six-Element Overview

There are six conceptual or tactical elements in EFT: (a) engage the client, (b) focus treatment, (c) emphasize client strengths and competence, (d) think "short term," (e) reframe issues in a positive light, and (f) emphasize mutual respect and equality (Slavik et al., 2000).

Engage the Client. Efficient Adlerian therapy emphasizes the crucial necessity of engaging clients in cooperation and collaboration at the outset of therapy. Cooperation and collaboration are necessary for communicating expectations in therapy, tailoring treatment, and preventing premature termination of therapy (Slavik et al., 2000).

Focus Treatment. Efficient Adlerian therapy stresses that the client's presenting complaint is the focus of treatment. The client, in collaboration with the therapist, defines, clarifies, and specifies the problems; generates solutions and action plans; and indicates when sufficient progress has been made (Slavik et al., 2000).

Emphasize Client Strengths and Competence. A basic belief of EFT is that clients are competent and have the ability to solve their problems. Clients have strengths, competencies, talents, and skills that may be brought to bear in solving problems. The therapist's job is to help the client rediscover abilities and assets and to develop latent or underdeveloped ones (Slavik et al., 2000).

Think "Short Term." Efficient Adlerian therapy's brief or time-limited focus helps the therapist frame the client's problems as "practical issues whenever possible, resorting to 'psychological' solutions only when necessary" (Slavik et al., 2000, p. 253). When issues are framed as problems of living, they can be broken down into small steps to create manageable short-term goals that facilitate more rapid opportunity for clients to experience success.

Reframe Issues in a Positive Light. Because EFT affirms that all problems and all solutions are social and relational in nature, Slavik et al. (2000) believe that the therapist should, when possible, reframe the client's issues in social and relational terms: "Casting others' and clients' behavior and intentions in a positive social light reframes issues as relational [and] often allows clients to think better of themselves and others" (p. 253). However, EFT focuses more on successful behavior than modifying convictions: "Successful behavior—that is, behavior that alleviates the problem—changes the way one looks at life and . . . changes one's feelings" (Slavik et al., 2000, p. 235).

Emphasize Mutual Respect and Equality. A foundational tenet of the approach, EFT stresses that an egalitarian and mutually respectful relationship is crucial for therapeutic success. Consequently, issues of status and dominance and submission are often less problematic than in other therapies, and clients are more inclined to actively enter into the problem-solving process (Slavik et al., 2000).

Efficient Adlerian Therapy: The 10-Step Treatment Process

Slavik et al. (2000) described the following 10 steps as a "process rather than a procedure" (p. 254). Rather than a linear or lock-step set of procedures, these steps describe a way of thinking about the process of therapy:

1. *The therapist invites the client to begin with a statement of the problem.*
2. *The therapist helps the client clarify the presenting problem, simplify it, or cast it in concrete, transactional terms.*
3. *The therapist asks the client for the best solution, if any, that is under his or her control.* Here the therapist might ask "If you could have it any way you wanted, how would you solve this problem?" (Slavik et al., 2000, p. 255). If the solution sounds reasonable, the therapist might recommend that the client implement the solution. However, sometimes clients may respond with hesitation and offer reasons why the solution is not plausible. In addition, some clients may want to defer to the therapist's "expert" opinion on how to solve the problem.

4. *If the client offers no best solution, the therapist may suggest one that he or she believes might easily work.* Slavik et al. (2000) recommended that the suggestion be offered in a tentative fashion, for example: "Here's a suggestion. I don't know if it would work for you. You might try. . . . What do you think?" (p. 256). The suggestions offered by the therapist can be accepted, rejected, or modified. Slavik et al. noted that how the client chooses to respond to suggestions is informative and may provide the therapist with greater knowledge of the client.

5. *If a client offers a best solution, the therapist encourages it.* Slavik et al. (2000) suggested that therapists, on hearing the potential solution, ask the client "What could you do to make this happen?" (p. 256). The solution may need some modification so as to be sufficiently specific and under the client's control. Nevertheless, it is often a direct way to generate ideas for solving problems that clients find plausible and agreeable.

6. *The therapist looks for and encourages strengths.* The therapist looks for and encourages cooperative, socially useful behavior that the client already knows how to do. The therapist affirms behavior that shows signs of healthy functioning—related to the solution or not—and seeks to help clients use these strengths in improving their situation and increasing their morale (Slavik et al., 2000).

7. *If a solution is not found in such practical ways, the therapist may ask for early memories and interpret them.* According to Slavik et al. (2000), therapists can use the information from early recollections to "inform, guide or modify the client's direction of movement in cooperative directions that make sense to the client" (p. 257).

8. *The therapist discriminates between the discouraged client and the pessimistic client.* Discouraged clients are best suited for brief therapy, because encouragement and the experience of success are typically what they need from therapy. According to Slavik et al. (2000), pessimistic clients need "well-structured, collaborative, long-term therapy and self-education" (p. 257).

9. *As a last resort, particularly for the pessimistic client, the therapist may suggest an assessment and describe the procedure and its purpose.* Slavik et al. (2000) noted that the purpose of the assessment is to encourage the client to consider longer term treatment. They recommended a phenomenological assessment (e.g., life style assessment) because it potentially allows for a deeper client–therapist relationship to develop in which clients feel safer to reveal more about themselves.

10. *The therapist may use other techniques.* If the client is amenable, the therapist may use additional techniques to help the client better understand him- or herself or as alternative methods for addressing the client's presenting problem. The therapist may use direct or indirect methods, depending on the client's situation and expectations (Slavik et al., 2000).

CONCLUSION

Hoyt (2002) noted that the fundamental distinguishing characteristics of brief therapy are the establishment of a collaborative therapeutic alliance and an emphasis on clients' strengths, assets, and abilities in the process of achieving the goals of therapy:

> The goal of brief psychotherapy, regardless of the specific theoretical approach or technical method, is to help the patient resolve a problem, to get "unstuck" and to move on. Techniques are specific, integrated, and as eclectic as needed. Treatment is focused, the therapist appropriately active, and the patient responsible for making changes. Each session is valuable, the therapy ends as soon as possible. (pp. 279–280)

According to Ansbacher (1972/1989), Adlerian therapy was the first brief therapy approach. Although this is not well known outside Adlerian circles, Adlerian therapists have had a long history of doing brief, time-limited psychotherapy. Adler practiced brief psychotherapy and emphasized many of the characteristics found in the contemporary brief therapy literature. These characteristics—such as rapid development of a strong therapeutic alliance; clear problem focus and goal alignment; rapid assessment and application of this focus and goal alignment to treatment; emphasis on active, direct therapeutic activity and cooperation; a focus on clients' strengths and abilities and an optimistic expectation of change; a present and future (or "now" and "next") orientation; and time sensitivity that tailors treatment based on the unique needs of clients—are replete in Adlerian therapy. Thus, Adlerian psychotherapy—brief or otherwise—clearly resonates with the characteristics common to the brief therapies and, consequently, is a useful model for brief, time-limited psychotherapy.

9

BRIEF COUPLES THERAPY

The tradition of couples therapy is strong within Adlerian psychology. In 1922, Adler began establishing clinics for the purpose of couples and family counseling in Vienna. Eventually, more than 30 were created. In this chapter, we focus on Adlerian contemporary approaches to brief couples therapy.

FALLACY OF DIVORCE AS A SOLUTION

The United States has become a "throw-away" society, in a sense. Many people do not plan for things to last or be permanent. When a marriage is not going well, it is often the case that a person looks not at him- or herself but rather at perceived failings of his or her partner. Oftentimes, the solution is divorce. A recent research study, which was a collaborative effort among several leading scholars from different academic settings (Waite et al., 2002), seems to highlight the fallacy of this thinking.

According to this collaborative study, unhappily married adults who divorced or separated were no happier, on average, than unhappily married adults who stayed together. On average, divorce did not reduce symptoms of depression for unhappily married adults, or raise their self-esteem, or increase their sense of mastery, compared with unhappy spouses who stayed married. The vast majority of divorces (74%) occurred between adults who had been happily married 5 years previously. Unhappy marriages were less common than unhappy spouses. Staying married did not typically trap unhappy spouses in violent relationships. Two out of three unhappily married adults who avoided divorce or separation reported being happily married 5 years later. Many currently happy married spouses have experienced extended periods of marital unhappiness, often for quite serious reasons, including alcoholism, infidelity, verbal abuse, emotional neglect, depression, illness, and work changes.

COMPONENTS OF A HEALTHY COUPLE RELATIONSHIP

What does a satisfying relationship look like? Carlson and Dinkmeyer (2003) highlighted 10 components that are present in couples who have satisfying relationships.

1. They individually accept responsibility and develop self-esteem.
2. They choose to encourage each other.
3. They identify and align their relationship goals.
4. They communicate their feelings with honesty and openness.
5. They listen empathically when feelings are being expressed.
6. They seek to understand the factors that influence their relationship.
7. They demonstrate that they accept and value each other.
8. They choose thoughts, words, and actions that support the positive goals of the relationship.
9. They solve relational conflicts.
10. They commit themselves to the ongoing process of maintaining an equal relationship.

Many couples seem to know what is wrong and what to avoid but need to be as clear about what works and what creates satisfaction.

RELATIONSHIP EDUCATION AND SKILLS

As we discuss further in chapter 12, Adlerians believe that the skills found in satisfying relationships can be learned. For example, developing and maintaining a good couple relationship requires a time commitment. It is often the case that counselors have their clients bring in their calendars and show them how to schedule time for the relationship.

Adlerians believe that the specific skills essential to a healthy relationship can be learned. No one is born with a good relationship skill gene. We learn (or do not learn) these skills from our families. It is understood that change often takes time, but all change begins with the individual. One person really can change a relationship. Adlerians also accept that feelings of love and caring that have diminished or disappeared often return when behavior changes. These changes do not have to be monumental: Small changes are very important in bringing about big changes. The primacy of the relationship is the key to satisfying relationships. Happy, stable couples make their relationship a priority and frequently use the words *us* and *we* (Carlson & Dinkmeyer, 2003).

Time-efficient therapists know that couples need to learn skills if they are going to create and maintain satisfying relationships. Although therapists need to know the skills, they cannot spend therapy time teaching them. Bibliotherapy, videos, or study groups are helpful ways to teach these basic skills.

WHAT IS INTEGRATIVE TREATMENT?

Adlerian brief couples therapy (ABCT) uses a variety of techniques and strategies. Therapists must be able to integrate a variety of treatment strategies to fit the unique needs of the individual and the couple. At times, the therapist needs to fix the structure, and at other times he or she needs to create honest and direct communication. Therapists may be called on to intervene in a crisis or to make a context safe for intimate communication to occur. Some couples need work on feelings, whereas others need to work on thoughts or behaviors. Therapist flexibility is needed so that the best of the many strategies available can be integrated.

The Adlerian approach is one that helps couples use their resources. The concept of encouragement gives the couple hope and the ability to continue to challenge adversity. ABCT uses the core factors identified in Lambert and Ogles's (2004) summary of outcome data in psychotherapy. Lambert and Ogle discovered that change occurs as a result of the same common factors, which we discuss in the following sections.

Clients' Extratherapeutic Factors

Forty percent of change is due to the client or his or her life circumstances (Lambert & Ogles, 2004). This category consists of a client's strengths, supportive elements in the environment, and even chance events. This is what clients bring to the therapy or change process, such as a good job, a supportive grandmother, membership in a religious community, a sense of personal responsibility, being lucky, or being physically healthy.

Client–Therapist Relationship Factors

Thirty percent of the reason for a successful outcome can be attributed to the relationship and such things as caring, empathy, warmth, acceptance, mutual affirmation, and encouragement. Placebo, hope, and expectancy are accountable for 15% of successful change. This has to do with whether the client believes in the therapist and process. Model/technique—that is, the specific approach or theory that is used—accounts for 15% of the change.

BASIC ADLERIAN PRINCIPLES

Adlerian psychology is essentially a systems theory that is holistic, purposeful, cognitive, and social. It focuses on the relationship or the patterns of interaction between partners. Adler realized that people are social beings and therefore that all problems are based in a social context. He contended that couples issues and conflicts were less likely to reflect personal pathology and more likely to be problems of cooperation between the partners.

The couple relationship is understood as an interpersonal social system in which input from each partner can either improve the relationship or stimulate dissonance and conflict.

Adlerians often say "Trust only movement." The interaction, communication, and movement between the partners are purposive and goal directed. The movement reveals intentions, feelings, and values that influence the system. It is essential to understand the psychological movement between the couple that creates cooperation or conflict. Are they moving together or apart?

Therapists must concentrate on observing and understanding what partners do instead of focusing on what they say. There has historically been too much interest on verbal communication between the partners. Recognizing movement that is cooperative and movement that is resistive is what attracts individuals to each other. This is also the basis for what causes relational conflict. What attracts individuals to each other also is the basis for their relational conflict (Hendrix, 2001).

Dreikurs (1946) was one of the first to observe that the qualities that initially attract individuals to each other are basically the same factors that create discord and conflict and lead to divorce. Pat Love (2001) provided a clear rationale for how the attraction process occurs. Dreikurs (1946) also noted that any human quality or trait can be perceived in a positive or a negative way. A person can be considered kind or weak, frugal or cheap, strong or domineering, and so on, depending on the individual's point of view. Dreikurs suggested that one person does not like or dislike another for his or her virtues or dislike that person for his or her faults. Instead, an emphasis on a person's positive qualities grows out of affection for that person, just as an emphasis on weakness grows out of rejection. This emphasis on the individual's weakness or negative trait provides an excuse for having to communicate, to negotiate, and to resolve conflicts. As Dreikurs (1946, 1967) has noted, this process of relabeling—that is, of perceiving formerly ideal qualities as despised qualities—has much to do with cooperation. He stated that whatever two people do to and with each other is based on a mutual agreement and full cooperation, be it for good or bad. He also noted that people are so accustomed to using the term *cooperation* for constructive interactions that they overlook the fact that one person cannot fight without the other's full cooperation. Cooperation is an orderly, harmonious effort in which both people work together toward a common objective, whether it be positive or negative. Positive cooperation is the expression of a sense of belonging together, a sense of self-confidence, a sense of confidence in each other, and the element of courage. Dreikurs (1946) believed that these four qualities are the sources of positive cooperation, whereas hostility, distrust, inferiority feelings, and fear are the basis of negative cooperation. These components are similar to Gottman, Driver, and Tabares's (2003) "Four Horsemen of the Apocalypse" in relationships: (a) criticism, (b) contempt, (c) defensiveness, and (d) stonewalling.

Each person is viewed as an individual, social, decisive human being whose actions have a purpose. "The attitude of every individual towards marriage is one of the expressions of his (her) style: We can understand it if we understand the whole individual and not otherwise" (A. Adler, 1956, p. 434).

Each partner has the creative capacity to choose and create his or her own perceptions and meaning. The couple is helped to see that their goals and the ensuing conflict are chosen. Choice is an essential component of all behavior, but it is frequently denied in human relationships. Couples are helped to see that through their beliefs, behaviors, and attitudes they make new choices (Glasser & Glasser, 2000).

Each partner has the responsibility to make decisions, and each is responsible for his or her behavior. When each person is responsible, then equilibrium and solutions exist instead of dysfunction and blaming. Change in the relationship always begins with oneself, not with one's partner. Personal responsibility is a frequent focus of treatment.

The beliefs, behavior, and feelings that exist in the system between the partners are the result of subjective perception. Behavior is a function of one's perception. Therapists look at what certain experiences mean to a particular person because each individual constructs his or her own reality. The partners are helped to understand the meaning they are giving to their experiences. It is often helpful for the therapist to point out that relationship patterns are often transgenerational. Relationships have the potential for continuous miscommunication, because each partner responds in the way he or she learned in the family of origin.

The couple's happiness is based on each person's self-esteem, social interest (the capacity to give and take), and a sense of humor. These are the ingredients for happiness in a relationship. *Self-esteem* is the individual's sense of worth and acceptance, *social interest* is the desire to cooperate, and *sense of humor* is the ability to see the relationship in perspective.

Relationships are also influenced strongly by the belief systems of the couple. Belief systems are related to priorities. Some of the priorities significant in the couple relationship include the following: control, perfection, pleasing others, self-esteem, and expectation. The personality priorities are based on perceptions and reveal what people believe they must do to belong and be accepted (Carlson & Dinkmeyer, 2003).

An important factor in understanding relationships is how the life styles of each partner fit together. This interaction, according to Dreikurs (1946), is evident in one's choice of a partner. We choose a partner "who offers us an opportunity to realize our personal patterns, who responds to outlook and conceptions of life, who permits us to continue or revive plans that we have carried with us since childhood" (Dreikurs, 1946, pp. 68–69). Adlerians see this as complementarities in the give-and-take of the partners' life styles. A couple relationship "is not merely one of a conscious choice and logical conclusions; it is based more profoundly upon the integration of two personalities" (Dreikurs, 1946, p. 83). This involves the fitting together of both the similarities and differences of a couple. Recent research suggests that we are attracted to individuals who are genetically different from us so that our offspring will have the greatest immunity to illness (Fisher, 2004; Love, 2001).

Dealing with the differences in relationships is imperative. Many couples believe that partners must be the same in order to be together. This will never happen. Couples need to learn how to be different and remain connected. Differences are not something that must be avoided. Whether we are talking about sexual desire or parenting styles, it is normal for two people to have differences and to disagree on more than a few issues. Some experts state that even the best relationships have 10 to 12 issues that will never be resolved. Differences, when they are accepted, keep relationships exciting.

PROCESS OF BRIEF THERAPY

Like most brief therapy models, there is an acknowledged time-limited context to the ABCT process. The focus of each session is to work on a single key area or issue. The therapist provides an optimistic and directive counseling style in which symptoms are viewed as solutions to problems. Each session concludes with assignments or behavioral tasks (Bitter & Nicoll, 2000). The focus of the intervention entails asking questions such as "Who is each person?", "Who are they as a couple?", "What does each person want from therapy?", "What are they doing (or not doing) that has led to an unsuccessful outcome?", and "What did they do when the relationship was satisfying?"

In the initial stages of ABCT, the therapist targets the intervention, making sure that the couple is given what they want from therapy. The therapist pays careful attention to the couple's degree of commitment to the therapy process.

Goals of Adlerian Brief Couples Therapy

The goals of ABCT are broad; however, they provide the general guidelines of treatment. Throughout the treatment process, the therapist fosters social interest, helps couples overcome feelings of discouragement and inferiority, helps couples modify their views and goals by changing their life styles, changes the couple's faulty motivations, helps them to feel a sense of quality in the relationship, helps them be contributing members of society, and provides skill-building and skill-using opportunities. This involves helping people to develop skills they lack and to understand why, if they already possess those skills, they do not use them. Finally, the therapist understands the behavior exchanges, the thoughts that underlie them, the way the partners process information, and the way each person creates his or her own reality. In essence, the ABCT therapist seeks to create solutions to problems, increase the couple's choices, and discover and use their individual and collective resources.

Four-Step Process of Adlerian Brief Couples Therapy

The treatment involves identifying unhelpful coping mechanisms and developing alternative approaches. The focus is on the cognitive aspects of the counseling process. The therapist realizes that the partners are discouraged and behave ineffectively because of faulty cognitions that have led to their beliefs and goals. Adlerian therapists believe that once partners are aware of and correct basic mistakes, they will feel and behave better. Therefore, the therapist tends to look for major mistakes in thinking involving issues such as mistrust, selfishness, underconfidence, and unrealistic expectations. The therapy session is structured around the following four central objectives that correspond with the four phases of the therapeutic process:

1. *Step 1: Relationship.* Establish an empathic relationship in which the couple feels understood and accepted by the therapist. The therapist helps each client to connect to his or her internal and external resources. This tends to create movement and empowers the couple to be hopeful about the possibility of a more satisfying life together. According to Bitter and Nicoll (2000), a quality relationship is based on mutual respect, requires an interest in and fascination with the couple and what they bring to therapy, and is facilitated by a col-

laboration that seeks to make an immediate difference in the couple's life.

2. *Step 2: Assessment.* Help couples understand their beliefs, feelings, motives, and goals that determine their life styles. This involves both formal written assessments and process assessments. Couples can fill out inventories prior to therapy that provide information about what the problem is; when it started; precipitating events; a medical history, including any current medications; a social history; and why they are in therapy. Other forms also are helpful. A mini life style interview is conducted; the imago inventory, genograms, marital inventories, and personality devices also are helpful. The therapist also needs to assess the level of marital conflict and the stage of change. All of this information is imperative to tailoring the treatment to the specific couple.

3. *Step 3: Insight.* Help couples to develop insight into mistaken goals and self-defeating behaviors and to find meaning, which will increase the level of participation and degree of tailoring.

4. *Step 4: Reorientation.* Help couples to consider alternatives to the problems, behaviors, or situations and make a commitment to change. Therapeutic gains are maintained over time through relapse prevention strategies.

CASE EXAMPLE

Information about the following couple was collected prior to the first meeting and is summarized as follows.[1]

Scott is a 38-year-old Caucasian man who has been married to Leslie (age 31) for almost 8 years. They have 10-year-old twins and a 6-year-old son. Scott was born the middle of three children and was the youngest boy. He reports that he had a younger sister who was the parents' favorite. He also reports problems of depression, obsessive–compulsive disorder, temper, and aggression. Leslie is the youngest of four girls. She believes her husband's major problem is his temper, whereas he believes her major problem is her attitude, that she is too argumentative. Both report a strong desire to work on the relationship.

Session 1

In approaching Leslie and Scott, the therapist wanted to identify what each person's role was in the unsatisfying marital relationship, to help them

---

[1]The initial session with this couple is available on videotape from Microtraining and Multicultural Development, 25 Burdette Avenue, Framingham, MA 01702.

learn where they learned their roles from, to help them develop clear goals of how they would like things to be different, and to become aware of and use the solutions that they have used in the past.

Therapist (T):   Leslie and Scott. You are both very kind and filled out some forms that help me to understand you guys. If I understand things correctly, Scott is 38, and Leslie is 31, and you have three children. You have a set of twins, age 10, and a 6-year-old. All of the kids must be in school? Can you tell me in your own words what is going on and what you want to work on? What is happening that you don't like?

Leslie (L):   We are going through some tough times in our marriage.

T: Can you talk about what makes them tough times for you?

L: His anger and temper are really getting tough for me to take.

T: So, if it were one word that was the problem, it would be either temper or anger?

L: [Nods in affirmation]

T: How about for you, Scott?

Scott (S):   Attitude.

T: Attitude with a big capital A?

S: Yeah.

T: What do you mean by attitude?

S: Her attitude towards me. I know I am bringing it on with my temper. But my temper is something that I can't just turn off.

The therapist has established that both partners have a problem in the marriage. Both partners contribute to the unhappiness.

T: What is the best solution you have found so far?

L: We haven't.

S: One of us has got to go.

T: One solution is that it is a little better if one of you leaves?

S: It seems to be OK. I'm not at home now.

T: So currently the solution is that you guys are not living together right now.

L: Currently, yes, but it has only been one week.

T: Does that help? Have you done this before?

L: This is the first time.

T: So this is the first time, so that means that things are probably at their lowest right now?

L: Yeah, I would think so.

This exchange allows the therapist to understand that this problem is probably at its worst and that the couple does not seem to have any effective problem-solving methods at this time, other than separation.

T: What do you think each of your roles are in the problem? If you had to put it into your own words, what do you contribute to the problem?

L: Well, I am sure that I contribute a lot. He has told me this before. But it's his temper and how fast that he gets mad is still such a hard thing for me to deal with because it is not just the two of us, he gets the kids involved as well . . .

T: So what is your role? His role is getting angry. So often we have a good picture of what our partner's role is, but not our own. What is your role? He says attitude.

L: Oh, yeah [*laughing*]. Yeah, I do have an attitude when things start going wrong. I do get an attitude and argue back.

T: Is that what an attitude means to you? Arguing back?

S: Yeah, pretty much. She argues back and is just spiteful.

L: I don't feel that I am spiteful or out to get revenge or anything like that. I don't feel that I am that way.

T: (*Nods head*)

L: You know, I just try to prove a point to him if he is acting a certain way, especially if the kids are involved, I try to get him to see it my way.

S: Yeah, your way.

T: How does that work?

L: It doesn't work.

S: Yeah, because it has to be her way.

T: So the idea is to prove a point, and proving a point means to do it my way? To see it my way?

L: Seeing it other than he is seeing it. If he is treating a certain individual in the household in a certain way and I would consider it damaging, I would like to see him stop that.

T: OK. When this is going on that is a good time for you to take a teaching moment? You try to teach him or help him learn something?

S: There is no teaching going on at all. She tells me I am acting pretty much like an ass and she is going to let me know it.

T: I see.

S: What I am trying to do when something like that happens is to get up and get away from it all. Get away from her, the kids or whatever else might be.

T: OK. I think I understand this. Where did you guys learn this from?

S: What, the temper?

T: Well, what you do. This way of interacting is always learned behavior.

L: I have no idea.

S: Well, my getting up is something that I have just started since we have been together. Because there is no telling what is going to happen if I really get going.

T: Well, what I am thinking is where did you learn to handle your frustration in a particular way. It sounds like you have learned that when you are frustrated you need to get angry. And it sounds like when you get frustrated you have learned that you need to keep talking.

L: [Grins]

T: That grin is what we sometimes call a "recognition reflex." Can you think of where you learned this? Often we learn this from our parents.

L: It could be. I was taught to talk things out in order to work out a problem. Not necessarily fight, but to work things through and talk things out.

T: How about from your end, Scott?

S: I would say the temper is just a natural thing. It comes from . . . there are a lot of people in my family that have a hot temper.

T: So you observed that when you were growing up that was the way other people solved problems?

S: Well, I don't think it really solved anything.

T: OK, but that is how people attempted to solve problems. I find that couples often do not have a very good problem-solving strategy and that they just keep using it over and over again even if it doesn't work for them. It probably didn't work for their parents and won't work for you. But you don't have any other ones. You are stuck. I don't know if that makes any sense to you guys?

L: Absolutely.

The therapist has created a situation in which both partners are beginning to see that they have a role in the problem. They are also learning that what they do was learned elsewhere and they should not take their partner's response personally.

T: Yeah. You try harder and harder to do the things you are doing even if they don't really work. One thing we might do is to think about if there is anything else that you might do when you get in a situation like this. An example you gave was dealing with the kids where evidently Scott was doing something. Can you think of a specific time when this happened and what you did and then what your partner did?

L: Are you talking about a time when the kids did something wrong?

T: Well, something that got you guys going at it with one another.

Some additional conversation occurs as the couple tries to settle on an example. The therapist wants to understand the interaction process that leads to conflict for the couple.

L: I wasn't raised in a household where there was violence. I feel there is a certain way to discipline kids. He comes too close to, if not crosses, the line where it becomes excessive and of course I interfere. My job is to protect the kids as their mother and then we end up getting into an argument because of how he handles a situation.

T: Well what led up to this specific one?

S: We have a situation to talk about. Her and me. It has to do with the kids. We were trying to talk privately. We sent the two big ones out. Ashley comes out or comes back in the house. Tyler is in the house. Christopher comes bopping around doing something, and Ashley and Tyler just won't leave us alone. We finally sent them away.

T: We?

S: The two of us.

T: So that was something you agreed on?

It is helpful to look for area of agreement. During conflict, couples feel they disagree on everything.

L: Uh-huh.

S: Yeah, we had to talk and it was pretty important. . . . We were trying to talk it out and Ashley and Tyler were in there just making us frustrated. We finally sent her away. She went into the dining room and was doing something in there. Tyler ran off up to his room saying "I hate you guys. I don't love you anymore" and all that kind of stuff. I said "come here" and gave him a big hug and a kiss and was sitting on the sofa with him. He got wound up and ended up jumping on my legs.

L: And then what happened?

S: I jumped up and grabbed my shoes off the floor and my t-shirt and I went outside.

L: It wasn't that simple. You jumped up and were hollering and swearing at Tyler. Tyler is a 6-year-old and for what he had done I feel you threw a real temper tantrum at that point and then when you started to walk out the door, Ashley was going to walk outside and you started yelling at her and she had nothing to do with the situation.

S: Well, the thing was that she wouldn't go away, and she asked if we could go talk. She was bothering us. Tyler bothered us and I don't think I directly swore at Tyler or anything. I got up and I was swearing about the whole incident.

T: So, let me make sure I get this right. You were having a really emotional topic that you guys have to work on.

L: Yes.

T: So you probably were a little bit worked up anyways.

S: Oh yeah. I was definitely worked up over this.

T: And then the kids bothered you and you are talking about this issue and another child bothers you.

S: And then I went out of the house and now Ashley won't leave us alone either and I am going outside and she says "Where are you going?" and I said I was going outside and she said "Well, I am going with you" and then I said "No, you are not. You are going to stay in the house like you were told and you are going to leave us alone and that is it. I am going outside to get away from you guys."

L: It is not that simple. You holler and you scream and you swear at them and you even call them names. You get in this rage and all she wanted to do was go outside. Not necessarily to be by you, but she just wanted out.

S: But she wouldn't go outside when she needed to.

T: And this is the time that you become really reasonable?

S: No, she wasn't being reasonable.

L: I asked him why he was yelling at her. I asked why she was yelling at him. She didn't do anything to him. She just happened to pass him in the hallway.

S: She is going to go outside now when Dad is going outside and her not going outside and her not doing what she was asked to do was part of my frustration.

L: But your frustration wasn't with her. See, this is just one incident. If he is frustrated at something that is not even a person, let's say something falls out of a cabinet, he gets frustrated. He carries on with his temper tantrum and the very next thing that walks into the room whether it be a dog, one of the kids or me, he turns on that person at that time, and I think that is wrong.

T: So how does that work for you guys?

L: It doesn't work.

T: Oh yeah?

S: Now it is not working at all.

T: Well, it works in some ways though. We usually do things that somehow work for us.

The therapist is helping the couple to see that we seldom do things that don't in some way work. Somehow, each person is getting reinforced for his or her part in this inappropriate dialogue.

S: It is venting. It is just venting on my part.

T: So, what would be different if you knew this problem wasn't there anymore? I don't mean the one that you were talking about with the way that you dealt with one another. If you were to wake up in the morning, and his anger was gone and your attitude was gone, what then?

This is what solution-focused therapists refer to as the "miracle question." Adlerians called it "The Question."

S: Things would be very different.

T: How so?

S: She would be easier to live with.

L: It's a mutual feeling.

T: Huh?

L: I said it is a mutual feeling. It is hard living with somebody who has a temper.

T: Well, OK. But so the advantage of this then is that you live in a struggle? There is always a struggle, that you don't have an easy life?

S: Well, I wouldn't say always. A lot of time there is a struggle.

T: So that is why you do this? To keep life interesting?

S: No, it is kept interesting because this happens.

L: I wish that it could all change is what I want.

T: But then you would have to get close together.

L: What do you mean?

T: If you weren't acting like this wouldn't you be very close together? Very close with one another?

The therapist is stating something that is obvious. Couples often are not aware of the messages that their behavior sends.

L: We probably would be.

T: Would that be a good thing?

The therapist uses a "Columbo" style question (i.e., strange or unusual questions) to help the couple think in a different manner.

L: Yeah, it probably would be.

T: Now, have you had that before in your lives?

L: Back when, I say back before when the kids were very small.

T: So early in your marriage when you guys were maybe infatuated a little bit with one another?

L: Maybe. Even beyond the infatuation part I would think.

T: What was that like? How did you guys live differently at that time?

The therapist helps the couple realize they already know how to act to create a happy marriage.

S: How did we live differently?

T: Yes, what was different about that time?

The therapist helps the couple to clearly see the behavior that was successful.

L: Well, when the kids were little there wasn't too much to make him angry.

T: OK, well, what did you do then if you didn't argue?

L: What do you mean?

T: How did you talk or did you play games with one another? How did you spend your time?

The therapist is helping the couple become more specific about the ways in which they enjoyed being with one another.

S: When they were little we were working.

L: Yeah, we worked a lot.

S: I worked a lot.

L: Yeah, but we spent time with each other and with the kids doing whatever. You know, even if it was watching movies on TV or whatever. Or maybe it was just going somewhere.

T: I see. And now somewhere along the line you get into this role of having these temper outbursts and you get into this role of being kind of a critic.

The therapist hopes they will see that they made a choice even if they were not aware of it.

S: She is more like a referee.

L: Yeah, that is what I feel like. I feel like I have to referee what is going on.

T: What would happen if you stopped that?

L: Somebody is going to get hurt.

T: Hmm. And what would happen if somebody got hurt?

S: I would be in jail.

L: Yeah. He would be in jail all right.

T: So you appreciate what she does?

The therapist uses another statement that helps the couple view each other's actions from a different perspective.

S: If I were hurting somebody I would appreciate it but . . .

T: Are you likely to hurt one of the kids if she . . .

S: Not one of the kids. Never.

This was a strong statement that seems to verify that Scott has control over his anger even though he might not always choose to use it.

T: So if . . .

S: I would not outright just hurt anybody.

L: He may not do it on purpose, but when he loses his temper he loses his frame of thinking.

S: My temper. You are right. I have had a lot of people, her father, for one, tell me that he has never seen anything like my temper before.

T: So this is probably one of the things that you are best at. You are best at having a temper?

The therapist uses this reflection to help Scott to see that he is somehow proud of this self-defeating characteristic.

S: Well, I don't know if I am . . .

T: I mean, you are known for this?

S: I have been for the last 10 years, anyway. I know that I didn't take a whole lot from people when I was younger either. I didn't take any lip from anybody.

T: It sounds like that is still what sort of happens when the kids have lip right now. You don't take much.

S: Yes, well it is the lip. I can take some of it, but if they don't do what they are told . . . you know I don't want to beat the kids. You know I just don't want to beat kids.

L: But you have physically grabbed them and yanked on their arms and done other things.

At this point in the interview, the therapist needs to remember that, as a mandated reporter of suspected child abuse, he or she must assess for physical and emotional child abuse. In this case, the clinician was not worried that this was occurring, because intake forms indicated that the situation had already been evaluated by the Department of Children and Family Services.

S: Well, I got to make them go where they are supposed to be going.

The therapist can hear that Scott believes that Leslie is not firm enough with the children.

L: But I don't think you need to be physical like that.

S: I need to make them go upstairs or something like that.

T: So the part where it gets physical, is this when he steps over the line for you, Leslie?

L: Yes, well, a lot of times it is with his words and then he gets to the physical part.

T: So how far would you let it go?

L: Now? Not very far at all. Now I try to interfere before things have gotten out of hand because this has actually taken a real toll on the kids.

T: It sounds like it has taken a real toll on you guys, too.

The therapist helps them realize that everyone in the home is suffering from this relationship pattern.

L: Well, it is very much so and we have had the same argument about his temper for probably seven years.

T: Is the biggest part of the problem for you what the kids do, or is the biggest part of the problem his reaction to what happens? Because I think I could help you handle the kids a little differently. I think we could probably work at that.

The therapist attempts to separate the issues to make the problem more manageable.

S: A lot of it is a discipline thing. I don't think that they really had, and it is not their fault and it is not my fault solely. They have never . . . well I was pretty harshly disciplined and I am not necessarily the one who wants to go out there and beat my kids but when they don't do what they are told something is going to happen. It is like "Straighten up your room." They don't straighten up the room. All right, fine, then I am going to take you and make you and show you where it is at.

T: Leslie, how would you do it if the kids didn't straighten up their room up?

S: She would do it herself.

L: Well, if they didn't straighten up their room they would be grounded.

T: So somewhere . . .

S: But she would be straightening up the room.

L: Or I would go up there and help. The older ones, no, but my 6-year-old, yes. I would help him.

T: So it sounds like you don't approve of his ways and he doesn't approve of your way.

The therapist helps the couple to realize that both of their ways are not acceptable.

S: Now what did you just do over this past weekend? You went through and cleaned their rooms because they couldn't do it the way you wanted.

L: That is dusting and stuff. I prefer to do that myself as far as doing the housework overall but they can just straighten up their own room.

The therapist did not respond to this "reacting" type of communication, which had become a habit for the couple.

T: So, do you think it would help if you guys had some agreed way of handling the kids that you respected? Like if it is Scott's problem, he will handle it and you will stay out of it as long as he handles it this way, or if it is Leslie's problem and Scott you will stay out of it as long as she handles it this way. Have you ever had a class in parenting?

S: No, we kind of jumped right into this. Wham, bam and here we are.

T: Kind of like the rest of us. There are not a lot of prerequisites for this other than physical.

The therapist "joins" the couple to let them know they are not alone.

L: Yeah. Right, right.

T: So it sounds like Scott is really good at being firm and Leslie is really good at being kind. You have got kind of a good cop/bad cop sort of a deal going on here. There is a system that works really simply and it is deceptively simple but I am wondering . . . well when you said that you would ground them. I wonder what would happen if the kids came in and you were talking and you just said this very simple thing that is called 1-2-3 Magic (Phelan, 1995). Have you ever done this?

The therapist attempts to identify each partner's strength. The 1-2-3 Magic program is a deceptively simple approach that is easy to learn and works quickly.

L: You know what, we have. We learned that through the school.

S: Yeah, and it never . . .

T: How did that work?

S: We never did follow up with it all that much.

L: It worked while we stuck to it.

T: I see.

The therapist acknowledges that they could solve this problem if they choose.

L: I mean, every now and then I catch myself using it but we were getting to the point where with my six-year-old we would tell him that it was 1 and he would tell us it was 2. He was starting to rebel against it.

S: And then when he says that you say "3, go to your room" he would say "6."

L: Uh-huh.

T: So you guys, when you learned that at school it worked OK. I mean that you guys thought that it was a good idea and while you did it it worked.

L: I think it worked. I think it worked. It seemed to go over a lot easier with the older ones because they learned it the first time . . .

T: That is really impressive. When I asked you guys before if you had a solution for this and you said you didn't but this sounds like a solution for as long as you did it.

The therapist is identifying a strength the couple possesses.

S: I guess maybe that is something that we have to stick to.

L: But it is remembering to do it when you are all heated up.

T: That is important. You see part of this approach to parenting is staying out of each others' roles. In other words, "I respect you enough to raise the kids the way we agreed to" and then if you don't, you know . . . if she cleans the room or picks up their stuff or if you should happen to yell at them later on you bring it back and say "Can we talk about what happened?" I don't know if something like that works for you guys. You see, there is one thing that I find that happens, and it sounds like it is going on with you guys, is that when you get into these situations that very quickly escalate. I learned that once your heartbeat gets above 96 beats a minute, do you know what happens?

The therapist is providing psychoeducation.

S: All bets are off.

T: Yeah, it is fight or flight for you. It is getting defensive. Somehow you have to get some way for you guys to soothe things a little bit. To keep things down a little bit and if you had an agreed-upon strategy to use that might really be helpful. You know, this 1-2-3 Magic. Do you have the book or something?

The therapist realizes that teaching "soft start-up" and "soothing" (Gottman, Driver, & Tabares, 2003) will need to occur in a future session.

L: We saw a videotape.

S: It was a set of two videotapes that we went to see with a counselor or somebody at the school.

T: But you know how to do it.

S: Yeah. 1, you get the warning. 2 . . .

T: Five seconds later it is 2.

The therapist is making sure that they still remember this process. This type of rehearsal helps to increase treatment compliance.

S: If they keep it up it is 2.

T: Five seconds later 3.

S: Uh-huh.

L: Uh-huh.

T: And what it does, is that it stops you from talking. It stops you from yelling and escalating. It stops you from moralizing and it just goes "1-2-3. Go to your room and take 6" or "take 10."

S: What do you do when they go stomping up the stairs and they slam their door?

T: You either let it go or say "Five minutes more" and then you set a timer. I think if you can work at that it is a compromise between what the two of you do. I think that is why it sounds like it was a pretty good idea because something would be done and that is what you want to see happen, Scott. You don't want to see the kids getting away with stuff and it would be done kindly, which is what you want to see happen, Leslie, because it sounds like relationships are really important for you. You kind of are like a lot of men and women because the guys are more the action and the doers and the women are more concerned with the relationship and what goes on inside the family. One is more with the rules and the other with relationships.

The therapist attempts to convey to them again that they are not alone.

S: I have always kind of . . . I don't know. I guess I am supposed to be the one who does the discipline.

L: I totally disagree.

T: Did you happen to see her head when you said that?

S: Yeah.

T: So, in the family that you grew up in the father was the disciplinarian.

S: Yeah.

T: And in the family that you grew up in?

L: It was both parents.

T: I think that is the way that most families are now. We expect husbands and wives both to do discipline. Because what happens if you do the discipline? You are not going to be liked. You are going to be coming into situations that you don't really understand and are accepted to be a referee or a judge.

The therapist responds to let Leslie know that she needs to take more action and for Scott to realize the downside of his efforts.

S: Well, I have always thought that if she is having a hard time with them then I will poke in and say "All right, fine. Now this is the way things are going to happen."

T: Well, let's check this out. Leslie, do you appreciate when he does that?

The therapist checks out Scott's mistaken assumption.

L: No. Not unless I ask.

T: So what would happen if that were the rule? Assume that you are not needed, Scott, that she really wants to learn how to do discipline. She wants to learn how to be firm like you and to handle these situations but she needs practice and she won't get practice if you keep sticking your . . .

S: Nose in.

T: You know, it is just a thought.

The therapist is attempting to influence Scott without directly telling him what to do.

S: We can give it a shot.

T: We call it respect. I respect that she can handle this, and for you it is going to be respect too. You know what I find that might be helpful for you? You may have to leave if he starts to work with the kids.

L: OK, but what happens when we get to the point of . . . yes, you mean leave with the kids?

T: No, no, no. I am glad that you clarified that. No, what I am suggesting is that like if you go 1 and you go 2 rather than saying anything, she needs to keep quiet and needs to respect you and to tell herself that you will handle it.

L: Well, that is fine as long as he sticks to that but often when he gets angry with the name calling and physically grabbing the children . . .

T: We have agreed that that is unacceptable. He said he doesn't want to do that anymore, and if you can agree not to comment on him anymore I think we have got one place to start with this.

L: I could do that if he is doing the 1-2-3 Magic. I know I could.

T: What else could we do to help? One of the things that I noticed on the questionnaires is that both of you reported some depression. Did you know that, or is that just something that is recent because you are separated? I noticed that there was trouble with sleeping.

S: No, this is something that I have been trying to deal with and treat for awhile, and I don't know. Maybe sometimes we went about things in the wrong way. We get depressed, don't like where we are staying, sell that house and buy another.

T: So that is your treatment for depression? To buy a new house?

S: I don't know if that was actually what it was but it seemed like when it got really bad there for awhile, he would get rid of it, all of it.

T: So just get a new situation . . . a new challenge?

S: Why not, just a fresh start with new people around.

L: It didn't work.

S: It didn't work, no. Well, it worked for maybe a year.

T: This is when you were married you did this?

S: Yes. Like I said, this is something I have been trying to treat. I have been going to more extensive steps now.

T: What else have you tried other than buying and selling a house?

L: Medication.

S: I went to a new doctor. I was on Prozac, and that didn't do anything. I went to Paxil and then BuSpar. The Paxil I didn't like what it did to me when I got started on it. I didn't like what it did to me coming off of it and I just stopped. I was sick for about two weeks trying to get over the withdrawal from the medication.

T: Did you notice any change when he was on the medication, Leslie?

L: The Prozac was bad. He was even worse but the first time he was on BuSpar . . .

S: The Paxil was the one that was doing it.

L: Yeah, whichever one it was. The first time he was on it there was some kind of a change. He was more mellow, but the last time he was on it, it was almost like he got immune to it.

T: So there is some hope by looking at maybe some medication to treat the physical part of the problem. There are a couple of other things that have been known to be really helpful and I don't know how these things fit into your lifestyle. Do you exercise?

S: Not as far as off the job. What I do is kind of physical.

The therapist suggests strategies that might treat the depression as well as help with self-management and self-control.

T: That is one thing that they say works. Riding a bike, running, walking vigorously and getting your heart rate up and keeping it up for about 40 minutes. If you can do this four times a week and again I don't know your schedule . . . I know you work hard and that you are going to say . . .

S: I could probably go out there . . .

T: The kids would probably go with you.

S: I am going to ride my bike and be racing and getting my heart rate up like. They ain't going to stay with me.

T: OK, so that is a possibility but in the winter I suppose it could be a stationary bike or something. Now how about you, Leslie, you have had some depressive symptoms, too.

The therapist attempts to make it clear that both partners have the problem.

L: Yeah, but mine have only been like going on for six months to a year.

S: Longer than that.

L: No it hasn't.

T: So, you think it is longer? OK.

L: It is just because of finally being fed up with the situation but I have never been on medication for it or anything.

T: Do you have anything that works? Something that is helpful to you?

L: So far, well, he left . . .

T: Did that help? Have you slept better?

L: I actually have slept better. I have had a little more relaxation and have been able to function at a higher level.

T: So maybe a change in the situation helps. If you can change the situation you can feel safer, and maybe that helps the depression. A second thing that really works, and I don't know you well enough about this one either, but they have done some studies with some really angry people, actually prisoners. They have been so angry that they ended up in prison and they had them meditate and they found that people who meditated for 30 minutes a day did better than the group that went to therapy and better than the group that took medicine.

S: Well, maybe I had better meditate, exercise, take therapy and get some medicine!

T: You don't want to leave any stones unturned, you know.

S: I am hitting all the bases. I have got to get this stuff straightened out, you see.

T: What meditation is, is basically where you just focus on relaxing and breathing. There are many different kinds of meditation that you can follow. It might be worth either talking to somebody or getting a meditation tape that you can work with.

S: I have gotten this new doctor and I am on a different medication. I started with the therapist because I went and talked with the doctor and he said that I have some underlying and deep-seated anger problems. I had begun to go to a group called Rage-Aholics and then there was another problem. I had OCD. [obsessive–compulsive disorder]

T: So that was one thing that worked until this event happened. At least you were making some progress at it. You may have these underlying issues, and I think it is good that you see a therapist and talk those through but after you get those issues out, you still are going to need some new ways to be with others. That is why I think if you could start some kind of exercise program and maybe even taking some time to meditate daily, I think that is going to reduce this problem significantly for you so that you are going to have more of a pause before you respond. I think what happens is that something happens and this is like a knee jerk reaction for him.

The therapist explains the purpose of this recommendation.

L: Uh-huh.

T: He needs to condition himself so that he can stop when he wants to and then not respond. It also sounds like you have a lot of things and ingredients that couples have when the relationship "goes south." They are negative ingredients like criticism. It sounds like that is going on. Then there is contempt where you look at somebody in a negative way. It sounds like that is also present and then each of you are defending your position. You are defensive. You defend your right to do what you are doing. You defend your attitude. You defend your anger and then there is this stonewall that you put up sometimes where you just won't talk. You remove yourself from one another. Those are the four things that really make a relationship go bad. If you can learn how to pause, you can have some choices. You can choose rather than defending maybe you can take a deep breath and you can say "So, if I understand you right, you think we need to have the kids leave us alone so we can talk" and then he will say "Yeah, that is exactly right" and you will say "I agree with you." How should we handle it? I think there is some real cooperation that you guys show when you keep your heart rates down a little.

S: Yeah, mine is so fast to go up, though.

T: Well, that is why I think you guys need some of this other training. I don't think it is just going to happen by talking. I think you are going to have to do some work. You are going to have to do some training. The one thing I wonder . . . what do you guys do for fun? I couldn't tell on the forms.

S: [*Laughing*] Fight.

T: OK, fight. You guys must have lots of fun, then?

L: You know, I used to because I am a talker, believe it or not, but I used to enjoy just sitting and talking to him as long as he would stay awake and listen. You know, just spending time with one another used to be fun. We do things every now and then over the years but it has become less and less.

The client is engaged and seems to have remembered some enjoyable times as a couple.

T: Is there a reason why that is? Maybe it is because you have not been getting along?

The therapist makes a guess at the obvious.

L: Well, that is part of it. Finances and stuff like that. Always busy working and trying to take care of the household.

S: We got bills to pay and work to do, and you know you can't always work on the fun.

T: Well, they say that relationships are satisfying depending on the amount of positive exchanges that go on between the couple. You probably had a lot of them when you were dating because you took the time to be with one another and to do some of the things with one another. I am wondering if you could start dating again.

S: Oh, and lead up to this?

T: What you do on a date is you agree that no issues will be raised so that when you go out the purpose is just to enjoy one another, so if somebody starts to say something negative, the other one goes "Time out. This isn't the time for that," and you can take turns arranging the date. So this week might be your date, Scott, and if you want to go every week or every other week then it would be your date next, Leslie. If you take her to a baseball game, she might want to take you to a ballet. You might want to go for a walk, and she might want to go to a movie, but whatever the person says . . . you are going to go. "Bring your hiking boots because we are going out for a trek through nature" if that is the date. You say "Cool" and you just agree with it, and if he says "I just want to do something" you say "Fine." This is what you need to do to get some fresh air in your relationship. Could you imagine yourself doing that?

S: That would be cool. Enjoying being around her would be a lot more fun.

L: [Nods her head and looks at Scott]

T: Somewhere along the line you guys have got to put some boundaries on a few of these things and really learn some different ways to be with one another. We talked about dating. We talked about maybe exercising. You are already doing other stuff with medication. We talked about meditation. We talked about discipline. There is a lot of stuff we came up with here. Is this what you were hoping for? Is this the kind of thing that might be helpful for you? Some of these tools?

The therapist summarizes some of the general recommendations.

S: Yes.

L: I would think so.

Session 2

The couple returned for the second session indicating that they had some good and bad times together this past week. Scott spent all day Saturday and Sunday at home and did not lose his temper. They felt they both did well using the 1-2-3 Magic Program (Phelan, 1995) solutions. Scott reported that he had not started an exercise program but had thought about it. He also had thought about doing some meditation.

T: What does it mean when you think about doing something?

S: What do you mean?

T: Is this a step you take before actually doing something or the step you take when you are not going to do something?

S: Oh! Well, I guess I am going to do both of these but have not found the time.

T: Does the time look better for next week?

S: No, but I will do it.

Leslie kept quiet during this exchange and did not make any negative or positive comments.

T: What was going on with you while Scott and I were discussing his week and future plans?

L: At first I was angry that he was procrastinating again, but the more I let him talk the more I believe he will do it next week.

T: So, what did you learn?

L: I guess I need to be patient and let Scott work things out alone.

T: Scott. Would that be helpful?

S: Damn straight it would.

The session progressed, and Scott and Leslie agreed that they would go out together this coming week for a date. It was agreed that Leslie would arrange the date this week and that no problems could be raised or discussed during date time. This was a time for positive exchanges and pleasurable activities.

Sessions 3–5

In these sessions, the couple continued to learn to respond to each other in a different fashion. Leslie learned to stay silent and to be supportive of Scott. Scott learned to use the 1-2-3 Magic Program (Phelan, 1995) and also read a book on positive discipline (Nelsen, 1996). He was concentrating on being more a positive support for his children and less of a disciplinarian. Perhaps most important was that he did daily meditation and was exercising four or five times each week and reported that this is the best he had felt in years. The therapist realized that the couple's conflicts were often created by the language use.

L: Scott just can't handle it when the kids speak up.

S: I shouldn't have to handle it. I am not going to have MY children disrespect me.

T: Can we stop for a moment? What just happened?

L: He can't take feedback and becomes a jerk.

S: She thinks the kids can do whatever they damn well please.

T: Would you be interested in a different explanation? [*Both nod their heads*] My guess is that Scott reacts to what he thinks is an attack by you, Leslie. I understand that is not your intent. You actually hope that by pointing things out to Scott he will be able to correct them and make the needed changes to improve relationships. [*Both nod their heads again*] Leslie, I am wondering if you would be willing to talk in a manner that will increase the likelihood that Scott can hear you?

L: Sure.

T: I wonder how Scott would respond if you were to provide a "softer start-up" to your comments?

L: I don't understand what you are talking about.

T: Maybe an example of another way to say what you said a moment ago will help. How about something like this, "Scott, you do so many things so well. If I were in need of protection or help you would be my rock. However, I am really puzzled that whenever the kids seem to respond or talk back to you, you like fall apart." What would you say back to that, Scott?

S: Well, I guess I'd say that I had not looked at it that way. [*Looking at Leslie*] Is he right that I would be the one you would look to for help?

L: Of course. We have been through so much together.

T: Did you notice what I did that was different?

Scott and Leslie spent the last 15 minutes of the fourth session learning how to use editing to raise issues in ways that decrease defensiveness. Both seemed surprised at the difference a few words can make. Despite Scott's strong presence, he was fragile and needed to hear some positive messages from Leslie. Leslie was relieved when Scott finally heard what she was saying and confirmed her observations about his actions.

Scott moved home, and the couple decided to stop treatment but agreed that if either felt the other was sliding back they would call for an appointment.

The couple was able to make some positive progress in a short five-session treatment. Although there still were many unaddressed treatment issues, the couple did not choose to continue therapy. This is a common occurrence, as many clients tend to stop once the presenting problem is treated. It is significant that the couple agreed to return for additional treatment if the need arises.

CONCLUSION

Brief couples therapy is a natural fit with Adler's theory. Interventions can occur in a brief time period with long-lasting results. The approach is active, directive, and optimistic. The therapist focuses on specific issues and assigns behavioral tasks. The case example of Scott and Leslie demonstrates how the therapist integrates strategies from many different theories to produce a positive outcome.

10

GROUP THERAPY

Adlerians view all problems as social and interactive by nature. Group psychotherapy, therefore, is a great resource for influencing an individual's attitude and behavior. Because all people are trying to fit into the social world, and our behavior is holistic and purposive, group interaction is viewed as most appropriate and central to the Adlerian model of helping. The focus of group therapy or counseling ranges from working with normal development issues to dealing with problems of personality or life style. In this chapter, we present a rationale and a clear, step-by-step process for conducting Adlerian group therapy with adults. We also offer many practical insights into group dynamics and the therapeutic forces that are present.

Alfred Adler was one of the first mental health workers to use group methods in a deliberate and systematic fashion (Hoffman, 1994). According to Moreno (1953), Adler started group therapy in 1910. The techniques that he used were unrelated to the concepts and practices of individual therapy. In 1931, Moreno (1953) coined the term *group psychotherapy*, which then became the formal name of this approach. In his work in the child guidance clinics in Vienna, Adler met with groups of teachers and parents and talked to them about problems they were experiencing with the children in their lives. This procedure became his open-forum counseling process. The goal of these sessions was to help the greatest number of people in the shortest amount of time.

In 1928, Rudolf Dreikurs published an article entitled "The Development of Mental Hygiene and Beyond" (Terner & Pew, 1978). In it, he described in detail the dynamic differences between individual therapy and group therapy. He also began using groups in his private practice at this time (Terner & Pew, 1978).

It is not surprising that Adler was involved with the development of group work, as this is a natural tool for addressing relationships. In groups, members can experiment with interactions and produce changes in their mistaken goals and faulty logic. The history of counseling and psychotherapy has been based on the assumption that privacy is an imperative; however, the need for privacy fits better in an autocratic society than a democratic one. Group therapy stands in opposition to the concepts of isolation and inequality. The group takes individual problems and makes them a common concern of the entire group. It has been said that group work is both a product of democracy as well as a tool for meeting its goals.

RATIONALE FOR GROUP THERAPY

Perhaps the best learning is experiential learning, in which people can learn about social problems and their solutions firsthand. The group itself becomes both the problem and the solution. The group process allows members to interact in a unique and individual fashion, sometimes with nonverbal communication and sometimes with verbal work.

The group environment provides a safe milieu in which individuals can learn how to have a voice in life. Group members learn how to understand and accept differences as well as to identify and understand universal thoughts and feelings. Providing support for members is perhaps the group's most important function. Group members both give help and receive help. This setting is a safe one that is noncompetitive, caring, and supportive.

The group setting also provides situations in which individuals can practice social skills, as opposed to individual therapy, where they can talk about life and life's issues without having the opportunity to practice social skills. The goal of the group is to create an atmosphere of social equality in which everyone in the group has worth, value, and rights.

In an era when people are shrinking and withdrawing from one another, group therapy can be very useful. A recent book, *Bowling Alone: Collapse and Revival of the American Community* (Putnam, 2000), indicated that more and more people are bowling each year, and yet fewer and fewer bowling leagues are being formed. Individuals are becoming separated from the groups to which they could belong. Group counseling provides involvement with others rather than withdrawal. The group approach also assists individuals in the formation of values.

NATURE OF THE GROUP PROCESS

The beliefs, feelings, and behaviors of the members are the focus of the group process. Values, attitudes, and purpose also are considered. The interpersonal nature of the group makes it possible for the members to not only become aware of their mistaken and self-defeating beliefs and actions but also to feel encouraged to change them. The group also uses encouragement to help group members be aware of their assets and the efforts they are making in pursuit of their stated goals. The group is a work group. Each person comes to the group with problems and is ready to acknowledge and work on those problems. The focus of the group is on helping members establish personal goals and, by challenging their perceptions, enable them to cope effectively with the tasks of life.

The group therapy situation is structured. Structure brings order to human interactions. The members of the group cocreate the structure, as in a democratic society. The group leader is trained and understands how to create structure within the group setting. According to Sonstegard, Dreikurs, and Bitter (1982), Adlerians work on many levels but anticipate that the groups will do the following: form and maintain interactive relationships, the more therapeutic of which are characterized by acceptance and mutual respect; examine the purposes and motivations underlying members' actions and behaviors and replace criticism with understanding; help individuals understand the goals they are pursuing through tentative psychological disclosures; and support reorientation and redirection when a member's life warrants it.

GROUP INTERACTION

People are involved in ongoing social interaction. At some point in their lives, they must face the challenge of deciding between serving their own interest and those of the groups to which they belong. In the group, Adlerians watch very carefully the psychological movement of the individual. Some members will move toward being a part of the group, whereas others will move away from the group. In very simple terms, some people try very hard to please and to be part of the group, whereas others might feel that "I belong only if I get my way."

Adlerians believe that the balance between social interest and self-interest can best be served through involvement in the give-and-take of the group. Because we are social beings, we live in and are influenced by others in the social system, and we behave in such a way as to belong by getting the approval of others. Each individual strives to belong and to be accepted and valued by others. The methods and strategies that a person uses to find significance and recognition will indicate how he or she chooses to belong.

The group will become a microcosm of the members' experiences. It is believed that group members will interact in the group as they do in other real life social situations. Sometimes, group members seek the same position they held in their family constellation. People also display their faulty beliefs with ineffective approaches to meeting the tasks of life. Through their actions in the group, the participants' life styles are revealed, as are their assumptions about people and relationships. The therapist, instead of simply listening to stories about how people behave, can actually observe and experience the participants and their behavior.

INTERPERSONAL LEARNING

According to Dinkmeyer and Sperry (2000), interpersonal learning facilitates change through the following process. First, the group becomes a social microcosm that represents each member's social world. Group members, through feedback and self-awareness, become aware of the purpose and consequences of their interpersonal behavior. For communication in the group to be effective, the transaction must be real and genuine; the participants must communicate their involvement and feelings about what they are experiencing as well as the feelings provoked by other group members' communication. Change occurs as a result of awareness, involvement, and commitment to make specific changes. These changes are contingent on the degree to which the member feels he or she belongs to the group and the resultant importance he or she places on being accepted and valued by the other members as well as encouragement from both group members and the group leader. Through the process of trying on new behaviors and beliefs, and learning that it is safe to change, the group member gains the courage to continue making positive movement.

The whole process can be described as setting into motion a cycle in which the following occur: perceptions and beliefs change; courage and a sense of belonging enable members to try on new behaviors; involvement and risk-taking are rewarded by acceptance and belonging; fear of making a mistake is replaced by the courage to be imperfect, which reduces anxiety and insecurity; and group members become able to try additional change as their self-esteem and self-worth develop (Dinkmeyer & Sperry, 2000, p. 178).

STEP-BY-STEP PROCESS

The Adlerian model for group therapy is presented in Figure 10.1. Adlerian group therapy is an integration of Adlerian psychology with socially

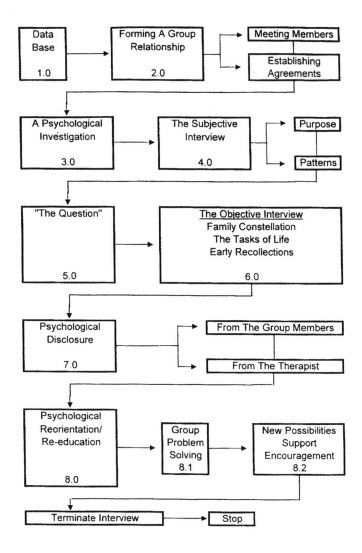

Figure 10.1. Adlerian group therapy, step by step. From *Adlerian Group Counseling and Therapy: Step by Step* (p. 61), by M. A. Sonstegard and J. R. Bitter, 2004, New York: Brunner Routledge. Copyright 2004 by Brunner Routledge. Reprinted with permission.

constructed systemic and brief approaches and is based on the holistic approach developed by Rudolf Dreikurs (1960, 1997) and Manford Sonstegard and James Bitter (2004).

Creating a Database

Information about clients and potential group members is often available to the therapist. An early database can help the therapist form initial guesses about the group by making hypotheses that can later be confirmed or disregarded. To be useful, these initial hypotheses require at least some initial data that are psychologically relevant, for example: where the person fits in his or her family constellation, how the person describes his or her personal concerns, a description of strengths and weaknesses, what the person hopes to get out of the group experience. Adler's hypotheses were often so accurate that in an initial meeting with clients his guesses were immediately confirmed (A. Adler, 1970).

Although the prescreening of group members is common today, Adlerians typically reject this procedure. Prescreening too often is used to eliminate from the group the people who could most benefit from the experience (i.e., those who are disruptive, self-absorbed, or isolated). Adlerians have no objection, though, to pregroup meetings that provide potential members with information about group process and dynamics and help them establish goals for the experience.

Forming a Group Relationship

For groups to get off to a smooth start, it is important for the group leader to address certain logistics, such as size, location, and balance of group members. Most of these issues require the therapist to reflect on what would constitute optimal conditions (Yalom, 1995):

- How many people can the therapist maintain fully engaged for an hour or more?
- Is there a location available that is private, free from distractions and noise, and with good lighting?
- What balance of men and women, age, and culture, or how much homogeneity versus heterogeneity, is needed in the group?

If these logistics can adequately be addressed, most group psychotherapy sessions take place in a moderately comfortable setting with chairs placed in a circle.

Meeting Members

Therapists must learn to begin the group process with a presence and interest in the people they meet. They must learn to concurrently observe the group as a process entity. A number of questions facilitate such an observation:

- Who sits with whom?
- How do people enter and find a place in the group?
- Who talks to whom?
- What is the level of comfort or discomfort in the room?
- What kind of atmosphere seems to be present?
- What initial impressions are being formed?

We conduct our group sessions in the following manner. When everyone is present, we catch everyone up on how the group was formed and any hopes or desires that we have for the group process, and then we ask the group members to briefly introduce themselves.

By focusing on relationships from the very beginning, we are laying a foundation for cohesiveness and connection. Although these initial introductions are important, they do not have to take up the entire session, or even a major portion of it. Introductions are a chance for group members to break the ice, to use their voices perhaps for the first time in a group setting.

When group members have had a chance to introduce each other, we generally ask them what agreements they would like to have in the group. As much as possible, Adlerians want group members to establish their own agreements for the group experience. We do not use the concept of group rules, or even ground rules, which are terms that suggest and too often reflect therapists' authoritarian history and the superior–inferior relationships inherent in that history.

Although these decisions may seem rather basic, they give group members some control over the group structure, and they lay the foundation for dealing with more important issues. Is the group open or closed? Can members come and go as they please, or do they need to always be present? Can a group member choose to be silent, to observe and not talk? What will the use and limitations of confidentiality be, and how will this essential concept be defined?

The Psychological Investigation

Adlerian psychological investigations focus on personal patterns and motivations expressed and enacted within the group and the social context experienced by individual group members. Although most such investigations start with a subjective interview that allows group members to bring up various issues, Adlerians may introduce more objective inquiries, including The Question, family constellation and birth order, an evaluation of the life tasks, or early recollections.

At first, what members choose to discuss in group sessions can be completely open. It is often enough to start by asking "So, what should we talk about?" When the group leader opens with such an invitation, he or she must be prepared to be tested on the integrity of the offer. Regardless of the topics chosen, however, each person's storyline, interaction processes, and group contributions will always reveal individual patterns and motivation.

The most common Adlerian interventions during an initial psychological investigation of the group include asking members to provide the group with specific incidents to which they attach meaning, asking group members to indicate how they feel in the midst of specific interactions, and watching the effect of individual contributions on the group as a whole.

The Subjective Interview

The subjective interview seeks to develop both individual storylines and a group consensus about what is relevant and important to most of the members. Finding a common language of inquiry often is a first step in this process.

Balancing the development of individual storylines with the need for group interaction is critical. Finding or asking about commonalities that exist in the presentations of multiple members also helps build a sense of cohesiveness in the group. Even if group members do not have similar life experiences, they can be asked to speculate about what meaning individual stories might have for the persons telling them. What seems to matter to the person? What does it say about the storyteller? What goals or purposes seem to motivate the person?

Often, group members will say things that seem on the surface to be contradictory. For example, Jim might note that he tries to please his parents but that he also gets angry at them and explodes. Adlerians treat such statements as two points on a line. In effect, they want to know how both of these statements can be true.

The Question

Adler (1927) used to ask his clients "What would you be like if you were well?" Dreikurs (1997) adapted what became known in Adlerian circles as "The Question" in the following manner. "What would you be doing if you didn't have these symptoms or problems?" Or, "How would your life be different if you didn't have these symptoms or problems?" Dreikurs used The Question for the purpose of making a differential diagnosis. The answer could help differentiate whether a problem was physical or psychological.

The Objective Interview

Many Adlerian therapists will skip the objective interview when they have developed enough of an understanding of the people in the group from the subjective interview or through the use of The Question. Standard Adlerian assessment procedures include an understanding of each member's family constellations, his or her personal approaches to the life tasks, or an interpretation of each individual's early recollections. Some therapists use one or more of these assessment tools to confirm what they already suspect about member patterns and motivations. Other therapists, however, prefer a more intensive process called the *life style analysis* (Powers & Griffith, 1995; Shulman & Mosak, 1988).

An assessment of the family constellation will allow the therapist to identify major influences in the client's life, interpretations the client generates about his or her position in the family, experiences the person had with his or her parents that set a guideline for gender identity, and his or her interpretation of life in society as put forth by the parents.

Within this assessment, the client's phenomenological interpretation of birth order is essential. Across cultures, siblings tend to have a greater influence on personality development than parental involvement (McGoldrick, Watson, & Benton, 1999). Listening to each individual's interpretation of his or her sense of place in the family helps the therapist understand the client's overall place in the world.

An assessment of life tasks allows the Adlerian therapist to discover coping patterns that individuals use to handle life's problems, to look for areas of support and dysfunction in daily living, and to observe the extent to which group behaviors manifest themselves in other parts of people's lives.

Adlerian therapists use early recollections (Clark, 2002) for different purposes, including an assessment of each person's convictions about the self, others, life, and ethical stances; an assessment of group members' stances and relation to the group process in the therapy relationship; verification of coping patterns and motivations; and an identification of strengths, assets, or interfering ideas or mistaken notions in each person's life.

Because Adlerians use early recollections as a projective technique (Mosak, 1958), we tend to introduce them with an open-ended request: "Think back to when you were very little and tell me something that happened to you one time." Most people have between 6 and 12 early age (under age 10) memories. These memories are self-selected stories that the individual uses to maintain a sense of constancy about the self and life (A. Adler, 1927, 1957). The content of memories is not as important as the reasons why the client has them. The client's life position in the memory is often as revealing as thinking about the memory as a story with a moral (a specific meaning). Interpretations are achieved collaboratively within groups, with group members offering guesses about possible meanings. In the end, each person must agree with or recognize the interpretations that have personal meaning

Psychological Disclosure

Psychological disclosures might happen at any point in the group process. Although initial disclosures tend to come from the group leader, it is important to involve group members in the process as soon as possible. The group is invited to investigate meaning in each others' lives as a foundation for working with each other and considering desired changes. Psychological disclosures are used to create understanding by making unconscious processes conscious, confronting useless interactions in the group, or exploring possible motivations behind behaviors.

Psychological Reorientation–Education

Psychological reorientation is the endpoint of therapy and is about changing group members' stances in life. This involves helping people to cope and approach life tasks in a useful manner. Adlerians define this usefulness as creating a sense of belonging and feeling valued in one's community. This requires a movement away from self-absorption, withdrawal, isolation, or self-protection toward the development of a community feeling and social interest. The enactment of traits commonly associated with a community feeling such as courage, acceptance of imperfection, confidence, a sense of humor, a willingness to contribute, an interest in the welfare of others, and a friendly approach to people is also present (A. Adler, 1956; Bitter & West, 1979).

Sometimes, psychological reorientation is accomplished through the modification of a motivation, a creation of new meaning, or the development of new possibilities or options. The most common reorientation process is group problem solving.

Group Problem Solving

Successful group problem solving depends on, and flows from, the establishment of a psychological understanding of the self and other people involved in any problem. Group problem solving and the generation of new possibilities tend to go hand in hand. In a sense, this step in group problem solving has been part of the group process from the beginning. Problem-solving mechanisms include establishing an atmosphere of safety and mutual respect, clarifying a psychological understanding of the group members' interactions, asking the group member whether he or she is open to input from others, generating as many options as possible, and identifying a constructive possibility that seems to fit that client.

Enactment of new possibilities almost always requires support and encouragement. It is not uncommon for Adlerians to use role playing or other psychodramatic techniques to aid group members in the practice of proposed solutions (Corsini, 1966). Support and encouragement also come in the form of having groups of peers standing in your corner and believing in you. Being part of the group also means that you never have to experience success alone. Therapy groups are ideal places in which to celebrate members' successes.

Although most group sessions seem to arrive at a natural stopping point, one of the group leader's tasks is to be cognizant of time and to not generate new material or processes when the end of the session's work is nearing. Indeed, even though most groups are ongoing, Adlerians treat each group as an entity in itself; that is, the group process for the session may serve as a goal or a purpose, propose or complete some work for one or more group members, or facilitate a new learning or meaning. Summarizing the achievements of sessions lays the groundwork for the eventuality that the group itself will one day terminate.

PROGRESS IN THE GROUP

The method for measuring progress is one's increased capacity to meet the tasks of life, to give and take, and to cooperate in what Adlerians call *social interest*. An individual's capacity to interact effectively with other members of the group is a measure of his or her social growth, which is one of the goals of the group experience.

An effective group offers its members opportunities to belong and be accepted, receive and give love and to have a therapeutic effect on others, see that one's problems are not unique but experienced universally, develop one's identity, and try on new approaches to the various social tasks of life.

UNDERSTANDING THE GROUP

Each person is a member of the group. The social meaning and context of each member's behavior is important. The following four principles of group interaction help the leader to understand and determine how to make an intervention.

1. People Are Social Beings

Most people want to belong to clubs, form friendships, and be a peer group member. Few people, unless they are extremely discouraged, want to be left out of groups. Most people are members of at least three groups: (a) family, (b) work/school, and (c) friends. Social interaction is inherent in human behavior.

2. All Behavior Has Social Meaning and Purpose

Each person's behavior reflects a search for his or her unique place in the group. Finding this unique place can be challenging; however, the social meaning and purpose (the goal) of the behavior or misbehavior do not have to make sense to the individual.

3. Life Style Is Expressed Through Behavior

A person's behavior is the means through which the goals of life are presented. If a person is not doing well in one area of work but seems capable of the work, what goal is he or she pursuing? If one looks to external reasons, one may find some legitimate contributing factors; these might include nutrition, distractions in family life, or personal conflict. It is more helpful to look at the internal reasons. Individually chosen behaviors are expressed through the person's life style. For some people, the life style will lead to the choice to do well or to do nothing at all in a particular area of life, regardless of one's ability. Faced with challenges in a particular area, a person may give up. From that individual's point of view, this makes sense; it is consistent with the context of his or her beliefs about the self. There is a simple rule that applies to all persons: Look at what a person does, not what he or she says. Adlerians have rephrased this as "Trust only movement." Consider the following examples of actions and words. A friend says "Let's have lunch soon" but never calls. Your boss says you need more time for planning but continues to give assignments that make planning impossible. Your wife says she understands that you have to work late; however, when you come home, she is angry at you. In each of these examples, the words and actions are inconsistent. Behaviors are a more useful and accurate indication of the person's intention.

4. Stimulating Social Interest Is Essential

Social interest is a willingness to cooperate for the common good of the group. When a person wants to do a job for his or her family, that person is expressing social interest. When a person is not willing to cooperate on an assignment, he or she is showing little social interest.

GROUP DYNAMICS

The field of group dynamics is concerned with the nature of the group, the development of and relationships among individuals, groups, and institutions. Group dynamics is concerned with all forces affecting social change. Therapists operate with an awareness of group dynamics. This should be not incidental but central to the therapist's role and function.

The therapist needs to be aware that the individuals in the group are inextricably intertwined. The mixture of group and individual personalities should result in the development of a group of persons who are aware of these relationships and move toward a mutually acceptable goal. Understanding how to change a group can come from various perspectives, which we now discuss.

Cohesiveness

People who are to be changed, and those who attempt to influence change, must have a strong feeling of belonging to the same group. Through equal participation, a feeling of psychological interdependence must be developed.

Attractiveness

The more attractive a group is to the members, the greater the potential influence of the group will be. This suggests that a critical issue is the selection of group members and of doing things that enhance the group's attractiveness. This is most often achieved by ensuring that people who are socially powerful or attractive become members of the group. Group attractiveness is also influenced by the time and location of the meetings.

Values and Attitudes

To achieve change, a person must first identify the values and attitudes that form the basis for his or her attraction to the group. Values and attitudes that group members have in common can be used for forces of change. The group will have less influence on attitudes that are not related to the basis for group membership.

Prestige of a Group Member

The greater the prestige of a group member in the eyes of the others, the more significant his or her influence will be. The implications of this for the therapist include that he or she must assess the prestige of each group member.

Group Norms

Efforts to change individuals or groups to make them deviate from group norms will encounter resistance. The pressure to conform to group norms must be considered in any strategy to achieve change.

Perception of a Need for Change

If the source of pressure for change is to lie within the group, then every group member should share a perception of the need for change. Members must have a clear conception of purpose and personal commitment to individual and group goals.

Communication

Changing the group requires the opening of communication channels. All persons affected by the change must be informed about the need for change, plans for change, and the consequences of change.

Change and Strain

Changes in one part of a group produce strain in other, related parts. The strain can be removed only by eliminating the change or readjusting the parts. Frequently, a change in the substructure, such as a pairing of friends or opponents, will create increased tension in the total group.

Goals

Some of the most significant forces in the group include goals, aspirations, leadership, anticipations, attitudes, and cohesiveness. For a group to become meaningful, a group goal must emerge. The group should be working toward some announced goal, and until that goal is clarified the group will tend to be unproductive.

Aspiration

Moderate but realistic increases in the level of aspiration tend to generate a comparable increase in performance. Aspirations are essential to a group that wants to succeed, and these aspirations need to result in both individual satisfaction and increased group performance. Therefore, moderately increasing the level of aspiration toward the group goal will usually result in a corresponding increase in the group's level of performance.

THERAPEUTIC FORCES

Therapeutic forces help us understand the need for a climate of growth, cooperation, and understanding. They are therapeutic in the sense they contribute to the well-being of the group. Time spent developing these attributes contributes to the overall benefit of the group.

The nine forces important in the development of a healthy group (i.e., therapy, classroom, teacher, or parent) are presented in Table 10.1. In the following discussion, we present the important aspects of each therapeutic force.

Acceptance

The skill of acceptance and mutual respect is the cornerstone of an effective, helpful group. A therapist who can share the idea of reflective listening will promote acceptance. Most people are capable of listening and responding to others' statements.

TABLE 10.1
Therapeutic Forces in Groups

Force	Purpose	Example
Acceptance	To develop mutual respect and empathy among group members.	"I can see you're being sensitive to Joshua's feelings."
Ventilation	To acknowledge and promote the expression of feelings, often by using reflective language.	"You seem very angry about this idea."
Spectator learning	To help group members understand their own concerns as they listen to other group members discuss similar concerns.	"How can you apply our discussion of Jim's problem to your brothers and sisters?"
Feedback	To let group members know how others perceive their behavior, often by encouraging use of I-messages.	"Could you please tell Carlos how you feel when he teases you?"
Universalization	To help group members experiment with new behavior.	"Who else has wondered about that?"
Reality testing	To help group members experiment with new behavior.	"Let's role-play this problem and try out new ways of dealing with it."
Altruism	To encourage group members to help each other, rather than compete.	"Beth, I really appreciate your helping Ricky with his problems."
Interaction	To foster group members' social skills and help establish an encouraging group atmosphere.	"Meg, share with Joyce how you felt when she said she enjoyed going out after group."
Encouragement	To stimulate group members' courage and social interest. To help members become more optimistic about solving problems.	"I think your new habits will help with your project."

Note. From *Systematic Training for Effective Teaching (STET): Teacher's Handbook* (p. 206), by D. Dinkmeyer, G. D. McKay, and D. Dinkmeyer Jr., 1980, Circle Pines, MN: American Guidance Service, Inc. Copyright 1980 by American Guidance Service, Inc., www.agsnet.com. Reprinted with permission.

Mutual respect can be stimulated in a variety of ways. Group members can pick someone in the group to get to know better, by talking about interests, friends, work, or hobbies. Each group member then introduces that person to the rest of the group. Most people enjoy being the center of attention and through this activity develop an appreciation for the similarities and differences among group members. Another way to stimulate mutual respect is through discussions in which each group member shares one personal strength and identifies one strength in another group member. A final way to stimulate mutual respect is to encourage empathy among group members by simply noticing when they are being sensitive to each other. The modeling of empathy by the leader also sets the stage for these behaviors and attitudes in the group.

Ventilation

People express emotions in the group, whether the therapist "permits" this or not. In a democratic or effective group, members feel free to share their feelings. The leader can promote this in a variety of ways: expanding the feeling-word vocabulary, sharing appropriate feelings through I-messages, noting opportunities for members to share unexpressed emotions, and holding discussions that have as a focus the sharing of feelings.

During a typical group session, many different emotions are experienced. The purpose of acceptance and ventilation is to give group members an opportunity to express these emotions.

Spectator Learning

Members can learn from each others' similar concerns. The value of this lies in discussing problem situations, because doing so allows that problem to be discussed simultaneously and enables other members who have similar concerns to learn as spectators. Topics for such learning experiences include, but are not limited to, anxiety, disappointments about jobs, concerns for the future, handling rejection, learning how to make new friends, and how to solve problems.

Feedback

The purpose of feedback is to give members clues as to how they are coming across in the group. Self-awareness can be increased when feedback is used appropriately. Feedback does not blame, accuse, or expect change by the other party. It simply states how the person is being experienced by another person.

For example, consider a group member who is constantly interrupting the discussion. Feedback from either the therapist or group members would state something to the effect of "I feel upset when you dominate the discussion, because I/others can't say what I/they want." Although change is not expressed in this statement, the foundation for change is laid in the dissatisfaction.

Feedback is a term with which mental health professionals are familiar. It may even be overused or misunderstood. In the context of group therapy, feedback is seen as simply an expression of feeling without criticism, but with the encouragement for change.

Universalization

A good group depends on how well the group members realize their similarities with each other. Universalization is the process of working with group members so they can see these similarities. This can be expressed in the following ways: "Has anyone else ever _____ (referring to a situation likely to be experienced by others)?" "Who else has ____?" Individuals can also learn about mutual similarities through discussions of topics that are likely to have broad appeal for group members. This is similar to the idea of spectator learning.

Reality Testing

The opportunity to experiment with new ways to respond to people is called *reality testing*. Although the concept sounds abstract, each of us tests reality anytime we do something different.

One of the best ways to incorporate reality testing into a group is to have the group leader model the ability to try new things. This can be done, for example, by encouraging small steps and seemingly minor movements or by modeling the courage to be imperfect.

Altruism

The process of encouraging cooperation, at the expense of competition, is called *altruism*. Although competition is a necessary part of life, it is overemphasized and has negative effects. Altruism is also known as "finding ways to help each other." Fostering altruism is a process of creating opportunities for the group members to help each other.

Interaction

Some therapists report that they want the group members' interaction to be polite and cooperative at all times. Interaction between themselves and the group members, and among the group members, should be polite. Encouraging positive interactions among group members, such as opportunities to work together without supervision, fosters opportunities for appropriate interaction.

Encouragement

Although we have left this group force as the last one, it is perhaps the most important. Focusing on strengths and assets, stimulating social interest, and increasing an optimistic attitude are all part of the encouragement process.

The nine therapeutic forces in groups can be used to recognize and encourage positive behaviors in the group. The usefulness of these forces is summarized as follows: The group develops its cohesiveness around guidelines for freedom and responsibility. Group members help set goals, make decisions, and institute changes. Whenever possible, group members proceed at their own level, reducing competition and stressing cooperation. They talk openly and honestly with each other and with the therapist. An atmosphere of mutual respect and trust is thereby developed, and encouragement is the prime motivator.

COHESIVENESS

Cohesiveness plays a significant role in group dynamics; in group therapy, it can be seen as akin to the relationship in individual therapy. *Cohesiveness* refers to the positive pull or attraction that members of the group feel for one another, the forces that enable members to experience a feeling of belonging, solidarity, and a common bond. This cohesiveness creates conditions whereby individuals feel not only understood, accepted, and valued but also free to reveal themselves and accept feedback from group members. A cohesive group is one in which members have a high level of mutual understanding and acceptance. Cohesiveness helps supply the feeling of belonging that is essential to all the other therapeutic forces.

The significances of cohesiveness is best understood when one recognizes that many people who come to a group for assistance have problems in establishing and maintaining a sense of personal worth and self-esteem. The group, because of its unique social climate, develops cohesiveness and provides an excellent corrective experience for these specific problems.

ROLE OF THE GROUP LEADER

The group leader is responsible for forming, establishing, and keeping the group going. In the early stages, the group leader is the only person with whom all the members of the group are familiar. Members expect the leader to assume responsibility for the group's growth and direction.

Group leaders must be sensitive to the forces that make their group a therapeutic experience. They are facilitators who both create and encourage situations in which participants provide emotional support, universalization, feedback, and opportunities to try new behaviors. These processes promote learning, personal growth, and cohesiveness.

Leaders must participate actively in the development of norms that facilitate growth and interpersonal learning. They intentionally establish the structure for the group and indicate guidelines for behavior, such as congruence, open interaction, involvement, nonjudgmental acceptance, confrontation, and commitment. Much of our social behavior is characterized by façades, surface interactions, the inhibited expression of feelings, and other modes that are destructive to the development of a productive group. It is crucial to understand that the norms that govern the group do not come about automatically as a result of forming a group. Their development requires deliberate effort on the part of the leader.

Therapists must recognize that as group leaders they must provide a model as well as expertise to stimulate movement. In the formative stage of a group, leaders may need to use specific therapy exercises as they create productive interaction. They may explicitly point out interactions that do not implement therapeutic goals and reinforce and encourage any attempts of members to effectively use the group's therapeutic forces. Some leaders like to believe that productive groups emerge without their guidance and even consider the kind of intervention we have discussed as manipulation.

Spontaneity is an important factor in effective group work. This is often referred to as the "here and now," and it enables leaders to pick up on what is happening and turn the interaction into a growth-promoting experience. Leaders must use all their creativity and spontaneity because both of these accelerate the progress of the group and provide a valuable model for the participants.

LEADERSHIP SKILLS

Group leaders must be able to function in following the process with all members regardless of how different their beliefs, feelings, and intentions are. They must be able to create an atmosphere in which members can achieve their goals and learn to help one another.

Leaders pay attention not only to the content of members' messages but also to the method, setting, and timing of messages. How are the feelings conveyed? With considerable involvement, or apathetically? Does the message indicate that the person is trying to focus the interaction on himself or that he wants to stay with the here-and-now transaction? Leaders are always aware of the purpose of a member's communication and, when appropriate, they confront group members with their beliefs, feelings, and intentions. Therefore, although leadership requires people who are open, honest, accepting, spontaneous, understanding, and congruent, these personality traits alone are not enough. Leaders must also possess the skills that we discuss in the following sections.

Structuring

Structuring is the most important group skill. The leader establishes the guidelines for the discussion or activity, clarifies any misunderstanding, and states the purpose of the session.

Example 1: "Let's talk about how much time we waste getting started—we need to do something. Who'd like to start?"

Example 2: "The purpose of this group is to introduce new ideas you might use in your life, to practice these ideas, and to receive support from others."

Comment: Structuring is often understood as the art of stating the obvious. This is correct! Too often, a discussion does not achieve its objectives when those objectives are left unstated. It is a rare meeting, discussion, or therapy group that does not benefit from structuring statements.

Universalizing

Universalizing is the process of helping others realize that their concerns are shared. It can be verbalized by the comment "Who else has felt that way?" when the group leader senses that the topic has been felt or experienced by others. Universalization is a process, not a single comment. It is fostered by the therapist creating opportunities for the group members to share similar concerns and challenges.

Linking

Linking occurs when the therapist points out group members who have something in common, for example, "It seems like Jim and Julie have an interest in poetry in common." This is an effort to link Julie and Jim on the concept of poetry.

Redirecting

Redirecting occurs when the therapist wants the group members to talk directly with each other instead of through the therapist as a switchboard operator of sorts. If a group member is directing a comment to another member, then he or she should address that person directly.

Goal Disclosure

Goal disclosure occurs when the group is working on behavioral problems. For each incident that is discussed, the purpose is to guess the person's goal or purpose in having performed that behavior.

Brainstorming

Brainstorming is the process of accepting all ideas when a solution is sought, without evaluating or negating any of the ideas. This can be particularly helpful when new strategies are being considered.

Blocking

Blocking is the important process of intervening in destructive communication. Therapists do not have to be solely responsible for blocking, but they must set the tone through structure, rules, or modeling.

Summarizing

Summarizing can occur at any time, but it is particularly helpful when one wants to learn what has happened in the group. This skill provides each member an opportunity to share what has been important for him or her. It also allows the leader to learn what has been important for the members. It can be started by the direction to complete the sentence "I learned. . . . " Summarizing is an excellent opportunity for everyone to give an equal amount of time to the group.

Task-Setting and Obtaining Commitments

Task-setting and obtaining commitments relate to the process of making discussions and ideas into concrete, behavioral actions. For example, a group member might say, "I want to do better at work." This is vague and gives only a general intent. Task-setting is the process of deciding what it will take to achieve doing "better" at work. This also helps the entire group set tasks.

We have found that group members have a similar tendency to have good intentions but not necessarily the ability to make their intentions specific. In this case, the therapist's task is to make the group member aware of what will be different, as specifically as possible. General ideas, such as "I want to do better" or "My office staff should be more cooperative with each other," have more specific counterparts that can be identified through task-setting and obtaining commitments.

Commitments should be as behavioral as possible and should identify a specific period of time. The therapist should be wary of statements such as "I'll never do that again" or "I'll try that idea." Most therapy group relationships have opportunities for follow-up; make a commitment for only the period of time between sessions. From this basis, the group members can build some momentum toward their goals.

Promoting Feedback

Promoting feedback is the process of exploring how one is perceived by others in the group. It is directly related to the therapeutic force of feedback within groups.

Promoting Direct Interaction

Promoting direct interaction allows group members to speak directly with each other. Instead of mediating disputes, the therapist should allow members to work out their differences.

Promoting Encouragement

Promoting encouragement is the process of finding what is right or okay in the group members, and letting them know it. It is the ability of the therapist to discover the assets and abilities of each group member. From that knowledge, encouragement helps the members to consider alternatives.

The process of memorizing these group forces and group leadership skills will not make one a better group leader. The process of working with groups with an awareness of these forces and skills does make one a better leader.

CONCLUSION

In this chapter, we have presented the fundamental aspects of Adlerian group therapy. We all live and work in groups and must understand how we affect and are affected by them. The step-by-step method developed by Sonstegard and Bitter (2004) provides a helpful explanation of Adlerian group therapy in practice. Successful therapists are able to use the dynamics of the group to help people change in ways that would not be possible in individual therapy.

11

PLAY THERAPY

Children of every era have played to comfort themselves and make sense out of their often-tragic life situations. For example, D. S. Sweeney (1997) discussed how children in the Nazi concentration camp at Auschwitz used play to cope as they prepared to die and as they witnessed the horrors of war. Children living during the Black Plague of the Middle Ages created the game "Ring Around the Rosie":

> The "rosie" refers to the red blotches and lesions from contracting the plague; the "pocket full of posies" refers to the flowers for the dead and the practice of putting flowers into the pockets of plague victims to ward off the smell of death; and "ashes, ashes, we all fall down" alludes to the imminent death of the plague-stricken and the practice of burning the bodies of plague victims. (D. S. Sweeney, 1997, p. 21)

Children use play to cope with and make meaning of difficult and meaningless situations.

A RATIONALE FOR THE USE OF PLAY IN PSYCHOTHERAPY

Play is essential to the development of cognitive, language, motor, and social skills in children. The fundamental importance of play to the development and well-being of children is evident by the fact that the United Nations proclaimed play as a "universal and inalienable right of childhood" (Landreth, 2002, p. 10). Play is the focal activity of childhood, and children "do not need to be taught how to play, nor must they be made to play. Play is spontaneous, enjoyable, voluntary, and nongoal-directed" (Landreth, 2002, p. 10). Furthermore, children communicate through play. According to Landreth (2002),

> Children's play can be more fully appreciated when recognized as their natural medium of communication. Children express themselves more fully and more directly through self-initiated, spontaneous play than they do verbally because they are more comfortable with play. For children to "play out" their experiences and feelings is the most natural dynamic and self-healing process in which they can engage. (p. 14)

Schaefer (1993) stated that play "has the power not only to facilitate normal child development but also to alleviate abnormal behavior" (p. 3). Consequently, play is a useful and appropriate method for psychotherapy with young children. Most children under age 10 do not have the abstract reasoning and verbal abilities to clearly express their thoughts, feelings, reactions, and attitudes. Thus, many therapists who work with children use toys and other play media to help young children communicate their experiences; reactions to experiences; desires and goals; and perceptions about themselves, others, and the world. According to the Association for Play Therapy, play therapy is the "systematic use of a theoretical model to establish an interpersonal process in which trained play therapists use the therapeutic powers of play to help clients prevent or resolve psychosocial difficulties and achieve optimal growth and development" (1997; cited in Kottman, 2003, p. 1). Play therapy is typically used with children between the ages of 3 and 10, but it may be used with older children as well (Kottman, 2003; LaBauve, Watts, & Kottman, 2001).

It is important to note that therapists interested in using play therapy may need to make a paradigm shift from a primary therapeutic focus of conversation and verbal skills to a primary focus of using play, toys, play media, and metaphors for communication and to facilitate change. It appears to be a simple change to make but is actually a complex conceptual shift that many adults may find difficult. Kottman (2001b) explained,

> Play therapists look at themselves, children, and the world from a different perspective than talk therapists do. Before they can begin to acquire the skills involved in using play to communicate with children, potential play therapists must learn a completely different way of understanding communication—to a symbolic, action-oriented model in which actions of puppets and animal figures are important pieces of information and in which a shrug, a smile, or a turned back can be an entire "conversation." (p. 20)

BENEFITS OF PLAY THERAPY

Play therapy is useful for establishing and maintaining a therapeutic alliance with children; helping therapists understand children and their interactions and relationships; helping children express feelings that they are unable or unwilling to verbalize; helping children behaviorally and constructively express feelings of anxiety, frustration, or hostility; helping children learn and practice social skills; and creating an environment in which children feel safe to "test limits, gain insight about their own behavior and motivation, explore alternatives, and learn about consequences" (Kottman, 2001b, p. 4).

Schaefer (1993, pp. 5–13) listed 14 therapeutic factors or mechanisms whereby children benefit from play therapy:

1. *Overcoming resistance.* Children usually do not make the choice to come for psychotherapy. Consequently, they are often reluctant to engage in the therapeutic process. Play is an excellent vehicle for establishing and maintaining the therapeutic alliance because it is "interesting, enjoyable, and natural to children" (Schaefer, 1993, p. 6).

2. *Communication.* Play is the natural language of children, and it is primarily nonverbal and symbolic. Through play, children are able to express conscious thoughts and feelings that they cannot express verbally. They also express unconscious thoughts, feelings, and wishes. As therapists listen to the natural language of children—and respond using the language of play therapy—children will feel progressively more free to express themselves.

3. *Mastery.* There are few areas in life where children have a sense of control, self-efficacy, or mastery. Play therapy provides an environment in which children can explore and engage in activities that "contribute to a sense of power, control, and mastery of the environment" (Schaefer, 1993, p. 7).

4. *Creative thinking.* Play therapy encourages creativity and flexibility and gives children the opportunity to enhance their problem-solving skills.

5. *Catharsis.* Play therapy gives children the opportunity to be in a relationship with a caring, empathic adult who accepts them unconditionally. Consequently, children feel permission to express intense feelings that previously they were unable, or did not feel permission, to express. Expression of these intense emotions can be a significant growth experience for children.

6. *Abreaction.* In the safety of the play therapy situation, children are often able to reexperience past traumatic events and

the concomitant feelings in a different and, it is hoped, more positive manner. Children can re-create in play those events, gain a sense of mastery over the situations, and advance in their development.

7. *Role play*. Through pretend play, children are able to initiate and explore alternative behaviors. In play therapy, children often initiate behaviors they have not previously considered, explore the experience of the new behavior, and evaluate the consequences of behaving this new way.

8. *Fantasy*. Play enhances children's ability to access their imagery capabilities. In fantasy, children can expand their world beyond its present difficulties and limitations. They can feel a sense of power or control over their world even when such power or control does not actually exist. Children can use their imagination to make sense of their world and cope with or transcend painful experiences.

9. *Metaphoric teaching*. By using stories, fantasy play, or artwork, play therapists can help children create new ways of under-standing—and generate more adaptive solutions for—problematic situations.

10. *Attachment formation*. Children presenting for play therapy often have limited healthy attachment to others. Replicating positive aspects and behaviors of the parent–infant relationship through shared fun, sensorimotor and fantasy play, role playing, and the like may help children establish feelings of secure attachment.

11. *Relationship enhancement*. As the play therapist creates a safe and nurturing environment for children by demonstrating warmth, unconditional acceptance, and respect, a therapeutic relationship may develop that is characterized by mutual feelings of warmth and closeness. This positive therapeutic relationship significantly increases the potential of a positive therapeutic outcome.

12. *Enjoyment*. Children enjoy playing. This is the most fundamental and obvious aspect of play and play therapy. Because children enjoy play, it may help them develop a sense of happiness or well-being and motivate them to do significant work in play therapy sessions.

13. *Mastering developmental fears*. In play therapy, children can reduce anxiety through the process of systematic desensitization. Children can express their feelings and develop a sense of mastery and self-efficacy by using various toys and play media to experience and respond to the anxiety-producing stimulus.

14. *Game play*. Games help children develop better social and communications skills, because the players must agree to, and abide by, pre-established rules. Games also help distractible children sustain focus on a task and teach children that choices have consequences.

BRIEF HISTORY AND OVERVIEW OF ADLERIAN PLAY THERAPY

Historically, Adlerians have regularly worked with children in family and school settings. As Kottman (1993, 1999b) has noted, however, very few addressed the developmental constraints that may hinder children from using language in therapy—or elsewhere—to directly communicate about their difficulties and concerns. Play therapy uses children's most natural means of communication (i.e., play). For this reason, it is particularly appropriate for work with children (Kottman, 2003; Landreth, 2002).

Although Adlerians have regularly worked with children, very few have discussed techniques commonly used in play therapy. Yura and Galassi (1974) and Nystul (1980) have suggested that play therapy methods might be useful for Adlerians in working with children; however, neither one of the articles presents specific information regarding the systematic use of Adlerian therapy in conjunction with the principles and procedures of play therapy with children. In response to this void in the play therapy literature, Terry Kottman began developing Adlerian play therapy in the late 1980s (Kottman, 1993, 1997, 1999b, 2001a, 2001b, 2003; Kottman & Warlick, 1989, 1990).

Adlerian play therapy integrates Adlerian psychology and psychotherapy with play therapy principles and procedures. Therapists using Adlerian play therapy communicate and build relationships with children by using the basic facilitative skills of play therapy (e.g., tracking, reflecting feelings, reflecting content, returning responsibility, limit-setting, etc.) while conceptualizing issues and relationships—with children and parents—and selecting therapeutic interventions from an Adlerian perspective. Adlerian play therapy is a process in which the play therapist

> (a) builds an egalitarian relationship with the child; (b) explores the child's lifestyle; (c) develops hypotheses about the intrapersonal and interpersonal dynamics of the child's difficulties (from the perspective of the child and from the perspectives of other people in the child's life); (d) designs a treatment plan for the child and for any other individuals who strongly influence the child (parents and teachers); (e) helps the child gain insight and make new decisions about self, the world, and others; (f) teaches the child new skills for relating to others; (g) helps the child practice new skills for interacting with others; and (h) consults with parents and teachers, working with them to develop more positive

perspectives on the child and to learn more encouraging strategies for interacting with the child. (Kottman, 2003, p. xi)

Research suggests that play therapy is a useful strategy across a broad range of problems, especially with children between the ages of 3 or 4 and 11 or 12, depending on their level of development. For example, Bratton and Ray (2000; cited in Kottman, 2003) presented a comprehensive play therapy literature review of 100 case studies and 82 experimental research studies. The case studies indicated that clients in play therapy consistently showed more well-functioning behavior and decreased levels of symptomatic behavior compared with their behavior before play therapy. The experimental studies suggested that play therapy can be helpful for children with problems such as "social maladjustment, conduct disorder, problematic school behavior, emotional maladjustment, anxiety/fear, negative self-concept, being 'mentally challenged,' and having a physical or learning disability" (Bratton & Ray, 2000, cited in Kottman, 2003, p. 13).

Adlerian play therapy is especially appropriate with children who have (a) control and power issues (e.g., bullying behavior, power struggles with parents and teachers, temper tantrums), (b) experienced an event they perceived as traumatic (e.g., adoption, death of a significant figure in the child's life, divorce of parents, natural disaster), (c) poor self-concepts (easily discouraged, minimal effort put forth on work, self-deprecating remarks), (d) problems cooperating with family members (sibling conflicts, fights with parents, conflict with classmates), and (e) weak social skills (difficulty making and maintaining friendships; Kottman, 1999c, 2001b, 2003).

APPROPRIATE PLAY MEDIA AND PLAY SPACE FOR ADLERIAN PLAY THERAPY

In Adlerian play therapy, the playroom or play space is equipped with a variety of toys similar to the toy selection in client- or child-centered playrooms and spaces. Kottman (2003) stated that it is essential to have toys that children can use to explore and express feelings related to family influences and dynamics and relationships with others; consider maladaptive beliefs, perceived threats, and past traumas; examine control, power, and trust issues; express their idiosyncratic manner of gaining significance and feeling a sense of belonging; express their creativity and imagination; and develop new cognitive and behavioral responses.

According to Landreth (2002), toys and materials must be carefully selected—not collected—because they are an essential part of the communication process for children. So that children may be free to express all aspects of their experiences, Adlerian play therapists purposefully select toys for their playroom or portable play kit that are representative of five distinct categories: (a) family/nurturing toys, (b) scary toys, (c) aggressive toys, (d) expressive toys, and (e) pretend/fantasy toys.

Family/Nurturing Toys

Children use toys in this category to develop a relationship with the play therapist; explore their thoughts and feelings about their relationships with family members, friends, and peers; and re-create relationships and events external to the play therapy situation. In addition, children often use these toys to play out their family atmosphere, express the desire for belonging, and to request or provide nurturing.

Toys in the family/nurturing category include dolls (including baby dolls); bendable doll families; a dollhouse; a cradle; animal families; people puppets; baby clothes; stuffed toys; a child-sized rocking chair; a warm, soft blanket; kitchenware (e.g., dishes, pots, pans, silverware); cleaning items (e.g., broom, dustpan); sand and sandbox; "humanlike" figures that could be used for a family; empty food containers (e.g., cans and cereal boxes); and wooden or plastic kitchen appliances (if space is available; Kottman, 1997, 1999c, 2001b, 2003).

It is important to have dolls from culturally diverse groups so that children can explore similarities and differences between groups of people as well as within their own ethnic group. It is helpful to have several families of each group so that children may be able to explore traditional, blended, and nontraditional family arrangements. It is also helpful to have several plastic animal families in case the child is not comfortable working with toys that look like a human family. Finally, for children who are not ready to explore family dynamics, small figures such as clowns or trolls are helpful because they look even less like people and are less clearly identifiable as a family (Kottman, 2003).

Scary Toys

Children use scary toys to address both real and fantasy fears. Using these toys, children can act out being frightened, protect themselves, or ask the play therapist for protection.

Toys in the scary category include a variety of scary puppets (e.g., alligator, bear, wolf), dinosaurs, alligators, insects and spiders, rats, sharks, plastic snakes, plastic monsters, and other toys that children might perceive as frightening (Kottman, 1997, 1999c, 2001b, 2003).

Scary toys help children explore and express their fears, maladaptive beliefs, perceived threats, and past traumatic events. Kottman (2003) offered specific recommendations regarding scary toys. First, whereas children have differing reactions, it is important to have a variety of scary toys that may invoke anxiety reactions. Second, it is useful to have several of each type of scary toy so that children can create families or differentiate between "good" and "bad" scary toys of the same type. Third, the play therapist's toy collection should include several snakes and an alligator or shark with a hollow body and sharp teeth. Children who have been sexually, physically, or psychologically abused commonly use these toys in their play. Finally, if a child has a specific fear, or has experienced a specific anxiety-provoking situation, it may be helpful to secure a toy that more specifically represents the particular fear or situation.

Aggressive Toys

Children use aggressive toys to express feelings of anger and fear; explore issues of control, power, and trust; and symbolically act out their aggression. They may use such toys to protect themselves from symbolic dangers, for example, from a scary toy. This helps children gain a sense of mastery and control and increase their perceived self-efficacy. Children also use aggressive toys to test limits and develop self-control.

Toys in the aggressive category include handcuffs, a stand-up punching bag/bop bag, toy soldiers and military vehicles, weapons (e.g., dart guns, play pistols, rubber knives, swords), small pillows for pillow fights, foam bats, and plastic shields (Kottman, 1997, 1999c, 2001b, 2003).

Kottman (2003) indicated some specific qualifications regarding aggressive toys. First, the weapons in play therapy should not resemble real weapons. Instead, they should be brightly colored or, for example, look like futuristic ray guns. Second, handcuffs should have a catch release for safety reasons and because the keys are often misplaced.

Expressive Toys

Expressive toys that are artistic or creative in nature, and other art media are useful for understanding how children understand themselves, others, and their world. Children use these toys and media to express thoughts and feelings, explore and express feelings about relationships with family members and others, conceptualize problems and consider solutions, and express their creativity and imagination.

Toys in the expressive category include clay or play dough; construction paper; crayons and markers; an easel and tempera paint; finger and watercolor paints; brown lunch bags; egg cartons; glue; magazines, for potential pictures and words for collages; markers; newsprint; pencils; pipe cleaners; posterboard; scissors; Scotch tape; and yarn (Kottman, 1997, 1999c, 2001b, 2003).

Kottman (2003) mentioned that expressive toys can be messy and that play therapists who may be concerned about paint spilling and the like will need to give due consideration to which expressive toys and art media they will include in their play materials.

Pretend/Fantasy Toys

Children use pretend/fantasy toys to express feelings, explore different roles, examine alternative behaviors and varying solutions to problems, and act out situations that they have observed. These toys also help children explore various relationships and practice new attitudes, feelings, or behaviors. Pretend/fantasy toys include costumes, hats, jewelry, purses, and other dress-up clothes; masks; a doctor kit; magic wands; blocks and other building materials; human figure puppets; animal puppets; a puppet theater; broom, iron, ironing board; telephones (two); transportation toys (e.g., airplanes, cars, trucks); and zoo and farm animals (Kottman, 1997, 1999c, 2001b, 2003).

Children often use pretend/fantasy toys as projective objects, "imposing their own ideas and identities on the toys" (Kottman, 2003, p. 9). To facilitate this projection process, it is important to avoid selecting toys with preconceived identities. If a toy has a well-established/defined identity prior to the child's experience of it in play therapy, he or she will typically not deviate from the preconceived identity.

It is not necessary to have all of these toys to engage in Adlerian play therapy; however, it is important to have representative toys from all five categories of play media. Whereas play is the most natural language of children, toys and play media are the words they most naturally use to express themselves. Therefore, the more play media choices children have for expressing themselves, the higher the likelihood that they will have sufficient resources to clearly express themselves in play therapy (Kottman, 1999c, 2003; Landreth, 2002).

The toys should be arranged in an open space and set within easy reach of the child client. In addition, toys should be arranged according to their specific categories; in other words, aggressive toys should be arranged with other aggressive toys, family/nurturing toys should be placed in close proximity to other family/nurturing toys, and so forth. This consistent, predictable arrangement helps children experience the play therapy situation as one in which they feel safe and comfortable (Kottman, 1999c, 2003; Landreth, 2002).

The ideal setting for play therapy is a spacious, custom-designed playroom. However, many therapists working with children have limited funds and must share space with other mental health professionals or travel to multiple locations. Fortunately, play therapists can conduct Adlerian play therapy in myriad locations by bringing a box or bag with selected toys from each of the aforementioned categories with them. Play therapists work in schools, go to children's homes, and go to hospitals and do play therapy on a hospital bed. What is necessary to engage in play therapy is a relatively quiet space with sufficient room where the play therapist can set out the toys and where the child and therapist can have sufficient privacy so that the child can be assured of confidentiality in the play therapy sessions. The most important consideration regarding play therapy space is the comfort level of the therapist. The play therapist must feel comfortable wherever play therapy occurs so that he or she is able to express his or her creativity and flexibility with clients (Kottman, 1997, 1999c, 2003; Landreth, 2002). Therapists considering the creation of a room solely dedicated to play therapy should consult Landreth (2002) and Kottman (2003) for thorough and practical considerations regarding the "ideal" playroom.

THE ADLERIAN PLAY THERAPY PROCESS

Adlerian play therapy consists of four process phases. Phase 1 focuses on developing an egalitarian relationship between the child and the play therapist. In Phase 2, the play therapist explores the child's life style, goals of behavior, and maladaptive beliefs. In Phase 3, the play therapist assists the child in gaining insight into his or her life style, goals of behavior, and maladaptive beliefs. The final or reorientation/reeducation phase focuses on helping the child consider new ways of striving for significance and interacting with others (Kottman, 1994, 1997, 1999a, 1999b, 1999c, 2001b, 2003).

Although the phases of Adlerian play therapy are sequential, they are by no means separate or discrete. Because the Adlerian play therapy process is fluid rather than static, developing and maintaining an egalitarian relationship between the child and the play therapist is an important consideration throughout the play therapy process. In each phase of play therapy, the therapist attempts to help children grow toward positive goals of behavior, or what are called the "Crucial Cs": *connecting* with others (the goal of cooperation), feeling *capable* (the goal of self-efficacy and self-reliance), feeling as though they *count* (the goal of belonging and contribution), and having the *courage* to engage life challenges (the goal of resiliency; see Bettner & Lew, 1996; Lew & Bettner, 1996). The therapist does not have to wait until the child has an extensive understanding of his or her own life style before helping the child to begin to gain an understanding of it. Also, the therapist can use procedures from the reorientation/reeducation phase whenever a child seems ready to change a maladaptive belief or behavior, even if the child has limited insight into other aspects of his or her life style (Kottman, 1994, 1997, 1999a, 1999b, 1999c, 2001b, 2003).

The goals of Adlerian play therapy are to help the child consider alternative perceptions to maladaptive beliefs about the self, others, and the world; help the child move from self-destructive goals and misbehavior toward constructive ones; facilitate the child's growth in the Crucial Cs; help the child understand and embrace his or her abilities, assets, and strengths, thereby decreasing his or her discouragement; and, ultimately, enhance the child's social interest (Kottman, 2003).

Phase 1: Building the Therapeutic Relationship

The primary goal of Phase 1 of Adlerian play therapy is to build egalitarian relationships with both the child and the parents (or parent). These relationships are foundational, because success in the subsequent phases of Adlerian play therapy is predicated on creating and maintaining relationships whereby the child and the parents feel safe and acceptably comfortable with the play therapy process. During this first phase, the Adlerian play therapist is essentially nondirective, working to keep the child in the lead. The basic skills used to build the relationship with a child in play therapy include tracking behavior, reflecting feelings, reflecting content, encouraging, responding to questions and making tentative hypotheses, actively interacting with the child, setting limits, and cleaning up the room together. The Adlerian play therapist uses these skills throughout the play therapy process to build and maintain an equal relationship with the child (Kottman, 1994, 1999a, 1999c, 2001b, 2003).

Tracking Behavior

Tracking is a play therapy technique common to most theoretical approaches to play therapy and is used to help build the therapeutic relationship. When a play therapist tracks behavior, he or she tells the child what the child is doing and how the child is using a toy (without labeling the toy). Tracking behavior is intended to communicate to the child that the child's behavior in the playroom is important and that he or she has the therapist's full attention. Tracking is done more frequently in earlier sessions and less frequently in later ones (Kottman, 1999c, 2001b, 2003; Landreth, 2002).

> Example: A child picks up a toy airplane and moves it around in the air.
> Response: "You're picking that up" or "You're moving it around in the air."

When tracking a child's behavior, it is important not to label toys, play media, or behaviors. If the play therapist labels something, the child usually feels obligated to use the therapist's label. By not labeling the toy, the child's imagination is not stifled, and he or she can decide the identity of toys or behaviors (Kottman, 2003; Landreth, 2002).

Reflecting Feelings

Reflecting feelings, which is a skill common to all forms of therapy, in Adlerian play therapy is intended to communicate to the client that the affective component of his or her play and words is understood and accepted. The play therapist acknowledges more obvious feelings expressed by the child in play or words and may choose to make tentative guesses about less obvious feelings indicated by the child's nonverbal behavior or on the basis of background information about his or her life situation or experiences (Kottman, 1999c, 2001b, 2003; Landreth, 2002). The following is an example of reflecting feelings in Adlerian play therapy.

> Example: A child is playing in the sandbox with a car he calls his "dune buggy." He is having difficulty keeping the sand out of the car, furrows his brow, and makes noises indicative of his annoyance.
> Response: "Sounds like you're feeling frustrated."

Reflections of feelings should be worded simply and clearly. The purpose is for the play therapist to communicate to the child that he or she understands what the child is feeling.

Reflecting Content

Reflection of content, which is similar in purpose to tracking behavior, is often used by Adlerian play therapists to communicate to the child that what he or she says is important. In reflecting content, the play therapist restates or paraphrases what the child has communicated in play or words (Kottman, 1999c, 2001b, 2003; Landreth, 2002).

> Example: The child has a little boy doll and a father doll. Using a deep voice, the child has the father doll say, "I know I said I'd take you, but I can't right now," and then the child has the father doll turn his back to the child doll.
> Response: "That little boy's dad said he would take him, but now he has changed his mind."

Encouraging

From an Adlerian perspective, encouragement helps children understand and acknowledge their abilities, assets, and strengths (Kottman, 2003; Watts & Pietrzak, 2000). A play therapist can encourage a child by (a) conveying unconditional acceptance, (b) demonstrating faith in the child by pointing out improvement and progress, (c) focusing on effort rather than a completed product, (d) focusing on strengths and assets rather than weaknesses and disabilities, (e) focusing on deeds rather than the doer, (f) demonstrating interest in the interests of the child, (g) not doing anything for the child that the child can do for him- or herself, (h) modeling the courage to be imperfect by acknowledging that we all make mistakes and can learn from them, and (i) helping children discover positive ways to belong and gain significance. There are many ways for therapists to encourage a child in play therapy. Key elements in the encouragement process include emphasizing the child's feeling of self-efficacy and pride and avoiding evaluative language (e.g., *good* or *well*; Kottman, 1999c, 2001a, 2003). Examples of encouraging statements in play therapy include,

- "You figured that out for yourself."
- "You're working hard on that."
- "You're building it just the way you want it."
- "Looks like you've got a plan."
- "You are really proud of the picture you're drawing."
- "You're really excited about getting a new puppy dog. Tell me more about your puppy."
- "I didn't set that back up very well. Thanks for helping do it better."
- "I see you're concerned about spilling that water. Sometimes accidents happen in here."
- "I'm not sure how to do that. Show me how you think it should work."

Returning Responsibility to the Child

It is discouraging and disrespectful to children when adults do or decide things for them that they can do or decide for themselves. The primary way that play therapists avoid doing this is by returning responsibility to the child. When returning responsibility, the play therapist communicates to the child that the child has the capability and responsibility for doing and deciding for him- or herself. This method can be very powerful for children who have a low sense of personal agency and low perceived self-efficacy (Kottman, 2001b, 2003; Landreth, 2002).

> Example: Child asks "Will you put my coat on for me?"
> Response: "I think that's something you can do for yourself."

> Example: Child asks "Should I draw or play in the sand?"
> Response: "That's something you can decide."

Asking and Responding to Questions

Children will occasionally ask questions during the process of play therapy. They will ask questions about their relationship with the therapist, the procedures in play therapy, basic logistical matters, or the personal life of the therapist. It is important when children ask questions or request information that the play therapist responds simply and honestly. Children's questions typically fall into one of four categories: (a) practical, (b) personal, (c) relationship, and (d) process questions. *Practical questions* ask for factual information; for example, "Where is the bathroom?" *Personal questions* are often attempts by children to make a connection with the play therapist or to lower their level of anxiety; for example, "Do you have any children?" *Relationship questions* typically have both overt and covert meanings and typically are the child's way of testing the strength of the relationship between the child and the play therapist; for example, "Do other children play in the playroom with you?" When asking *process questions*, children are usually attempting to define the boundaries of their relationship with the play therapist and delineate the parameters of the play therapy process; for example, "What do you think I should do next?" (Kottman, 2003; Landreth, 2002; O'Connor, 2000).

The child's questions are another opportunity to develop the relationship and better understand the child and his or her world. When children ask practical questions, they are usually only asking for factual information, and a direct factual response is in order. With process questions, a returning responsibility to the child response is necessary (see "Returning Responsibility to the Child" section). Adlerians believe that children have a purpose or goal in asking personal and relationship questions, however, and it is important to understand that purpose or goal. Therefore, when a child asks a question, the Adlerian play therapist makes a guess (tentative hypothesis) about the purpose of the question and then chooses to answer the question or, if the therapist deems the question too personal, responds by saying, "That is a question I choose not to answer." The child's response—verbal or nonverbal—to the guess about the purpose of the question often provides important information about his or her purposes and goals and the developing play therapy relationship (Kottman, 1994, 1999c, 2001b, 2003).

Asking questions is an important technique for both building rapport and for getting to know the child. Integrating questions into the natural flow of play and conversation in play therapy, the therapist inquires about the presenting problem, current events or social contexts in the child's life, or the child's life style. Kottman (2003) suggested two ways—general and specific—of asking questions about the presenting problems or current events and social contexts in the child's life. The general form is the "How is it going with . . .?" question format. For example, if a child has history of sibling rivalry issues, the play therapist might ask, "How is it going with your (sister or brother)?" The specific form of asking questions about presenting problems or current events and social contexts is to ask a "How could you change one particular aspect of . . . ?" question. For example, if the child's presenting problem is learning to appropriately express anger, the play therapist might ask "How could you tell your teacher that you are mad without getting into trouble?" How and when the play therapist uses these types of questions typically depend on the age of the child, his or her level of cognitive development, and the degree to which the child is comfortable with talking about the particular issues. Furthermore, Kottman (2003) recommended that play therapists limit the number of questions and allow children the freedom to choose whether to answer the questions. This helps avoid creating an interrogatory environment in play therapy.

Questions regarding the child's life style are usually asked in Phase 2 (Exploring the Child's Life Style; later in this chapter) and fall into four broad categories: (a) questions about the family atmosphere and family constellation, (b) questions about school, (c) questions about friends/social contexts, and (d) general questions. Play therapists should not bring a long list of questions into the playroom. Instead, they should gain sufficient familiarity with life style questions so that they can blend the questions into the normal flow of conversation with children (Kottman, 2003).

Interacting Actively With Children

Adlerian play therapists often play with child clients. The play therapist's inclusion in play can be at the child's request or at the initiative of the therapist, and the play can include role play or simple playful interaction. In role playing various situations, the child is able to take the lead and control the direction of the role play. Interactive play that allows the child to be in the lead helps build and maintain the play therapy relationship. Interacting actively by choosing to play with a child should be a continuation of the play therapy process. The play therapist must continue to make therapeutic comments, such as tracking, reflecting content and feelings, attending to nonverbal behavior, and encouraging. The temptation to become so involved in playing with the child that one loses sight of one's role as therapist must be avoided (Kottman, 1994, 1999c, 2001b, 2003).

Limit-Setting

Setting limits is an important tool in building the play therapy relationship. Limit-setting helps children understand that certain behaviors are inappropriate in the playroom. It anchors the play therapy process to reality and provides a sense of consistency and predictability. Non-negotiable limits in play therapy include harming self, the therapist, or others in the playroom; damaging toys or other parts of the playroom; and leaving the playroom before the session is completed. Other limits are negotiated on the basis of the play therapist's comfort level (e.g., whether water is allowed in the sandbox and, if so, how much) but should be reasonable and realistic (Kottman, 1999c, 2003; Landreth, 2002).

Adlerian limit-setting is a variation of the child-centered approach to setting limits (see Landreth, 2002). It consists of four steps:

1. In Step 1, the play therapist states the limit in a nonevaluative manner (e.g., "It is against the playroom rules to . . . ").
2. Step 2 consists of the play therapist reflecting the child's feelings and/or making a guess about the purpose of the behavior (e.g., "You feel angry," "Seems like you wanted to show me that I can't tell you what to do").
3. In Step 3, the play therapist engages the child in creating alternative behaviors that are acceptable in the playroom. The play therapist and the child then negotiate an acceptable appropriate behavior (e.g., "I bet you can think of something else you can shoot with the dart gun").

4. In Step 4, if the child will not engage in the creation and negotiation of an acceptable appropriate behavior, or does not follow through with the negotiated agreement, then the play therapist engages the child in creating possible logical consequences for future limit-breaking behavior (e.g., "If you choose to shoot me with the gun, you choose not to play with the gun anymore today"; Kottman, 1994, 1999c, 2001b, 2003).

Putting all four steps together in Adlerian limit setting, might look like the following example:

Billy is angry at the play therapist, points the dart gun at her and says, "I'm going to shoot you."

Play therapist (PT): It's against the playroom rules to shoot me with the dart gun.

Billy: Well, I'm going to do it.

PT: You're angry, and you want to show me that I can't tell you what to do.

Billy: Yeah!

PT: Well, I bet you can figure out something else in here to shoot.

Billy: No, I'm going to shoot you. [*He fires the dart gun and just misses the therapist.*]

PT: Billy, if you choose to shoot me with the dart gun you choose not to play with it anymore today.

Cleaning the Play Space Together

Adlerian play therapists typically invite children to help put away toys and clean up the play space. This reinforces the notions of egalitarian relationships and shared responsibility that are central to Adlerian theory and play therapy. If cleaning the room seems appropriate for the child client, then 10 minutes prior to the end of the session the play therapist tells the child that in 5 minutes they will begin cleaning the room together. With 5 minutes remaining in the session, the play therapist asks the child what the child would like to pick up and what he or she would like the therapist to pick up. The play therapist and the child then work together in the cleaning-up process (Kottman, 1994, 1999c, 2001b, 2003).

Phase 2: Exploring the Child's Life Style

In the second phase of Adlerian play therapy, the therapist explores the child's family atmosphere, family constellation, goals or purposes of behavior, and early recollections so that he or she can formulate an understanding of the child's life style.

Family Atmosphere

The family atmosphere is the general emotional climate of a family and the resulting relational patterns therein. The family atmosphere has a significant impact on the family member's life styles. Aspects of family atmosphere include the parents' attitudes toward their children; the parents' perspectives on approaches to discipline; the parents' life styles; the family's values (largely based on the parents' values); the family atmosphere of each parent's family of origin; the relationship quality of the marital dyad; the parents' parenting skills; and any personal problems of the parents that may impede their ability to provide respect, warmth, and a clear but flexible structure for their children (Kottman, 1994, 1999c, 2003).

The play therapist can assess the child's perceptions of the family atmosphere by observing the child's play with dolls and the dollhouse, puppets, kitchenware, and in the sandbox; observing parent–child interactions before and after play therapy sessions; using art therapy strategies (e.g., kinetic school and family drawings); and by asking the child and the parents questions about methods of discipline and family relational patterns (Kottman, 1994, 1999c, 2003).

Family Constellation

Rudolf Dreikurs (1952–1953) noted that the family constellation is a "sociogram of the group at home during the person's formative years" (cited in Kottman, 2003, p. 195). According to Adlerian psychology, the family constellation is significantly influential on the development of the child's life style because the family structure—along with the family atmosphere—affects the child's core attitudes and perspective on life. In the Adlerian approach, birth order is understood in terms of psychological position in the family constellation. This psychological position is significantly more influential on the development and maintenance of family members' life styles than mere chronological birth order position. Adlerian play therapists use methods to explore the family constellation that are similar to the ones they use in investigating the family atmosphere. Central to this exploration is assessing the degree to which the child's thoughts and behaviors are characteristic of his or her psychological birth order, because each position has both distinctive strengths and limitations (Kottman, 1994, 1999c, 2003).

Goals or Purposes of Behavior

According to Lew and Bettner (1996; Bettner & Lew, 1996), well-functioning children strive toward positive goals of behavior, or the Crucial Cs (connecting, feeling capable, feeling as though they count, and courage). If children believe they are unsuccessful in achieving positive goals of behavior, they become discouraged and begin striving toward negative goals (see also Kottman, 1999b). Dreikurs and Soltz (1964) classified the misbehavior of children according to four goals or purposes: (a) attention, (b) power, (c) revenge, and (d) proving inadequacy. In Phase 2 of Adlerian play therapy, the therapist seeks to identify the child's goals of misbehavior by observing the child's behavior during play therapy, being aware of his or her emotional reaction to misbehavior by the child, listening to descriptions by parents and teachers of the child's misbehavior and their emotional reactions to the same, and asking questions about and observing the child's responses to correction by parents and teachers (Kottman, 1993, 1999c, 2001a, 2003).

Early Recollections

According to Adlerian theory, people selectively recall specific early memories because the memories are indicative of their current view of the self, others, and the world. Thus, early recollections can help the play therapist understand the child's life style. Soliciting early recollections in play therapy typically occurs with children over 8 or 9 years of age (Kottman, 2003).

To secure early recollections, the therapist can ask the child to describe something that happened when he or she was small or to draw a picture of the experience. In addition, the play therapist may ask the child to use dolls or puppets to communicate an early recollection. Collecting six to eight early recollections often reveals patterns in the family atmosphere, family constellation, and purposes of behavior, thereby providing valuable information about the child's life style (Kottman, 1994, 1999c, 2003).

Life Style Conceptualization

The purpose of gathering all the life style data is to help the play therapist gain a holistic understanding of the child and his or her world and thereby help the child gain insight into the child's life style and consider changes in attitudes, perceptions, emotions, and behaviors. The play therapist integrates information obtained through observation of the child's play themes, relationships with others, artwork, and behavior in and out of play therapy sessions; attention to the child's responses to questions asked by the play therapist; and (if appropriate) interviews with parents and teachers (if appropriate).

Using the life style data, the therapist creates a life style conceptualization that is the basis for treatment planning in Adlerian play therapy with the child and consultation with significant adult figures in the child's life (Kottman, 2003).

Phase 3: Helping the Child Gain Insight

In moving from Phase 2 to Phase 3, the Adlerian play therapist uses the data gathered from Phase 2 to discover patterns in the goals or purposes of behavior, family atmosphere, family constellation, and early recollections and begins to formulate hypotheses about the child's life style and the private logic and core convictions contained therein. As he or she develops these hypotheses, the therapist also begins to design strategies for sharing these ideas with their clients (Kottman, 1994, 1999c, 2001b, 2003).

In Phase 3 of Adlerian play therapy, there is a major shift in the therapist's expectations for change as he or she begins sharing the aforementioned hypotheses with the child to help the child gain insight into his or her life style. Helping the child gain insight serves as a characteristic prelude to the final phase of therapy, in which he or she considers, and possibly begins implementing, attitudinal and behavioral changes. Strategies used to help the child better understand his or her life style include tentative interpretations (hypotheses), metacommunication, artwork, play metaphors, bibliotherapy, and connecting play therapy to the real world (Kottman, 1994, 1999c, 2003).

Tentative Interpretations

The Adlerian play therapist offers interpretations of both play and words to children in the form of tentative interpretations (hypotheses or guesses). The therapist may offer guesses about the child's family atmosphere or family constellation patterns and how the child interacts and gains significance within the family and other social contexts (e.g., school); the child's perception of self, others, and the world; the relationship between the child's attitudes and his or her behavior; and the child's goals or purposes of behavior. The interpretations may be offered directly to the child or indirectly, by using play media. Hypotheses are offered tentatively so that the child may correct the play therapist if the guess is incorrect or if the child is not ready to address the ramifications of a correct interpretation. Children often do not respond verbally to interpretations. However, they almost invariably respond by offering some form of nonverbal recognition reflex, a disruption in play behavior, or a metaphoric response within their play (Kottman, 1994, 1999c, 2003).

Some examples of direct and indirect tentative hypotheses are the following:

> Example: The female child client puts a baby doll in bed with mommy and daddy dolls. She then puts a little girl doll on the living room couch and has the doll begin to cry.
>
> Direct response: "You feel sad because your mommy and daddy spend so much time with your baby brother. My guess is that you wish your mommy and daddy spent more time with you."
>
> Indirect response: "She sounds really sad. I'm wondering if she is sad because her mommy and daddy spend so much time with the baby and she wishes her mommy and daddy would spend more time with her."

Metacommunication

Metacommunication, a strategy often used immediately following a tentative interpretation, consists of communication by the play therapist about the child's verbal and nonverbal communication. The play therapist uses metacommunication by making an observation about the child's response to an interpretation or question, taking note of patterns in the child's communication and offering hunches about what the child's nonverbal behavior is communicating. For reasons similar to those for using interpretations, metacommunication is offered to the child in a tentative manner (Kottman, 1999c, 2003).

Artwork, Play Metaphors, and Bibliotherapy

Adlerian play therapists often use artwork to help children gain insight. Kottman (1999c, 2003) has noted that sometimes children will spontaneously produce artwork, and the therapist can ask the child questions about both the process and the product. On other occasions, the therapist may specifically ask the child to create artwork (e.g., family drawings, kinetic home and school drawings, etc.).

Adlerian play therapists also use play metaphors to communicate with children. Situations in the lives of children may be so painful or stressful that they will not be comfortable talking about them directly. Consequently, children often create a pretend narrative through play to communicate what is occurring in their lives. Because children often use play metaphors to communicate, it is typically most productive for the play therapist to respect their use of metaphor and respond indirectly through the metaphor rather than directly interpreting it (Kottman, 1994, 2003).

Adlerian play therapists can also create a therapeutic metaphor or use bibliotherapy with a child to develop perceptual alternatives or help the child better understand various aspects of his or her life style. The play therapist can create a story about animals, dolls, puppets, or another child; engage in mutual storytelling; or read a book about a character in a situation similar to that of the child client. As the play therapist uses these procedures, he or she should watch for nonverbal communication indicative of the child's experience of the metaphor. Some children will benefit by the play therapist's use of metacommunication regarding the child's reaction to the metaphor, whereas other children are best served by the therapist not responding to their reaction (Kottman, 2003).

Connecting Play Therapy to the Real World

In the process of helping children better understand their thoughts, feelings, and behaviors, the play therapist must strive to help children generalize these insights beyond the play therapy situation to other settings and relationships. Clients may not automatically generalize what they learn in therapy to the rest of their lives. To facilitate the transfer of learning, the Adlerian play therapist can delineate parallels between how the child thinks, feels, and behaves in the process of play therapy and how he or she thinks, feels, and behaves at home, school, and in other contexts. By noting these parallels, the therapist helps the child begin generalizing his or her insights in play therapy and thus begin considering potential changes the child wants to make (Kottman, 1994, 1999c, 2003).

Phase 4: Reorientation/Reeducation

In the final phase of play therapy, the Adlerian play therapist moves to a more directive, teacher–encourager role. The therapist in this reorientation/reeducation phase helps the child generate perceptual and behavioral alternatives and learn and practice new attitudes and skills so that the child can implement them in relationships and situations outside of the play therapy situation (Kottman, 1994, 2001a, 2003).

Helping Children Generate Perceptual and Behavioral Alternatives

As children gain insight into their life style and consider alternative perceptions of themselves, others, and the world, they typically are ready to consider alternative ways of interacting with others. Children often already possess sufficient knowledge and skills to engage in successful interactions but fail to appropriately apply these assets. Kottman (1999c, 2003) has suggested that the therapist help such children recall specific experiences and situations in which they would like to act more cooperatively and constructively. If appropriate for the child, the play therapist can directly engage him or her in a conversation. The therapist can first ask the child to recall thoughts, feelings, and behaviors regarding specific situations and then ask him or her to think of perceptual, emotional, or behavioral alternatives for past or future occurrences. With other children, an indirect engagement may be more appropriate. For indirect engagement, Kottman (2003) suggested using therapeutic metaphor, bibliotherapy, or mutual storytelling to help children explore other ways of thinking, feeling, and behaving. The therapist can use role play, dolls, puppets, artwork, and other creative arts strategies to reenact specific past or anticipated experiences or situations and engage the child in a dialogue regarding alternative perspectives, emotions, and behaviors.

Helping Children Learn New Skills and Behaviors

Some children have difficulty generating perceptual and behavioral alternatives, even with help from the play therapist. Other children may have skill or learning deficits that limit their ability to create solutions to their problems. With these children, the play therapist may choose to provide information and teach skills. Again, the therapist can use direct or indirect means in the teaching process. In the direct approach, the play therapist provides information about a subject or explains how the child would accomplish a task. In the indirect approach, the therapist can use dolls, puppets, toys, role models from stories or books, or role play to provide the information or demonstrate the desired behavior (Kottman, 1994, 1999c, 2003).

Helping Children Practice New Skills and Behaviors

As children create perceptual alternatives and behaviors or learn new attitudes and skills, they need an opportunity to practice thoughts, feelings, and behaviors in a safe, secure environment. The play therapy relationship gives children this opportunity. Again, depending on the child's needs, the play therapist can use direct or indirect means to help children practice. The play therapist usually begins the practice process using an indirect approach. Children rehearse what they and others will think, feel, say, and do using dolls, puppets, toys, other play media, or storytelling. Play therapists can also use a more direct approach in asking children to practice new attitudes and skills by role playing real or anticipated situations (Kottman, 2003).

Kottman (2003) suggested that as a child's sense of self-efficacy with the new attitudes or skills increases, he or she might benefit by interacting with others—parents, a sibling, a child friend, or another child client. The play therapist can invite the significant person or persons into the safe and supportive environment of the play therapy situation, thereby giving the child opportunity to practice with actual members of his or her life.

Throughout this phase of play therapy, the child will benefit from ample encouragement. The play therapist serves as a cheerleader, acknowledging the child's efforts and affirming the progress made, taking note of the child's abilities and strengths, and reflecting the child's feelings of pride and accomplishment. Encouragement helps the child anchor the successful changes in thoughts, feelings, and behaviors (Kottman, 1994, 1999c, 2003).

CONCLUSION

Adlerian play therapy is a four-phase process that integrates principles and procedures from play therapy with Adlerian psychology and psychotherapy. This approach to therapy with children can be very effective in helping clients better understand themselves and their relationships with others; learn new ways to view themselves, others, and the world; and develop new skills and access latent abilities that enhance their sense of self-efficacy and their interactions with significant others.

Regardless of one's theoretical orientation, it is essential to get training and supervision in play therapy from experienced play therapists. Terry Kottman, the creator and foremost authority on Adlerian play therapy, created *The Encouragement Zone* largely to provide training and supervision in play therapy (see "Selected Readings and Resources for Further Study" at the end of this volume).

Concomitant to the ongoing play therapy process with the child, Adlerian play therapists consult with parents and, if appropriate, teachers. Parents and teachers can provide invaluable information regarding the child's developmental history, learning styles, and relational patterns. Their support of the child's efforts to change in play therapy also can be invaluable (Kottman, 2003). Parental involvement is particularly important in the play therapy process. Children may make some productive changes in play therapy without parental involvement, but substantial and long-lasting progress most often occurs when parents are actively involved. Teacher involvement is particularly important when the child's presenting problem relates to situations at school or when the problem is hindering the child's academic performance.

As with changes in the family system, sometimes changes in the classroom/school interactional patterns are needed to help facilitate or maintain changes in play therapy. In the next chapter, we discuss parent and teacher consultation.

12

CONSULTATION AND PSYCHOEDUCATION

Adlerian psychologists have a long tradition of educational interventions. Alfred Adler became the first psychological educator when he conducted public counseling demonstrations in Vienna in the 1920s. The goal of the family counseling sessions was to educate and inform a public audience in the skills needed for healthy family living. In these programs, Adler not only provided facts but also demonstrated how these facts could be applied to the lives of both the people who were on stage and those in the audience.

Adlerians believe that, when possible, training should come before treatment. Many people have problems in their daily living because they have been trained in autocratic, power-driven skills. These skills provide problems in today's democratic world. Adlerians have applied their educational ideas in schools and community centers as well as in the therapy relationship. Clients are viewed as students who want to learn the necessary skills for a more satisfying life style. In this chapter, we look at ways of working with teachers, parents, families, and couples from an educational model. Two specific ways of Adlerian psychological education will be highlighted: (a) consultation and (b) psychoeducation for parents and couples.

Consultation is typically an outgrowth of the problems that lead children and teens into individual therapy. The consultant is often (but not always) the individual therapist, and he or she usually consults privately with teachers in school or parents in the therapy setting. Psychoeducation is conducted by trained psychoeducators in groups and can be invaluable either as a stand-alone intervention or as a part of therapy for children and couples.

First, we describe consultation and offer an example of how a consultative interview might proceed. Next, we discuss parent education groups and describe the roles of leaders and members in these groups. Finally, we describe a couples education group model. Again, such groups can be stand-alone interventions or valuable adjuncts to couples therapy.

CONSULTATION

The consultant must have a clear understanding of the task of consultation. In its most basic sense, consultation can be summed this way: When someone has a problem, he or she goes to see the consultant/therapist about that problem. Often, the problem is another person, and the individual who brings the problem to the consultant is a teacher or parent. Consultants often talk about the child with whom the person is concerned. In consultation, the Adlerian consultant speaks directly to the teacher or parent about their problem: the child. The task is to help the person who brings the problem (the consultee) to become more aware of his or her inner resources and more sensitive to the beliefs that prevent effective functioning in the problem child. Consultants are agents for change and facilitators of human potential. Through this feedback process, the consultant helps the consultee learn new skills (Carlson & Dinkmeyer, 2002; Dinkmeyer & Carlson, 2001).

Consultants need to understand how to develop collaborative relationships. Cooperation and an equal commitment toward changing the status quo of the system in which we live are the elements of this relationship. Working within the system, a consultant creates change with consultees and, in essence, changes the system with the cooperation and alliance of the consultee.

The collaborative relationship initiated by the consultant is based on his or her essential beliefs about how to change behavior, attitudes, and beliefs. Consultation is enhanced by cooperative problem-solving approaches. It is impeded by advice-giving or other superior–inferior methods. Teachers and parents need more than ideas; they need to be consulted, not simply advised. The consultee's concern is not solved by a superficial string of answers. Consultants help consultees integrate new ideas and skills with their beliefs and emotions.

An Adlerian consultant does not play the role of expert. Consultants who are always engaged in crises are often people whose life styles seek excitement or the creation of these types of dependent relationships. Thus, consultants need to be aware of their beliefs and their own relationship style.

It can be flattering to receive a request for help with a problem. It can be exhilarating to think that one might be able to provide a ready answer and solve a problem for a parent or teacher. This is a trap that Adlerian consultants avoid. By doing so, they can teach parents and teachers how to understand and solve their own problems.

THE SEVEN-STEP CONSULTING PROCESS

Individual consultation with teachers or parents follows a seven-step process.

Step 1: Establish the Tone

In this first step, the consultant establishes a sense of mutual respect, rapport, or perceived equality. Privacy and confidentiality are established. Open, honest, and direct communication is crucial; this is an educational process, not a medical diagnosis. Nobody will be blamed; everyone can be part of the solution. Consultants must help the teacher or parent understand how this is a problem for that particular individual.

Step 2: Get a Specific Description of the Problem

The consultant should ask the consultee, "Can you give a specific example of when the child was a problem *for you?* Pick something in the last day or two." Follow-up questions can include "What, specifically, did he or she say or do?", "How did you respond, and how did you feel when responding?", and "What did he or she do then?" The consultant should ask the parent or teacher to repeat the exact words, in the way that the child said them. If the consultee cannot remember, ask him or her to paraphrase.

Steps 3 and 4: Get a Second Specific Example and Clarify the Goal of Misbehavior and the Teacher's or Parent's Troubling Belief

Get a second example by repeating Step 2. Summarize the pattern by restating what the child did, how the parent or teacher responded and felt, and what the child did next. Solicit a guess as to the child's goal of misbehavior. See the chart on the goals of misbehavior in chapter 1.

Step 5: Review the Guidelines for Reaching This Goal

In this step, the consultant reviews with the consultee guidelines that will help them reach their desired goal. These include the following: attention (catch the child being good, create attention-getting moments), power (give the child choices, create choice opportunities; don't fight or give in), avoid revenge (give chances for fairness, refuse to be hurt), avoid displays of inadequacy (do not give up despite extreme discouragement; instead ask a question such as "One asset is . . . ?"). The consultant also should identify ways the consultee has successfully worked through this goal of misbehavior in other situations. Together, they review what could be done that the consultee has not yet tried.

Step 6: Solicit Tentative Suggestions

In Step 6, the consultant and consultee work on one problem at a time. The consultant should break the goals down into realistic steps that can be achieved in about a week. The consultant should be concrete and anticipate that things will get worse before showing improvement. He or she should remind the parent or teacher that changes are only for 1 week and are renegotiable. Direct suggestions should be avoided; instead, the consultant should ask questions such as "Have you thought about ____?", "What would happen if you did ____?", and "Would you be willing to consider ____?"

Step 7: Attain Closure

In this final step, the consultant should get the consultee's commitment to implement specific solutions. Both should review exactly what the consultee will do. Last, a follow-up meeting is scheduled.

CASE EXAMPLE

The consultation process just described can be best understood by following an example of a brief consultation in a school setting. The consultant is in this case the play therapist who has been working with Phil, the student of a frustrated teacher. Therapists who work with children will be able to see how consultation with parents about the disruptive behavior of a child in the home would be very similar.

Teacher (T): I really need some help with Phil. He's driving me insane.

Consultant (C): Can you give me an example of when Phil has been a problem to you in the last day or two?

T: Every time I start to teach, he gets up and walks around the room. Sometimes he just leaves the classroom.

C: How about today? Did he get up and walk around the classroom? Exactly what happened? Can you go right to the point where he was a problem for you?

T: Yeah, I was teaching science, and I thought I had a pretty good lesson prepared. The students were sitting in a group and all of a sudden Phil starts to cough real loud. I thought maybe he needed to get a drink, so I said "Phil, if you need to get a drink, go ahead." He answered "Oh, no. That's OK." I proceeded to teach, and suddenly he gets up and leaves my classroom. I ask "Where are you going?" He says, "I am going to get a drink. You said I could." But this was 25 minutes later.

C: Can you say again how you said "Where are you going?"

T: "Where are you going?" [*in an angry tone*]

C: How did you feel when he did this?

T: I am always angry whenever he does something like this. He really makes me mad.

C: What did you do?

T: I told him to get back in his seat. Sometimes I try to ignore him.

C: When you tell him to go back, does he do it right away?

T: Oh yeah, he's usually pretty good. He might look out the window a few minutes, but he eventually strolls back to his place. He's not bold or anything.

C: Do you have any idea why Phil does this? What is the purpose of his behavior?

T: Well, I think he does it to get my attention. He knows that every time that he walks around or leaves the classroom that I'm going to stop what I'm doing and ask him what is wrong. I think he is really a boy who craves attention.

C: Do you have any other possible ideas about what it is that Phil is doing?

T: I'm not really sure.

C: Could it be that Phil wants to be the boss? That he wants to do things on his terms and not yours?

T: I guess I really never looked at it that way.

C: Could it be that Phil and you are in a power conflict and he wants to be in charge of this class?

T: Boy, that makes a lot of sense to me.

C: Have you got any ideas how you might get out of a power conflict? Has there been a time in the past where you have been in a power conflict and have gotten out successfully?

T: Well, I probably have, but right now I can't really think of it.

C: Is there anything else that you have thought about doing that you haven't done with Phil?

T: I have thought at one time about telling him that when he leaves the classroom that he can't come back in. That once you leave you are gone.

C: That's an interesting idea. Do you think something like that might work with Phil?

T: Well, I don't know. I'd be willing to try it.

C: What exactly would you do?

T: I guess I could say "Phil, you have a choice. You can either sit down or leave."

C: Wow, I wonder what would happen, and if he left what would happen then?

T: He would have to go to the office, or I could call down and someone could come and get him to make sure that he got there.

C: Would you be willing to do that this week and see if that helps?

T: Sure. I'll talk to you next week.

In this situation, Phil and the teacher were in a power conflict. The teacher was unwittingly supporting Phil's behavior by thinking that Phil just wanted attention. If Phil just wanted attention, then he would have returned to the desk in a fashion that would have let the teacher know he was being cooperative. Instead, Phil returned on his terms, and he got up to go to the bathroom when he wanted to and not when he was allowed to. Often, when teachers can understand their role in supporting goals such as power, attention, revenge, or inadequacy, they can change their behavior and therefore directly solve the problems they are facing. The consultation model does not simply solve a problem for the teacher or parent; it actually teaches them the problem-solving process.

PARENT EDUCATION

Parents rarely have adequate experience, training, and educational background to enable them to function effectively in their role as child caregivers. In the Adlerian approach to parent education, "normal" or adequate parents are given the opportunity to increase their child-rearing skills. One need not necessarily be sick, deviant, or troubled to be assisted.

The attitudes, ideas, and interrelationships of parents are frequent sources of problems. The struggle involves obtaining independence from their own autocratic background or permissive patterns. This however, does not help parents to establish democratic approaches to dealing effectively with their children. The acquisition of new techniques and democratic management of children is a matter no longer of choice but of necessity. A healthy family unit is the most important ingredient in a healthy society.

Parent education is an increasingly important function for psychotherapists. It provides an opportunity in an educational setting to maximize growth in the family. The attention given to the development of parent education programs has been increasing. Available programs in the parent education field are evidence of the growth of this particular dimension of mental health.

The therapist needs to not only listen to the parents' problems but also teach them the skills to solve their problems. Working in the actual life space of parents helps the family members develop solutions to their problems. The therapist must go beyond just knowledge. Knowledge defines a problem, but it does not solve it. The therapist should be eager and willing to help formulate ideas but not a judge, umpire, or dispenser of criticism.

A program of parent education that centers on weekly parenting group discussions is an integral mental health component in that it allows parents to take an active role. Such groups are formed to help parents understand and work with the affective and cognitive aspects of dealing with their children. Once a program of this nature is begun, it becomes self-supporting. Despite common misconceptions, our experience has been that parents, regardless of socioeconomic status, intellectual level, or ethnic background, want and will seek out and support this activity.

Perhaps the effectiveness of parent education can be attributed to the many advantages that parents derive from it. Parents find that their concerns are often similar to concerns raised by other parents. Each group member is a qualified expert in the field of raising children. Although there are problems that each of us does not know how to handle, there are other problems that we have already mastered. Groups provide opportunities for parents to learn from one another. Parent education is a method that provides new ideas, skill practice, and encouragement to place the new ideas and skills into each family. Parent education groups are cost-effective, too, in that they reach not only the 10 to 12 participants but also the participants' children and spouses.

Adlerian psychotherapists are well acquainted with the parent educational materials that are available at present and have developed the skills of being competent parent education leaders. Therapists who are interested in reaching the greatest number of people will develop a training program that permits them to train additional parent group leaders. Most of the current parent education programs are well organized and come with detailed leader's manuals. Active Parenting (Popkin, 1994) and Systematic Training for Effective Parenting (STEP) are the two most popular Adlerian-based programs.

Both have similar content and pedagogy. In the next section, we discuss the STEP program to provide a better understanding of parent education.

SYSTEMATIC TRAINING FOR EFFECTIVE PARENTING

The STEP (Dinkmeyer, McKay, & Dinkmeyer, 1998) program is the most widely used Adlerian parent education program. STEP and its companion, STEP/Teen (Dinkmeyer, McKay, & Dinkmeyer, 1990), which is designed for the parents of teenagers, have reached approximately 4 million parents, either in parent education groups or through their own reading.

The STEP program is organized so that consultants can teach the program the first time and then start to identify parents who, with a minimum of training, can become facilitators of the program. Consulting becomes most effective as the leaders are permitted to have a leadership role and an opportunity to train additional numbers of parents.

The content of the STEP program focuses on nine major concepts:

1. Understanding children's behavior and misbehavior,
2. Understanding more about your child and about yourself as parent,
3. Encouragement: Building your child's confidence and feelings of worth,
4. Communication: How to listen to your child,
5. Communication: Exploring alternatives and expressing your ideas and feelings to children,
6. Natural and logical consequences: A method of discipline that develops responsibility,
7. Applying natural and logical consequences to other concerns,
8. The family meeting, and
9. Developing confidence and using your potential.

The STEP program is organized systematically as a skill-building program that has a systematic instructional sequence. The process usually involves a discussion of the previous week's activity assignment. Parents are asked to do something specific with their children or to observe their children and then report back on the results.

A discussion of the assigned reading is held, focusing mostly on how this reading applies to parents' work with their children. Charts are used as visual aids that describe the major concepts and principles of the program; these charts are discussed to reinforce the major concepts.

Parent education groups often consist of approximately 12 members and usually meet once a week for about 1.5 to 2 hours, for 6 to 9 weeks. Attendance is usually voluntary, although we have observed an increasing use of parent education as part of the judicial system's attempts to remediate abusive and neglectful parents. Most groups are closed; when a group has begun, no new members are allowed to join.

Although the mix is heterogeneous, the recommendation is that parents have a least one child of about the same age so that themes or common challenges particular to an age group can be enhanced. For example, the parents of a teen are often bored by discussions of bed-wetting or the challenges of toddlers. Similarly, parents of toddlers are often horrified to learn of the challenges of adolescence to greet them in a decade!

Systematic Training for Effective Parenting of Teens (STEP/Teen) has the same philosophy and psychology as the STEP program. The content adds material to help the parents understand personality development and emotions in adolescence as well as their own emotional responses. The STEP/Teen program also goes into much greater detail with the special challenges that occur during the teen years (Dinkmeyer et al., 1990).

A third program, Early Childhood STEP, has been developed for parents of younger children, ages birth to 6 (Dinkmeyer, McKay, & Dinkmeyer, 1989). A companion for STEP and STEP/Teen, the program offers similar concepts at age-appropriate levels. For example, the age range is divided into three areas: (a) babies, (b) toddlers, and (c) preschoolers. Specific developmental information is presented so that parents know what to expect from their children.

THE LEARNING CYCLE IN PARENT EDUCATION GROUPS

Parent education groups function successfully when the consultant understands the areas of leadership skills, the learning cycle, and the stages of the group.

Leadership Skills

The group's time, topics, size, and scope are structured. Several chapters in the program can be compressed if time limitations deem it necessary. The topics of the group should be structured to reflect the educational nature of the group. The group is not therapy.

The leader seeks to universalize the experiences of the group members. Most parents have had similar challenges raising their children: bedtime, chores, and motivation are examples of the typical issues. However, parents usually do not recognize that their experiences are similar to those of others in the group. The group leader has the task of pointing out this similarity.

Another avenue for universalizing is regarding parents' expectations for their children. Most parents want their children to do well in life, to learn from their mistakes, and to try hard. These goals can be explored, and methods for reaching them are one purpose of the parent education group.

Encourage, encourage, encourage. A leader can never be too encouraging with parents in the group. Even when court-ordered, discouraged parents are in the group, the leader must seek to find what is right or okay about these parents. Simply being in the group is an asset, which can be acknowledged.

The Learning Cycle

New ideas are presented through discussions of the readings and charts. In most chapters, the ideas presented are new ones, compared with more commonly used ideas. For example, in the chapter on motivation, the new idea of encouragement is contrasted with the idea of praise.

The ideas are then translated into specific skills. If the parents understand the idea of encouragement, how do they encourage? What is said or done that is encouraging? Parents practice the skill through role play, discussion of problem situations, and audio- or videotaped incidents.

The importance of using the learned skills with children is stressed through practical applications. In most group meetings, the consultant makes certain parents know what their homework for the week will be. This can then be checked and discussed at the start of the next group session.

Stages of the Group

It is helpful to understand that the group will go through three very different stages. Each stage requires the use of different leadership traits.

"Great Expectations"

At first, most parents are usually excited and involved but believe the group will teach them how to "fix" or change their children. Group leaders should spend time structuring the group so that parents understand the goals of the group. Universalizing is also necessary to allow members to begin to recognize the commonality of their concerns. This stage of the group often lasts two or three sessions.

"You Mean I Have to Change?"

Here parents begin to recognize that the parent group offers ideas to change themselves, not the children (although changes in children do result as a consequence of the parent's new behaviors and attitudes). Parents who have no interest in changing their behaviors may become discouraged. This transition stage is an opportunity for the consultant and leader to understand human behavior and encourage any positive movement.

Cohesiveness and Commitment

The final stage of the groups is characterized by cohesiveness and a commitment to change. Many groups find it difficult to end, because the experience has been beneficial for the participants.

THE NEXT STEP

The Next STEP (Dinkmeyer, McKay, & Dinkmeyer, 1987) is an advanced program designed for parents who have completed STEP, STEP/Teen, or Early Childhood STEP. It provides basic introductory concepts while developing a problem-solving procedure. The program is organized to help parents apply the STEP concepts to specific problems. In the course of the program an opportunity is provided for parents to become more familiar with their own life style and how it affects their parenting effectiveness.

Optional content is available to be covered by a particular group. Some of the options include building your and your child's self-esteem; your child as an achieving person; learning how to make responsible choices; gentle strength and firm love; discipline; special concerns of parents of infants and toddlers; and special concerns of intermediate teens and handicapped children. Units are also devoted to stress in the family and the issue of single parents and step-parents.

THE PARENT C GROUP

The C group is a method for helping group members acquire knowledge and evaluate their own beliefs and attitudes. In the C group there is an opportunity to go beyond the study of principles. The group involves not only the demonstration of procedures and ideas but also helps members become more aware of how their beliefs and attitudes affect their relationships with their children (Dinkmeyer & Dinkmeyer, 1976).

The power of the C group comes from the parents' awareness that a belief such as "I must always be right" or "No one's going to challenge my rules" interferes with effective relationships and caring communication. Parents are helped to see that their belief results in resistance and struggle for power. However, if the belief is modified to "I prefer to be right, but I can make mistakes" or "It would be easier if my authority weren't challenged as part of growing up," then the possibility for conflict resolution is increased.

Leaders of C groups prefer to work with parents who have been in study groups or STEP programs because a common awareness of the fundamentals of human behavior and common ability to use basic parenting skills exists. The C group leader then integrates this awareness with parents' feelings, beliefs, and attitudes so that they can apply the principles to very specific situations. Leaders of C groups require much more skill in managing group dynamics than in dealing with problem solving.

The approach was titled C *group* because the forces that make it effective begin with a C. The specific components include the following:

- *Collaboration*: working together on mutual concerns as equals is a basic requirement.
- *Consultation*, which is received and provided by the members.
- *Clarifying* of member's beliefs and feelings is accomplished.
- *Confrontation*, which produces more honest and realistic feedback. A norm is established so that each individual sees his or her own purposes, attitudes, and beliefs and develops a willingness to confront other members with their beliefs.
- *Concern* and *caring*, which permeate the relationships.
- *Confidentiality*: whatever is discussed within the group stays within the group.
- *Commitment*, which requires that each person make a decision to participate fully and become involved in working on his or her own personal concern.
- *Change*, which is the purpose of involvement; each member determines his or her goals for change.

THERAPEUTIC FORCES IN PARENT GROUPS

Parent education groups provide a unique opportunity for all parents to become more aware of their relationships with their children. They are allowed to experience feedback from other parents in regard to the impact that their parenting procedures have on their children. This opportunity for mutual therapeutic effect is constantly available. Concurrently, provision is made for the creation of a strong bond, which takes advantage of the universal problems that confront parents. They experience a realization that all parents have problems and that solutions are available. The opportunity for parents to help each other and to mutually develop new approaches to parent–child relationships is provided. Corrective feedback from peers has a tremendous effect on the participants.

Therapists who conduct parent groups must be careful not to establish the groups as if its intentions were to provide information and to deal only with cognitive ideas. This is not a lecture, or a discussion, but truly a group experience. This necessitates the use of group mechanisms and dynamic processes that are present in any well-organized therapeutic group. A primarily educational group can have therapeutic results.

The therapist realizes the necessity of reassuring and encouraging the parents (even if only by their good intentions to help the child). The therapist should lead, not push or tell. The parent group is much different from the traditional parent meeting. The parent group emphasizes the treatment of parents as whole people and as equals. They are not lectured at or told how they should be; instead, they are dealt with in relation to their own concerns and to where they are.

Some of the group mechanisms that are particularly pertinent to group work include group identification or a communal feeling, which encompasses the idea that all members are concerned about common challenges and have a willingness to help parents live more effectively with their children; the opportunity to recognize the universal nature of child-training problems; the opportunity to not only receive help but also to give help and love to others; the opportunity to give encouragement and support; and the opportunity to listen, which not only provides support but also, in many instances, provides spectator therapy. Someone else's idea may enable parents to start a new approach to transactions with their child. The mechanism for feedback is the benefit the individual gains from listening to and observing others.

STARTING GROUPS

Organizers of group programs for parents may face the problem of having more participants than can be accommodated in a single group. Groups should have approximately 10 to 12 members so that each member can enjoy the advantages of a small group. It is important that the participants have children of about the same age so that the basis of their experiences and challenges are somewhat similar.

Programs such as STEP provide an introductory 8-minute videotape that outlines the focus of the program and some of the topics that will be covered. Parents can obtain some sample program materials and find that their need for education is not a sign of weakness but rather a sign of intelligent commitment to the growth of their children and themselves as a parent.

This point is especially important and deserves the therapist's full attention. In the absence of past explanations, parents must deal with many possible reasons for becoming involved in an education program. Often, a parent rationalizes "This worked for my parents, so it will work for me" yet realizes that this defensive posture does not work. In such cases, the therapist must help the parent appreciate the shift from autocracy to democracy, which has left many parents without effective strategies for dealing with their children. It is not that parents lack ability but that they lack skills and models. It is up to the therapist to point out to parents this essential difference and the possible implications.

GROUP LEADERSHIP STYLE

Parent group leaders must use skills to make group experiences constructive. These skills are similar to those used in Adlerian group psychotherapy, but the focus is on learning and on universalizing the qualities of being a parent.

Structuring

Structuring allows the group to know exactly what will be expected of each member; meeting times and place, lengths of sessions, and purposes and goals will be used to structure the group. Structuring occurs during the group's first sessions. As the group progresses, the leader must be constantly aware of what is going on in the group so that he or she can determine whether the current situation is in the best interest of the group's stated goals and purposes.

Universalizing

Universalizing helps members become aware that their experiences are similar to those of others. Groups provide many opportunities for group members to realize how much they have in common. It is up to the leader to tap this well of common experiences and bring the similarities to the surface for everybody's benefit. When a member shares a problem with the group, the leader can elicit reactions from the others by asking "Has anybody had a similar difficulty?" or some similar open-ended questions that invites participants to share experiences. Often, a parent reacts spontaneously—verbally or nonverbally—in agreement, and the leader can then encourage additional responses from that member.

Linking

Linking is the process of identifying common elements in the group member's comments. The leader often finds that an idea keeps coming up as a theme of the member's experiences. With parent groups this may be "bedtime is usually pretty difficult" or "sometimes spanking is really the only way to get the message across." It is important for the leader to use these themes in positive ways to link members in the early stages of the group. Linking and universalizing promote cohesiveness, a feeling of togetherness, and a sense of purpose. Once a theme is expressed and detected, the leader can articulate the common element with comments such as "I sense that Don and Sally feel connected about their middle child." The group can then briefly discuss the problems common to most middle children and possible new ways to deal with middle children.

Focusing on the Positive

It may be difficult for parents to see the positive side of their children while they are immersed in a power struggle or other conflict. The parents' ability to focus on the positive and to encourage their children's skills and assets often helps facilitate change in the children's behavior. The leader can model encouraging behavior by looking for assets and efforts. Parents often do not see improvement until others in the group help them realize the changes that have taken place.

Commitment

Leaders help stimulate commitment to the group. It is important that each group member make a commitment to attend all sessions, participate in discussion, and apply the ideas in his or her family relationships. Thus, homework is an essential part of the group process. A leader asks for specific commitments at the end of the session and at the start of the next session by asking members to share their experiences.

Summarizing

The summary at the end of the session deals with the feelings and ideas as they occurred at any time during the session. It may focus on the content of the meeting or on the commitment that each member has made for the upcoming week. The leader can begin by asking each participant to complete the sentence "I learned _____." This procedure allows members to share what they have gained during the session and gives them an opportunity to correct or clarify confusions or doubts.

Encouragement

Encouragement is a skill that parents may find especially difficult. It is often mistaken for praise, which is a more widespread form of motivation in U.S. culture. The essential difference between the two is that praise generally focuses on external results, whereas encouragement recognizes inherent abilities and positive expectations.

The next section is devoted to psychoeducation for couples. The aforementioned skills are the same ones that are used with couple education groups.

PSYCHOEDUCATION IN THE TREATMENT OF COUPLES

The movement to enrich marriages and to provide education rather than therapy for couples is usually credited as having begun a little over 40 years ago. The historical roots of marriage enrichment are generally traced to

Barcelona, Spain, where a group of married couples met in January 1962 for a weekend marriage enrichment retreat with Rev. Gabriel Calvo. It is from this meeting that the worldwide network of Marriage Encounter resulted.

Rudolf Dreikurs published the book *The Challenge of Marriage* in 1946. This book was based on the thoughts that he had developed 10 or more years earlier. Dreikurs predicted correctly that "normal" people would need help dealing with "normal" problems and frustrations of living together. He saw the shifting switch from autocratic to democratic living and hoped to help partners learn to live as equals. Study groups of couples gathered to learn the skills needed to live a more satisfying life.

Since that time, many programs have been developed to help couples learn how to build loving, satisfying, and lasting relationships. Most married couples want to stay married. They want the advantages of a satisfying marriage: a longer, healthier life; love, acceptance, and emotional support; greater economic achievement; and children. Couples need skills for living in today's companionate relationships. Traditional marriage was based on roles fixed by gender. Men worked and provided home and food, while women bore children and nurtured the family. Marital success was judged by how well these roles were fulfilled. In companionate marriages, marriage roles and relationships are discussed and negotiated. Both partners have the skills necessary to identify and align their goals with their partners; encourage their partners, including through "encouragement meetings" and "encouraging days"; develop honest, congruent communication; develop an understanding of how their beliefs, feelings, and goals influence their communication; listen empathically, express feeling accurately and practice these skills in marriage meetings; learn to make helpful choices in their marriage; develop a process for resolving skills; and develop self-help skills for building and maintaining an equal marriage.

Training in Marriage Enrichment (TIME; Dinkmeyer & Carlson, 2003) is a marriage education program based on the work of Alfred Adler. It is an educational program designed to help married couples learn the skills they need to build a loving and supportive relationship. In TIME groups, couples develop skills that enable them to enrich their marriages and to deal with particular challenges that they experience. Couples define the marriage that they want and develop and retain the skills to maintain that relationship. Participation in a TIME group does not imply that a couple has an ineffective marriage or marriage problems but rather that they want to grow and strengthen their relationship.

BASIC PRINCIPLES OF THE TRAINING IN MARRIAGE ENRICHMENT PROGRAM

The TIME program was developed on several principles of marriage. Developing and maintaining a good marriage relationship requires a time commitment. For marriage to succeed, couples must make their relationship an important priority now and in the future.

Specific skills that are essential to a healthy marriage can be learned. When partners understand how a marriage works, and what the necessary skills for building a successful marriage are, they can develop skills that create a positive and rewarding relationship.

Change often takes time, but all change begins with the individual. The first step in enriching a marriage involves a commitment to change. Partners begin by understanding how each of them has shaped their marriage and what each can do to make desired changes. Couples are encouraged to be patient with their rates of progress.

Feelings of love and caring that have diminished or disappeared will often return with behavior changes. Romantic feelings, intimacy, and love can diminish over time in a marital relationship. When feelings change, many couples needlessly believe that their relationship is over. A change in feelings may mean that partners are not being reinforced in the marriage and that the relationship deserves a higher priority. By viewing their relationship as intimate and satisfying, the couple can establish new behaviors and feelings.

Small changes are very important in bringing about big changes. A happier relationship results from many small changes over a period of time. Even though both partners are committed to change, there may be times when unwanted patterns reappear. This does not mean their new skills are not working. Couples are encouraged to continue focusing on the positive relationship they want.

Marriage Skills

The TIME program is organized systematically. Each of the 10 sessions is designed to present the principles and provide opportunities to practice the necessary skills for enriching the marriage. The goal is to help the couple apply and integrate the ideas and skills into their marriage relationship. The goal is achieved through reading, meaningful discussions, and application of the ideas and activity assignment and exercises. The couple is expected to work on specific skills each week.

Process

Couples join a TIME group and agree to meet for the next 10 weeks. Each session lasts approximately 2 hours; however, it can be shortened or lengthened with suggestions provided in the leader's manual. Most of the same procedures used in parent education apply to marriage education as well. The leader does not need to be an expert on relationships or have a perfect marriage. He or she does, however, need to be able to facilitate a group and follow the session outlines provided in the leader's manual. The expert on relationships is not the leader but rather the book *Time for a Better Marriage* (Carlson & Dinkmeyer, 2003). The leader teaches people how to have a satisfying marriage by following the material in the book.

Each week, the couple is asked to read a new chapter from the book and to practice the skill that was taught for the week. The skill activities are structured, and guidelines are provided on cards at the back of the book. Some couples have very good skills in some areas, such as communication, but may need help in other areas, such as problem solving. Not all couples are strong in all skills. The group setting is a good place for couples to help one another and to learn that they are not alone.

The leader has the knowledge that all people are socially embedded and seek personal significance through belonging in social systems. Most problems in the couple reflect some form of alienation or feeling of a lack of worth and acceptance from their partner. The leader facilitates the discussion so that members have an opportunity to learn these ideas while seeing their personal relevance.

The power drive is generated by the need of both the individual and the couple to improve, or protect themselves. The leader watches the process of action and the methods used to reach their goal. The leader, as well as the group members, begins to understand each partner's beliefs and goals.

When social interest is present, the power drive is directed toward the caring of others, and the behaviors will be constructive. If the social interest is underdeveloped, then the power drive will be against or away from others. The couple's mutual interdependence requires that they be concerned about one another and learn to cooperate and work together. Developing social interest and overcoming alienation are a major focus of all Adlerian educational or therapeutic interventions.

Differences between the partners provide for growth through negotiation and cooperation. When tension and stress are elevated, a power conflict is occurring, and repeated problems signal that a standoff is taking place. The leader needs to model and teach the negotiation of differences as well as to have other couples discuss how they were able to work through similar problems.

The couple is a separate dynamic entity created by the interaction between the partners. It is a unit that is different from each individual. Couples often need to understand that decisions that are good for individuals are often not good for the couple relationship. The leader can ask "Is that the best decision for the marriage?"

The couple's interactions are guided by the goals, life style, and private logic of each partner and the couple as a unit. The leader has to work with both the couple as a unit and the individual members who create the marriage. The couple interactions are mediated by values held in common; the negotiation of differences; and interdependency between one another for survival, development, and significance.

The characteristic ways of pursuing the challenges of life and solving problems evolve as part of the couple's life style through the development of rituals, myths, and rules. They are expressed over time as continuing patterns and themes of behavior. Discussions about rituals that each couple has can be enlightening and provide good ideas for the creation of new rituals.

Therapeutic change takes place in the couple system as a result of new subjective perceptions, goals, information, and skills; improved communication patterns; and the reorganization of places and roles in the system. These are the things that take place when a marriage education group has been successful.

MAINTAINING AND EXTENDING SKILLS: THE *LIVING LOVE* VIDEOS

The *Living Love* video series (Carlson & Love, 2000) provides a helpful way for couples to extend the learning they achieved in the TIME program. The seven-volume video set provides the essential skills for couples to create and maintain satisfying relationships. Each video introduces a set of exercises and activities that are taught by leading experts in couples education and demonstrated by real couples. Each video highlights an important area for extended study. The video topics are loving sexuality, keeping passion alive, a great relationship is a matter of choice, creating connection, conscious communication, cocreating a positive relationship, and getting unstuck.

CONCLUSION

Adlerians work to help people learn the skills needed to live democratically. These skills are provided through consultation procedures and psychoeducational groups of parents and couples. Effective psychologists need to be able to help their clients to develop these skills. Many problems that are presented to psychologists will respond better to training as opposed to psychotherapeutic treatment. Effective psychologists need to be able to provide consultation and educational services.

CONCLUSION

We are hopeful that you have gained an appreciation for just how useful Adler's ideas are for contemporary psychotherapy. These ideas are helpful for a wide variety of problems and can be easily integrated with other approaches. We also hope that the friendliness and practical nature of the approach has not left the impression that Adler's ideas are not of significance or substantive. It is important to remember that, almost 100 years after their origin, they are still in use around the world.

Adler was not a gifted writer, and as a result his ideas were not easily disseminated. He preferred to talk or demonstrate. Even today, many Adlerians similarly would rather practice or speak than write or do research. They seem drawn to the practical effectiveness and friendly nature of the ideas. It is fortunate that there are many good Adlerian writers today who are sharing these ideas with a large audience. Many are writing in the self-help areas.

Adler's ideas seemed out of step with the *zeitgeist* of his times. Today's world is perfectly suited for Adler's ideas. More and more people seem to be searching for answers to how to be a happy and satisfied person. Adler's practical, down-to-earth methods are being used in school, child-raising, and clinical settings.

Adler's ideas have not been very well known, and when they were presented it was often done in an inaccurate fashion. These ideas are taught as a main approach in most counseling graduate programs; however, in clinical psychology, family therapy, or social work programs, Adlerians are seldom mentioned.

THE "LACK OF RECOGNITION" QUESTION

As we have noted throughout this volume, Adlerians have traced the influence of Adler's work on many theories of personality and psychotherapy developed subsequent to the era of the so-called "three pillars": Freud, Adler, and Jung. Despite the identification of many apparent lines of influence from Adler to modern theories, the Adlerian scholars have documented a widespread lack of understanding of Adlerian contributions to mainstream applied psychology. "Adler once proclaimed that he was more concerned that his theories survive than that people remembered to associate his theories with his name. His wish was apparently granted" (Mosak, 2000, p. 58).

In addition, some non-Adlerian scholars have noticed the lack of recognition of Adler and the Adlerian perspective in psychology and psychotherapy theory and practice. For example, in his expansive text on the history of psychodynamic psychology, Ellenberger (1970) offered the following comments, which echo Mosak's (2000) statement:

> It would not be easy to find another author from which [sic] so much has been borrowed from all sides without acknowledgement [of] Alfred Adler. . . . There is the puzzling phenomenon of a collective denial of Adler's work and the systematic attribution of anything coined by him to other authors. . . . His teaching has become to use a French idiom, an "open quarry" (une carrier publique), that is, a place where anyone and all may come and draw anything without compunction. An author will meticulously quote the source of any sentence he takes from elsewhere, but it does not occur to him to do the same whenever the source is Individual Psychology; it is as if nothing original could ever come from Adler. (p. 645)

More than 23 years later, Singer and Salovey (1993) presented a similar estimation regarding Adler's work:

> It is a poignant and somewhat troubling historical fact that the essence of what we have to say about meaningful memory, and what Bruhn . . . McAdams . . . and Tomkins . . . have to say was said by Adler . . . in the first decades of this century. . . . Adler, alone among all theorists in the clinical and experimental circles, argued for the centrality of memory to the understanding of personality. He proposed that one's earliest memories are merely reflections of the most valued current tendencies and life goals of the individual. Memories are revised and shaped in the service of one's enduring attitudes. Rather than veridical accounts of past experiences, they are tendentious fictions that encapsule in their manifest content what is now most important to the person. For Adler, the memory contained the projective content of personality; further free association of mining the memory for its latent meaning was unnecessary and possibly obfuscating. . . . Adler's emphasis on manifest content of memory and its relationship to the major themes within personality captures an

essential argument of contemporary personality theorists. Why, then, this fifty- to sixty-year gap in mainstream attention to Adler's position?

Freeman (1993) noted that the lack of attention paid to Adler's theory in clinical and counseling psychology programs is "incredible, given the Adlerian contributions to the development of psychotherapeutic theory, clinical practice, and delivery of psychological services" (p. iv):

> [Adlerian psychotherapy] has been the basis for Frankl's Logotherapy and the contemporary Ego-analytic approaches of the psychoanalysts, and has been one of the major influences for the development of present day Cognitive Behavior Therapy. . . . The structured, strategic, systemic, and dynamic focus that was developed by Adler . . . has become so much a part of Cognitive Therapy. (pp. iv–v)

In terms of contemporary psychology in general, and contemporary approaches to psychotherapy specifically, Adlerian psychology and psychotherapy remain obscure and are often misunderstood and misrepresented. The following are three potential reasons why Adler and Adlerian psychology and psychotherapy have not been more widely recognized.

1. *Adler was not a gifted writer.* Although his ideas were far ahead of their time and are replete in contemporary psychological theories and therapies, Adler was a mediocre and unsystematic writer whose primary interests were in being with and helping people. Thus, as Maniacci (1999) indicated, Adler wrote few books for professional audiences, especially after World War I. By then, his ideas were progressively taking on a social-psychological emphasis, and his books were largely targeted toward the general population, both in Europe and in America. "Adler kept his language simple, his concepts (relatively) clear, and his style minimal" (Maniacci, 1999, p. 59). Singer and Salovey (1993) suggested that although Adler's writings are visionary, they nevertheless possess "a fragmentary and outmoded style" (p. 19) that may have had "a severe impact on the attention it has received from subsequent scholars and scientists" (p. 20).

2. *Adler's ideas were out of step with the* Zeitgeist *of his day.* The psychological mindset of Adler's time (the early decades of the 20th century) was primarily mechanistic. Consequently, Adler's movement to a socially embedded, phenomenological, and nondeterministic theoretical perspective was generally considered unscientific and unworthy of note by Freudians and behaviorists. In the history of psychology, we see numerous examples of the "power as knowledge" political phenomenon that social constructionists have borrowed from

Michel Foucault. Common wisdom says that "Knowledge is power." Foucault (1980) suggested that, instead, "Power is knowledge." In other words, whoever has the power determines what is worth knowing, what is true or right. For a long time, psychoanalysts and radical behaviorists controlled both the academy and therapy training institutions. They had the "power," and so they determined what "knowledge" was worth knowing. Psychoanalysts, who held a virtual monopoly on psychiatric training centers and hospitals, either ignored Adler or misrepresented him because Adler was a dissident who had rejected classical psychoanalysis. Behaviorists, who possessed a similar monopolistic grip in universities and psychology departments, ignored Adler because his subjectivistic, socially oriented theory was considered unscientific. Consequently, students in subsequent years—who ultimately created their own theories of psychotherapy—were provided little or no introduction to Adlerian theory and therapy, and they consequently developed ideas that sounded remarkably like Adler's but with little or no acknowledgment of him (Mosak & Maniacci, 1999; Singer & Salovey, 1993; Watts & Critelli, 1997).

3. *Adler's theory is often poorly presented in the literature.* Many secondary source textbooks and journal literature have provided inadequate and erroneous presentations of Adlerian psychology and psychotherapy (Silverman & Corsini, 1986; Watts & Critelli, 1997). For example, Adler's theory often is erroneously described as "neo-Freudian" and placed alongside discussions of other psychoanalytic theories. Although it is true that the neo-Freudians were strongly influenced by Adler (Ellenberger, 1970), it is not true that Individual Psychology was merely the first neo-Freudian position.

Part of this misrepresentation problem may be explained by the lack of attention non-Adlerian authors have paid to the evolution of Adler's theory. Adler was a colleague—not a disciple—of Freud's. In the years between 1902 and 1911, Adler attempted to work within the boundaries of orthodox psychoanalysis as defined by Freud. However, Adler's fundamental assumptions were different than Freud's, and eventually the tension between the two reached a breaking point. According to Mosak and Maniacci (1999), in 1911, Adler left the Freudian Psychoanalytic Society and formed a new group, originally named "The Society for Free Psychoanalytic Research." He later renamed it "The Society for Individual Psychology," "with 'individual' meaning 'indivisible,' that is, holistic (derived from the Latin *individuum*)" (Mosak & Maniacci, 1999, p. 6).

Early in its inception, its primary focus was upon psychoanalysis. Adler himself maintained his private practice as a psychiatrist, but after World War I (during which time Adler served as a military physician) Adler turned much more social in his orientation and began working full force for many of the social issues listed previously. Hence, his work falls approximately into two periods: Prior to the First World War, Adler was a psychoanalyst, and that can be seen in his two most important, early works—*The Neurotic Constitution* (1912/1983b), and *The Practice and Theory of Individual Psychology* (1920/1983d). These are the two works Adler himself wrote on his own, with the latter being a collection of his papers that he assembled. After World War I, Adler wrote increasingly as a philosopher, social psychologist, and educator, with works such as *Understanding Human Nature* (1927/1957), *The Science of Living* (1929c), *The Education of Children* (1930/1970), *What Life Should Mean to You* (1931/1958), and *Social Interest: A Challenge to Mankind* (1933/1964f) being directed to the lay public. These works are primarily based upon lectures and notebooks of Adler and were assembled by members of his group, with his approval. (Mosak & Maniacci, 1999, pp. 6–7)

Adler's early works up until and during World War I focus primarily on abnormal human behavior and sound rather psychoanalytic. However, after World War I, Adler was more interested in normal human behavior and progressively developed his mature theory, which is "holistic, phenomenological, teleological, field-theoretical, and socially-oriented" (Manaster & Corsini, 1982, p. 2). In the main, contemporary Adlerian psychology and psychotherapy is based on Adler's later period and subsequent developments by later Adlerians (e.g., Rudolf Dreikurs).

Because of its evolution, during Adler's time and afterward, it is difficult to place Adlerian theory and therapy into a single theoretical category and this may be yet another reason why Adler's theory is misunderstood and misrepresented. The Adlerian approach can be categorized as cognitive, systemic, existential, and psychodynamic. More recently, as we noted earlier, some Adlerians have begun describing it as a constructivist or constructionist theory and therapy.

It is difficult to say what the future will bring for Adler's ideas. It seems that Adler's statement of 75 years ago remains on target:

It must be about twenty years since I tried to foretell the future of Individual Psychology in some such words as these. Individual Psychology, which is essentially a child of this age, will have a permanent influence on the thought, poetry and dreams of humanity. It will attract many enlightened disciples, and many more who will hardly know the names of its pioneers. It will be understood by some, but the number who misunderstand it will be greater. It will have many adherents, and still more enemies. Because of its simplicity many will think it is too easy, whereas those who know it will recognize how difficult it is. It will bring its followers neither wealth nor position, but they will have the satisfaction of learning from their opponent's mistakes. It will draw a dividing line between those who use their knowledge for the purpose of establishing an ideal community, and those who do not. It will give its followers such keenness of vision that no corner of the human soul will be hidden from them and it will ensure that this hard-earned capacity shall be placed in the service of human progress. (A. Adler, quoted in Dreikurs, 1950, p. vii)

GLOSSARY

Biased (Ap)perception: A perception with meaning attached to it.

Compensation: An attempt to make up for a deficiency.

Discouragement: Lacking courage; the inverse of encouragement, when people feel they do not belong in a useful, constructive manner.

Early recollections: A single incident an individual can recall from under the age of 10; it must be able to be visualized, have a narrative (even if sparse), and should have a feeling associated with it and a part that vividly stands out.

Encouragement: Instilling courage in individuals, such as by showing faith in them, expecting them to be responsible for themselves, and valuing them for who they are.

Encouragement (in therapy): The process of helping clients to feel they have worth as they are; when therapists demonstrate social interest to and for their clients.

Family atmosphere: The emotional tone of the family, typically established by the parents' relationship toward each other but also influenced by how the siblings got along with each other and their parents.

Family constellation: The early developmental influences on a person, typically comprising siblings, parents, other key persons, and the neighborhood and community.

Helpful parenting styles: Methods of raising children that foster social interest, typically emphasizing encouragement, responsibility, love, and respect.

Inferiority: Something that is deficient in form or structure and is objective, measurable, and contextual.

Inferiority complex: A behavioral manifestation of a subjective feeling of inferiority.

Inferiority feeling: An appraisal of deficiency that is subjective, global, and judgmental.

Life style: The attitudes and convictions people have about how to find their place in the world; the instructions for how to belong.

Life style convictions: The attitudes and beliefs that direct the person's sense of belonging. They almost always are nonverbal.

Life tasks: Adler originally defined three (work, love, and community); the main challenges that life presents to all humans. All three must be addressed in order to function.

Mistaken goals: Goals that are detrimental to others, such as those that run counter to social interest, for example, wanting to be better than others as opposed to helpful to others.

Normal goals: Goals that are beneficial to others, that do not interfere with others, for example, striving to be excellent at a task as opposed to being better than others.

Private or faulty logic: Convictions that run counter to social interest, that are unique to the individual and do not facilitate useful, constructive belonging.

"The Question": A technique in which Adlerian therapists ask the client "What would be different in your life if you didn't have your symptoms?" The response can reveal the purpose for which the client is generating the symptoms and, potentially, whether the symptoms are more psychogenic or somatogenic in origin.

Safeguarding mechanisms: What other systems of psychotherapy have called *defense mechanisms*; the behaviors or attitudes individuals select to evade responsibility and not meet the life tasks.

Self-concept: All of the convictions and attitudes individuals have about themselves that can complete either of two sentences: "I am . . . " or "I am not . . . "

Self-ideal: All of the convictions and attitudes that people have about themselves that can complete either of the following two sentences: "In order to belong, I should . . . " or "In order to find my place, I should not . . . "

Social interest: An interest in the interest of others, behaviors and attitudes that display a sense of fellow feeling, responsibility, and community with others, not just for today but for generations yet to come.

Unhelpful parenting styles: Methods of raising children that discourage social interest; in other words, methods that emphasize external control, frightening or intimidating children, and valuing children not for who they are but rather who they should be.

SELECTED READINGS AND RESOURCES FOR FURTHER STUDY

Adlerian Organization

North American Society of Adlerian Psychology (NASAP)
50 Northeast Drive
Hershey, Pennsylvania 17033
Telephone: 717-579-8795
Web site: http://www.alfredadler.org

Professional Journal

The Journal of Individual Psychology is available from NASAP or the University of Texas Press.

Training Centers

NASAP can provide a list of the 58 Adlerian organizations and institutes. The Adler School of Professional Psychology in Chicago offers fully accredited master's and doctoral programs:

Adler School of Professional Psychology
65 East Wacker Place, Suite 400
Chicago, Illinois 60601
Telephone: 312-201-5900
Web site: http://www.adler.edu

Recommended Readings

Ansbacher, H. L., & Ansbacher, R. R. (Eds.). (1956). *The Individual Psychology of Alfred Adler: A systematic presentation in selections from his writings.* New York: Harper Torchbooks. This has been the main source of Adler's writings. The editors' comments are very helpful in understanding Adler's theory and practice.

Carlson, J., & Slavik, S. (1997). *Techniques in Adlerian psychology.* Philadelphia: Taylor & Francis. This is a collection of classic articles from the *Journal of Individual Psychology* that deal with techniques and practice.

Dinkmeyer, D., Jr., & Sperry, L. (2000). *Counseling and psychotherapy: An integrated, Individual Psychology approach.* Columbus, OH: Merrill. This is a complete basic text on counseling and psychotherapy from an Adlerian perspective.

Dreikurs, R. (1971). *Social equality: The challenge of today*. Chicago: Adler School of Professional Psychology. Even though this book is dated, it is an important book on Adler's theory and modern issues of living.

Hoffman, E. (1994). *The drive for self: Alfred Adler and the founding of Individual Psychology*. Reading, MA: Addison-Wesley. This is the best biography on the life of Alfred Adler.

Hooper, A., & Holford, J. (1998). *Adler for beginners*. New York: Writers and Readers. This is an easy-to-read primer about the life and contributions of Alfred Adler.

Mosak, H., & Maniacci, M. (1999). *A primer of Adlerian psychology: The analytic-behavioral-cognitive psychology of Alfred Adler*. New York: Brunner Routledge. This is a good source about the "nuts and bolts" of Adlerian psychology.

Watts, R. E. (Ed.). (2003). *Adlerian, cognitive, and constructivist therapies: An integrative dialogue*. New York: Springer. This book includes Adlerian, cognitive, and constructivist authors addressing the integrative possibilities between Adlerian therapy and cognitive and constructivist approaches to psychotherapy.

Demonstration Videos

Carlson, J. (1998). *Psychotherapy with the experts: Adlerian psychotherapy*. Boston: Allyn & Bacon. Dr. Carlson works with an African American woman struggling with her divorce and overfunctioning approach to life.

Carlson, J. (2004). *Adlerian psychotherapy*. Washington, DC: American Psychological Association. Dr. Carlson works with a young man with issues of perfectionism. In one 45-minute session, significant change occurred.

Carlson, J. (2002). *Child therapy with the experts: Adlerian parent consultation*. Boston: Allyn & Bacon. Dr. Carlson provides an example of an individual parent consultation with a single mother and a parent group consultation.

Carlson, J. (2003). *Brief integrative Adlerian couples therapy*. Available from Microtraining and Multicultural Development, 25 Burdette Avenue, Framingham, Massachusetts 01702. Dr. Carlson works with a couple with problems of anger and abuse.

Carlson, J., Love, P., & Nelsen, J. (2005). *Parenting with the experts: Positive discipline*. Boston: Allyn & Bacon. This is an entertaining video that teaches an audience of parents the basic skills of positive discipline.

Carlson, J., Kjos, D., & Bitter, J. (1998). *Family therapy with the experts: Adlerian family therapy*. Boston: Allyn & Bacon. This program clearly demonstrates Adlerian family therapy with a large family. The key concepts are clearly illustrated.

Carlson, J., Keat, D., & Kottman, T. (2003). *Child therapy with the experts: Adlerian play therapy*. Boston: Allyn & Bacon. This video presents the rationale for Adlerian play therapy and includes a complete therapy session with a real client.

Web Site

People who are interested in training with, or being supervised, by Dr. Terry Kottman are encouraged to visit The Encouragement Zone site: http://www.geocities.com/encouragementzone/

REFERENCES

Adler, A. (1924). Syphilophobia. In *The practice and theory of individual psychology* (P. Radin, Trans.). New York: Harcourt, Brace. (Original work published 1911)

Adler, A. (1927). *The practice and theory of Individual Psychology*. New York: Harcourt, Brace.

Adler, A. (1929). *Problems of neurosis*. (P. Mairet, Ed.). London: Kegan Paul, Trench, Trubner.

Adler, A. (1931). *What life should mean to you* (A. Porter, Ed.). New York: Little, Brown/Blue Ribbon Books.

Adler, A. (1956). *The Individual Psychology of Alfred Adler* (H. L. Ansbacher & R. R. Ansbacher, Eds.). New York: Basic Books.

Adler, A. (1957). *Understanding human nature* (W. B. Wolfe, Trans.). New York: Premier Books.

Adler, A. (1964). *Social interest: A challenge to mankind* (J. Linton & R. Vaughn, Trans.). New York: Capricorn. (Original work published 1933)

Adler, A. (1970). The case of Mrs. A. In H. L. Ansbacher & R. R. Ansbacher (Eds.), *Superiority and social interest* (Rev. ed., pp. 160–170). Evanston, IL: Northwestern University Press.

Adler, A. (1979). *Superiority and social interest* (3rd ed., H. L. Ansbacher & R. R. Ansbacher, Eds.). New York: Norton.

Adler, A. (1992). *What life could mean to you* (C. Brett, Trans.). Oxford, England: Oneworld. (Original work published 1931)

Adler, A. (2002). *The neurotic character: Fundamentals of Individual Psychology and psychotherapy* (C. Koen, Trans., & H. T. Stein, Ed.). San Francisco: Classical Adlerian Translation Project. (Original work published 1911)

Adler, K. (1967). Adler's Individual Psychology. In B. B. Wolman (Ed.), *Psychoanalytic techniques: A handbook for the practicing psychoanalyst* (pp. 299–337). New York: Basic Books.

Adler, K. (1989). Techniques that shorten psychotherapy. *Journal of Individual Psychology, 45*, 62–74. (Original work published 1972)

Allred, G. H., & Poduska, B. (1985). Evaluating interviewing skills through the AIAT. *Individual Psychology, 41*, 187–203.

American Psychiatric Association. (2000). *Diagnostic and statistical manual of mental disorders* (4th ed., text rev.). Washington, DC: Author.

Anchin, J. C. (2003). Integratively oriented brief psychotherapy: Historical perspective and contemporary approaches. *Journal of Psychotherapy Integration, 13*, 219–240.

Ansbacher, H. L. (1977). Individual Psychology. In R. J. Corsini (Ed.), *Current personality theories* (pp. 45–82). Itasca, IL: F. E. Peacock.

Ansbacher, H. L. (1989). Adlerian psychotherapy: The tradition of brief psychotherapy. *Journal of Individual Psychology, 45*, 26–33. (Original work published 1972)

Ansbacher, H. L. (1990). Alfred Adler's influence on three leading cofounders of humanistic psychology. *Journal of Humanistic Psychology, 30*, 45–53.

Ansbacher, H. L. (1991). The concept of social interest. *Individual Psychology, 47*, 28–46.

Ansbacher, H. L. (1992). Alfred Adler's concepts of community feeling and social interest and the relevance of community feeling for old age. *Individual Psychology, 48*, 402–412.

Ansbacher, H. L., & Ansbacher, R. R. (Eds.). (1978). *Cooperation between the sexes: Writings on women, love, and marriage.* New York: Anchor.

Arciniega, G. M., & Newlon, B. J. (1999). Counseling and psychotherapy: Multicultural considerations. In D. Capuzzi & D. F. Gross (Eds.), *Counseling and psychotherapy: Theories and interventions* (2nd ed., pp. 435–458). Upper Saddle River, NJ: Merrill/Prentice Hall.

Asay, T. P., & Lambert, M. J. (1999). The empirical case for the common factors in therapy: Quantitative findings. In M. A. Hubble, B. L. Duncan, & S. D. Miller (Eds.), *The heart and soul of change: What works in therapy* (pp. 33–55). Washington, DC: American Psychological Association.

Association for Play Therapy. (1997). Play therapy definition. *Association for Play Therapy Newsletter, 16*(2), 4.

Bachelor, A., & Horvath, A. (1999). The therapeutic relationship. In M. A. Hubble, B. L. Duncan, & S. D. Miller (Eds.), *The heart and soul of change: What works in therapy* (pp. 133–178). Washington, DC: American Psychological Association.

Beck, A.T. (1976). *Cognitive therapy and the emotional disorders.* New York: Meridian.

Beck, A. T., Rush, A. J., Shaw, B. F., & Emery, G. (1979). *Cognitive therapy of depression.* New York: Guilford Press.

Bettner, B. L., & Lew, A. (1996). *Raising kids who can: Leader's guide.* Newton Centre, MA: Connexions Press.

Bitter, J., & Nicoll, W. G. (2000). Adlerian brief therapy with individuals: Process and practice. *Journal of Individual Psychology, 56*, 31–44.

Bitter, J., & West, J. (1979). An interview with Heinz Ansbacher. *Journal of Individual Psychology, 35*(1), 95–110.

Botella, L., & Herrero, O. (2000). A relational constructivist approach to narrative therapy. *European Journal of Psychotherapy, Counselling, and Health, 3*, 407–418.

Botella, L., Herrero, O., Pacheco, M., & Corbella, S. (2004). Working with narrative in psychotherapy: A relational constructivist approach. In L. E. Angus & J. McLeod (Eds.), *The handbook of narrative and psychotherapy: Practice, theory, and research* (pp. 119–136). Thousand Oaks, CA: Sage.

Brack, G., Hill, M. B., Edwards, D., Grootboom, N., & Lassiter, P. S. (2003). Adler and Ubuntu: Using Adlerian principles in the new South Africa. *Journal of Individual Psychology, 59*, 316–326.

Broderick, C. B., & Schrader, S. S. (1991). The history of professional marriage and family therapy. In A. S. Gurman & D. P. Kniskern (Eds.), *Handbook of family therapy* (Vol. 2, pp. 3–40). New York: Brunner/Mazel.

Budman, S. H., Friedman, S., & Hoyt, M. F. (1992). Last words on first sessions. In S. H. Budman, M. F. Hoyt, & S. Friedman (Eds.), *The first session in brief therapy* (pp. 345–358). New York: Guilford Press.

Burns, D. D., & Auerbach, A. (1996). Therapeutic efficacy in cognitive–behavioral therapy: Does it really make a difference? In P. M. Salkovskis (Ed.), *Frontiers of cognitive therapy* (pp. 135–164). New York: Guilford Press.

Carich, M. S., & Willingham, W. (1987). The roots of family systems theory in individual psychology. *Individual Psychology, 43,* 71–78.

Carlson, J. (1989). Brief therapy for health promotion. *Individual Psychology: Journal of Adlerian Theory, Research, and Practice, 45*(1–2), 220–229.

Carlson, J. (2005). *Adlerian therapy* [DVD/videotape]. Washington, DC: American Psychological Association.

Carlson, J. M., & Carlson, J. (2000). The application of Adlerian psychotherapy with Asian-American clients. *Journal of Individual Psychology, 56,* 214–225.

Carlson, J., & Dinkmeyer, D. (1999). Couple therapy. In R. E. Watts & J. Carlson (Eds.), *Interventions and strategies in counseling and psychotherapy* (pp. 87–99). Philadelphia: Accelerated Development/Taylor & Francis.

Carlson, J., & Dinkmeyer, D., Jr. (2002). *Consultation* [Videotape]. New York: Brunner Routledge.

Carlson, J., & Dinkmeyer, D. (2003). *Time for a better marriage.* Atascadero, CA: Impact.

Carlson, J., & Love, P. (2000). *Living love* [Videotape]. Phoenix, AZ: Zeig Tucker & Theisen.

Carlson, J., & Slavik, S. (Eds.). (1997). *Techniques in Adlerian psychology.* Washington, DC: Accelerated Development.

Carlson, J., & Sperry, L. (1998). Adlerian psychotherapy as a constructivist psychotherapy. In M. F. Hoyt (Ed.), *The handbook of constructive therapies: Innovative approaches from leading practitioners* (pp. 68–82). San Francisco: Jossey-Bass.

Carlson, J., Sperry, L., & Lewis, J. A. (1997). *Family therapy: Ensuring treatment efficacy.* Pacific Grove, CA: Brooks/Cole.

Carlson, J., Sperry, L., & Lewis, J. (2005). *Family therapy techniques: Integration and tailoring.* New York: Brunner Routledge.

Chandler, C. K. (1991). The psychology of women: Approaching the twenty-first century. *Individual Psychology, 47,* 482–489.

Chernin, J., & Holden, J. M. (1995). Toward an understanding of homosexuality: Origins, status, and relationship to individual psychology. *Individual Psychology, 51,* 90–101.

Christensen, O. C. (Ed.). (1993). *Adlerian family counseling.* Minneapolis, MN: Educational Media.

Clark, A. (2002). *Early recollections: Theory and practice in counseling and psychotherapy.* New York: Brunner Routledge.

Cooper, J. F. (1995). *A primer of brief psychotherapy.* New York: Norton.

Corey, G. (1991). *Theory and practice of counseling and psychotherapy* (4th ed.). Pacific Grove, CA: Brooks/Cole.

Corsini, R. J. (1966). *Role playing in psychotherapy.* Chicago: Aldine.

Cowen, E. L., & Kilmer, R. P. (2002). "Positive psychology": Some plusses and some open issues. *Journal of Community Psychology, 30,* 449–460.

Davis, T. E., & Osborn, C. J. (2000). *The solution-focused school counselor.* Philadelphia: Accelerated Development/Taylor & Francis.

Day, S. X. (2004). *Theory and design in counseling and psychotherapy.* Boston: Lahaska Press.

DeJong, P., & Berg, I. K. (2002). *Interviewing for solutions* (2nd ed.). Belmont, CA: Brooks/Cole.

de Shazer, S. (1985). *Keys to solution in brief therapy.* New York: Norton.

de Shazer, S. (1991). *Putting differences to work.* New York: Norton.

Dewey, E. A. (1971). Family atmosphere. In A. G. Nikelly (Ed.), *Techniques for behavior change: Applications of Adlerian theory* (pp. 41–47). Springfield, IL: Charles C Thomas.

Dinkmeyer, D. (1972). Use of the encouragement process in Adlerian counseling. *Personnel and Guidance Journal, 51,* 177–181.

Dinkmeyer, D., Jr., & Carlson, J. (2001). *Consultation: Creating school based interventions* (2nd ed.). New York: Brunner Routledge.

Dinkmeyer, D., & Carlson, J. (2003). *Training in Marriage Enrichment (TIME).* Bowling Green, KY: Communication and Motivation Training Institute Press.

Dinkmeyer, D., Jr., & Dinkmeyer, D. (1976). Adlerian family counseling and therapy. In A. Horne (Ed.), *Family counseling and therapy* (pp. 383–401). Itasca, IL: F. E. Peacock.

Dinkmeyer, D., Dinkmeyer, D., Jr., & Sperry, L. (1987). *Adlerian counseling and psychotherapy* (2nd ed.). Columbus, OH: Merrill.

Dinkmeyer, D., McKay, G., & Dinkmeyer, D., Jr. (1980). *Systematic Training for Effective Teaching (STET): Teacher's handbook.* Circle Pines, MN: American Guidance Service.

Dinkmeyer, D., McKay, G., & Dinkmeyer, D., Jr. (1987). *Next STEP.* Circle Pines, MN: American Guidance Service.

Dinkmeyer, D., McKay, G., & Dinkmeyer, D., Jr. (1989). *Early Childhood STEP.* Circle Pines, MN: American Guidance Service.

Dinkmeyer, D., McKay, G., & Dinkmeyer, D., Jr. (1990). *Systematic Training for Effective Parenting of Teens (STEP/TEEN).* Circle Pines, MN: American Guidance Service.

Dinkmeyer, D., McKay, G., & Dinkmeyer, D., Jr. (1998). *Systematic Training for Effective Parenting (STEP).* Circle Pines, MN: American Guidance Service.

Dinkmeyer, D., & Sherman, R. (1989). Brief Adlerian family therapy. *Individual Psychology, 45*, 148–158.

Dinkmeyer, D., Jr., & Sperry, L. (2000). *Counseling and psychotherapy: An integrated, Individual Psychology approach* (3rd ed.). Upper Saddle River, NJ: Merrill/Prentice Hall.

Disque, J. G., & Bitter, J. (1998). Integrating narrative therapy with Adlerian lifestyle assessment: A case study. *Journal of Individual Psychology, 54*, 431–450.

Dowd, E. T., & Kelly, F. D. (1980). Adlerian psychology and cognitive–behavior therapy: Convergences. *Journal of Individual Psychology, 36*, 119–135.

Dreikurs, R. (1946). *The challenge of marriage.* New York: Hawthorn.

Dreikurs, R. (1950). *Fundamentals of Adlerian psychology.* New York: Greenberg Publishers.

Dreikurs, R. (1960). Are psychological schools of thought outdated? *Journal of Individual Psychology, 16*, 3–10.

Dreikurs, R. (1961). The Adlerian approach to psychodynamics. In M. I. Stein (Ed.), *Contemporary psychotherapies* (pp. 60–79). New York: Free Press.

Dreikurs, R. (1967). *Psychodynamics, psychotherapy, and counseling.* Chicago: Alfred Adler Institute of Chicago.

Dreikurs, R. (1971). *Social equality: The challenge of today.* Chicago: Adler School of Professional Psychology.

Dreikurs, R. (1997). Holistic medicine. *Individual Psychology, 53*, 127–205.

Dreikurs, R., & Soltz, V. (1964). *Children: The challenge.* New York: Hawthorn.

Duffy, T. H., Carns, M. R., Carns, A. W., & Garcia, J. L. (1998). The lifestyle of the middle-class Mexican American female. *Journal of Individual Psychology, 54*, 399–406.

Edwards, D. J., Dattilio, F. M., & Bromley, D. B. (2004). Evidence-based practice: The role of case-based research. *Professional Psychology: Research and Practice, 35*, 589–597.

Ellenberger, H. (1970). *The discovery of the unconscious: The history and evolution of dynamic psychiatry.* New York: Basic Books.

Ellis, A. (1970). Humanism, values, rationality. *Journal of Individual Psychology, 26*, 11.

Ellis, A. (1973). *Humanistic psychotherapy.* New York: McGraw-Hill.

Ellis, A. (1989). Rational–emotive therapy. In R. J. Corsini & D. Wedding (Eds.), *Current psychotherapies* (4th ed., pp. 197–238). Itasca, IL: F. E. Peacock.

Ellis, A. (1998). How rational emotive behavior therapy belongs in the constructivist camp. In M. F. Hoyt (Ed.), *The handbook of constructive therapies: Innovative approaches from leading practitioners* (pp. 83–99). San Francisco: Jossey-Bass.

Ellis, A. (2000). Rational–emotive behavior therapy. In R. J. Corsini & D. Wedding (Eds.), *Current psychotherapies* (6th ed., pp. 168–204). Itasca, IL: F. E. Peacock.

Evans, T. D., & Milliren, A. P. (1999). Open-forum family counseling. In R. E. Watts & J. Carlson (Eds.), *Interventions and strategies in counseling and psychotherapy* (pp. 135–160). Philadelphia: Accelerated Development/Taylor & Francis.

Exner, J. E. (2003). *The Rorschach: A comprehensive system. Volume I: Basic foundations and principles of interpretation* (4th ed.). Hoboken, NJ: Wiley.

Fisher, H. (2004). *Why we love: The nature and chemistry of romantic love.* New York: Henry Holt.

Foley, V. D. (1989). Family therapy. In R. J. Corsini & D. Wedding (Eds.), *Current psychotherapies* (4th ed., pp. 455–500). Itasca, IL: F. E. Peacock.

Forgus, R., & Shulman, B. (1979). *Personality: A cognitive view.* Englewood Cliffs, NJ: Prentice Hall.

Foucault, M. (1980). *Power/knowledge.* New York: Pantheon.

Frank, J. D., & Frank, J. B. (1991). *Persuasion and healing: A comparative study of psychotherapy* (3rd ed.). Baltimore: Johns Hopkins University Press.

Freeman, A. (1981). Dreams and images in cognitive therapy. In G. Emery & R. C. Bedrosian (Eds.), *New directions in cognitive therapy: A casebook* (pp. 224–238). New York: Guilford Press.

Freeman, A. (1993). Foreword. In L. Sperry & J. Carlson (Eds.), *Psychopathology and psychotherapy* (pp. iii–vi). Muncie, IN: Accelerated Development.

Freeman, A., & Urschel, J. (2003). Individual psychology and cognitive–behavioral therapy: A cognitive therapy perspective. In R. E. Watts (Ed.), *Adlerian, cognitive, and constructivist psychotherapies: An integrative dialogue* (pp. 71–88). New York: Springer.

Frevert, V. S., & Miranda, A. O. (1998). A conceptual formulation of the Latin culture and the treatment of Latinos from an Adlerian psychology perspective. *Journal of Individual Psychology, 54,* 291–309.

Friedman, S. (1997). *Time-effective psychotherapy.* Boston: Allyn & Bacon.

Garfield, S. (1986). Research on client variables in psychotherapy. In S. Garfield & A. Bergin (Eds.), *Handbook of psychotherapy and behavior change* (3rd ed., pp. 213–256). New York: Wiley.

Garfield, S. (1994). Research on client variables in psychotherapy. In S. Garfield & A. Bergin (Eds.), *Handbook of psychotherapy and behavior change* (4th ed., pp. 190–229). New York: Wiley.

Gergen, K. J. (1999). *An invitation to social construction.* Thousand Oaks, CA: Sage.

Gergen, K. J. (2001). *Social construction in context.* Thousand Oaks, CA: Sage.

Glasser, W. (1998). *Choice theory: A new psychology of personal freedom.* New York: HarperCollins.

Glasser, W. (2000). *Reality therapy in action.* New York: HarperCollins.

Glasser, W., & Glasser, C. (2000). *Getting together and staying together: Solving the mystery of marriage.* New York: HarperCollins.

Goldenberg, I., & Goldenberg, H. (2000). Adlerian psychotherapy. In R. J. Corsini & D. Wedding (Eds.), *Current psychotherapies* (5th ed., pp. 375–406). Itasca, IL: F. E. Peacock.

Gottman, J. M., Driver, J., & Tabares, A. (2003). Building the sound marital house: An empirically derived couple therapy. In A. S. Gurman & N. S. Jacobson

(Eds.), *Clinical handbook of couples therapy* (3rd ed., pp. 373–399). New York: Guilford Press.

Grizzle, A. F. (1992). Family therapy with the faithful: Christians as clients. In L. A. Burton (Ed.), *Religion and the family: When God helps* (pp. 139–162). New York: Haworth Pastoral Press.

Hanna, F. J. (1998). A transcultural view of prejudice, racism, and community feeling: The desire of striving for status. *Journal of Individual Psychology, 54,* 336–345.

Hartings, M. J. (1976). *Inferiority complex: An Adlerian approach to Rorschach shading responses.* Unpublished paper, Alfred Adler Institute, Chicago.

Hedberg, C., & Huber, R. J. (1995). Homosexuality, gender, communal involvement, and social interest. *Individual Psychology, 51,* 244–252.

Hendrix, H. (2001). *Getting the love you want: A guide for couples.* New York: Owl Books.

Herring, R. D., & Runion, K. B. (1994). Counseling ethnic children and youth from an Adlerian perspective. *Journal of Multicultural Counseling and Development, 22,* 215–226.

Higgins, R. L. (2002). Reality negotiation. In C. R. Snyder & S. J. Lopez (Eds.), *Handbook of positive psychology* (pp. 351–365). New York: Oxford University Press.

Hoffman, E. (1994). *The drive for self: Alfred Adler and the founding of individual psychology.* Reading, MA: Addison-Wesley.

Hoyt, M. F. (Ed.). (1994). *Constructive therapies.* New York: Guilford Press.

Hoyt, M. F. (1995). *Brief therapy and managed care.* San Francisco: Jossey-Bass.

Hoyt, M. F. (2000). *Some stories are better than others: Doing what works in brief therapy and managed care.* Philadelphia: Brunner/Mazel.

Hoyt, M. F. (2002). How I embody a narrative constructive approach. *Journal of Constructivist Psychology, 15,* 279–289.

Hubble, M. A., Duncan, B. L., & Miller, S. D. (1999a). Directing attention to what works. In M. A. Hubble, B. L. Duncan, & S. D. Miller (Eds.), *The heart and soul of change: What works in therapy* (pp. 407–447). Washington, DC: American Psychological Association.

Hubble, M. A., Duncan, B. L., & Miller, S. D. (Eds.). (1999b). *The heart and soul of change: What works in therapy.* Washington, DC: American Psychological Association.

Hubble, M. A., Duncan, B. L., & Miller, S. D. (1999c). Introduction. In M. A. Hubble, B. L. Duncan, & S. D. Miller (Eds.), *The heart and soul of change: What works in therapy* (pp. 1–19). Washington, DC: American Psychological Association.

Jones, J. V., Jr., & Lyddon, W. J. (2003). Adlerian and constructivist psychotherapies: A constructivist perspective. In R. E. Watts (Ed.), *Adlerian, cognitive, and constructivist psychotherapies: An integrative dialogue* (pp. 38–56). New York: Springer.

Jones, S. L., & Butman, R. E. (1991). *Modern psychotherapies: A comprehensive Christian appraisal.* Downers Grove, IL: InterVarsity Press.

Kelly, E. W., Jr. (1994). *Relationship-centered counseling: An integration of art and science.* New York: Springer.

Kelly, G. (1955). *The psychology of personal constructs* (2 vols.). New York: Norton.

Kern, R. M., Hawes, E. C., & Christensen, O. C. (1989). *Couples therapy: An Adlerian perspective.* Minneapolis, MN: Educational Media Corporation.

Kern, R. M., Yeakle, R., & Sperry, L. (1989). Survey of contemporary Adlerian clinical practices and therapy issues. *Individual Psychology, 45,* 38–47.

Kopp, R. R. (1989). Holistic metaphorical therapy and Adlerian brief psychotherapy. *Individual Psychology: Journal of Adlerian Theory, Research and Practice, 45*(1–2), 57–61.

Korobov, N. (2000). Social constructionist "theory hope": The impasse from theory to practice. *Culture and Psychology, 6,* 365–373.

Koss, M. P., & Butcher, J. N. (1986). Research on brief therapy. In S. Garfield & A. Bergin (Eds.), *Handbook of psychotherapy and behavior change* (3rd ed., pp. 627–670). New York: Wiley.

Kottman, T. (1993). The king of rock and roll. In T. Kottman & C. Schaefer (Eds.), *Play therapy in action: A casebook for practitioners* (pp. 133–167). Northvale, NJ: Aronson.

Kottman, T. (1994). Adlerian play therapy. In K. O'Connor & C. Schaefer (Eds.), *Handbook of play therapy* (Vol. 2, pp. 3–26). New York: Wiley.

Kottman, T. (1997). Adlerian play therapy. In K. O'Connor & L. M. Braverman (Eds.), *Play therapy theory and practice: A comparative presentation* (pp. 310–340). New York: Wiley.

Kottman, T. (1999a). Group applications of Adlerian play therapy. In D. S. Sweeney & L. E. Homeyer (Eds.), *The handbook of group play therapy* (pp. 65–85). San Francisco: Jossey-Bass.

Kottman, T. (1999b). Integrating the Crucial Cs into Adlerian play therapy. *Journal of Individual Psychology, 55,* 288–297.

Kottman, T. (1999c). Play therapy. In R. E. Watts & J. Carlson (Eds.), *Interventions and strategies in counseling and psychotherapy* (pp. 161–179). Philadelphia: Accelerated Development/Taylor & Francis.

Kottman, T. (2001a). Adlerian play therapy. *International Journal of Play Therapy, 10*(2), 1–12.

Kottman, T. (2001b). *Play therapy: Basics and beyond.* Alexandria, VA: American Counseling Association.

Kottman, T. (2003). *Partners in play: An Adlerian approach to play therapy* (2nd ed.). Alexandria, VA: American Counseling Association.

Kottman, T., & Warlick, J. (1989). Adlerian play therapy: Practical considerations. *Journal of Individual Psychology, 45,* 443–446.

Kottman, T., & Warlick, J. (1990). Adlerian play therapy. *Journal of Humanistic Education and Development, 28,* 125–132.

LaBauve, B. J., Watts, R. E., & Kottman, T. (2001). Approaches to play therapy: A tabular overview. *TCA Journal, 29*, 105–114.

LaFountain, R. M. (1996). Social interest: A key to solutions. *Individual Psychology, 52*, 150–157.

LaFountain, R. M., & Garner, N. E. (1998). *A school with solutions: Implementing a solution-focused Adlerian-based comprehensive school counseling program.* Alexandria, VA: American School Counseling Association.

LaFountain, R. M., & Mustaine, B. L. (1998). Infusing Adlerian theory into an introductory marriage and family course. *The Family Journal, 6*, 189–199.

Lambert, M. J. (1992). Psychotherapy outcome research: Implications for integrative and eclectical therapists. In M. R. Goldfried & J. C. Norcross (Eds.), *Handbook of psychotherapy integration* (pp. 94–129). New York: Basic Books.

Lambert, M. J., & Barley, D. E. (2001). Research summary on the therapeutic relationship and psychotherapy outcome. *Psychotherapy: Theory, Research, Practice, Training, 38*, 357–361.

Lambert, M. J., & Ogles, B. M. (2004). The efficacy and effectiveness of psychotherapy. In M. J. Lambert (Ed.), *Bergin and Garfield's handbook of psychotherapy and behavior change* (5th ed., pp. 139–193). New York: Wiley.

Landreth, G. L. (2002). *Play therapy: The art of the relationship* (2nd ed.). New York: Brunner Routledge.

Lazarus, A. A. (2000). Adlerian psychotherapy. In R. J. Corsini & D. Wedding (Eds.), *Current psychotherapies* (5th ed., pp. 340–374). Itasca, IL: Peacock.

Leman, K. (1985). *The birth order book: Why you are the way you are.* New York: Dell.

Lew, A., & Bettner, B. L. (1996). *A parent's guide to understanding and motivating children.* Newton Centre, MA: Connexions Press.

Littrell, J. M. (1998). *Brief counseling in action.* New York: Norton.

Lombardi, D. L. (1973). Eight avenues of life style consistency. *Individual Psychologist, 10*, 5–9.

Love, P. (2001). *The truth about love.* New York: Fireside.

Mahoney, M. J. (1991). *Human change processes: The scientific foundations of psychotherapy.* New York: Basic Books.

Mahoney, M. J. (1995). Continuing evolution of the cognitive sciences and psychotherapies. In R. A. Neimeyer & M. J. Mahoney (Eds.), *Constructivism in psychotherapy* (pp. 39–68). Washington, DC: American Psychological Association.

Mahoney, M. J. (2002). Constructivism and positive psychology. In C. R. Snyder & S. J. Lopez (Eds.), *Handbook of positive psychology* (pp. 745–750). New York: Oxford University Press.

Mahoney, M. J. (2003). *Constructive psychotherapy: A practical guide.* New York: Guilford Press.

Manaster, G. J. (1989). Critical issues in brief psychotherapy: A summary and conclusion. *Individual Psychology, 45*, 243–247.

Manaster, G. J., & Corsini, R. J. (1982). *Individual Psychology: Theory and practice.* Itasca, IL: F. E. Peacock.

Maniacci, M. P. (1990). *An Adlerian interpretation of the comprehensive system of the Rorschach inkblot test.* Unpublished doctoral dissertation, Alfred Adler Institute.

Maniacci, M. P. (1996a). An introduction to brief therapy of the personality disorders. *Individual Psychology, 52,* 158–168.

Maniacci, M. P. (1996b). Mental disorders due to a general medical condition and other cognitive disorders. In L. Sperry & J. Carlson (Eds.), *Psychopathology and psychotherapy: From diagnosis to treatment* (2nd ed., pp. 51–75). Muncie, IN: Accelerated Development.

Maniacci, M. P. (1999). Clinical therapy. In R. E. Watts & J. Carlson (Eds.), *Interventions and strategies in counseling and psychotherapy* (pp. 59–85). Philadelphia: Accelerated Development.

Maniacci, M. P. (2002). The DSM and Individual Psychology: A general comparison. *Journal of Individual Psychology, 58,* 356–362.

Maniacci, M. P. (2003). A cognitive conundrum: Where's the thinking in cognitive? In R. E. Watts (Ed.), *Adlerian, cognitive, and constructivist therapies: An integrative dialogue* (pp. 107–121). New York: Springer.

Maniacci, M. P., & Sackett-Maniacci, L. A. (2002). The use of the DSM–IV in treatment planning: An Adlerian view. *Journal of Individual Psychology, 58,* 388–397.

Mansager, E. (Ed.). (2000). Holism, wellness, spirituality [Special issue]. *Journal of Individual Psychology, 56*(3).

Martin, J., & Sugarman, J. (1997). The social–cognitive construction of psychotherapeutic change: Bridging social constructionism and cognitive constructivism. *Review of General Psychology, 1,* 375–378.

Martin, J., & Sugarman, J. (1999). *The psychology of human possibility and constraint.* Albany: State University of New York Press.

Master, S. B. (1991). Constructivism and the creative power of the self. *Individual Psychology, 47,* 447–455.

McGoldrick, M., Watson, M., & Benton, W. (1999). Siblings through the life cycle. In B. Carter & M. McGoldrick (Eds.), *The expanded family life cycle: Individual, family, and social perspectives* (3rd ed., pp. 153–166) Boston: Allyn & Bacon.

Metcalf, L. (1995). *Counseling toward solutions.* San Francisco: Jossey-Bass.

Miranda, A. O., & Umhoefer, D. L. (1998). Depression and social interest differences between Latinos in dissimilar acculturation stages. *Journal of Mental Health Counseling, 20,* 159–171.

Moreno, J. L. (1953). *Who shall survive?* New York: Beacon House.

Mosak, H. H. (1958). Early recollections as a projective technique. *Journal of Projective Techniques, 32,* 302–311.

Mosak, H. H. (1977). *On purpose.* Chicago: Alfred Adler Institute.

Mosak, H. H. (1979). Adlerian psychotherapy. In R. J. Corsini (Ed.), *Current psychotherapies* (2nd ed., pp. 44–94). Itasca, IL: F. E. Peacock.

Mosak, H. H. (1987). *Ha ha and aha: The role of humor in psychotherapy.* Muncie, IN: Accelerated Development.

Mosak, H. H. (1989). Adlerian psychotherapy. In R. J. Corsini & D. Wedding (Eds.), *Current psychotherapies* (4th ed., pp. 64–116). Itasca, IL: F. E. Peacock.

Mosak, H. H. (1995). Adlerian psychotherapy. In R. J. Corsini & D. Wedding (Eds.), *Current psychotherapies* (5th ed., pp. 51–94). Itasca, IL: F. E. Peacock.

Mosak, H. H. (2000). Adlerian psychotherapy. In R. J. Corsini & D. Wedding (Eds.), *Current psychotherapies* (6th ed., pp. 54–98). Itasca, IL: F. E. Peacock.

Mosak, H. H., & Maniacci, M. P. (1993). Adlerian child psychotherapy. In T. R. Kratochwill & R. J. Morris (Eds.), *Handbook of psychotherapy with children and adolescents* (pp. 162–184). Boston: Allyn & Bacon.

Mosak, H. H., & Maniacci, M. P. (1998). *Tactics in counseling and psychotherapy.* Itasca, IL: F. E. Peacock.

Mosak, H. H., & Maniacci, M. (1999). *A primer of Adlerian psychology: The analytic–behavioral–cognitive psychology of Alfred Adler.* Philadelphia: Accelerated Development/Taylor & Francis.

Mozdzierz, G. J. (1998). Culture, tradition, transition, and the future. *Journal of Individual Psychology, 54,* 275–277.

Murray, E. J., & Jacobsen, L. T. (1978). Cognition and learning in traditional and behavioral therapy. In S. Garfield & A. Bergin (Eds.), *Handbook of psychotherapy and behavioral change* (pp. 661–687). New York: Wiley.

Neimeyer, R. A. (1995). Constructivist psychotherapies: Features, foundations, and future directions. In R. A. Neimeyer & M. J. Mahoney (Eds.), *Constructivism in psychotherapy* (pp. 11–38). Washington, DC: American Psychological Association.

Neimeyer, R. A. (2000). Narrative disruptions in the construction of the self. In R. A. Neimeyer & J. D. Raskin (Eds.), *Constructions of disorder: Meaning-making frameworks for psychotherapy* (pp. 207–242). Washington, DC: American Psychological Association.

Neimeyer, R. A. (2003). Two paths diverge into a wood: Cognitive/constructivist contrasts and the future evolution of Adlerian psychotherapy. In R. E. Watts (Ed.), *Adlerian, cognitive, and constructivist psychotherapies: An integrative dialogue* (pp. 122–137). New York: Springer.

Nelsen, J. (1996). *Positive discipline.* New York: Ballantine.

Neuer, A. (1936). Courage and discouragement. *International Journal of Individual Psychology, 2,* 30–50.

Newlon, B. J., & Arciniega, M. (1983). Respecting cultural uniqueness: An Adlerian approach. *Individual Psychology, 39,* 133–143.

Nichols, M. P., & Schwartz, R. C. (1995). *Family therapy: Concepts and methods* (3rd ed.). Boston: Allyn & Bacon.

Nicoll, W. G. (1999). Brief therapy strategies and techniques. In R. E. Watts & J. Carlson (Eds.), *Interventions and strategies in counseling and psychotherapy* (pp. 15–30). Philadelphia: Accelerated Development/Taylor & Francis.

Nicoll, W. G., Bitter, J., Christensen, O. C., & Hawes, C. (2000). Adlerian brief therapy: Strategies and tactics. In J. Carlson & L. Sperry (Eds.), *Brief therapy with individuals and couples* (pp. 220–247). Phoenix, AZ: Zeig, Tucker, & Theisen.

Nikelly, A. G. (1971a). Private logic. In A. G. Nikelly (Ed.), *Techniques for behavior change: Applications of Adlerian theory* (pp. 61–64). Springfield, IL: Charles C Thomas.

Nikelly, A. G. (Ed.). (1971b). *Techniques for behavior change: Applications of Adlerian theory*. Springfield, IL: Charles C Thomas.

Norcross, J. C. (Ed.). (2002). *Psychotherapy relationships that work: Therapist contributions and responsiveness to patients*. New York: Oxford University Press.

Nystul, M. (1980). Nystulian play therapy: Applications of Adlerian psychology. *Elementary School Guidance and Counseling, 15*, 22–29.

Nystul, M. (1999). Problem-solving counseling: Integrating Adler's and Glasser's theories. In R. E. Watts & J. Carlson (Eds.), *Interventions and strategies in counseling and psychotherapy* (pp. 31–42). Philadelphia: Accelerated Development/ Taylor & Francis.

Oberst, U. E., & Stewart, A. E. (2003). *Adlerian psychotherapy: An advanced approach to individual psychology*. New York: Brunner/Routledge.

O'Connell, W. E. (1965). Humanistic identification: A new translation for *gemeinschaftsgefuhl. Journal of Individual Psychology, 21*, 44–47.

O'Connell, W. E., & Stubblefield, S. A. (1989). The training of the encouraging therapist and the 30-minute psychiatric interview. *Individual Psychology: Journal of Adlerian Theory, Research, and Practice, 45*(1–2), 126–142.

O'Connor, K. J. (2000). *The play therapy primer* (2nd ed.). New York: Wiley.

O'Hanlon, W. H., & Weiner-Davis, M. (1989). *In search of solutions: A new direction in psychotherapy*. New York: Norton.

Parry, A., & Doan, R. E. (1994). *Story revisions: Narrative therapy in a postmodern world*. New York: Guilford Press.

Pepper, F. C. (1971). Birth order. In A. G. Nikelly (Ed.), *Techniques for behavior change: Applications of Adlerian theory* (pp. 49–54). Springfield, IL: Charles C Thomas.

Peven, D. E., & Shulman, B. H. (2002). *"Who is Sylvia?" and other stories: Case studies in psychotherapy*. New York: Brunner-Routledge.

Pew, M. L. (1989). Brief marriage therapy. *Individual Psychology: Journal of Adlerian Theory, Research, and Practice, 45*(1–2), 191–200.

Phelan, T. W. (1995). *1-2-3 Magic: Effective discipline for children 2–13*. Glen Ellyn, IL: Child Management.

Popkin, M. (1994). *Active parenting*. Atlanta, GA: Active Parenting.

Powers, R. L., & Griffith, J. (1987). *Understanding lifestyle: The psycho-clarity process*. Chicago: AIAS.

Powers, R. L., & Griffith, J. (1989). Single-session psychotherapy involving two therapists. *Individual Psychology: Journal of Adlerian Theory, Research, and Practice, 45*(1–2), 99–125.

Powers, R. L., & Griffith, J. (1995). *IPCW: The Individual Psychology workbook (with supplements)*. Chicago: AIAS.

Prochaska, J. O., & Norcross, J. C. (1994). *Systems of psychotherapy: A transtheoretical approach* (3rd ed.). Pacific Grove, CA: Brooks/Cole.

Prochaska, J. O., & Norcross, J. C. (2003). *Systems of psychotherapy: A transtheoretical approach* (5th ed.). Pacific Grove, CA: Brooks/Cole.

Propst, L. R. (1996). Cognitive–behavioral therapy and the religious person. In E. P. Shafranske (Ed.), *Religion and the clinical practice of psychology* (pp. 391–408). Washington, DC: American Psychological Association.

Putnam, R. D. (2000). *Bowling alone: Collapse and revival of American community*. New York: Simon & Schuster.

Raimy, V. (1975). *Misunderstandings of the self*. New York: Jossey-Bass.

Raskin, N. J., & Rogers, C. R. (1989). Person-centered therapy. In R. J. Corsini & D. Wedding (Eds.), *Current psychotherapies* (4th ed., pp. 155–194). Itasca, IL: F. E. Peacock.

Reddy, I., & Hanna, F. J. (1995). The life-style of the Hindu woman: Conceptualizing female clients of Indian origin. *Individual Psychology, 51*, 216–230.

Roberts, R. L., Harper, R., Tuttle Eagle Bull, D., & Heideman-Provost, L. M. (1998). The Native American medicine wheel and Individual Psychology: Common themes. *Journal of Individual Psychology, 54*, 135–145.

Rogers, C. R. (1951). *Client-centered therapy*. Boston: Houghton-Mifflin.

Rogers, C. R. (1967). Autobiography. In E. W. Boring & G. Lindzey (Eds.), *A history of psychology in biography* (Vol. 5, pp. 343–384). New York: Appleton-Century-Crofts.

Rogers, C. R. (1969). *Freedom to learn: A view of what education might become*. Columbus, OH: Merrill.

Rogers, C. R. (1980). *A way of being*. Boston: Houghton Mifflin.

Rogers, C. R. (1989). *The Carl Rogers reader* (H. Kirschenbaum & V. L. Land, Eds.). Boston: Houghton Mifflin.

Safran, J. D., & Muran, C. (2000). *Negotiating the therapeutic alliance: A relational treatment guide*. New York: Guilford Press.

Salzman, M. B. (2002). A culturally congruent consultation at a Bureau of Indian Affairs boarding school. *Journal of Individual Psychology, 58*, 132–147.

Sattler, J. M. (1982). *Assessment of children's intelligence and special abilities* (2nd ed.). Boston: Allyn & Bacon.

Sauber, S. R. (Ed.). (1997). *Managed mental health care: Major diagnostic and treatment approaches*. Bristol, PA: Brunner/Mazel.

Schaefer, C. E. (1993). What is play and why is it therapeutic? In C. E. Schaefer (Ed.), *The therapeutic powers of play* (pp. 1–15). New York: Aronson.

Schneider, M. F., & Stone, M. (Eds.). (1998). Narrative therapy and Adlerian psychology [Special issue]. *Journal of Individual Psychology, 54*(4).

Schramski, T. G., & Giovando, K. (1993). Sexual orientation, social interest, and exemplary practice. *Individual Psychology, 49*, 199–204.

Scott, C. N., Kelly, F. D., & Tolbert, B. L. (1995). Realism, constructivism, and the individual psychology of Alfred Adler. *Individual Psychology, 51*, 4–20.

Seligman, M. E. P. (2002). Positive psychology, positive prevention, and positive therapy. In C. R. Snyder & S. J. Lopez (Eds.), *Handbook of positive psychology* (pp. 3–9). New York: Oxford University Press.

Sexton, T. L., & Whiston, S. C. (1994). The status of the counseling relationship: An empirical review, theoretical implications, and research directions. *Counseling Psychologist, 22*, 6–78.

Sexton, T. L., Whiston, S. C., Bleuer, J. C., & Walz, G. R. (1997). *Integrating outcome research into counseling practice and training.* Alexandria, VA: American Counseling Association.

Sherman, R. (1999). Family therapy: The art of integration. In R. E. Watts & J. Carlson (Eds.), *Interventions and strategies in counseling and psychotherapy* (pp. 101–134). Philadelphia: Accelerated Development/Taylor & Francis.

Sherman, R., & Dinkmeyer, D. (1987). *Systems of family therapy: An Adlerian integration.* New York: Brunner/Mazel.

Shulman, B. H. (1973). *Contributions to Individual Psychology.* Chicago: Alfred Adler Institute.

Shulman, B. H. (1985). Cognitive therapy and the Individual Psychology of Alfred Adler. In M. J. Mahoney & A. Freeman (Eds.), *Cognition and psychotherapy* (pp. 243–258). New York: Plenum.

Shulman, B. H. (1989). Some remarks on brief psychotherapy. *Individual Psychology, 45*, 34–47.

Shulman, B. H., & Mosak, H. H. (1988). *Manual for life style assessment.* Muncie, IN: Accelerated Development.

Silverman, N. N., & Corsini, R. J. (1986). What psychology students are "learning" about Individual Psychology: A study of textbooks. *Individual Psychology, 42*, 96–106.

Singer, J. A., & Salovey, P. (1993). *The remembered self: Emotion and memory in personality.* New York: Free Press.

Slavik, S., Sperry, L., & Carlson, J. (2000). Efficient Adlerian therapy with individuals and couples. In J. Carlson & L. Sperry (Eds.), *Brief therapy with individuals and couples* (pp. 248–263). Phoenix, AZ: Zeig, Tucker, & Theisen.

Snyder, C. R., & Lopez, S. J. (2002). Preface. In C. R. Snyder & S. J. Lopez (Eds.), *Handbook of positive psychology* (pp. ix–x). New York: Oxford University Press.

Sonstegard, M. A., & Bitter, J. (2004). *Adlerian group counseling and psychotherapy: Step-by-step.* New York: Brunner Routledge.

Sonstegard, M. A., Dreikurs, R., & Bitter, J. (1982). The teleoanalytic group counseling approach. In G. Gazda (Ed.), *Basic approaches to group psychotherapy and group counseling* (3rd ed., pp. 507–551). Springfield, IL: Charles C Thomas.

Sperry, L. (1987). ERIC: A cognitive map for guiding brief therapy and health care counseling. *Individual Psychology: Journal of Adlerian Theory, Research, and Practice, 43*, 237–241.

Sperry, L. (1989). Contemporary approaches to brief psychotherapy: A comparative analysis. *Individual Psychology, 45*, 3–25.

Sperry, L. (1993). Psychopathology and the diagnostic and treatment process. In L. Sperry & J. Carlson (Eds.), *Psychopathology and psychotherapy* (pp. 3–18). Muncie, IN: Accelerated Development.

Sperry, L. (1995). Sexual orientation and psychotherapy: Science, ideology, or compassion? *Individual Psychology, 51*, 160–165.

Sperry, L. (Ed.). (2002). *DSM–IV* in clinical practice today [Special issue]. *Journal of Individual Psychology, 58*(4).

Sperry, L. (2003). Commonalities between Adlerian psychotherapy and cognitive therapies: An Adlerian perspective. In R. E. Watts (Ed.), *Adlerian, cognitive, and constructivist psychotherapies: An integrative dialogue* (pp. 59–70). New York: Springer.

Sperry, L., & Carlson, J. (1991). *Marital therapy: Integrating theory and technique*. Denver, CO: Love.

Sperry, L., & Carlson, J. (Eds.). (1996). *Psychopathology and psychotherapy: From DSM–IV diagnoses to treatment* (2nd ed.). Washington, DC: Accelerated Development.

Sperry, L., Carlson, J., & Kjos, D. (2003). *Becoming an effective therapist*. Boston: Allyn & Bacon.

Sperry, L., Carlson, J., & Peluso, P. (2005). *Couples therapy*. Denver, CO: Love.

Sperry, L., & Maniacci, M. P. (1992). An integration of *DSM–III–R* diagnoses and Adlerian case formulations. *Individual Psychology, 48*, 175–181.

Stein, H. T., & Edwards, M. E. (1998). Alfred Adler: Classical theory and practice. In P. Marcus & A. Rosenberg (Eds.), *Psychoanalytic versions of the human condition: Philosophies of life and their impact on practice* (pp. 64–93). New York: New York University Press.

Stuart, R. B. (2000). Brief integrative behavior therapy with individuals and couples. In J. Carlson & L. Sperry (Eds.), *Brief therapy with individuals and couples* (pp. 3–32). Phoenix, AZ: Zeig, Tucker & Theisen.

Sundberg, N., & Tyler, L. (1976). *Clinical psychology*. New York: Appleton-Century-Crofts.

Sweeney, D. S. (1997). *Counseling children through the world of play*. Wheaton, IL: Tyndale.

Sweeney, T. J. (1998). *Adlerian counseling: A practitioner's approach* (4th ed.). Muncie, IN: Accelerated Development.

Terner, J., & Pew, W. L. (1978). *The courage to be imperfect: The life and work of Rudolf Dreikurs*. New York: Hawthorn Books.

Vaihinger, H. (1925). *The philosophy of "as if": A system of the theoretical, practical, and religious fictions of mankind*. New York: Harcourt, Brace.

Vann, G. (1995). Marital therapy with managed mental health care. *Individual Psychology: Journal of Adlerian Theory, Research, and Practice, 51*, 398–405.

Waite, L., Browning, D., Doherty, W., Gallagher, M., Luo, Y., & Stanley, S. (2002). *Does divorce make people happy?* Washington, DC: Institute for American Values.

Walter, J. L., & Peller, J. E. (1992). *Becoming solution-focused in brief therapy*. New York: Brunner/Mazel.

Wampold, B. E. (2001). *The great psychotherapy debate: Models, methods, and findings*. Mahwah, NJ: Erlbaum.

Watkins, C. E. (1997). An Adlerian reaction in the spirit of social interest: Dialogue worth reckoning with. *Journal of Cognitive Psychotherapy, 11*, 211–214.

Watkins, C. E., & Guarnaccia, C. A. (1999). In R. E. Watts & J. Carlson (Eds.), *Interventions and strategies in counseling and psychotherapy* (pp. 207–230). Philadelphia: Accelerated Development/Taylor & Francis.

Watts, R. E. (1992). Biblical agape as a model of social interest. *Individual Psychology, 48*, 35–40.

Watts, R. E. (1995). Social interest and the core conditions: Could it be that Adler influenced Rogers? *Journal of Humanistic Education and Development, 34*, 165–170.

Watts, R. E. (1998). The remarkable similarity between Rogers's core conditions and Adler's social interest. *Journal of Individual Psychology, 54*, 4–9.

Watts, R. E. (1999). The vision of Adler: An introduction. In R. E. Watts & J. Carlson (Eds.), *Interventions and strategies in counseling and psychotherapy* (pp. 1–13). Philadelphia: Accelerated Development/Taylor & Francis.

Watts, R. E. (2000). Entering the new millennium: Is Individual Psychology still relevant? *Journal of Individual Psychology, 56*, 21–30.

Watts, R. E. (2001). Addressing spiritual issues in secular counseling and psychotherapy: Response to Helminiak's view. *Counseling and Values, 45*, 207–217.

Watts, R. E. (Ed.). (2003a). *Adlerian, cognitive, and constructivist therapies: An integrative dialogue*. New York: Springer.

Watts, R. E. (2003b). Adlerian therapy as a relational constructivist approach. *The Family Journal: Counseling and Therapy for Couples and Families, 11*, 139–147.

Watts, R. E., & Carlson, J. (Eds.). (1999). *Interventions and strategies in counseling and psychotherapy*. Philadelphia: Accelerated Development/Taylor & Francis.

Watts, R. E., & Critelli, J. W. (1997). Roots of contemporary cognitive theories in the Individual Psychology of Alfred Adler. *Journal of Cognitive Psychotherapy, 11*, 147–156.

Watts, R. E., & Phillips, K. (2004). Adlerian psychology and psychotherapy: A relational constructivist approach. In J. D. Raskin & S. K. Bridges (Eds.), *Studies in meaning: Exploring constructivist psychology* (Vol. 2, pp. 267–289). New York: Pace University Press.

Watts, R. E., & Pietrzak, D. (2000). Adlerian "encouragement" and the therapeutic process of solution-focused brief therapy. *Journal of Counseling and Development, 78*, 442–447.

Watts, R. E., & Shulman, B. H. (2003). Integrating Adlerian and constructive therapies: An Adlerian perspective. In R. E. Watts (Ed.), *Adlerian, cognitive, and constructivist psychotherapies: An integrative dialogue* (pp. 9–37). New York: Springer.

Wolfe, W. B. (1934). *Nervous breakdown: Its cause and cure.* London: Routledge.

Wubbolding, R. E. (2000). *Reality therapy for the 21st century.* Philadelphia: Brunner-Routledge.

Yalom, I. D. (1995). *The theory and practice of group psychotherapy* (4th ed.) New York: Basic Books.

Young, J. E. (1999). *Cognitive therapy for personality disorders: A schema-focused approach* (3rd ed.). Sarasota, FL: Professional Resource Press.

Young, J. E., Klosko, J. S., & Weishaar, M. E. (2003). *Schema therapy: A practitioner's guide.* New York: Guilford Press.

Yura, M., & Galassi, M. (1974). Adlerian usage of children's play. *Journal of Individual Psychology, 30,* 194–201.

INDEX

299

in contemporary practice, 63
contemporary relevance of, 21–22
as directive, 9
efficient (EFT), 164, 171–174
four phases in, 70
group therapy, 208–215
as integrative and eclectic, 10
lack of recognition for, 273–274
multicultural considerations in, 31–34
and narrative therapy, 28–29
play therapy, 231–249
and positive psychology movement, 34–36
and postmodern approaches, 26
as present and future oriented, 8–9
"The Question" in, 110, 137–138
and solution-focused brief therapy, 27
and systemic approaches, 24–26
validation of, 36–40
Adolescence, life style interview information on, 122
Affection, 49
Aggression, as safeguarding mechanism, 60, 97
Aggressive toys, for play therapy, 234
Alliances, in life style interview, 116, 121–122
Allport, 34
Alternative explanations tactic, 149–150
Altruism, as force in groups, 219, 221
Ambiguity, tolerance for, 48, 62
American Psychiatric Association, 63
Anchin, J. C., 155
Ancillary services, 113, 114
Anger, 62
Ansbacher, H. L., 66
Antisuggestion tactic, 142
Anxiety
    as safeguarding mechanism, 61
    tactics for reducing, 148–149
Apathy, 62
Apperception
    biased, 45
    schema of, 24
Arciniega, G. M., 32–33
Arranger, life style as, 45–46
Artwork, in play therapy, 246
Asay, T. P., 68, 73–74
"As if," 27, 144
Aspiration, in group therapy, 218
Assessment, 103–128
    clinical summary, 111–112

general diagnosis (initial interview), 103–111
in group therapy, 212–213
movements within treatment, 114–115, 122–124
psychological testing, 124–127
special diagnosis (life style interview), 115–122
treatment plan, 112–114
Association for Play Therapy, 228
Assuming another's perspective, 140–141
Atmosphere, family. See Family atmosphere
Attachment
    as goal, 49, 50
    and love, 62
    in play therapy, 230
Attention, as goal, 14
Attention-seeking behavior, 13
Attitudes, in group therapy, 217
Attitudinal therapists, 22–23
Attraction process, 178–179
Attractiveness, influence in group and, 217
Axes, diagnostic, 98–100, 112

Bachelor, A., 70
Background data, in general diagnosis, 108–109
Backward movement, 60
Beck, A. T., 22–23
Behavior
    ABT understanding/treatment of, 165–169
    as adaptation, 84
    children's goals of, 243–244
    emotion and changes in, 267
    as function of perception, 179
    as goal oriented, 13–15
    immediate behavior tactic, 141
    life style as expression of, 215–216
    as socially embedded, 11
    social meaning/purpose of, 215
    in therapeutic relationship, 74–75
    tracking (in play therapy), 237
Behavioral therapy, Adlerian therapy and, 160
Being-in-the-world, 91
Beliefs
    in couple relationships, 180
    viewpoints becoming, 12
Biased apperception, 45
Bibliotherapy, in play therapy, 246
Biological factors

Hope, success of psychotherapy and, 38–39
Horvath, A., 70
Hoyt, M. F., 155, 174
Hubble, M. A., 37–39
Human behavior. *See* Behavior
Human nature
    social aspect of, 215
    theories of, 3–4
Humor
    in couple relationships, 180
    as therapy tactic, 144–146
Hypotheses, in play therapy, 245

Idealization, 60
Ideas, screened, 11–12
Ideational shifts, law of, 144
IDE (interpersonal–developmental–experiential) therapy, 160
Identifying information (general diagnosis), 106–107
Illogic, identifying, 139–140
Imagery tactics, 146–147
Immediate behavior/movement tactic, 141
Impulsive–global people, 48–49
Inadequacy
    as goal, 14
    and self-concept statements, 133
Individualism, 30
Individual Psychology. *See* Adlerian (Individual) Psychology
Inferiority
    acceptance of vs. compensation for, 132
    defined, 48
    and life style development, 58–59
    and neurotic disorders, 97
    of organs/organ systems, 46–47, 83, 90
    perceived, compensating for, 14
    and personality disorders, 97–98
    and private logic, 87
    and psychotic disorders, 96–97
    and vulnerability to psychopathologies, 90
Inferiority complexes, 49
    and *DSM* diagnostic categories, 100
    encouragement for giving up, 132–133
Inferiority feelings, 48–49
    complexes manifesting, 89
    elimination of vs. living with, 132
    and self-concept statements, 133
Information processing, 47–49
Informing behaviors, in therapeutic relationship, 75

Initial interview. *See* General diagnosis
Insight, 143, 244–247
Integration of psychotherapies, 29
Integrative, Adlerian therapy as, 10
Integrative treatment (brief couples therapy), 177–178
Interaction
    in couples, 268
    as force in groups, 219, 221
    in group therapy, 226
    in play therapy, 241
Interdependence, 50
Internal conflicts, creation of, 138–139
Internal–external locus of control, 48
Interpersonal–developmental–experiential (IDE) therapy, 160
Interpersonal learning, in group therapy, 208
Interpersonal psychotherapy, 160
Interpreting behaviors, in therapeutic relationship, 75
Interrelatedness of psychopathologies, 100–101
Interventions. *See also specific therapies*
    medical, 113
    tailoring of. *See* Adlerian theory
    targeted, 133
Interviews
    assessment, 103
    diagnostic. *See* General diagnosis; Special diagnosis
    summaries of, 136
Intimacy, as life task, 13

Jokes, 145

Kelly, E. W., Jr., 73
Kilmer, R. P., 35
Koss, M. P., 158
Kottman, T., 228, 231–249

Labeling
    in play therapy, 237
    relabelling, 179
LaFountain, R. M., 32
Lambert, M. J., 68, 73–74, 177–178
Landreth, G. L., 228
Law of ideational shifts, 144
Lazarus, Arnold, 10
Leadership
    for group therapy, 223–226
    for parent education groups, 259–260, 264–265

Learning
    experiential, 5, 206
    in group therapy, 208
    in parent education groups, 260
    spectator, 219, 220
Lessons from the past tactic, 143
Levelers, 48
Lewis, J. A., 26
Life style, 43–62
    behavior as expression of, 215–216
    biological factors influencing, 46–50
    client's grip on, 93
    and convictions about what is, 56
    and convictions about what should be,
        56–58
    convictions underlying, 24
    in couple relationships, 180
    defined, 11–12
    and degree of activity, 50–51
    development of, 46–55
    and early recollections of childhood, 13
    and goodness of fit concept, 54–55
    as guide, 44
    ideas screened through, 11–12
    and inferiority, 58–59
    as limiter, 44
    and meaning-making, 44–46
    in play therapy, 240–244
    as predictor, 44–45
    private logic as foundation for, 12
    and psychological processes, 61–62
    and psychopathology, 90–91
    psychosocial dynamics in, 51–54
    and safeguarding mechanisms, 59–61
    and self-concept, 56
    and worldview, 56
Life style interview. See Special diagnosis
Life style vulnerabilities, 90–91
Life tasks, 13, 109
Limiter, style of life as, 44
Limit setting, in play therapy, 241–242
Linking, by group leader, 224, 264
Littrell, J. M., 163
Living Love video series, 269
Locus of control, 48
Logic, private. See Private logic
Logistical issues in therapeutic relationship,
    70–72
Long-term goals, 113–114
Long-term therapy, 7
Lopez, S. J., 34
Love, 62, 69

current functioning questions about,
    109
as life task, 13, 86
Love relationships, 49–50

Mahoney, M. J., 27
Maladjustment, perspective on, 162–163
Managed care, 158
Manaster, G. J., 9, 10, 159
Maniacci, M., 23, 275
Maps, cognitive, 144
Marriage, 266. See also Couples therapy
Martin, J., 29–30
Maslow, Abraham, 34
Mastery, in play therapy, 229
Meanings, 26
    and difficulty of life, 83
    of life, 116
    making, 44–46
Medical interventions, 113
Medication evaluations, 113
Memory, life style and, 61–62
Mental disorders, 89
Mental health, in terms of social interest,
    11
Mental Research Institute (MRI), 25, 160
Metacommunication, 245–246
Metaphors, in play therapy, 230, 246
Middle children, 52–53
Miller, S. D., 37–39
Minus to plus tactic, 143
Misbehavior, goals of, 14, 15
Mistaken convictions, 90
Model, success of psychotherapy and, 39–40
Mosak, H. H., 23, 33–34, 69, 275
Motivational tactics, 148
Motive system, 119
Movement(s)
    immediate movement tactic, 141
    through life, 87
    within treatment, 114–115, 122–124
    trusting, 139, 216
MRI. See Mental Research Institute
Multicultural considerations, 31–34
Multimodal therapy, 154
Multiple psychotherapy, 115
Mustaine, B. L., 32

Naming the demon tactic, 148–149
Narrative therapy, 26, 28–29
Narrow scanning, 48
Needs

data collection for, 115–116
duration of, 115
summary of, 136
Spectator learning, as force in groups, 219, 220
Spectator therapy, 3
Sperry, L., 23, 26, 74, 160, 208
Spirituality, 13, 33–34
Spitting in the soup tactic, 142
Spontaneity, in group work, 223
Standing still, 60
Stated values, 54
STEP. *See* Systematic Training for Effective Parenting
STEP/Teen. *See* Systematic Training for Effective Parenting of Teens
Stewart, A. E., 24, 79
"Stick and carrot" tactic, 148
"Storied" lives, 28
Strain, in groups, 218
Strategies, 134
Stress
defined, 90
external, 91–92
and vulnerability to psychopathology, 90
Striving, styles of, 87
Structuring, by group leaders, 223–224, 264
Style of life. *See* Life style
Subjective condition, 109
Subjective interview, 212
Substituting useful beliefs tactic, 150
Successful outcomes of therapy, 37–40
and collaborative formulation of goals, 77
in groups, 214
guarantees of, 78
payments contingent upon, 72
and therapeutic relationship, 38, 70, 76–77
Sugarman, J., 29–30
Summarizing, by group leader, 225, 265
Summary(-ies)
of the Early Recollections, 116–119
of the Family Constellation, 116–118
presenting clients with, 136
Superordinate constructs, 27
Sweeney, D. S., 227
Sympathetic compensation, 47
Symptoms
congruency between life style convictions and, 138

with neurotic disorders, 95
"The Question" related to, 110, 137–138
as safeguarding mechanisms, 60
as secondary to life style convictions, 93–94
shift in, 100
target of, 107
Systematic Training for Effective Parenting of Teens (STEP/Teen program), 258, 259
Systematic Training for Effective Parenting (STEP program), 257–259, 263
Systemic therapies, 24–26, 160

Tactics, 134–150
anxiety-reducing, 148–149
appropiateness of, 135
assuming another's perspective, 140–141
change, 143–144
for conflict resolution, 138–140
confrontation, 141
countering, 149–150
for differential diagnostics, 137–138
of efficient Adlerian therapy, 171–172
encouragement, 142–143
humor, 144–146
imagery, 146–147
motivational, 148
for orienting client to therapy, 136–137
paradoxical, 142
theoretical grounding of, 135
Taking over tactic, 149
Targeted interventions, 133
Tasks
of life, 13, 85–86
set by group leader, 225
in therapeutic alliance, 76
of therapists, 68
Task setting tactic, 144
Techniques, 134
in Adlerian therapy, 76
empty chair technique, 139
as factors in success of psychotherapy, 39, 40
multiple psychotherapy, 115
tactics for use of, 134
Termination of therapy, criteria for, 79
Testing, psychological, 124–127
Theories
Adlerian, 4, 5, 7, 11–16, 274

ABOUT THE AUTHORS

Jon Carlson, PsyD, EdD, ABPP, has earned doctorates in counseling and clinical psychology and holds an advanced certificate in psychotherapy. He is Distinguished Professor in the Division of Psychology and Counseling at Governors State University in University Park, Illinois, and director of the Lake Geneva Wellness Clinic in Lake Geneva, Wisconsin. Dr. Carlson is a fellow of the American Psychological Association and holds a diplomate in family psychology from the American Board of Professional Psychology. He has authored 35 books and 140 professional articles and has developed over 200 commercial and professional videos and DVDs. He serves as the founding editor of *The Family Journal* and is past president of the International Association of Marriage and Family Counseling.

Richard E. Watts, PhD, received his doctorate in counseling from the University of North Texas and is professor of counseling in the Department of Adult Leadership and Counseling at Sam Houston State University in Huntsville, Texas. Prior to his current post, he held faculty positions at Texas A&M University—Commerce, Kent State University, and Baylor University. His interests include Adlerian, cognitive, and constructivist–constructionist approaches to individual and couple and family counseling; counselor supervision and counselor efficacy; ethical and legal issues; play therapy; and religious and spirituality issues.

Michael Maniacci, PsyD, is a published author and former core faculty at the Adler School of Professional Psychology. He is on the board of consultants for many parents and family organizations and has published several book chapters, articles, and books on Adlerian psychology and psychotherapy. He maintains private practices in Chicago and Naperville, Illinois.